In Search of a Better World

Age 5, Calcutta 1926, photo taken at Woodburn Park, Calcutta.

after Senior Cambridge Exam, Calcutta, 1936.

As a college student, probably 1938.

In Search of a Better World
Memoirs

by
Jolly Mohan Kaul

Foreword
by
Amlan Datta

Samya

In Search of a Better World: Memoirs
was first published in February 2010 by SAMYA,
an imprint of Bhatkal and Sen,
16 Southern Avenue, Kolkata 700 026

ISBN 81-85604-99-1
978-81-85604-99-2

Rs 550.00

Lines quoted from *The Prophet* by Kahil Gibran
on pages 330 and 331 are reproduced courtesy
Gibran National Committee, Bsharry, Lebanon.

Design by Samya and typesetting by Krishna Gopal Das
74T Sultan Alam Road, Kolkata 700 033
and printed by Web Impressions (India) Pvt Ltd
34/2 Beadon St, Kolkata 700 006.

Published by Mandira Sen for SAMYA,
An imprint of Bhatkal and Sen,
16 Southern Avenue, Kolkata 700 026.

To the memory of my wife, Manikuntala Sen.
This book is a modest attempt
to repay the huge debt I owe to her.

Foreword

I have known Jolly Mohan Kaul since the middle of the last century. Over this period of roughly six decades, his ideas have changed notably. Outwardly this change is very striking, although it is not really exceptional; I have known other persons who have passed through a similar transformation. Inwardly, Jolly remains much the same; a steady gentleness is a persistent trait of his character. Equally steady is his deeper quest stated in the title of his book, the search for a better world. In his Introduction Jolly writes: 'I venture to suggest that if they [my critics] are patient and read on they will find a thread linking the different phases and the variety of activities that I have been involved in as I have searched for a better world.'

When we first met, Kaul was a communist and a Marxist. We were, so to speak, in opposite camps and got involved in public debates. But he was a gentle Marxist and we confronted each other without any harsh feelings. In the early 1960s his world-view was transformed. Things changed dramatically after the Chinese attack. 'It was the Chinese attack', Kaul sharply observed, 'that gave the jingoists and the fascist elements in the country an upper hand.' In his letter of resignation from the Communist Party of India submitted in January 1963, Kaul wrote: 'I remain as interested as ever in the cause of democracy, socialism and peace for which I had been working so long but I do not feel confident that by remaining in the Party I shall be able to further that cause.'

As a communist, Jolly was deeply involved in the trade union movement. Today, he continues to work on the labour front but of a distinctly different character. He is in the company of Gandhians these days. Recently, he invited me to speak at the Gandhi Shram Pratishthan (Labour Foundation) where, joyfully, Jolly and I find ourselves in the same camp. For him this has been a long journey conscientiously undertaken over the span of a long life.

It is characteristic of the author of this autobiography that he made his own 'experiment with truth' in his humble way. At every turn of his long journey, he tried honestly and tenaciously to learn from his varied confrontations with reality, struggling all the while to arrive at a more adequate idea of truth as an instrument of achieving a better world. Political labels can be deceptive as words provide only an approximate way of expressing truth. Socialism, Mohandas Gandhi once said, is a beautiful word. Quite early in life, Jolly Mohan Kaul started calling himself a socialist. He stays wedded to that word. However, with the progress of his life the word has acquired for him new meaning. Equality, fraternity and freedom remain cherished ideals. But the form in which these ideals ask to be enshrined has undergone change. This is the result of staying ready to learn from one's experiment with truth.

The remarkable changes in Kaul's areas of activity and the evolution of his ideas are not simply of interest in terms of his personal life. They have also a wider significance for the history of this age, the epoch to which he and the rest of us jointly belong. This is why all of us have something to learn from Kaul's faithful report on his search for a better world.

Kolkata
12 May 2009

Amlan Datta

Contents

Foreword by Amlan Datta		vii
Preface		xii
Introduction		xiii
Illustrations follow		176
1	The Youngest of Six Brothers	1
2	To Calcutta and School	9
3	Community Spirit or the Lack of It	29
4	The In-Between Experience	32
5	College and the Extra-Curriculars	34
6	The Cultural Movement	51
7	Going Underground	54
8	Into the Trade Union Movement	70
9	Famine and Beyond	88
10	Strike Wave: The Great Calcutta Killing	94
11	Lessons from the Port Strike	102
12	The South-East Asia Youth Conference	113
13	The Second Party Congress	116
14	Jail, 1948-1951 and the New Party Line	121
15	Kakababu	147
16	New Constitution, Freedom, Party Reorganization	151

17	The First General Elections	160
18	The Order Changeth	175
19	Marriage at the Time of Strife	177
20	The Tram Movement	181
21	The 1950s Food and Other Movements	185
22	The Twentieth Party Congress of the CPSU	189
23	The Kerala Experience	197
24	Money Matters	201
25	Of Worker Cadres	216
26	Heading for a Split: The Extraordinary Congress at Amritsar	224
27	Conflict of the Giants	232
28	India-China Relations: The Vijayawada Congress	241
29	The Chinese Attack	245
30	Severing Party Links	249
31	The Struggle for Survival	265
32	The Corporate World	276
33	Back to Journalism	288
34	Manikuntala and I	299
35	Ramgarh: Village in a Valley	318
36	Adrift on the Open Sea	327
37	Kanti Mehta's Gandhi Labour Foundation	332
38	Whither Better World?	349
	Afterword by Aditi Roy Ghatak	371
	Index	375

Preface

I started writing these memoirs at the turn of the millennium in the year 2000. At that time I had not thought of ever publishing what I wrote nor was I sure that I would ever complete the task. I felt, however, that it was incumbent on me to keep a record, particularly of the years during which I was active in the communist movement, and so I plodded on, sometimes stopping for months at a stretch, at other times managing to write a few paragraphs.

As the social and political environment of the country continued to deteriorate and the idealism that had inspired me in early life turned into cynicism, there were periods of depression when it seemed to me that nothing could save the world from impending doom and it was not worth continuing with the exercise that I had undertaken. At other times, when friends who had got to know that I had started work on the project asked me why I was making such slow progress, I said haltingly that perhaps the last chapter of my life story had yet to unfold. I also thought that I was still searching for answers to the many questions that had arisen in my mind. Had it not been for these periods of doubt and uncertainty it would not have taken me as many as eight full years to finish the work.

As it turned out it was indeed fortunate that I waited so long, for the last eight years have been eventful, and the experience I have gained particularly during the time I spent at the Gandhi Labour Foundation, where I had the privilege of the company of Kanti Mehta, an eminent trade unionist and a Gandhian and of Justice C. S. Dharmadhikari (Retd), another outstanding Gandhian, has been extremely rewarding. My stint of nearly six years there has, to some extent, helped me to find the answers to the questions that were troubling me.

While writing my memoirs, I have sometimes written comments from today's perspective. Interspersed in the text, these have been divided from the main body of the chapter by a short line at the beginning and at the end and set in a smaller size, so that the two, the story of the past and my reflections of today, could be offered separately.

Now that the book is about to be released I wish to acknowledge the debt to the many friends and relatives who have helped to bring this project to fruition. First of all I wish to thank all those—too many to be named in this short preface—who encouraged me to write and prodded me to go on till I completed the memoirs. But for their encouragement and their confidence in me this task would never have been finished.

At a time when I was still doubtful whether what I had written was fit for publication the first person to whom I sent the manuscript was Anita Kaul, my niece-in-law (is there such a word?), currently a senior official in the Education Department of the Government of India, who went through the manuscript promptly and gave a favourable verdict on its suitability for publication. Her help and advice have been of immense value to me.

I would also like to thank my nephew Ranjan Kaul and my friend Sunanda Datta-Ray for their suggestions. Thanks are also due to Arun Ghosh who did the necessary research for checking the references, dates and other facts. I also wish to acknowledge the assistance received from Aditi Roy Ghatak who has been a pillar of support all along, giving advice, editing the manuscript and checking the proofs repeatedly. I am grateful to the Gibran National Committee of Bsharry, Lebanon, for graciously granting permission to quote lines from *The Prophet* by Kahil Gibran on pages 330 and 331. And finally I would like to offer my thanks to the publishers for being so helpful.

Introduction

I am now in my eighty-ninth year. The average lifespan of an Indian being just a little over sixty years, this has been a long innings; an eventful life. The world has changed enormously since I first looked at it as a child. My country and the city in which I have lived almost the whole of my life, except the first five years, have changed beyond recognition. This is hardly surprising. Even as a child I knew that change would surely come. Indeed, it was to change things that I spent the best years of my life. What is surprising is the way people have changed; how attitudes and values have changed; how the way people look at things has changed. These have not always been along the lines that I had contemplated. At times, it is almost as if I am living on a different planet.

I too have changed but it seems to me that the wheel has turned full circle and that today I am more like I was when in school. Does this happen in all cases? It occurs to me that this is somewhat similar to what happened to my wife. Her last years brought her very close to her early years. Is this why old age is called second childhood . . . when one is overcome with a feeling of helplessness especially with the loss of many faculties—the memory and the slowing down of reflexes?

I have certainly slowed down; I am physically much weaker and am capable of much less effort but I do not think that there has been any significant decline in my faculties; in my memory, for instance, or in my capacity to reason and analyse. In fact, I think that, in many respects, I now have a clearer mind. The child sees the reality a little better because its mind is not clouded by ideologies and isms that distort vision. Only the child could cry out that the 'emperor wears no clothes'.

I have no intention of sitting in judgment on the generations that have come after me but I do believe that they would be well served if they had some knowledge of what the world was like in the early part of the last century and how it affected the generations that grew up in those years. I was fortunate enough to have been associated with the trade union and the communist movements in their formative years, both before and after Independence. Those who have been or still are in the Left movement have often asked me to write about those years. Some not directly associated with the Left but academically interested have also asked me for information.

Even though I spent (what are generally called) the best years of one's life—eighteen or nineteen to the age of forty-one or forty-two from the late 1930s and early 1940s till the early 1960s of the last century—as a whole-time activist of the undivided Communist Party of India (henceforth the Party), my life did not end with my exit from the Party. Nor has my life afterwards been either dull or monotonous. It has been a life full of interesting experiences from which I have continued to learn, to grow. Even as these lines are being written, I am learning; still trying to find answers to the many questions that have been and still are in my mind.

My active life having begun in the late 1930s, I have spent more than two-thirds of it after I left the Party. Much of the book deals with the post-Party phases. Those who are or were in the communist movement may feel that it has little relevance to their areas of interest. I venture to suggest that if they are patient and read on they will find a thread linking the different phases and the variety of activities that I have been involved in as I have searched for a better world. After all, it was to build a better world, a better society, a classless society, free from exploitation that the communist movement set out on its Long March with the publication of the *Communist Manifesto* in 1848.

My life's journey has been marked by amazing twists and turns. I have lived several different lives, as it were. Those who have seen me in one incarnation find it difficult to recognize me in another. I myself wonder how these transformations took place and in retracing my life's journey, I am trying, to some extent, to understand myself better. This book represents an attempt to set down these experiences over fast-changing times. I venture to think that I have been able to look at the world with a clearer vision and from a broader perspective after I left the Party even though my Marxist background and my years as a communist greatly shaped my ideas.

While the pursuit of a better world has always been constant, these nine decades have seen very interesting changes within me and without. These memoirs are not just about what I did but more about what I have become; how and why this has happened. Much of my learning has come from books and from ideas that others have shared with me but, most of all, it is from life that I have learnt.

ONE

The Youngest of Six Brothers

I was born in Simla (now Shimla), then the summer capital of the Government of India; the youngest of six brothers. We had a tubercular brother and some sisters too who died fairly young. So, we were really five, all surviving till their eighties and beyond. It was 1921; the month September; the date twenty-second, and my brothers told me that the time was twenty minutes past seven. It was easy to remember the exact time because of the drama that accompanied the announcement, as they have repeatedly told me. One evening, when they were relaxing on the verandah of our house, an ayah rushed in and proudly proclaimed: *'Saat bujkay bees minut per baba hua'* (at twenty minutes past seven the baby was born).

Unlike my brothers who were ushered into the world by midwives, my mother was taken to a hospital and I was helped out of her womb by a gynaecologist. The hospital was named after Lady Reading. I understand that it still exists and plan to visit it before I leave this world. The distinction—the birth in a hospital—conferred on me did not only indicate an improvement in the living standard of the household but also a sign of the influence of modern ideas; of the declining hold of traditional customs in middle class households in the cities.

My father, Shyam Mohan Nath, was born in a traditional Kashmiri family but had struggled all along against traditional concepts that he thought were outmoded. He was a great believer in adopting modern ideas which, to him, meant 'western' ideas. This explains a unique feature in our Kashmiri Pandit family: all the children were given English names, Prince, Major, Little, Young, Victor and Jolly! Even families far more westernized than ours did not experiment with names.

When my eldest brother, Prince, was getting married, my father insisted on cutting out the elaborate rituals that traditionally lasted over a whole week and opted for a one-day ceremony, performed by a renowned Sanskrit scholar. He retained the essentials of a Hindu marriage but kept out the frills. In another break with tradition, the sacrificial fire, the *havan*, was lit all right but, instead of sitting round it on the floor, the bridal couple sat on sofas and my brother was dressed in a suit. This may be common today but was rather unusual at that time and was the subject of some sarcasm in our community magazine, *Bahar-e-Kashmir*.

My father had a strong personality and all his children were greatly influenced by him. The small Kashmiri Pandit community has exerted an influence on Indian culture and politics far greater than would be warranted by its numbers. It has also contributed to the economic, cultural and intellectual life of the country. My father was quite proud of his ancestors and was able to draw the family tree going right back to the first Pandit who migrated from Kashmir in 1750. Some of these ancestors had held important positions in the Mughal court or as dewans of some of the native states.

By the time my grandfather, Bishambar Nath, was born, the family was in straitened circumstances. As the eldest surviving son—there was an elder brother who died early—my father had to shoulder the responsibility of getting the younger brothers on their feet and the sisters married. This he managed to do on a paltry salary on which he began his career in the Railways. His life was a story of tremendous determination, grit and patience. There are two sentences that recur in the diary that he maintained for more than half a century. 'Everything comes to a man who waits' and 'Thy will be done'.

These sentences bring out the character of the person and help to understand how he rose from a humble clerk to a highly respected accounts officer. A matriculate, he passed several departmental examinations for which he studied while doing a full-time job—often working 18 hours at a stretch—something that he would write about in his diary. He also had to manage his large household with its many problems single-handed. Shortly after my birth, my mother, Shyamvati, became incapable of attending to the household chores. So Papa had to multi-task.

Even without a college education, his English was excellent and his accent closer to the genuine English than my own. This was probably because of his regular interaction with senior officials of the Railway Board, many from England or Scotland and some Anglo-Indians. His diaries talk of a school principal, who seemed to have been an Englishman, Mr. Alcott. Papa was equally proficient in Urdu and Persian, which he had picked up as a child, when he went to a local madarsa (the traditional school that mainly taught Urdu and Persian).

Papa's early years were particularly hard. He could go to high school only because he had won a scholarship on the basis of the results of his middle school examination. In his career, too, he had to make his way up by dint of hard work. I remember that he once came back on a tonga as late as 2 o'clock in the morning. Late nights were a regular feature especially when the Railway budget was being prepared or discussed. Papa's grit and determination obviously rubbed off on his children because all of them made a mark for themselves in their own spheres.

Apart from this inherited legacy, there were other aspects of the environment that moulded our lives. The 1920s and 1930s were years of turmoil. The national movement was gathering momentum. Gandhiji had emerged as the leader of the mass movement for Independence and his calls for civil disobedience were attracting hundreds of thousands of men and women of all ages. They were defying the law and filling the jails. Our cousin Suraj Kishen Munshi, whom we called Nannabhai (Nanna means 'child' in Hindi), a bright young man with a poetic temperament, took a leading part in the students' movement in Calcutta, then the hub of the national movement. Even from jail he would send long letters full of lyrical passages, describing his emotions. On release, he would recount his experiences and, given his poetic temperament, recite Tagore's poems that he had learnt in jail. He touched the right chords in our hearts and made us eager to be part of the national movement.

Tragically, Suraj Kishen died early; he committed suicide in 1933, when just 23, leaving behind a manuscript of his poems and much speculation about the cause. Was it unrequited love? After all, he did address a poem to one of his fellow girl students in the English Department of the Calcutta University. Although only twelve then, I was quite mature and had already read hundreds of novels, including many by Dickens, Thackeray, Scott, Victor Hugo, Jane Austen, Charlotte and Emily Brontë and many others. I am fairly certain that this was not so and believed that he took this extreme step because the future must have looked totally bleak to him. His family was not well off and, as the only son of a large family, his father and sisters were looking up to him to take up a job to augment the meagre pension that his father received from the government.

Having participated actively in the freedom movement, a government job was out of the question. An uncle of his who had contacts with the Indian business community in Calcutta's Burrabazar area had found one for him. It involved writing in English the accounts that a traditional businessman, operating from his *gaddi*, kept in his local vernacular. For a sensitive person with a poetic temperament the prospect of spending years at the *gaddi*, filling up the columns of the ledgers, on a mere pittance of a salary, must have been appalling. I suspect that sheer frustration drove him to taking his own life. Placed in his circumstances, with no other option, I too might have preferred death. I do not think the youth today realize how limited the choices were for the young in those days, especially for those who had a record of political activity and whose means did not permit them to start their own business. Small wonder that some chose suicide and others took to revolutionary politics.

My brother Lalit (Little) Mohan Kaul, whom we called Lytton, also joined the national movement and offered satyagraha along with many others while studying at the Jadavpur Engineering College. Little Mohan was too odd a name and so all of us, Papa included, used to call him Lytton. Victor, born shortly after Lytton, told us later that Lord Lytton had come on a visit to Simla round about that time and since Lytton was on everyone's lips at that time Little Mohan became Lytton. At a certain stage in his life, Lyttonbhai must have felt that he had had enough of Lytton and Little Mohan and formally changed his name to Lalit though none of the other brothers changed their names. I continue to be called Jolly, though I find it embarrassing at times. I do not always feel jolly but manage to project a cheerful image and people generally think that the name reflects my temperament.

Lalitbhai lived a long and useful life and died a natural death in January 1999 at the age of 85. His was a remarkable personality and we brought out a festschrift on him on the first anniversary of his death. Lalit stood out amongst the brothers not only for what he achieved without much help from others but also because of his generous nature and his unstinted service to the family. While a student at the Jadavpur Engineering College, Lalit responded to Gandhiji's call to join the civil disobedience movement. He was arrested with many others and sentenced to six months' rigorous imprisonment. In jail, he was subjected to every form of torture that he endured rather than submit to the dictates of the British Jail Superintendent, one Colonel Luke, who wanted him to salute him every morning with the invocation 'Sarkar Salaam'. After his release, he continued his studies and graduated with a degree in chemical engineering. However, as this was not a recognized institution (it was run by the National Council of Education that the government refused to recognize), he had difficulties in getting a proper job in his own profession.

Rather than remain dependent on the family, he took up a series of small jobs in several sugar factories as a chemist. These factories were all in UP and he had to switch jobs three or four times as these were temporary appointments and the salary was low, only Rs 50 a month, as far as I remember. One of the factories had been set up by the Japanese and I remember that the Japanese chief engineer came to India on one occasion to attend to the machines and stayed with us for a night before leaving for the factory. This was our first direct contact with a Japanese and we were surprised to see how little he ate and impressed us with his very simple life style. Lalitbhai finally secured regular employment in the newly-started Department of Central Excise. He retired as Collector of Central Excise. He was also of great help to me during my years in the Party even though he never fully agreed with its policies.

Each of my other brothers contributed to the formation of my personality and character. The eldest, Prince, was the only one who went abroad for higher studies and got both a Diploma in Public Health and his MRCP from England. Later, he joined the World Health Organization and rose to become its Deputy Director General. His letters and his accounts of life there upon his return served as our first direct introduction to the western world.

Majorbhai, had a totally different influence on the family and on me. He introduced us to Hindu philosophy (ideology) and gave us our first copy of the Bhagawad Gita (translated into English by Annie Besant). Under his influence, I read the Gita several times though I was only thirteen or fourteen then. I did not understand much, except the story elements in the Gita but it had a subtle though profound impact on me. Later, when a Jesuit Father in school tried to convince me about the need to accept Christianity, it was this influence that enabled me to stand up to his arguments even though I was impressed with the faith and dedication of the Jesuit Fathers. They had a lasting impact on me.

Victor, just above me even though six years older, was more of a friend than the others who were much older. We were very close and it was with him that I discussed all my problems. He too would spend hours talking about his experiences. It was from him that I derived my interest in and love for English literature and English poetry. It stood me in good stead later when I took up English literature as my honours subject for my graduation. It is apparent that I exerted a great influence on him for he too joined the communist movement shortly after I did.

I have very faint memories of Simla that I left when I was just five. As was the practice in those days, most central government offices shifted to Delhi for the winter and returned to Simla in summer. I have happy memories of these annual peregrinations, especially the journey from Kalka to Simla by train. We would count the many tunnels the train passed through and shriek with excitement whenever the train entered them. I have some memories of the house that we lived in. It was called 'Alicot' and stood on the lower mall; on the way to what was called the Lower Bazaar. Once, I fell from the verandah of the first floor of our two-storey house on to the field below. This could have been very serious but I was small and very light and, perhaps, like a cat that can fall many storeys without sustaining an injury, I was able to get away with only a few scratches and with no bones broken.

Just across the fence of our house was the compound of the St. Thomas School. When I was a little over three, my father handed me over the fence to one of the teachers and asked her to see whether I would enjoy attending school. I remember her name: Miss Lillian. I distinctly recollect across these many years having howled so much that I was promptly handed back. Evidently, the time was not right for me to join school. I went to that very school a year later and liked learning a few nursery rhymes and familiarizing myself with some letters of the alphabet. I do not think I progressed much further during the few months there. I do remember though about the class once being marched off to the mall with little Union Jacks in hand to wave when, possibly, the Viceroy passed that way. Later, we were brought back to the school after having stood for some hours, given some sweets and let off for the day. The practice of using small children to cheer dignitaries, now called VIPs, continues till this day, sometimes with disastrous consequences for some children.

I have been told that I was weaned very late, when I was three, giving my father a hard time getting me off breastfeeding. The habit is unhealthy when carried on till so late but was especially undesirable for me because by then my mother had begun to show signs of mental abnormality. I do not know if this had any significance for my later life; none that I am conscious of. The fact remained that it was my father rather than my mother who brought me up. My mother was always around and kept to herself in her room. She was very affectionate, though her mind did wander. That may have had some impact because normally it is the mother who brings up the child.

TWO

To Calcutta and School

In 1925, my father was transferred to Calcutta to handle the accounts of the railway bridge being constructed across the river Hooghly, connecting Bally with Dakshineswar. He came alone as the rest of the family could not be moved from Simla until a house had been rented, furnished and a domestic help engaged. The rest of the family, myself included, arrived a year later, in 1926. Surprisingly enough, I remember the date on which we arrived in Calcutta: it was 5 September.

Calcutta, as I saw it from the verandah of the house we hired—1B Elgin Road—was very different from what it is today. The Diocesan Girls School was right across the street that was wide, clean and well maintained. Road maintenance was so much easier because the traffic was limited to a few cars, a few cycles and a few hand-pulled rickshaws. I do not remember having seen motor cycles on that road. There were so few cars that sometimes my brother or a cousin and I would play a game of guessing how many cars would pass. Sometimes, no more than a couple of cars passed in the entire morning. Of greater interest was our buying a second-hand car around 1932. This was shortly before my father retired and my brother returned after medical studies in England. It was a second-hand Renault bought from the French Motor Company for the princely sum of Rs 3,000; petrol then was fourteen annas a gallon!

Calcutta was a fairly clean city. The streets were washed twice a day; at least Elgin Road was, as were many other roads in the city proper. Our knowledge of Calcutta was limited to the Bhowanipore area, where we lived, and Chowringhee right up to Dalhousie Square.

Papa's office was in Dalhousie Square; Fairlie Place to be precise, where the headquarters of the Eastern Railways still remain. We took a bus or a tram from the Elgin Road-Chowringhee crossing to go past Chowringhee and Esplanade to get there. Trams were the preferred mode of transport though the buses of the Walford Transport Company, especially the double-deckers with an open upper deck, were also good fun. Chowringhee was familiar terrain because the cinema houses showing English pictures were all situated along Chowringhee or the roads leading from it: Globe, Elphinstone Empire, later New Empire, Metro and Lighthouse. Balcony seats for the night show at the New Empire were only for those in formal dress suits.

In the south, Calcutta was limited to the Kalighat and Bhowanipore neighbourhoods, where we lived. Park Circus came up only in 1928 when a session of the Indian National Congress took place. The Congress Exhibition Road there bears witness to the event. In the north, the city extended up to Shyambazar and Baghbazar, where we sometimes went for the heavenly rosogollas, which were quite a sensation at that time.

Calcutta had many open spaces and parks and quite a few ponds. The Dhakuria Lakes were being developed and I distinctly remember seeing extensive digging going on. The Anderson Club pool and the one just south of that were dug up in the late 1920s or early 1930s. The pool south of the Anderson Club (now called the Indian Life Saving Society) one was used for yachting though the yachts that I remember were much smaller than those that we see in the yacht races these days.

We started visiting the Lakes quite early; going to the Lakes was like an excursion far out of the town. The surrounding areas were swamps with village huts perched on patches of high ground in between. One can get an idea of the area from an incident that remains etched in my memory. One day, on his way back from office, my father brought along a Bengali gentleman who, we were told, was an agent dealing in what we would now call real estate. Papa said that he would show us some plots of land that were on sale. We asked if Papa was thinking of buying land but he pooh-poohed the idea.

The agent took us to the Dhakuria Lake area and then across the railway line. This was the Sealdah-Budge Budge line that evidently had been built quite early because it was operational when we went there perhaps in 1930-1931. He pointed to a swampy area across the railway line and said that plots were on sale there. One could buy a plot of a bigha (one-third of an acre) or more at Rs 300 a bigha! From there, he took us further east and pointed to another swamp where land was on sale at Rs 500 a bigha! My father thanked the agent and said he would let him know his decision later. We knew that there was no question of our buying any of those plots as Papa was dead against buying any property. In fact, unlike most people, his priorities were quite different. He used to proudly say that his five sons were his best assets and that he did not need any other. As for the plots shown by the agent, the first was what is now Lake Gardens and, the second, Jodhpur Park! Land here sells at Rs 5 lakh or more per *cottah,* which is one-twentieth of a bigha. One might think that we would be cursing ourselves for not having bought the land but none of us brothers has ever regretted Papa's decision.

Calcutta at that time lived up to its reputation as a city of palaces and gardens. Not only was the Mullick Palace a real show piece, a veritable museum, there were numerous mansions and *rajbaris* (princely palaces) with sprawling lawns belonging to the big zamindars and others who had the title of rajas. With the major industries of that period, jute, tea, coal, engineering, insurance, shipping and banking located in Bengal, with their headquarters in Calcutta, it was also the commercial capital of the country. It already had a booming stock market and a jute futures market; perhaps the only city in India to have these. A hundred years ago, there was a vibrant and officially registered stock exchange there.

From the cultural perspective too, the city was in the forefront. Girish Ghosh, the dramatist, was making waves and even women artistes had started appearing on the stage. Binodini was only one of the celebrated names. Indigenous cinema started with the New Theatres Company and the stars of those years—Saighal, Pramathesh Barua, Devika Rani and Kananbala—are still remembered with pride by the older generation in the country. We never missed any of the New Theatre's films. The aura of Rabindranath Tagore, India's first Nobel laureate, had spread across the entire country and even far beyond. Presidency College and St. Xavier's College were the leading educational institutions of the day and Calcutta University built by stalwarts such as Sir Ashutosh Mookerjee was regarded as the premier university of the country.

My brothers, Victor and Lytton, were admitted into a school just a few yards from our house. This was the Cathedral Mission High School that, as far as I know, still stands there, though Elgin Road is changing so fast that I am not so sure. Coming from Simla, my brothers had some problems adjusting to the new syllabus and the new environment and needed tutors to guide them. I remember one in particular. He was a little pro-British because I remember entering into an argument with him when I expressed some rather radical views. I was no more than six or seven so my remarks amused everyone. I said something like: 'We must shoot down the British.' I think the tutor was a bit alarmed for some days later a man from the Special (Intelligence) Branch came to the house and talked to my brothers and myself. He evidently decided that a six or seven year old should not be taken seriously and that was the end of it. Nevertheless, this does reflect the atmosphere in the house and in the country generally.

As for myself, I had only done a few months in a nursery at the St. Thomas School, Simla. My father wanted me to go to a good English medium school and had set his sights on St. Xavier's of which he had heard a lot, probably from his colleagues in office but also very likely from cousin Suraj Kishen. The school, unfortunately, accepted only students from Standard I, for which the qualifying age was six plus. So I needed to go through a year of kindergarten and the obvious choice was St. John's Diocesan that was bang opposite our house.

I found it difficult to adjust to the new environment to which I was suddenly exposed and the memories of my one year in that school are not happy ones. The headmistress or principal was a certain Miss Belchambers, who was probably an Anglo-Indian. In January 1927, when I was admitted into this school, I was just a little over five. It was a girl's school but boys were admitted in kindergarten, though most of the kindergarten students were girls. I have faint memories of the year I spent in that school and remember that I disliked the arithmetic class because the lady teacher was ill-tempered. If we made mistakes, she would throw the copy book on our faces and shout at us.

Two other incidents, very different in nature, stand out in my memory across the years. One reflects a trait in my character, absent-mindedness, that persists till this day; a fairly common one but probably more pronounced in me. We used to have a mid-day break for tiffin at around half-past twelve. One day, when the bell rang for the break I thought it was the bell for the end of classes and I took my bag and walked across the road to our house. An uncle of mine who was at home was a little surprised to see me at that time and asked how I had come home so early. I told him that the classes were over and so I had come home. A couple of hours later, a durwan or watchman of the school came across with a letter from the principal complaining that I had run away from school. I think my father sent some sort of an explanation the next day but the school decided that I was not to be trusted and so one of the senior girls was instructed to guard me during the tiffin period and make sure that I did not run away. The girls took their job seriously and would hold my wrist so tight that it hurt. I complained to my father and I think the punishment was withdrawn after a few weeks. Fortunately, I was in the school for only a year.

The point is that I was neither running away from the school nor wanting to bunk classes. I resented the punishment and felt unhappy during my stay there. The second incident is of a different nature. It was the annual convocation of the St. John's Diocesan College. We could see the school even from our sitting room where we spent most of our time at home. We suddenly noticed that the place was swarming with police vehicles and that the policemen had surrounded the school. My uncle who was at home made enquiries and found out that during the convocation one of the girl students had brought out a revolver and had shot at the Governor but missed. This incident left an impression on my mind though I do not know who the girl student involved was.

Such incidents created a strong urge in us for freedom. We resented our status as a colony of the British empire and were attracted towards the national movement from a very young age. While we strongly supported the dominant strand of the national movement at that time, the non-violent mass civil disobedience movement led by Mahatma Gandhi of the early 1930s, we hailed every act of resistance by any group of patriots, no matter what form it took. I remember how thrilled we were when one morning someone in the house, my uncle or my cousin, read out the newspaper headline about the armed revolt in Chittagong by a group of revolutionaries, who had stormed the armoury, seized all the weapons and liberated the town. The revolt known in history as the Chittagong Armoury Raid was short-lived but it did rouse the whole country. It certainly made us dream of one day taking up arms and driving out the British rulers. Little did I know at that time that some of the leaders of this operation, Ganesh Ghosh, Ananta Singh, Kalpana Dutt, Subodh Roy, would be fellow members of the Party that I would join some years later.

Such acts were of a sporadic nature while the Gandhi led national movement was a constant presence. So, while thoughts of armed struggle remained a day dream, we felt that we had to make our contribution to the national movement in whatever way we could. That is why when the call for boycott of foreign goods, particularly of foreign cloth, was given, I remember that we all started wearing khadi and stopped seeing English films. That really meant not going to the cinema at all because only English films were shown in those days and we were very fond of them. It was, therefore, a great act of sacrifice on our part, particularly because a Parsi gentleman,

Minoo Dhotiwala, who had become a friend of the family, gave us free passes for all the theatres owned by his family. This included what was then known as the Madan Theatre and such others as the Globe and Elphinstone cinemas. It was in these halls that the latest and best English films including the Charlie Chaplin films were released

We also started spinning on the charkha and the *takli.* It was during this period that I joined my first political procession; one organized with the body of Jatin Das who died while on hunger strike in the Andamans. I was twelve or less but I marched along with the rest of the procession right up to Hazra Park from where his body was probably taken for cremation. The park was later named the Jatin Das Park.

Papa was in the meantime on the verge of retirement. The Railways being directly owned by the government, he was a railway officer and a government servant. How did he react to all that was happening in the country and within our family? While he did not start wearing khadi, he sympathized with all that we were doing and had great admiration for my cousin and some other relatives, who were participating in the civil disobedience movement. He too was very fond of going to the cinema but participated in the boycott of English films; all this while he admired the British, giving his sons English names. He was particularly impressed with their efficiency, their sense of discipline and the thoroughness with which they went about their jobs. I cannot say how far this represented the reality but this was his perception as he would often tell us. Many people of that generation, particularly government servants had this kind of a split personality: hating the British for having enslaved us while admiring their efficiency, management skills and discipline. Papa was no exception.

My schooling really began when I joined St. Xavier's. Getting into St. Xavier's is worth recounting because it brings out the sea change in the education scenario since my childhood days. My cousin, Suraj Kishen, was a good student, a good debater and public speaker and a dedicated political activist. He studied at St. Xavier's for some time but was later expelled for his political activities. Immediately after I finished kindergarten in December 1927, my father began looking out for a regular school where I could study right up to the School Final stage. Suraj Kishen was still in St. Xavier's and was asked to help. He took me to see Father Turmes, who was not the Prefect or the Rector but was fond of my cousin, probably because he was in charge of the Debating Society of which my cousin was the secretary or convenor. He took one look at me and said he would speak to the School Prefect or whoever was in charge of admissions. There was no admission test, no interview and I had been enrolled. The school bus was booked for me and one fine morning on a cold January day in 1928, I found myself walking down the corridor of the ground floor of an old building. This building has been demolished; in fact, the new building came up while I was in the college.

Had there been an admission test, I would surely have failed because I had not learnt to speak English and would not have been able to answer the kind of questions that I believe are now put to kids. However, my life in school, in the proper sense of the word, had begun. School life continued for nine years till the Senior Cambridge examinations in 1936. After that I joined college in the same institution till I graduated in 1940. These thirteen years comprise the first phase of my life. They were the formative years that helped to shape my character and personality. Later events and subsequent experiences modified the early mould considerably but the imprint of the early years remained throughout my life and is evident even today.

St. Xavier's then was very different. That was only natural because of the sea change that has taken place in our country since then. The boys in our school—it was a boys' only school then—were from different groups. There was a large number of Anglo-Indians—I presume most of them Catholics—some Jews, some Parsis and only a few Bengalis. There were two hostels, one for the Christian students and the other a Hindu hostel for college students only. The teachers were either Anglo-Indians or Jesuit Fathers, mostly from

Belgium with some from Ireland.

My first term in the school was unpleasant and could have been disastrous. I had several traumatic experiences especially with an Anglo-Indian teacher named Mr. Murphy. He must have been a sadist because he would beat the boys mercilessly. No one was spared and if one made a mistake in sums or failed to do the homework, cuts would flow from a long cane that he brought to class. The worst was reserved for a particular boy, whose name I still remember: Baker. There were days when Mr. Murphy would come into class and call Baker to come up the first thing. For apparently no rhyme or reason, at least none that was clear to any of us, he would start beating him. Baker would scream and shout but the caning would go on. Was this to frighten us or was it just an expression of his sadism?

My problem was different. Having spoken Hindustani at home and having picked up little else in the year at Diocesan or the few months at St. Thomas, Simla, except the alphabet and a few nursery rhymes, I knew no English. At Xavier's everything was in English that was the medium of instruction. The books were all in English and the boys spoke only English even amongst themselves. I was totally out of my depth. At the end of the first term the school wrote to my father asking him to withdraw me from school. I understand that Papa sent back a strong reply refusing to do so but assuring them that I would improve over time.

The second term was much better. A new teacher, Mr. Pires, took our classes as Mr. Murphy was on leave. He was a good person and though he used the cane occasionally, his punishments were reserved for gross mistakes or misdemeanours. He was also an excellent teacher and I started picking up quite fast. Learning languages is quite easy when you are very young especially when you hear only that language for nearly five or six hours a day and are forced to communicate only in that language. I also received help at home from my brother, Victor, who helped me to memorise English poems in our text book. Victor was fond of poetry even then and later instilled in me a love of English literature. I think he could have made a good poet for he did write a few poems but never took it up seriously.

Mr. Murphy was back for the third term but I managed to complete the year with my results just good enough to earn me promotion to the next class. The next year was a turning point in my school career. Mr. Pires was again our school teacher and I was a fast learner. If memory serves, I found myself standing first in one of the examinations. The drill in those days was that there was a weekly class test, generally on a Friday. The day before, Thursday, was a holiday when one prepared for the test. The boy who came first—the results were announced on the following Monday—was asked to take the class register with the results to the Rector, Fr. Vermiere. This system enabled the Rector to keep in touch with all the bright boys in the school.

I recall one or two incidents that sound amusing but caused me a lot of distress then. One boy, I still remember his name, George Talati, asked me to hold his tiffin while he locked up the doors of the classroom. The practice was that during the tiffin recess the rooms were locked up to prevent theft of books while the classrooms were empty. One of the boys was given the responsibility of doing this. Talati finished locking up the doors and turned to me for his tiffin. I had, in my absent-mindedness, eaten up his tiffin. I had not intended to do so and was carrying my own tiffin. Later, I found my own tiffin tucked in my pocket. Talati was, however, not going to take this lightly. He took me to the School Prefect and complained that I had eaten up his tiffin. I did not know what to say and started crying. I was only seven years old but the Prefect admonished me and said that if I felt hungry in future and did not have my own tiffin, I should go to him and he would give me something to eat. I remember being unable to explain to him that I had done this in a fit of absent-mindedness.

On another occasion, while I was having my tiffin—usually sandwiches—a kite swooped down and snatched it neatly from my hands. During tiffin time we would roam around the fairly spacious playing ground and eat out in the open. The sky above would be swarming with kites. We do not see kites nowadays. There are only crows and, of course, vultures who frequent places where carcasses are to be found. They are not interested in schoolboys' tiffin.

The next two years were rather uneventful. I continued to do well in class though I was not among the first two or three. In some examinations, we called them competitions, I did come first but I was poor in mathematics. I was reading a lot though, mostly fiction, Charles Dickens being my favourite. I must have read some of his books such as *Oliver Twist* and *David Copperfield* several times. We had Anglo-Indian teachers in these two classes who were strict but not sadists like Mr. Murphy. One of them, Mr. Bellety, had been a member of the Indian Olympic Hockey team.

I made a number of friends but was very close only to a few. One of them was Sunil Bose, who later became Bengal's top badminton player. After he retired from active sports he became sports correspondent of the *Amrita Bazar Patrika* and continued with the paper till he retired. He died some years ago. The other friend was Bablu (Debabrata) Bose. He was the grandnephew of Sir J. C. Bose and quite a bright boy but rather eccentric. Later, when I came in contact with the Party, I found that he too had joined the communist movement. I worked very closely with him during the Youth Cultural Institute years about which I will speak later. Over the years, he became increasingly eccentric and I lost touch with him when he went to England. He remained there for many years and I met him rather unexpectedly when I was editing the economic journal *Capital*. He would write on science subjects and on his granduncle.

Another person who was a year senior to me in school was Subroto Sengupta (SSG). When I joined the Standard I in 1928, he joined Standard II and right up to the Senior Cambridge class he continued to be a class ahead of me. He passed Senior Cambridge in 1935. I passed in 1936 and was in touch during the school years but became close friends in college. He was a brilliant student and used to win the first prize in some of the essay competitions that were open to all. Later, when I took up debating seriously, he used to accompany me to represent Calcutta University in inter-university competitions.

Subroto joined the communist movement and was active on the students' front. He was the editor of the journal published by the All India Students Federation. He dropped out of the Party in the 1950s after the turmoil following the Left-Adventurist line of 1948-1950 and took up advertising as a career. Later he emerged as the builder of Clarion, formed after D. J. Keymer closed down. I was again in close touch with him when I left the Party and returned from Delhi in 1964 and worked as a freelancer for Clarion that had, meanwhile, become Clarion McCann.

The other students with whom I came in close contact in school were Arun Bose and Bhaskar Mitter, who joined the school in 1934 when we were in Standard VII. Both were very bright and had evidently spent some time in schools in England. Arun Bose introduced me to socialist ideas. He was very well read and he talked of Bertrand Russell and Bernard Shaw and some other Fabian socialists. He had not become a Marxist then. Whether it was for want of access to Marxist literature or because he was more under the influence of the Fabian socialists is difficult to say. I do remember though that we used to sit for hours in the library talking about socialism and philosophy. These interactions were important because it was through them that I became interested in socialism. I read Bernard Shaw's *Intelligent Woman's Guide to Socialism* and his other books. I think I read all the three volumes of his plays.

Arun Bose went to England for his college studies and returned to India in 1940 as a communist. He was immediately taken into the Central Committee of the CPI and I met him on a few occasions during my Party years. He too left the Party in the early 1950s but continued to be a Marxist. He started teaching economics in Delhi and, after retirement, returned to Calcutta where I used to meet him occasionally at seminars.

Bhaskar Mitter, who also joined these discussions sometimes, became my main competitor in school. From Standard V onwards

I used to come first in class. In Standard VII too I was first, Bhaskar second and, probably, Arun was third. In Standard VIII, Bhaskar came first and I stood second. In the final Senior Cambridge exam, I was told that I had stood first though ranks were not announced then as they are for the Board exams now. In fact, Father Dobinson, our class teacher in the final year, told me that I had come first in India but no official merit list was published, unlike what is done for the *Madhyamik* results today, and I had no means of verifying the information.

Bhaskar was the son of Sir B. L. Mitter and went on to become chairman of many companies such as Andrew Yule, Indian Oxygen (now BOC)—the company in which I worked from the late 1960s right up to the early 1980s—CESC and perhaps many others. He also became President of the Bengal Chamber during which period I interacted with him on a number of occasions.

Another person I recall was a boy whom we knew as K. C. (Bhaya) Sen. He probably had an English mother though I learnt later that he was a grandson of the eminent Brahmo leader, Keshab Chandra Sen. He was a very nice person and at one stage, when we were allowed to bring out a class magazine of which I was made the editor, he worked closely with me. I met him again when I joined the University Rowing Club in 1937. He became our champion sculler and established quite a few records. He disappeared from my radar during my Party years.

I would meet him again quite often after I joined the Lake Club in 1972, until he finally migrated to England. I later learnt that he is running a pub there. I wonder what Keshab Sen's thoughts would be if he were looking down from heaven and seeing one of his descendants running a pub! Not that I thought less of KC because of this. He is a fine person and I do not believe that just because he was the descendant of a great spiritual leader he too should have followed in his footsteps.

Abhijit Sen, who later became chairman of the Sen Raleigh group, was another person with whom I had occasion to interact in the post-Party stage. I think he was a year junior to me but I remember having known him during my school years. No other name stands out; perhaps because most of the boys were either Anglo-Indians or Jews or Parsis. Among the Parsis was a Russi Anklesaria, who distinguished himself as a surgeon and whom I have met on one or two occasions. There was one Choksi, who too became chairman of some company and settled in Ireland. I met him and his wife suddenly at the Calcutta Club one day. He was very effusive as we had tea and snacks together. The Anglo-Indians and Jews left the country after Independence and settled in Australia, Canada or in England. Possibly many of the Jews went to Israel. We also had a Mallya in our class; possibly the father or uncle of the industrialist and Member of Parliament, Vijay Mallya.

The next important landmark in my school career and indeed in my life was the year 1932. I had now moved up to Standard V and for the first time a priest, Father P. Joris s.j., was our teacher. He had a very strong personality and it left a lasting impression on me. He was a good teacher too; a disciplinarian who never used the cane. I soon became his favourite student and it was from this year that I started coming first in class. I began to concentrate on my studies and even went in for extra classes in French when Fr. Joris offered to coach me. These used to be during the holidays. I never needed tutors during my school and college life; nor did any of the top boys in class. The Fathers were always available for any assistance either after school hours or during the holidays.

It was from this year that emphasis was placed on religious instruction. The classes usually started with the Lord's Prayer. The Christian boys repeated it but the others stood in silence. The daily repetition, sometimes twice or thrice a day, helped us to memorise it. I have not forgotten it till today. I did not use it during my years in the Party and for some years even afterwards but later I began repeating it. It is an excellent prayer and it certainly helps. We also had Bible classes and it was not compulsory for non-Christian boys to participate but we sat and listened all the same.

Were efforts made to convert us? Yes, by one Father and not in any crude manner. There was no pressure nor were any special incentives offered. There were long discussions and efforts to convince some of us who were attracted towards religion but not yet prepared to accept Christianity. As far as I remember, two students, one in the class above ours and one in my class had almost made up their minds to accept Christianity. While I accepted the existence of God and was convinced of the need for prayer, I was never tempted to accept Christianity. Strange as it may sound, it was only after reading Vivekananda that I came closer to Christ than I had been in my school, run by the Jesuits. In fact, I did my best to dissuade the two boys I have referred to from seeking conversion. They had started going to the chapel and saying their prayers there. Ultimately, they lost interest.

The Fathers in the later classes made no such attempt. Perhaps this was a personal effort on the part of Fr. Joris and not a policy decision of the Fathers. They concentrated on the Christian students, mostly Catholics. Even after Fr. Joris left school for another institution, he continued to write long letters to me. I had told him that I was not convinced that Christianity was the only true faith. He tried to convince me in his letters. I do not remember his arguments but I do remember the pages and pages of matter he sent. I soon stopped reading them or replying to the letters. Obviously, I was in no position to argue with him and yet I realized that there was no question of my converting to Christianity.

That I was able to resist this attempt is in a large part due to my home atmosphere. My father was never very religious minded in the sense that he never went to temples or offered any prayers at home. He did, however, have a strong faith in God and Majorbhai's introduction to the Gita enabled me to overcome Fr. Joris's influence. Despite this, I admired him greatly and later, after I left the Party, I contacted him again and we met from time to time even after he had become Prefect of the Commerce Department of St. Xavier's College. The impact of his personality remained with me throughout my life; the way he disciplined himself, the way he used every moment of his time in useful activity, his strong faith, were all traits that influenced me.

Many years later, probably some time in the 1980s, I attended a meeting called by some students to felicitate him when he retired. I got to know of it through an announcement in the papers and, when I went, I found that it had been called by the commerce students. Fr. Joris had, I think some time in the 1960s, become Prefect of the Commerce Department and it was his efforts that made the Commerce Department of St. Xavier's College the preferred destination for commerce students. Many of his students had risen to high positions in business and industry or in the professions. Tapan Mitra of Indian Aluminium and later Chairman of Haldia Petrochemicals, whom I had got to know through my rowing activities, was one of them. When the meeting ended and there was no reference to Fr. Joris' earlier stint in the school, I spoke to some of the Fathers and to some of the alumni of the Commerce Department who had called the meeting. It appears that none of them knew about his earlier stint in the school; not even the Fathers who spoke about him in that meeting.

After the meeting we were told that we could go up to his room and see him. He was too ill to come down and attend the meeting. So we went in single file and wished him as we went past him. I was tremendously impressed by what I saw. He was holding a rosary in his hand and there was a smile on his face and a faraway look as if he was seeing a vision. It was almost like a trance. Was this a kind of *samadhi*? He died shortly afterwards. We had had our farewell meeting.

The next year, Standard VI, was not so very eventful except that it was from this year that I started writing and developed an interest in English literature. I was writing essays and these were good enough to get me the first place. I was also reading the classics, especially Dickens and everything that the school library offered or those that my brother Victor brought from other libraries. Besides, there were many that I won as prizes. What a turnaround from the Standard I boy whom the school wanted to be withdrawn because of his inability to cope with the classes. Our class teacher now was Fr. Corbett who was not a Belgian. He was probably Irish.

In Standard VII, there was a Belgian, Fr. Mairlot, in charge of our class. Right from Standard V, special subjects like mathematics, history and geography were taught by other subject teachers. The last two were taught by an interesting person, Father Verbockhaven. He had written his own books and did not use the prescribed text books. I realized later that this was because he wanted to give the Catholic viewpoint for English history. He tried to make the lectures interesting by dramatizing the events. Had videos been in vogue, we would have surely been shown video clips.

Hindi was introduced as a subject from Standard VII. Earlier, right from Standard II or III, we had Latin as second language. Surprisingly, it was Fr. Mairlot who started taking our Hindi classes leading to some amusing incidents. There were 30 or 35 boys in our class of whom only some six or seven had Hindi/Urdu as their mother tongue. Till then, except for the script, there was no difference in the spoken language. When Fr. Mairlot wrote a Hindi sentence on the board, the Hindi/Urdu-speaking boys would stand up and shout: 'The sentence is incorrect, Father.' Embarrassed, he would explain that he had followed all the rules of grammar. 'We do not know the rules of grammar but this is not correct,' we would insist. He saw that this was not on and arranged for a separate class for the six or seven of us that was called the advanced Hindi class, taken by a Mr. Pandey, who taught Hindi in the college. He was very good but considering that this was the first time I was learning the Hindi alphabet, I was a little out of my depth in the beginning, especially when he taught us Tulsidas's *Ramayana* written in a form of Hindi that was quite different from the colloquial Hindi I was accustomed to. We all picked up very fast though.

Standard VIII was another milestone. Our teacher was an Anglo-Indian, a Mr P. O'Brien, whose son Neil and grandsons have made a name for themselves. Neil was on the board of Oxford University Press in India. Mr O'Brien taught us English literature and was an excellent teacher. He taught us how to appreciate English poetry, drama, essays and fiction. The grounding that I got during this year enabled me to do well when I took up English literature for my graduation. However, for the first time after the Standard V, I stood second. Bhaskar was first. This was partly due to my illness; I had been suffering from headaches though one thing good came out of it. I resolved to go in for sports and outdoor activity to ensure that I kept fit. I realized that all work and no play makes Jack a dull boy. I waited for a year until the final Senior Cambridge exams before I took up sports in right earnest. I had started playing football for the class team but was not very serious about it. I was not very good but was evidently improving because when we were playing against Ivan Surita's team he encouraged me saying: 'You are playing well, *bacchu* (kid).'

For the final year in school, in 1936, we had Fr. Dobinson as our class teacher. Although a Jesuit priest, he was very unlike conventional priests who had taught us. He was very jovial and would often stop teaching half an hour before the close and say, 'Let us have some jokes.'. Most of them he told himself but often we too joined in as he made us feel that he was one of us. I am grateful to him because he gave us—Arun Bose, Bhaskar Mitter, Bablu Bose and perhaps one or two others and me—a carte blanche to use the library. The keys of the almirah were given to us and we could take any book we liked. When I got my prizes for Standard VIII, all books—these were the only prizes given each year—I was unhappy with the books I got and told Fr. Dobinson so. He took me to Thacker Spink and Company—where the Peerless head office now stands—and asked me to choose as many books as I liked. It was this kind of help and encouragement that enabled me to top the list of those who appeared for the Senior Cambridge examination that year. Fr. Dobinson was most probably also Irish. Later, in the 1960s, after I gave up political activities and started visiting St. Xavier's again, I learnt that Father Dobinson had passed away. I was sorry to hear this because he was the one with whom I would have most liked to interact even though the other Fathers too were most sympathetic and willing to help.

School also provided me with my first stint as an editor of a journal. It was in Standard VIII or perhaps even earlier that we brought out a journal. Whether we mooted this ourselves or it came as a suggestion from the teachers I do not remember but there it was. I was asked to edit it and, I think, I chose the name: *The Medium*. We would collect articles and some school news and type it out after which it was cyclostyled and distributed among the students of Standards VIII and IX, the final classes in school. That was my first foray into the world of journalism and clearly a portent of things to come.

I also recall Subroto Sengupta's satirical piece when he was in Standard IX. He wrote about us, who were in the Standard VIII, a very well-written piece in which he called us the Highbrows and signed himself as a Lowbrow. He was possibly taking a swipe at people like Arun Bose who always talked about Bertrand Russell, Bernard Shaw and what were, for the majority of students, exotic subjects such as socialism and philosophy.

The next momentous event in my young life was the debate in which I participated in Standard VIII for the first time. I still remember the topic: 'It is better to be a scholar than to be a sportsman.' I spoke in favour of the motion but was a little nervous, spoke rather haltingly and did not make a very good impression. A beginning had, however been made of the many years of debating during which I became a good speaker and, more importantly, got over stage fright. In fact, the presence of a large audience always acted as a source of inspiration.

School was then a wonderful experience and I owe a lot to the school for the grounding it gave me; one that has stood me in good stead. I am still reaping the benefits: I learnt the importance of ethical behaviour. I acquired a sound education in the humanities. I saw what efficiency and discipline were all about. My contact with students from various backgrounds broadened my horizon. I learnt the English language well, was able to enjoy writing and to appreciate the greatness of English literature. It was through this literature that windows were opened into a different and a wider world. There is some criticism now-a-days, particularly from the Sangh Parivar, about the harm that Christian missionaries are doing. My experience tells me that the missionaries have played an important part in spreading education and science in the country and have also set examples of efficiency and discipline that have had a positive influence on our society. There have been aberrations; some have tried to run down our ancient culture and heritage though all that has changed now. St. Xavier's in Patna and Delhi have become Hindi medium schools.

THREE

Community Spirit or the Lack of It

Since we were coming to Calcutta for the first time, our first contacts were naturally with the Kashmiri Pandit community. Kashmiri Pandits had come and settled in the city long before our arrival. Sambhunath Pandit was a judge of the Calcutta High Court and eminent enough to have had a street, Sambhunath Pandit Street, and a hospital named after him. His house, or a part of the original, is listed as a heritage house. I remember our family being invited to the huge *haveli* on the western end of Sambhunath Pandit Street along with the rest of the *biradiri*, that is, the entire community.

At that time the biradiri consisted almost entirely of those members of our community who had left Kashmir a century or two earlier; many were not Kashmiri-speaking but Urdu-speaking. The official language for commerce, industry and all official work was English. On one or two occasions the biradiri was invited to our own house and I remember a long line of people sitting on the verandah of our ground floor with banana leaves placed in front of them on which food was served. Whenever an important event took place in the family, sweets and laddoos were distributed to the entire community. My brother's success in the MRCP exam in England was one such occasion. The entire biradiri was treated to sweets.

There were many older Kashmiri families in Calcutta. One was the family of Jeevanlal Pandit who served as the President of the Burrabazar Congress Committee in the late 1920s and early 1930s. The family was distantly related to us and we were in close touch. They had a son who was just a year older and a daughter, a couple of years older. Surprisingly, they spoke Bengali among themselves, their Hindustani accent was a little peculiar and we often made fun of that. Another family was that of Shyamsunder Kaul whose son, Pratap, whom we called Pattu, was just a little younger than I was. He later joined the Indian Civil Service and became the Finance Secretary in the Government of India and later Ambassador to the United States. They lived in the Bhowanipore area, not far from where we were, on Ray Street. I lost touch with them after the 1930s but I met him again much later when I was working as a journalist. Despite the long gap he recognized me and we chatted for a while.

There was also the Wanchu family with which we were in regular touch and often played badminton with their boys. They had bought a plot of land and built a house in the Park Circus area that had a small compound at the back. During the 1946 riots, their house was attacked and they managed to survive by taking shelter with a Christian family in the neighbourhood until they were rescued by an army patrol. They shifted to our house in Bhowanipore until the situation became normal but they could not bear to return to their house. They sold it and shifted to a rented flat.

Amongst my many interesting, amusing memories is that of Papa taking me on a visit to a farm house of some wealthy person, somewhere on the Howrah side of the Hooghly, when I was around ten or eleven. The person my father was meeting was Motilal Nehru, who was related to us and Papa used to meet him and other members of the family whenever they came to Calcutta. Papa's diary mentions that Motilal Nehru and his wife once came and stayed with us in Simla. I remember visiting Krishna, Jawaharlal Nehru's sister, with Papa, when she was in a hospital in Calcutta and presenting her with a bouquet of flowers. I also remember visiting Kamala Nehru in hospital; Jawaharlal also dropped in for a while. The meeting at the Howrah farm house was a little more interesting. As Papa and Motilal Nehru sat down for a chat, I was clearly feeling out of place when a girl, just a little older than I was, appeared and the two elders immediately asked her to show me round the garden and play with me. The girl took me around and showed me the different flowers in the garden for about half an hour. I did not ask her name, nor did she ask me mine and we were soon called in. Recalling that incident years later, I feel, that the girl must have been the person later known as Indira Gandhi.

Other memories of this period are of the poverty and destitution that one could see particularly around the bazars and market places. After returning from office, Papa would take one of the older boys to the market for making household purchases and I tagged along. I remember sitting in the car outside Jadubabu's Bazar in Bhowanipore while Papa and an elder brother went into the market. As I waited, staring out of the car window, a beggar would arrive with outstretched arms. I had nothing in my pocket and could only look on. After a while he moved away but another face appeared in front of the window. Some of these beggars were hideously deformed with leprosy. I was shocked but could only turn my eyes away and wondered why and how such poverty and misery existed. My wait in the car sometimes extended to as much as an hour or more. It is from then that I inwardly resolved to do something about such poverty and misery.

This resolve was strengthened by another phenomenon: domestic servants in every house we visited. Some came from the Garhwal hill areas, some from Nepal and others from Bihar or Orissa. Our own house was no exception. Again, I was forced to be a silent spectator as some of them were shouted at; some even beaten with sticks for minor transgressions. I had to do something about that. How could such things continue?

FOUR

The In-Between Experience

Princebhai's success in England meant far more than just a treat for the biradiri. Princebhai returned and had a great impact on our lives by simply sharing his experiences. Even his voyage to England provided us with an eye-opening experience because Papa, Victor and I travelled to Bombay to see him off. On the day of his departure, we went to Ballard Pier from where the ship—a P&O vessel—took off. I went inside the ship and was taken for a look at the cabins and other parts of the ship. This was quite a momentous occasion: my first time inside a ship. Then came Princebhai's weekly letters to which Papa would reply. He would dictate the reply to Victor and often I would see both the letter from England and the reply.

Through these letters and his first-hand account of conditions there after he returned, we learnt about life in England. He had brought with him a gramophone and a few records of popular English songs that gave us our first exposure to what was then western pop music; very different from the pop music of today. We also learnt how to set the table for dinner or lunch, how to lay the table with the right cutlery for the type of meal to be served and what is known as table manners. How did this help me in later life? It certainly helped when much later in life I took up a job in a British company. I felt immediately at home and had no problem of adjustment; not even when I visited the headquarters of the company in Hammersmith House, London. I was able to make a good impression.

Princebhai joined the Indian Medical Service (the Army medical service) and was later selected for the World Health Organization, where he rose to be the Deputy Director General. Throughout his career in the WHO and for some years after his retirement, when his services were on demand as a consultant, he lived abroad and most of his children were educated in Switzerland or New York. After retirement, he tried to settle down in India and built a house in New Delhi's Maharani Bagh but could not adjust to the conditions. With most of his children abroad, he finally settled down in Canada where he spent the remaining years of his life. He died at the ripe old age of 99. His was the western influence on the family for which Majorbhai's Hindu influence, with the yogasana culture, provided the perfect balance. Majorbhai too entered the corporate world and served as the director and chief executive of some companies.

At the risk of jumping a little ahead in my narrative, I might mention here that it was Princebhai who quietly suggested to me once in the late 1950s, during one of my visits to Delhi perhaps to attend a meeting of the National Council, that it was time to consider whether I should continue in the Party and move on to some other field of activity. I was then just approaching forty, and he explained that further hesitation might make it too late. This was some time after the Twentieth Congress of the CPSU and the de-Stalinization drive, when I had begun to feel the need to do some rethinking about my future. My mind was in turmoil but I had not, till then, considered the possibility of quitting the Party. In fact, such a course of action was quite inconceivable despite the revelations about Soviet reality. The little nudge from my brother made me realize that there was another option; I saw his point. At a later stage, much beyond forty, a change might not have been possible, even if I wanted it. The wisdom of his words came home to me many years later. In private conversations with me, two senior leaders of the Party confessed to me on separate occasions that they too had wanted to break away but found that they had nowhere to go; it was too late.

FIVE

College and the Extra-curriculars

Back to the pre-Party days, it was time to go to college and, of course, it was to be St. Xavier's. What was worrisome was the state of my health that had deteriorated in the last two years in school; I had blinding headaches. I understood then that looking after the body was as necessary as looking after the mind. One of the first things that I did after joining college was to join the University Rowing Club. I also joined a physical culture organization, as 'gyms' were then called. This was the beginning of my interest in sports that I have kept up with till this day. Sports and yogasanas account for my fitness despite my years. I have done yoga with occasional breaks right till this day with immense benefits to my health and total personality. Any education sans sports is incomplete. Quite rightly has it been said that Waterloo was won on the playing fields of Eton.

For me, it was yet another process of self-discovery; a strong pair of lungs that I had no knowledge of possessing and which made me good at long-distance running. I competed in the one-mile event at the inter-collegiate sports and was tied for the first place with a boy named Ahmed. We both got the first prize and were selected for the inter-university championship to be held in Lahore, probably in 1938. Not unexpectedly, Punjab University won the championship including the one-mile race but this was a great experience for me. In hindsight, the total lack of any coaching was a severe handicap; my tactics were absolutely wrong. I accelerated from the first, took the lead in the first round and tried to maintain the lead till the end. Obviously, I was absolutely out of breath by the time the last lap was being run. There was not a word of advice from anyone either in the college or in the university. No wonder standards were so poor here.

Sports and extra-curricular activities became a part of the college regimen for more than the three and a half years that I was in college. Some of our teachers were good, some just about average. Fr. Bryan who taught us English literature was very good and so was Fr. Schepers who taught us history. No other teacher made much of a mark. I took up Hindi as a second language and made fairly good progress with the help of our Hindi teacher, Mr Pandey. I even took part in Hindi debates because debating had become a serious interest for me.

I discovered that I was able to speak well and suffered from no stage fright. I was chosen to represent the college in inter-collegiate competitions and, to my joy, won the third prize in the very first competition that I participated in. This was perhaps the first All India Inter collegiate Debating Competition and remains one of the memorable events of my life. The Senate Hall of the Calcutta University (sadly demolished since with a most uninteresting structure in its place) was packed to capacity. There must have been over 3,000 people and I still meet some who remember me just because of that debate. In those days no attention was paid to preserving the heritage and that beautiful building was pulled down as was the frontage of St. Xavier's, which used to be the portico of the Sans Souci theatre. These were beautiful pieces of architecture and should have been preserved.

This debate had an enormous influence on the future course of my life. Earlier, I had no interest in politics apart from a vague sense of nationalism and an urge to make the country free. These debates, mainly on political themes, made me take serious interest in politics. The subject of that memorable debate was 'Gandhiji's path of truth and non-violence is the only way to win freedom for India' or something to that effect. I spoke in favour of the motion and won the third prize. The first and second prize winners were from Lahore colleges. Mazhar Ali, who got the first prize, became a renowned journalist in Pakistan. He ran a weekly that had a very progressive outlook. It required tremendous courage to run such a weekly in Pakistan but he persevered till the end. Some pieces from this journal were published in *Mainstream* and perhaps other Indian journals as well.

The girl who won second prize definitely deserved it. She may have been Perin Bharucha (who later married Ramesh Chandra, Secretary, World Peace Council), who also studied in Lahore and later joined the Party. I was able to keep track of Mazhar Ali and some of the other speakers. Purnendu Banerjee, from the Law College, got the fourth prize. He later got a diplomatic assignment and was ambassador or first secretary in an Indian embassy. By a strange coincidence, I was recently shown a manuscript written by him describing his experiences as a diplomat and asked to give an opinion as to whether it was fit for publication. I thought that the material was good but it needed a lot of editing. I do not know whether it was finally published.

The debate not only gave me a lot of publicity but was, in a sense, my first foray on to the political stage. Significantly, I took a stand in support of the Gandhian outlook. As this story unfolds, one will see how I took a U-turn shortly afterwards and accepted the viewpoint of the communist movement in India, well expressed in Rajani Palme Dutt's book, *India Today*, where he castigated Gandhi as the 'Jonah of Indian Revolution'. In an irony of fate, I have returned to Gandhi in the last years of my life.

Another important incident of the time, one of many that were gradually though somewhat imperceptibly prodding me towards my decision to plunge into politics, was the strike in St. Xavier's College. This strike was suddenly thrust upon the students; launched without any preparation or warning. The issue was whether the students could read an address on the Rector's Day without having it vetted by the college authorities. We were sitting in the auditorium when Kalyan Bose and Aurobindo Bose, nephews of the charismatic Subhas Chandra Bose, suddenly declared a strike because the authorities were insisting on censoring their address. They walked out and took with them about 50 per cent of the students.

For many of us in the auditorium this was a bolt from the blue. We did not understand why we were being asked to go on a strike without any notice or preparation. The next day I cycled up as usual to the Short Street gate of the college and found that there was picketing going on. We roamed around for some time and then scaled the wall to enter college and found more than 50 per cent of the boys present. The teachers were greatly concerned at the turn of events and, though the classes were held, we were not able to pay much attention; nor were the teachers in a mood to lecture seriously. We went again the next day but heard a commotion at the Park Street gate. Many picketers were squatting in front of the gate to prevent anyone from entering and the authorities had brought out hose pipes to squirt water on them.

This incensed the students further and many others from outside joined the picketers. For the first time I found student leaders from outside coming to the college and addressing what had by now become a large gathering. Among those who spoke were Sadhan Gupta and Biswanath Mukherjee, both of whom I saw for the first time. The provocations led to the strike becoming total. No one entered the college the next day though we went near the gate to see what was happening.

One day, a group of 30 or 40 students started marching towards Elgin Road; a short distance from Short Street. I joined them more out of curiosity than anything else. The procession entered the house of Subhas Bose on Elgin Road and the leader, known later as Netaji, came out and spoke to the students. He did not make a speech as such but spoke a few words quietly to the students. I do not remember what he said but very likely he encouraged them and promised them support. The strike was soon resolved though, following some sort of a settlement and classes were resumed and on the whole the incident made little impression on me.

The point I wish to make is that my entry into politics was not through the students' movement though that did create an awareness of the prevalent atmosphere. St. Xavier's remained practically insulated from politics for a long time though there had been a .

strike in 1930 or 1931, in which my cousin Suraj Kishen was involved (one that forced him to take a transfer to another college along with other strike leaders). Among the leaders of this strike was Saleque, an Urdu-speaking nationalist Muslim, whom I got to know rather well. He joined the Party and was later elected councillor of the Calcutta Corporation. He got to be known as Saleque Lucknowi because he would participate in *mushairas* (Urdu poetry festivals). Saleque, now in his nineties and rather ill, rang me up recently and recalled our days in St. Xavier's.

My increasing preoccupation with politics received another boost courtesy a study circle that we started at Somen Gupta's house. He was a fellow student whose parents had a fairly large house on Manoharpuker Road in south Calcutta. One of their rooms could be spared for our meetings. I am not sure when we started this but we met on Sunday afternoons during the St. Xavier's years. Although a purely academic exercise, it helped me to get in touch with the political trends in the student world of Calcutta at that time. In our group were communist students; some M. N. Royists, some who supported Subhas Bose, some who belonged to the Sri Sangha group of Lila Nag, and perhaps some who were not attached to any group though they were all left-minded. We used to invite one speaker from outside to give a talk that was followed by a discussion. Sometimes the speakers were from among the student leaders. Of the outside speakers that I recall were Jyoti Bose and Bhowani Sen.

I do not remember what Jyoti Bose spoke on but recall that he read out certain passages from Leontiev's book and made a few comments of his own. I was far more impressed by Bhowani Sen, who spoke on Dialectical Materialism and put across his point of view very well. We were none the wiser after his explanation though. This was sometime in 1938 or 1939. In this study circle, we started a typed journal that I was asked to edit. Quite a few issues were brought out and several copies were circulated amongst the members of the study circle. In one we supported the move to make Subhas Bose the President of the Congress. This was when the Tripura

Congress (January 1939) was held and Gandhiji's nominee, Pattabi Sitaramayya, lost.

To take a fast forward to the 1950s, 1960s and 1970s—when Jyoti Bose emerged as one of the most popular leaders and a very impressive speaker, many, even within the Party, wondered how despite his rather mundane style of public speaking, Jyoti Bose could get such amazing audience response. He surpassed others with far greater oratorical skills. I think, his down-to-earth, simple colloquial idiom, telling people about day-to-day developments taking place in the State Legislative Assembly and in the movement outside, went down much better with the people, particularly urban audiences, than the rhetoric of speakers who would generally be regarded as greater orators.

Behind Jyoti babu's huge success and popularity lay two factors. One, as an 'England-returned' *(bilet pherot)* barrister, he was ever the quintessential bhadralok and—unlike another Left Front minister who famously declared that he was not a bhadralok but a communist—never tried to hide it. In the pre-Independence Legislative Assembly, as practically the only voice of the opposition, who could stand up and argue with the great Dr. B. C. Roy—he soon became the darling of the Indian middle class.

In fact, it is an open secret that Dr. Roy, surrounded as he was by a set of very mediocre ministers, admired him for his courage and his debating skills, which enlivened the otherwise dull Assembly proceedings, and encouraged him all along. Also, Jyoti Babu never cared much for theory, relying entirely on his common sense. Thus, while other leaders were imprisoned in the straightjacket of a theory that could no longer provide a guide to action, he worked his way through the maze of Bengal politics, using what is now called pragmatism as his only lodestar.

No wonder, he has sometimes been called the Deng of the Indian communist movement.

Circumstances were gradually leading me into politics. The student community in Calcutta was in a state of ferment. Left politics was in the air and the communist Left had appeared as the dominant force, thanks to the Students Federation. In 1937-1940 it was a united organization of students of different political colours but the Left-minded students were an overwhelming majority.

Ultimately, it was through my debating activities that I was finally drawn into the communist movement. An inter-collegiate debate at the Calcutta University Institute on the subject 'The Soviet attack on Finland is an act of aggression' found me representing St Xavier's and in favour of the motion. From a common sense point of view this was obvious and I strongly condemned the aggression. By now I had become a fairly good speaker and my speech attracted attention. After the debate I was collared by two speakers who had spoken against the motion. One was Biswanath Dubey, a powerful speaker but of the demagogic type. He was a leader of the Labour Party (sometimes referred to as the Bolshevik Party) who tried to bully me into accepting his point of view. Finding that I would not yield, he gave it up as a bad job.

The other speaker, Prasanta Sanyal, who took hold of me after Dubey had given up, had a different approach. Soft-spoken and willing to listen to my point of view, he quietly put forth the case on the other side. I realized that there was some merit in what the other side was saying though I was not fully convinced. I went back and reported to Father Bryan that, surprisingly enough, the majority in the hall had rejected the motion. He just shook his head as if to say what a pity they cannot see the obvious.

This encounter had set me thinking and I felt that these students had a point of view. Soon many other communist students who had witnessed the debate—and probably been told by Prasanta about this student who was a good debater but was willing to listen to the other point of view—started approaching me. Sunil Sen, later of the *Kisan Sabha* and still later history professor at Rabindra Bharati University, Dilip Bose (who later worked with Rajani Palme Dutt in England and became an active worker of the Party) and some others got in touch with me and started giving me communist literature. The war had broken out by this time and been characterized by the communists as an imperialist war; the CPI had been declared 'illegal' and the literature was being clandestinely circulated. There was a certain thrill in this, a sense of adventure and a little fear too as to where all this was leading me to.

During this period in college, I made many friends but, except one, no one was very close. Neville Cambell was an Anglo-Indian with a very different outlook from many others whom I had known earlier. He was very intelligent and a good speaker but a Protestant in a college run by Jesuit priests, who were rather sectarian in outlook. At least Neville thought so and felt that he was being discriminated against. When two boys had to be selected for an inter-collegiate debate, I was the first choice. The judges, amongst our college Fathers, took a little time to select the second person. Cambell had spoken well and should have been selected but they chose one Antony d'Souza, a Catholic boy, instead who had clearly spoken from a memorised text whilst both Cambell and I had spoken extempore.

Neville and I became very good friends and visited each other's homes occasionally. His only relative there was an elder sister and I do not remember whether his parents were in some other town or had died. In any case, he never talked about them. Neville tried to identify with the Indian viewpoint and fully agreed with those who criticised British domination of India and wanted Independence for the country. Although both of us had taken English Honours, after graduation we felt that instead of proceeding along the beaten track and taking up English for post-graduation, we should try something different. We had been reading Freud and felt that in psychology lay the key to changing human nature and making better human beings and thus a better world.

Needless to say, like most young men at that time we had both been bitten by the 'we-must-devote-ourselves-to-making-the-world-a-better-place' bug and took admission in the Experimental Psychology Department of Calcutta University. This department was located in the Science College on what was then known as Upper Circular Road (now APC Road after the great scientist Acharya Prafulla Chandra) in the Rajabazar area. Neville went on to join the Indian Civil Service and was later posted in Darjeeling where he tragically died in a landslide some time in 1948 or 1949.

Thorough disillusionment awaited us at the Psychology Department. Except Dr. Girindra Sekhar Bose, who was a psychiatrist and took up cases of mentally abnormal patients, the teachers were boring and their subjects seemed irrelevant to us. Only Dr. Bose generated some interest and a very memorable event was the trip sponsored by the Psychology Department to the Ranchi mental hospital. We spent about two weeks there studying various types of mental abnormalities. Overall, however, the course was a far cry from our expectations of helping us to change the consciousness of the people and thus removing the ills of the world. I had completed one year of my post-graduate studies and even passed the fifth year exam but my heart was not in it. I spent most of the time during and after college hours in the University Arts Department on College Street either in the library or in activities close to my heart.

The University library was excellent and the librarians, particularly the assistant librarian, Shiv Sankar Mitra, and other staff were extremely helpful. We could get all the books we wanted within a short time of putting in our requisition. The idea of continuing with the dull psychology classes and appearing for the final exam at the end of another year during which I would have to read heavy books on a subject in which I had lost all interest appalled me. I would much rather be involved with the exciting political activity that was beckoning me.

I had read many booklets on Dialectical Materialism and on other Marxist concepts apart from the *Communist Manifesto*. The content of the latter was impressive and its style almost lyrical. Since the centre of student political activity was not the Science College but the Arts Department on College Street, I started spending all my time, barring the actual class periods—no more than four or five at the most—in the Arts Department. I had met the leaders of the Students Federation, Abani Lahiri, Ramen Banerjee, Netai Ganguly, Shankar Roychoudhry, Shyamal Chakravarty and others, whose names I cannot recall. They had already co-opted me into their circle. I was first given the charge of producing a wall newspaper. That I produced by taking a large sheet, putting all the bits of news that were given to me and some pieces of my own and arranging them in columns, as newspapers do. Someone, I do not remember who, would draw a few sketches or cartoons and I would type out the whole matter after which it would be pasted on a particular spot on the wall of one of the corridors. This was my first major venture into the world of journalism; the earlier one was as editor of *The Medium*. I carried on with this for about a year and saw it become quite popular with a respectable readership among the students of the Arts Department.

Neville too was getting attracted towards socialism. By this time I was getting some of the illegal Party literature; my first underground journal was 'The Proletarian Path to Independence' as distinct from what was then the Gandhian path of non-violence. It spoke of the unity of the working class and the peasantry and of attaining independence through mass struggles leading to general strikes and then on to insurrection. I passed on the literature to an equally interested Cambell. By now, I had become quite an active party worker; it was not considered safe to keep the literature in our house. Cambell would keep them in his house since he was not exposed as a communist sympathizer and took only an academic interest in the radical students' movement. It was a measure of his identification with the national movement and of his courage that he agreed to keep these despite the dangers inherent in such a course.

My foray into politics had taken me into the fringes of the movement but I was still a long way from taking the final plunge.

Even a couple of years before this, when I was in college (I joined the first year class in St. Xavier's in January 1937) if someone had told me that soon after my graduation in 1940, I would become a whole-time worker of the CPI, I would have considered him crazy. So would those who knew me in college. My family background was such that the possibility of taking the course that I finally did would have appeared very remote indeed. Things turned out otherwise, though, with the inter-collegiate debate in the University Institute becoming a turning point.

That debate set me thinking and brought me into contact with some of the brightest students in the university, who were practically all attracted by Marxism. Obviously, I too had attracted the attention of the communist group in the university that set about feeding me with Marxist literature. That alone might not have prompted me to take the plunge. The political environment of the late 1930s and the early 1940s made all the difference. The rise of fascism perturbed right thinking people the world over and we in India were no exception. Jawaharlal Nehru, the idol of the youth at that time, was speaking eloquently against fascism and so was Rabindranath Tagore, another icon on the national stage.

The civil war in Spain where the fascist General Franco was trying to overthrow a legally-elected government just because it was leaning towards the Left had stirred the conscience of people, particularly the youth. The ugly face of fascism had horrified almost all shades of political opinion in India. Intellectuals, writers, poets, artists, playwrights had condemned it even though the worst was yet to come. Franco was successful in establishing his dictatorship and then came the rise of Mussolini and, finally, Hitler. In Japan too a particular brand of fascism had emerged under Tojo. The portents were grim and the student community was in the forefront of the anti-fascist movement. Finally, the Second World War started in September 1939. Neither I nor those of our generation, born in the early 1920s, had seen the First World War but we had read about it, seen films such as *All Quiet on the Western Front* and knew that the war could bring untold sufferings on the common people of the world and lead to the death of millions. I felt that we could not just watch and stand by.

I appeared for my BA examinations in January 1940 and the results were out by March or early April. I was surprised to get a first class in English Honours because I had not worked as hard as I had for my Senior Cambridge examinations. Extra-curricular activities such as athletics, rowing and debates that involved participating in competitions even outside Calcutta took a lot of my time. There was also the political, sometimes illegal, literature that I was reading seriously; political study circles that I was attending; apart from reading books on socialism. Yet, I had only vague ideas of what it meant to be a communist; my picture of one was based on Maxim Gorky's *Mother* that I had read several times. I realized that it would mean suffering, imprisonment and even risking my life. I kept debating with myself as to whether this was the kind of life that I was prepared to lead. I had already decided not to sit for the ICS though this was what my father had hoped for. Much later I learnt that there were others too who were looking forward to my joining the civil service for reasons of their own.

I finally took the decision one day in April 1940. What impelled me? Some of the best students of the time were communists. They were advocating a far more militant nationalist line than the followers of Mahatma Gandhi. The war had broken out and we felt that capitalism-turned-imperialism meant war and a continuous struggle for a greater share of the loot from the colonies. Finally, there was this trait in my temperament that persists: whenever I take up any activity, I throw myself fully into it: no half measures or casual approach for me. The decision came to me while I was sculling on the lakes. I paused for a while and said to myself: 'Yes, this is what I must do', even as my heart was palpitating from a sense of unease and even fear of what I was letting myself in for. There was also the excitement around the course that I was committing myself to. I knew it spelt danger but also that it would bring adventures and experiences such as I would never have hoped for in a career as a bureaucrat. My years in the Party did bring experiences and adventures even more exciting and more hazardous than I had ever imagined.

My first assignment as a communist sympathizer (I was still a long way from becoming a party member) was to contest the election to the committee of the University Institute as a candidate of the Students Federation (then known as BPSF, the Calcutta unit of the AISF). This was my first experience of an election. I was guided by Sunil Sen. To begin with, I had to enrol some members for the Institute; that we did by going from hostel to hostel. I had to give class lectures, five minutes just before class started, asking students to vote for SF candidates. All this was very new and strange for me but I enjoyed the experience on the whole, even though it meant hard work. I had to do all this while continuing to attend my classes at the Science College.

On election-day, I went to the University Institute dressed in a dhoti and kurta that I wore for the first time. I was completely unknown at that time. I looked different from most Bengali boys and had a strange name (today Kaul is fairly well known) and was the subject of much speculation. Who is this boy? Who has put him up as a candidate? One lot of students who were opposed to the SF spread the rumour that he is from the Kolay family (Jagannath Kolay a well-known businessman and, if I remember right, a Congress leader). All this was a recipe for failure and I, expectedly, lost. It was my first appearance on the electoral scene and I had neither the background of any activity in any student organization nor of any political group. The main activity that I was associated with was the wall newspaper.

Another such 'activity' that I was engaged in was to conduct a study circle for some girls who were at this time moving close to the Party. There were not many, only three: Uma Chakravartty (Nikhil Chakravartty's sister), Roma Goswami and Anjali Sen, all university students. I am not sure whether I volunteered to do so or was asked by Nikhil Chakravartty himself or the Student Federation leadership. The atmosphere even in the co-educational university was such that mixing with girls was not as commonplace as it is today. Girls had a separate common room where they would wait till the teacher entered the class and then come into the class together.

It was during this period that I first met Indrajit Gupta who had recently arrived from England and had straight away been asked to work underground. Nikhil Chakravartty, who too had recently returned to Calcutta from England and had started teaching in the university, had evidently picked me up as a promising recruit for the Party. Perhaps to impress me even more he told me that I should meet a bright underground leader who might take a few classes for me exclusively if I could arrange a suitable meeting place.I tried to figure out what would be the best place and ultimately approached a Kashmiri relative, Kailas Razdan, who was then in the Hooghly Pilot Service. The pilots, who had to spend most of their time on sea bringing ships in through the rather tricky and treacherous channels on the Hooghly, had a place called the Chummery where they could spend time when in Calcutta. Kailas had a room in this building on Chowringhee. I requested him for his key so that I could use his room to take occasional lessons from a certain Professor Thomas from England. He readily agreed.

Accordingly, the message was sent and the place and time communicated to the comrade. I used this place twice or thrice as far as I can recall and there were no formal lessons as such; just some casual talk. The purpose was served though, because I was certainly impressed for, as I learnt much later, he was none other than Indrajit Gupta. In between, he visited our underground den sometime between September 1941 and April 1942. Even then his identity was not revealed. It was only after the Party was legalized that I learnt who he was.

Indrajit deserves a special mention, given my interaction with him during and after my years in the Party. Unlike some others who after returning from England were straightaway co-opted into the Central Committee of the Party, Indrajit began as an ordinary trade union organizer and was initially drafted for work in the Jute belt. Later, he worked closely with me in the Port union of which I was the Secretary and he was, for some time, President. He stepped down to make way for Nepal Bhattacharya under circumstances that I will go into later.

Indrajit was an excellent orator who could speak Hindustani well, having spent his early life in Punjab. In fact, he knew very little Bengali and I think it was in the underground den, which I have referred to earlier, where I gave him his first lessons in Bengali! This was very much a case of the blind leading the blind because at that time my own grasp of the language was poor. It still is. Many years later, as he lay on his deathbed while his wife stood beside him, I mentioned this fact to her. Indrajit nodded and as I held his hand there were tears in his eyes and a lump in my throat as we both realized that the end was near.

Of his qualities that I most admired was his capacity to remain aloof from the factional groupings that became a feature of the Party in the 1950s and 1960s till the split. He managed to do this by sticking to the working class movement and not trying to become a Party apparatchik. He did, of course, go on to become the General Secretary of the CPI. Even at that time, as far as I could see as an outsider, he refrained from the kind of politicking that is the hallmark of most of the current breed of politicians. As a Member of Parliament he earned respect as one who took his job seriously and whose speeches were always worth listening to.

My participation in the student movement under the aegis of the Student Federation did not last long because soon I was switched over to another front: the cultural front. I do not know which Party unit took this decision and was never curious to find out. It is possible that after the electoral fiasco the SF leaders thought that I was not quite fitted for the role of a student leader. Nikhil Chakravartty and Renu Roy, Dr. B. C. Roy's niece, had arrived from England and might have made that suggestion.

Something significant happened at this stage though I had not realized its import then. I decided to suspend my faith in God and religion, to accept the communist philosophy as explained in the booklets given to me and in the lectures that I heard. The Jesuits of St. Xavier's had left a deep impression on me and while rejecting the idea of conversion, the dedication and the conduct of the fathers had instilled in me a strong faith in religion. When I got involved in the communist movement, I wanted to know what its philosophical outlook was. The theory of Dialectical Materialism with its emphasis on atheism did appear strange to me. Why atheism, I wondered, though the excitement of being an iconoclast finally swayed me. Bhowani Sen's lecture at our study circle was significant and over time I became quite adept in taking classes on Dialectical Materialism and other aspects of communist theory. As for the attitude towards religion, we learnt that 'Religion is the opium of the people'.

Another question that I asked my leaders at that time was about the communist viewpoint on ethics. Rather flippantly I was told that whatever was in the interests of the revolution was moral. It followed that anything that was not was immoral. Although this was a casual and light hearted remark, I think this truly represented the outlook of the communist movement at that time and, in fact, does so even today. This leads directly to the major question of ends and means. Does the end justify the means? In other words, if the goal towards which one is striving is considered to be right, would any means, fair or foul, to attain it be acceptable? Then again, who decides what is in the interests of the revolution?

In the era of parliamentary democracy, 'revolution' is, of course, now interpreted as meaning power coming into the hands of the communists. It is this outlook that has determined the strategy and tactics of the communist movement, as the whole series of events in the last few decades has revealed. I have described some of these events in the chapters that follow. In fact, all 'politics' from Chanakya to Machiavelli has been guided by this basic principle of the 'ends justify the means'. The only thing is that some seem to make it a part of ideology, decry conventional ideas of morality as bourgeois morality and thus are not bothered by qualms of conscience while others at least pay lip service to 'ethics' and talk of 'value-based' politics.

SIX

The Cultural Movement

The decision to take up the cultural movement seriously was well thought out. The rationale was simple: with the outbreak of the war that we and the entire spectrum of national movements in the country considered imperialist, the Party was declared illegal and many of its leaders arrested. Others went underground. Not even the student movement, under the banner of the Students Federation, was spared. Under these circumstances it made sense to build up a strong cultural movement whereby the message of peace, freedom and of the rights of the people could be broadcast through songs, plays, exhibitions of posters and paintings without attracting the Defence of India Rules.

The movement was inspired by reports of a similar movement in China, where the message of the struggle against Japan and the other imperialist powers was carried across the country, deep into the rural areas through community singing. A book by Israel Epstein in circulation *(The Unfinished Revolution in China)*, at that time gave a vivid account of this movement in China. It provided a template for the formation of the Youth Cultural Institute (YCI). Its guiding spirits were Nikhil Chakravartty, Chinmohan Sehanovis, Renu Roy (later Chakravartty) and a few others. Among the students, apart from myself, there were Subrata Banerjee, Bablu (Debabrata) Bose, Ramkrishna Mukherjee, Uma Chakravartty (later Sehanovis), Anu Gupta (Sadhan Gupta's sister), Dilip Roy, who was a good singer. The well-known singer Debabrata (George) Biswas would train our singing squad. He and some others such as Sunil (Paltu) Chatterjee, Nobendu Chatterjee who were then with the Hindustan Insurance Company founded by the businessman Nalini Ranjan

Sarkar. They had an amateur drama group and were very happy to get an opportunity to stage plays under the auspices of the YCI. Subhas Mukherji's poetry was, of course, inspirational. I was asked to work as the secretary of the organization founded in 1940 and I did so till September 1941, when I left to work underground handing over the responsibility to Subrata Banerjee. I am sure he has written about this in his forthcoming autobiography.

I wrote a Hindi song during this period: *'Mazdur, mazdur hain, hum'*, and a satirical play in English, *'Politicians Take to Rowing'* that was first performed at the University Rowing Club and became very popular. There was such a demand for it that performances were organized at various colleges. The original cast included Kamal Basu (later Mayor of Calcutta), Subrata Banerjee, Subroto Sengupta Robin Mitter, Prasanta Sanyal, Sunil Sen (of Lakkhi Babu jewellers), another Sunil Sen (who was probably a student of the English Department in the university), Dilip Bose, and some others.. Sometimes I acted as Hitler, caricatured as a farcical yet hateful character. Notably, this was before the war had really heated up with the attack on the Soviet Union and with the entry of Japan.

I do not remember whether this was performed under the aegis of YCI or was later co-opted by YCI. Of interest is the fact that students researching the history of drama are looking at this and some other plays that we performed under the YCI banner as the precursors of the Indian Peoples' Theatre Association (IPTA) movement. Many years later, when I was invited to speak at a meeting where the early days of this movement were being recalled, Mrinal Sen, the film director, told me that this play had been performed in his college when he was a student.

Some other plays performed by the YCI group included: *'The Boy Grows Up'*: an anti-war play adapted from an English story by Bablu Bose and myself; *'Kerani'* the first Bengali play (written by Paltu Chatterjee) that we staged and *'Anjangarh'*, based on Subodh Ghosh's Bengali novel *Fossil.* Details about the YCI are contained in the volumes on the cultural movement edited by Sudhi Pradhan (*Marxist Cultural Movement: Chronicles and Documents,* 3 vols, National

Book Agency, 1979). Then there was a play portraying the Chinese resistance to Japanese aggression in which some of our girl comrades took part. Given the taboo against girls from respectable families appearing on the stage, we had, as a gesture to conservative opinion, to ensure that there were no boys in the scenes in which the girls appeared on stage.

My stint in the YCI was a very creative one. My faculties were at their height and I was developing both as an organizer and a creative writer. It was, in a sense, a continuation of my education. Some of the stalwarts of the day were associated with the YCI. There was Dr. Nihar Ranjan Ray of the History Department, Shahid Suhrawardy, President of our organization, who was Curator of Victoria Memorial and professor in the University and brother of a minister in the then Government of Bengal. There were Professor Hiren Mukherjee, Professor Nirmal Bose, the eminent Gandhian scholar, Chintamani Kar, a leading artist, who designed our logo, singer Debabrata Biswas, whose name is a byword for Rabindra Sangeet and many others whose names I cannot recall. Nikhil Chakravartty and Chinmohan Sehanovis were, of course, among the guiding lights of the YCI. With figures such as these actively associated with the organization, I was eagerly soaking up the rich culture of Bengal as well as that of the radical Left that was emerging all over the world.

SEVEN

Going Underground

On 22 June 1941, Hitler's Germany launched a full scale attack on the Soviet Union and thereby changed the course of history and of the war. By this time I had become a convinced communist. I had been working seriously for the CPI for more than a year, first in the Students Federation and later on the cultural front. I had also done a fair amount of reading and was particularly impressed by Sidney and Beatrice Webb's *Soviet Communism: A New Civilisation?* A subsequent edition of the book removed the question mark. It made me feel that at last a workers' state had come into being; a new civilisation was in the making and that the path for the liberation of mankind had, at last, opened out.

I was so inspired that I wrote a series of four articles, which were published in the *Hindusthan Standard*: marking my foray into the daily press. Given this mind-set, the news of the attack on the Soviet Union was very disturbing. The onward march of fascism threatened all the progress mankind had made and would lead to the worst form of barbarism. Even Jawaharlal Nehru and other world leaders were denouncing fascism and I felt that remaining on the periphery of the movement, just staging plays and singing songs, was not enough. I had to respond by taking the plunge without any reservations. The Party was illegal and a large number of its workers and leaders had gone underground. I had to go the whole hog and work as a whole-time Party worker and take part in the underground movement.

This was not an easy decision. Having got a first class in my BA examination, I was getting a monthly scholarship of Rs 32—a princely sum in those days—with which I could buy books: Bernard Shaw's plays, H. G. Wells' *History of the World* and many others. My family was looking forward to my going in for the ICS, the premier civil service in the country. Even my brothers and some other friends of the family had great expectations of me. There was also a girl towards whom I was attracted, though I never expressed my feelings; nor did I know if she reciprocated them. To leave all this behind and head for an unknown world and an uncertain future was a frightening prospect. Yet there were compelling factors, not the least was the complete disillusionment with the Experimental Psychology course that I had taken up.

There was also the oppressive atmosphere at home once Papa realized that I would not sit for the ICS. He had set his heart on it and my recalcitrance led to a total change in his attitude towards me. I had been his favourite son; he would boast of my achievements to all his friends and relatives and here I was determined to pursue a course that would shatter all his dreams. He could not countenance my resolve of not joining the civil service and had become extremely irritable; trying to hurt my feelings and sentiments in every way. I realized that I would not be able to live in this atmosphere very long.

Even more depressing was the news of the advances being made by the fascist forces. This was above all the main factor that influenced my decision. I, along with many of my contemporaries in the university, began to feel that what had appeared as a beacon of hope for mankind was in danger of being destroyed. This called for the extreme sacrifice from all of us and I could not shirk what I felt was my duty at this hour. So I sent word to the party centre in Calcutta that I was prepared to work whole time and to go underground. The leaders in Calcutta—I later learnt that they were members of the Provincial Committee Secretariat—evidently took my proposal seriously for I was summoned to an interview. I was taken to an underground den where I met people whom I did not know. Later, I found that one of them was Muzaffar Ahmad and the others were possibly Biswanath Mukherjee and Saroj Mukherjee. I do not exactly remember what was discussed at that meeting for my mind was in a daze. I was overwhelmed by the visit to an underground den and meeting some of the legendary leaders of the Party. Evidently they found me suitable because, shortly after, I received the message that my request had been accepted and I was to go underground. I was not told what my assignment would be nor where I would be located.

I clearly remember the day—23 September 1941—a day after my birthday on the 22nd. Very elaborate arrangements were made to ensure that my disappearance did not excite suspicion and that I would not be followed to my assigned den. Since I was already known in the Party's cultural and students' circles, it was necessary to ensure that our activists did not get any inkling of what was happening. So I was told to make up a story that would be credible and not excite suspicion even among the comrades who knew me. The story was that the straitened family circumstances had forced me to take up a job. I had received a good offer from Nagpur and was headed there. This reflected the reality in many middle class families at that time; it was accepted.

Quite a few friends sympathized with me and said they understood my compulsions. Subroto Sengupta, who was then a prominent student leader and editor of the *Student* (the AISF journal), called me over to his house and tried to persuade me to change my decision and to continue to work for the Party in Calcutta. I told him that my family insisted on my taking up the job and there was nothing that I could do. Of course, my family knew nothing about this and I was careful not to give them the slightest hint of what I was planning to do. Subroto felt very sorry but realized that no amount of persuasion would make me change my mind.

On the fateful day, I packed up my things in a small suitcase and got ready to go. I had been going out frequently for debates and other excursions organized by the college or the Psychology Department for the past few years and there was nothing unusual in my going away for a few days. My father had opened a savings account for me in the Central Bank of India (New Market branch). When I left the house, there was around Rs 130 in the account. I withdrew the money and closed the account. I do not exactly remember what story I made up for the family but I aroused no suspicion. I did, however, post a letter to my brother, Victor, telling him that I was going underground and that he should tell Papa and others in the family but ask them not to talk about it. This is how they all got to know. The letter, sent by ordinary post, must have reached them a day or two after I left.

I came out of the house and was met a little away from it by one of the 'tech men' (couriers and supporting staff for the underground organization) who was to escort me to the den. He was my friend Dilip Bose, who came from a rich zamindar family and even though he was taking part in our cultural movement, no one suspected that he was working for the Party. To avoid any possibility of suspicion Dilip Bose took me in his car, an old Chevrolet, to Howrah Station. There I was parked with my suitcase. Dilip's part of the operation was complete and he left.

At the appointed time another tech person came and escorted me to the final destination. Amidst the huge crowd at the station no one noticed that I had only come in a little while ago and was leaving again. The tech who took me was Ajoy Das. He escorted me to the den that I was supposed to be posted at. When I landed there I recognized Muzaffar Ahmad, universally known as Kakababu. There were a few others whom I did not know. The den was a small three-roomed flat in Park Circus, then considered to be in the outskirts of Calcutta. There were two ladies there and a couple of young persons. After the Party became legal, I came to know that one of the ladies was Sudhi Pradhan's wife and the other was Bela Chatterjee (later Lahiri). Sudhi Pradhan was also there at that time and so was another old gentleman.

One of my first acts was to hand over the Rs 130 that I had taken out of my account to Kakababu. I began the second phase of my life with not a penny in my pocket. The Party had now taken the responsibility of providing for my needs. We were paid an allowance of Rs 30 a month of which Rs 15 was deducted for food. The remaining Rs 15 was supposed to be our pocket money, used by most whole-timers, not the women, to buy bidis or cigarettes.

What I expected to be the most momentous days of my life became the most traumatic months. This shocking turn of events had nothing to do with bearing up with the discomforts at the den. In fact, the living conditions were not at all uncomfortable. We lived like a small family and the company was not unpleasant. We ate simple food but it was ample. On some special occasions, we even had chicken curry and pulao that Kakababu cooked. On such occasions, each of us contributed Rs 5 from the Rs 15 pocket money. The trauma was because I was not given any work even after I settled down.

After a few days, I asked Kakababu what I would be doing. He merely said that I would be told by and by. Since there was nothing else to do, I spent my spare time—after I had performed my allotted household chores—reading whatever literature was available in the den. There was not much till we started receiving some circulars issued by the Central Committee. A typed copy of the *History of the Communist Party of the Soviet Union* (CPSU) reached our den after a few weeks. That I read avidly; more than once. Whenever I asked what I was supposed to do, I was just told to wait. Having lived a hectic life in school and college this enforced idleness was beginning to tell on my nerves. I was also a little puzzled by this strange reluctance to allot work to me.

The mystery was soon solved when a comrade suddenly turned up. I was told that he was the Central Committee member in charge of the Bengal Committee. He called me and asked me to type out a letter. There was a typewriter in the den as well as a cyclostyling machine. Since I could type well, I had on my own started typing and I was occasionally being given some short letters to type. Circulars from the Provincial Centre to the districts were being sent in Bengali but correspondence with the Central Committee took place in English. Those letters had to be typed and my services were sometimes required. It was only natural that this Central Committee comrade called me to type a letter. He dictated the message, which I took down in long hand.

It was a short letter addressed to the Party General Secretary, P. C. Joshi, though no real names were used. The letter referred to me and told the General Secretary something on these lines: 'I found that he was already here when I came. We will now have to see what we can do with him.' I realized that instead of telling me directly that the Central Committee thought that it was a mistake to have brought me to the underground den, he had chosen this method to communicate this to me. This was a terrible shock to me. What followed was even more shocking. I asked him why the Central Committee felt that I should not have been brought here. He said that it was their experience that boys from backgrounds such as mine were not able to stand the rigours of underground life.

So, what happens to me, I asked. He said that since I had come to the den, I would have to stay on as there was a risk of exposure if I was sent back. There was no option but to keep me there. My next question was what would be the work assigned to me if I was to continue to stay there. I do not remember his exact words but the gist was: Petit bourgeois youth who wanted to work for the Communist Party would first have to declass themselves. This was not an easy task and would take some time. So for the present my job would be to swab the floors, to clean the utensils after meals and carry out such household chores as would be assigned to me.

I can hardly describe my feelings. I was not wanted and yet would perforce have to stay on so as not to endanger the safety of our leaders. I was literally trapped and felt claustrophobic. I later asked once or twice if I could occasionally be assigned some outdoor work. They said that even that would not be possible. My unusual appearance would immediately attract attention and arouse curiosity and might even lead the Special (Intelligence) Branch people to the den. So there was no question of my going out. I would have to stay put within the four walls of the den. If all this did not a prison make, I do not know what else would. The years I later spent in jail were a much happier experience for me than the period I spent in this den.

Here was I, with a brilliant academic record, acknowledged as one of the leading debaters of the university, already known as a writer of a few plays and songs that had created quite a stir, but considered unfit for any work by the Party for which I had sacrificed all; to which I had pledged my future. Surprisingly enough, I did not react the way I might have been expected to. I did not revolt even inwardly. There was no question of my running away as that would be cowardly, and I certainly was not a coward. I had decided to work whole-time for the Party and would stick to it no matter what the consequences and no matter what hardships I had to bear. I decided that I would consider this as a challenge; I would prove to the Party leaders, who had considered me a petit bourgeois who would not be able to withstand the rigours that working for the Party would entail, that they were wrong. So I accepted the decision, sought to declass myself and forget my bourgeois values. Eventually, I did indeed meet the challenge successfully and not only endured all the hardships of underground life, made even more onerous by the ban on my going out of the den even for a few moments, but earned the respect of even that CC comrade who had told me that it was a mistake to have brought me to the den.

The traumatic experience at the den had a serious impact on my psyche; the effects of which I continue to feel. Had I revolted even inwardly and said to myself that I would hit back when the opportunity arose—since there was no possibility of doing so at that time—perhaps the damage would have been less severe. Instead, I accepted this and began to think that it was only fair that I declass myself; curb my ego and do the work that was assigned to me, even if it was cleaning the floor and washing utensils.

Throughout the nearly nine months in the den my mind was in turmoil. Instinctively, I felt that the treatment meted out to me was unfair but I rationalized that after all I was a petit bourgeois youth. To become a true Bolshevik, I needed to surrender to the Party completely and to accept that their decision was correct. Was it not something of this kind of an attitude that made some leading members of the Central Committee of the Soviet Party confess that they had indeed taken an anti-Party stand and thus provide the alibi for their own liquidation?

The more serious consequences of the experience was a considerable loss of self-confidence; something that affects my working and my mind even today. Probably, this is the kind of attitude that is created in the soldier so that he may work like an automaton carrying out orders without questioning. ' Theirs not to reason why/Theirs but to do and die'. The curbing of the ego must have all been to the good but not the loss of self-confidence. I had not heard of the term brain-washing. It was much later that I learnt what it meant and realized that this was the beginning of that process. Had it not been for this, I may not have so readily submitted to some of the wrong policy decisions that the Party took in subsequent years.

An interesting sidelight to this episode is that on emerging from underground, I discovered that this CC comrade was none other than Somnath Lahiri, one of the founder members of the Communist Party in Bengal. Contrary to what might have been expected after this experience, I developed the best of relations with him in later years and admired him greatly for his political acumen, his abilities as a journalist (he edited our Bengali party journal *Swadhinata*) and as a public speaker. More importantly, I got to like him as a human being. I had occasion to clash with him in the debates on the National Front *versus* the Democratic Front that started after the Twentieth Party Congress of the CPSU; despite that I earned his respect and I continued to hold him in high regard.

It is unfortunate that after the Left-Adventurist period he was one of those sidelined and he was never able to reoccupy the position of leadership he had been in earlier. My assessment of him as a fine human being was strengthened when I learnt that he was one of the few in the Party who supported the revolt of Dubček and others, known as the Prague Spring and felt that the Soviet suppression of the revolt was not justified. He had been in a sanatorium in Czechoslovakia in 1968 and was able to get first-hand accounts of what was happening outside. This might not seem to tally with my experience of him in the den but I could see that when one is a part of a vast machine guided by a very sectarian and ruthless ideology, personal feelings have to be subordinated to the requirements of the Party, which means, of course, its top leadership. When I look back on my own functioning during the years I was Secretary of the Calcutta District Committee, I realize that sometimes my own actions were totally at variance with my natural temperament.

At the den, we anxiously followed the developing situation in the war. The Soviet army was still retreating and we wondered how the Socialist citadel that had been considered impregnable had begun to crumble so soon. The party line was that it was a war between the imperialist powers to decide who would get a larger share of the spoils of the colonies. I was equally concerned about my stay at the den that I feared would stretch for years, till the war ended. The situation took a new and unexpected turn very soon and there were three memorable incidents during the period.

The first was a message that my brother, Prince, was in Calcutta on a short visit. Victor who was in the Party as an unexposed cadre must have been asked to deliver the message to the Party that Princebhai was eager to meet me to see how I was getting on. I do not remember whether he was still in the Army Medical Service or had joined the World Health Organization. I was told he would like to meet me. The Party agreed and one evening I was carefully taken out of the den by one of our tech men in his car and after such precautions as changing cars, I was taken to a restaurant where our rendezvous had been arranged. I do not remember who else was there; possibly Victor. We had a Chinese dinner at Chung Wah; in one of the cabins that had curtains so that people could dine in privacy. Princebhai was quite pleased with the arrangement and felt assured that I was well and was being looked after properly. This was the only time that I went out of the den; save when we shifted. All of us moved out to the new den but that was hardly an outing.

The next incident was the stuff of adventure novels; fact is often more amazing than fiction. It was past midnight when I heard a commotion. I woke up to find that two comrades had arrived and would stay with us for a few days. I had no idea who they were. They were just given beds to sleep on for the night and we all went back to sleep. The next day I learnt that the two comrades had managed to escape from the high security Hijli detention camp and had made their way to Calcutta where they had contacted the Party and been brought to the safety of our den. They were Panchu Gopal Bhaduri and Nripen Chakravarty. The story of their escape has been told elsewhere and I will not repeat it save to say that it was an act of tremendous courage and daring but it also involved very careful planning. I got to know both of them well during the few days that they spent in the den. They were amongst the most outstanding leaders of the Party. Nripen Chakravarty was the builder of the Party in Tripura and later became Chief Minister. Even as the Chief Minister, he had a simple and austere lifestyle but was expelled from the Party under circumstances that are regrettable and speak a lot about the deterioration that had taken place in the Party. Nripen Chakravarty is no more. His party membership was restored shortly before he died at the age of 99 in December 2004.

The other comrade, Panchu Gopal Bhaduri, was also a gifted person and during the few years that he lived, he showed remarkable courage and determination. He was popular and easily won the State Legislative Assembly election though he was afflicted with a strange disease that gradually restricted his movements to such an extent that he had to be moved from place to place on a stretcher. Despite this, he fought and won elections, was active to the last and addressed factory gate meetings. If ever there were persons fitting the image of true revolutionaries, these were the two.

The third incident is also very revealing. One day, a comrade whom I knew well from our university days announced that someone who was 'the greatest intellect in Asia' would be coming to our den. I was not told his name since he too was underground and had been given a tech name. My tech name at this time was Madan and his was probably Ram. The 'intellect' came at the appointed time and spent a night with us. I recognized him from our schooldays; we were in the same class. I have talked about him earlier and to see him being referred to as the 'greatest intellect' increased the turmoil within me manifold. Bhasker Mitter and I beat him to the first and second positions regularly though I concede that performance in school is not necessarily the best criterion to judge a person's ability in the future.

What irked me was the thought that he had, after two or three years in college in England, walked straight into the Central Committee. How come the question of declassing did not come up in his case? I kept these thoughts to myself though these questions puzzled and pained me. I did not dare to draw the obvious conclusions that were shoved back into the deeper recesses of my mind. The impact of the colonial mentality is strong throughout the political spectrum even today. A degree from a foreign university—those days it was Oxford or Cambridge—was a passport to a bright future. This would be quite acceptable in the world of commerce and industry but that it should be a passport to a bright future in the political, even the communist movement, was indeed shocking.

A note from P. C. Joshi, the Party General Secretary, helped to assuage my feelings somewhat. It said that a true communist is one who does whatever work is assigned to him with full zeal so that he may prove to be the best in that field. Taking the cue from this, I spent a long time cleaning and polishing the utensils until they really shone. My efforts were noticed and the Central Committee member too was impressed. I was now being given some work; typing for one. When they saw how good I was, a lot of the correspondence came my way: circulars in English had to be typed and circulated. I was also asked to produce a Hindi Bulletin for which a Hindi typewriter was made available. Based on reports from the districts, I prepared the Hindi bulletin on stencils that were then cyclostyled. The cyclostyling machine was operated by the girl comrade at the den.

There had to be at least one lady to show that we were a family. In the beginning there were two. Later, one left and only Bela Chatterjee remained. She did all the cyclostyling and cooked the main morning meal of a fish curry with some vegetable thrown in. The evening meal, cooked by the male members taking turns, consisted of rice and a kind of mixed vegetable and dal curry that was just boiled together with a little bit of oil and some spices. This delicacy was known as Hot Pot; nutritious but quite insipid. One evening, the gruel placed before us emitted a foul smell. It had been the turn of one of the old comrades, Gopal Basak, one of the Meerut Conspiracy Case prisoners, to cook. We asked him about the stink and he sheepishly admitted that in an effort to make the curry more tasty he had saved up a piece of fish brought a few days ago and put it in the pot. He did not realize that the fish would rot. There was no fridge in the den but he had thought that it would produce something like the popular Bengali dish in which a fish head is put in the dal or one of the vegetable curries. Since rotten fish is no substitute for fresh fish, the meal had to be cooked all over again.

More interesting was the manner in which I saw the party line evolve through the stages during my stay in the den. The imperialist war became a People's War. Since I typed the letters and circulars, I also was privy to many decisions taken by the top Party leadership: the Politbureau where the two main figures were P. C. Joshi and Gangadhar Adhikari; the former playing the dominant role. Although I do not remember the exact sequence of events, there were three notes that came to the Provincial Committee (PC) den and played an important part in bringing about the change.

The first was a long note referred to as the Jail document. It appeared to have mainly been drafted by B. T. Ranadive but had the support of the others in the Bombay jail at that time. Its main thesis was that at every given moment the Party should identify its main enemy and concentrate fire on it. Even other enemies could be allies in the fight against the main enemy. I remember reading the document carefully and though I cannot recall the details, this was its essence. The main enemy was, of course, fascism, led by Hitler and the Nazis. It was suggested that we should, therefore, support the war effort and consider it a People's War. There was another note, probably from Rajani Palme Dutt (RPD), who was generally considered responsible for the Indian Party on behalf of the Comintern. This was a short note saying that with Hitler's attack on the Soviet Union it was the duty of all communists to support the allies against the fascist powers. There was a third note on similar lines from Tiger (the tech name of Jyoti Bose, as I learnt later) who too was underground but in a separate den. There may have been other messages sent directly to the Central Committee headquarters but these were the three that I saw.

After some time there came a long document from the politbureau, evidently drafted by P. C. Joshi. It was somewhat critical of the jail document though in essence it seemed to say very much the same thing. The only thing that PCJ emphasised was that, along with our slogan of People's War, we should put forward the demand for the release of the Congress leaders and others imprisoned after the Quit India call. I think his document was titled: 'For National Defence, National Unity and National Government'. This document was finally accepted as the party line. That this document was much the same as the others became clearer after the letters that PCJ wrote to Maxwell, Secretary of State for India in the British government, were revealed. These letters came into my hands as I was asked to type them out so that they could be kept in the files of the Provincial Committee.

PCJ made a plea for the legalization of the Party since it now considered this a People's War and was prepared to take part in civil defence. It would even be prepared to send its selected cadres for training in guerrilla warfare from British army experts. These squads would be useful in stemming the advance of the Japanese in case they entered Indian territory. There may have been, indeed, must have been, direct negotiations with representatives of the government because ultimately sometime in the first half of 1942 the ban on the Party was lifted, warrants against the underground leaders were withdrawn and, gradually, those who were in jail released.

What was my own reaction to these developments? I had suspended my critical faculties and had developed a frame of mind that was prepared to accept whatever the top leadership of the Party decided. True, I was a bit shocked when I saw the letters to Maxwell, copies of which I was asked to type but there was also a feeling of relief that this would lead to my emergence into the open. This, in fact, happened even sooner than I had expected. When it became clear that the legalization of the Party was imminent, I was told that since there was no warrant against me—the police were unaware of my existence as a party worker—I could go home as if I had just returned from Nagpur or wherever I had been working. In April or early May 1942, I was dropped off at a point from where I could get into a taxi and reach home.

By now I had decided that my future would have to be with the working class. Even though I was determined to go to the trade union front, the party leadership evidently still had doubts about my capacity to participate in the working class movement. It probably thought that I had not yet matured enough to take on the responsibility of a trade union leader. In those days employers were reluctant to recognize trade unions and did their best to break them, using strong arm methods whenever necessary. One had to be really tough to survive in the trade union movement. So the leadership suggested a via media. Since I had cut my teeth in the cultural movement, I was asked to continue with this but, for a change, to organize cultural groups amongst the workers.

This was virgin territory and I knew that I was trying to do something that had not been tried before. I was not daunted and quickly got down to working. The tram workers were the most advanced at that time and our union there was strong. The workers were mostly accommodated in 'messes'; buildings in which dormitory-like accommodation was provided by the company. This was an advantage as many workers were available at any given time since they worked in shifts. I contacted the union leaders and after discussions chose the Pratapiditya mess (in the Kalighat area of Calcutta) to try out my experiment.

The response was excellent, the workers enthusiastically accepted the idea and I prepared a small play for them. I do not remember whether it was in Hindi or in Bengali; most likely it was in Hindi. After many rehearsals the group was ready and performed not only before the workers of their own depot—Kalighat/Tollygunje but before workers of other depots as well. The movement spread and the next depot to form a drama group was Rajabazar. It was here that we discovered Dasratlal, a good folk singer, who could play the *dholak* as he sang. We also discovered Benoy Roy, a trade union organizer in the Beliaghata area of east Calcutta. Nobody had known about his talent for singing and music. He became a close friend. One of the songs that made him famous was one that I wrote in Hindi—'*Jag re mazdur jag re kisan/ aa raha hai Japan, lutera Japan*'. Dasratlal and Benoy Roy were both picked up by the central IPTA squad and performed all over India and even abroad. Benoy Roy later went to Moscow and, apart from working as a news reader for both Hindi and Bengali radio bulletins, he did his masters in philosophy. A promising future was unfortunately cut short when he died, knocked down by a car in Moscow while crossing the road.

How do I evaluate the eight months of underground life? First, my decision to go underground was a hasty one, taken without understanding the implications and without getting a clarification on what my exact duties would be. I was so eager to take the plunge into what I thought would be real revolutionary work and to surrender completely to the Party that I did not think the decision through. The price could have been very heavy but for the sudden turn of events that shortened my stay underground. I should have drawn the proper lessons from this but it seems that when I set my heart on doing something I take the plunge without weighing all the pros and cons.

Second, it showed the very casual functioning of both the state and the central party leaders. This continued and was evident in the 1950s and the 1960s, as long as I was there. I do not know whether it has persisted to this day. Third, it showed the scant regard that the Party pays to its human resources. The manner in which I was asked to come underground without being clear about what my role would be and where I would be fitted into the Party apparatus showed that human beings were regarded as mere cogs in the whole Party machine. Perhaps that is an inevitable part of secret underground functioning. There is no place in it for considering human beings as human beings. They have to function as robots. If asked to go as suicide bombers they have to go. Fourth, sycophancy and the colonial mentality were prevalent in the Party and perhaps persist till this day . . .

EIGHT

Into the Trade Union Movement

Interesting though organizing cultural groups among workers was, I was impatient for an opportunity to take up full-fledged trade union work. The leadership finally gave in and sent me to the trade union front. I was also asked to join the Red Guards, which was being set up with comrade Sambhu Bose as our trainer. The Party was still being attacked for its support to the war and the People's War slogan. The Red Guards was a volunteer corps set up to protect Party meetings. I had to rush wherever attacks on the Party were apprehended. On one occasion, there was an attack on the South Calcutta Party office and comrade Nripen Chakravarty was trapped inside.

I found a howling mob, baying for the blood of the 'communists' suspected to be inside. Most of the workers had managed to get out but there seemed to be no way of saving comrade Nripen Chakravarty. Enterprising as he was, he suddenly made a dash out of the building, taking those who had laid siege to the office unawares, and jumped onto a running tram. Some attackers did manage to get hold of him and plant a blow or two but he managed to escape lightly thanks to some quick thinking and great daring on his part. Those of us waiting outside to prevent an assault on the party office were greatly impressed by his courage and agility.

Comrades were being attacked everywhere but we managed to keep our activities going and win support from even those opposed to our political line. The selfless service that our comrades rendered to the people, especially in famine afflicted areas, was remarkable. Our slogan for opening fair price shops and the struggle of our women comrades to ensure that the food was distributed fairly helped us win over many apolitical people and some from other parties as well.

On one occasion, in August 1943, we learnt that the Socialists had called a students' strike and were going to take students to a central point for a meeting on the occasion of the first anniversary of the Quit India Movement. The Party decided that our comrades would spread out to different areas, especially near schools and colleges, to try to prevent students from collecting at one point because the police had mobilized a huge force to beat them up and, if necessary, fire on them. I was posted in front of Deshapriya Park near two schools: Tirthapati School and Kalidhan Institution.

Around mid-day, I found a procession of schoolboys—most of them not more than 10 or 12 and some even younger—emerging from one of these institutions and marching along Rashbehari Avenue, proceeding towards Kalighat. They were led by half a dozen or so young men, evidently cadres of the party that had called the strike. If this procession reached the meeting place, many of these children might not have been able to survive the police lathi-charge and worse. I rushed up and stood in front of the procession and shouted that the kids should not be taken to the meeting where they might be beaten up. The processionists were taken by surprise and my shouting and gesticulation led to quite a few boys leaving the procession. Seeing that their attempt to take these boys to the meeting was being frustrated, the cadres leading the procession pounced on me and started beating me.

Fortunately, bombs and pipe guns had not come into use at that time and, even though my clothes were torn, I was not seriously hurt. Things might have taken a turn for the worse but for the timely intervention of Ajoy Singh, a comrade and the boxing instructor at Ballygunje Institute, who was reputed to be a dare devil. He appeared suddenly and, on seeing him, my assailants fled. The arrival of Ajoy Singh was not fortuitous. One of our women comrades, also deputed to move around in the area, had seen me being beaten up, rushed to the Ballygunje Institute and asked Ajoy

Singh to hurry and rescue me. The woman comrade who saved me from a serious misadventure was none other than Manikuntala Sen. This, I got to know from Ajoy Singh who escorted me to safety but it never occurred to me to go up to her to thank her.

Since I had been active in Ballygunje, I was assigned to a trade union cell in that area. There was an industrial belt on what was then the outskirts of Calcutta, where a number of engineering and steel factories had come up. The largest of these was the Bhartia Iron and Steel Works. If memory serves, there were two working class comrades in that cell: Rahman, who became a whole-timer and Mohammad Nissar, who was still working in the factory, when I joined the cell. The cell secretary, the leader of the unit, was Abani Sen who had been an employee of the Tinplate Factory in Jamshedpur and had participated in the strike there. He was the only one with fairly extensive experience of the trade union movement. Apart from others, there was comrade Prakriti Mitra, a remarkable person, extremely hard-working, totally dedicated, a fine human being and an excellent organizer.

Shortly after I joined the cell, a group of workers from an engineering factory nearby, Beruck and Comens, asked us to organize a trade union in their factory. Till then, we only led the trade union at the Bhartia Iron and Steel factory and the cell asked me to organize the new union. Since this was my first experience, I asked Abani Sen to guide me in the nitty-gritty of forming a union and getting it registered. At a mass meeting, I was elected secretary of the union, an executive committee was formed comprising some leading workers who had taken the initiative to form the union. Steps were taken to get the union registered. We next formulated a charter of demands that I drafted after discussions in the executive committee. But who was to bell the cat? The union not being recognized, none of the worker leaders wanted to go to present the charter to the management. So I was asked to go.

Taking the papers in a portfolio bag, I walked straight past the factory gates where the security staff, not knowing who I was, made no attempt to stop me. I went right up to the office where the sahibs were sitting. The factory was run by a Dutch company and the management consisted entirely of expatriate Dutchmen. Seeing me they were livid with rage (they actually turned red) and shouted: 'Who are you? How did you get here?' I said that I was the secretary of the union and that I was associated with the Bhartia Union. This enraged them even more and they refused to have anything to do with me. Had I had not walked away quietly, they would surely have had me thrown out but I had learnt my lesson on the management attitude towards unrecognized unions. Perhaps it still is the same in many parts of India.

I reported the matter to the executive committee and it was decided that we would send our charter of demands by registered post, which we did. The company's response was prompt. They sacked Bireswar Baidick, the worker leader of the union but accepted some of the demands, thereby creating a dilemma for us. On the one hand, if we did not register our protest against this attack, the union would lose faith in us and would be weakened considerably. On the other hand, we realized that as the demands concerning wages and such others had been met partially, there would be a division amongst the workers if we decided to go on strike. I discussed this in our cell and it was decided that we should ask the workers to go on strike. This was endorsed by the executive committee as well as by the general body though the workers did this because they felt that having reposed faith in us they should accept our decision. The strike was successful on day one. We had organized picketing and, except the management and clerical staff, no one went in save a few loyalists, prompted by personal reasons.

After a few days some workers started reporting for work. The company's henchmen escorted them and our picket lines were broken. The workers of this factory were involved in a strike for the first time; the union was only a few months old. Out of desperation some leading workers suggested that a dreaded goonda in the locality be roped in. They thought that an offer of money would persuade him to do the job for us. This was obviously a fatal mistake because the management was keeping track of our moves and was obviously in a position to offer much more than our fledgling union could.

The goonda did turn up the next morning with some gang members and forcibly pushed the workers into the factory. Many workers who had assembled near the factory gate to know what was happening were pressed into service to break the strike. Our volunteers, who stood in awe of these ruffians, just stood by and watched. It was clear that the strike would not continue. The union office was just a few yards away from the factory gate. Every morning some of our worker volunteers would assemble there to take up positions at the various points where we had set up our picket posts. On the day these events were taking place, one by one the workers quietly left the office and walked away, leaving me alone. There was the gang forcing the workers to go in and they were entering the factory gates, with their heads bowed. They did feel ashamed but they saw that there was no alternative if they wanted to save their jobs. This was my first experience of a strike.

Standing alone in the office of a union that had clearly lost the battle, I realized that I was in a vulnerable position. There was the distinct possibility of the ruffians attacking the union office. In an unsuccessful strike, the management's stooges quite often smash up and even set fire to union offices. I knew this could happen. Strangely though, I felt no fear. In fact, I stood right in front within a few feet of the goondas and prepared for the worst. Evidently they felt that their purpose had been achieved; a very large number of workers had been pushed in; the strike had been broken and it was clear the rest of the workers would join the next day. After a couple of hours, the gang left and all was quiet; a very death-like quiet.

I closed the union office and went to my cell leader and other members to discuss what should be done. Some suggested that another desperate effort should be made to save the strike by more vigorous picketing the next morning but we thought that it would be futile and decided to call off the strike, which was only a formality because the workers had, even without our prompting, decided to join work. Looking back, I question the decision to call a strike.

The war had started, the Defence of India Rules had come into force. Even the People's War line had been adopted by the Party. If this issue had come up a few months later, the decision would have been against strike. In fact, we would not even have sent the strike notice because this factory was possibly supplying items to the defence forces.

Even had it not been so, would the strike have been justified in normal circumstances? The company had partially met the workers' demands. The workers felt that they had gained something. To strike on the issue of the dismissal of one worker, even though he was a union leader, could not have been very popular with the workers. We should also have realized that the workers had formed a union for the first time and had no previous experience even of any struggle, not to speak of a strike. What we should have done is to claim victory when the concessions were made because it was after the strike notice that the reliefs had been announced. We could have said that we would fight for the reinstatement of the sacked worker through legal channels and through the conciliation process. Meanwhile, we could have asked the workers to set up a fund for the maintenance of the dismissed worker and contribute to it from their wages. They would definitely have responded to this as they had all gained from the package the company had announced.

This would have saved the union and enabled it to build up a fund of its own for future struggles. The biggest mistake was to try to get the support of goondas to counter the efforts of the company's henchmen. Where workers cannot defeat the strike breakers on their own, it is suicidal to get hired thugs because the management can always better the payment and use the same thugs to break the strike. I was learning fast. As we had feared, following the unsuccessful strike, a few other workers who had played a leading role in organizing the strike were also dismissed. Fortunately, a friend of one of my brothers was heading the Jamalpur railway workshop. With the war on, they were recruiting and the dismissed workers were all skilled technical hands. I was able to get them employed in that workshop.

The next important learning experience for me was the strike at the Bhartia Iron and Steel factory where our union was an old and established one. The workers too had earlier experiences of strikes. This union was within the purview of our cell and I was associated with the strike right from the preparation stage until the final settlement. The leadership was provided entirely by Abani Sen in consultation with the district party leadership and the executive committee comprising leading workers from all the departments of the factory. In fact, it was the worker leaders who played the main role in organizing the strike. This was the plus point here; a seasoned and experienced working class leadership. The strike had the support of the overwhelming majority of the workers, who were worked up because of the spiralling inflation. Wages were low; an unskilled worker got only Rs 12 or so per month and the skilled workers no more than Rs 30 or Rs 40. The concept of dearness allowance was unheard of. When prices started shooting up, survival became virtually impossible.

With the active participation of a large number of worker leaders and volunteers, the strike was successful. It lasted for nearly a month when the management capitulated. The worker leaders were called for negotiations (outsiders like us were not allowed) and were able to negotiate from a position of strength. They struck a good bargain; there was a substantial increase in emoluments and some other facilities. This struggle of the workers was yet another rich learning experience for me and by the time the strike ended I felt that I had become an experienced trade unionist. During the entire period of the strike I stayed in a workers' bustee along with Abani Sen and one or two cell members in rather primitive conditions. Subsequently too, when we moved out of the bustee, we lived in a rented room within the working class area in a house that belonged to a sympathizer, Professor Niren Roy.

By this time I was participating in party meetings in which problems of the iron and steel industry as a whole were discussed. It broadened my horizon and improved my understanding of the trade union movement. In recognition of the work that I had done in the trade union movement, I was elected to the General Council of the All India Trade Union Congress (AITUC). I recall having attended my first All India Conference of the AITUC in Nagpur in 1943 in which, along with many others, Promode Dasgupta was a delegate from West Bengal. N. M. Joshi the liberal, non-party trade union leader was the AITUC General Secretary and steered the entire proceedings even though S. A. Dange and Ranadive (BTR) and other communist trade union leaders were present.

At this and other AITUC conferences, which I attended later, there would be 'fraction' meetings of all the Communist Party members who were attending. These meetings were always addressed by BTR. I remember being highly impressed by the speeches that he delivered. He would present the class angle in every issue and could present the stand of the Party as one that was in the best interests of the working class.

In early 1943, the party leadership wanted me to move to the Kidderpore area. There were developments in the Port union that opened out possibilities and serious challenges. The Port Trust Employees Association, as it was then called, was established by a group led by the popular Nepal Bhattacharya. It was one of the earliest unions registered under the Trade Union Act and had even been accorded recognition by the Port Trust authorities, a rare achievement for those times. In the early stages, its membership was mostly confined to the clerical staff and its activities consisted of sending petitions and taking up individual cases with the management but its influence had gradually extended to other sections of employees.

With the outbreak of the war and the Defence of India Rules coming into force, the government had 'externed' Nepal Bhattacharya from the city. As a result, the group which had been active along with him and called itself the Workers Party, comprising a handful of relatively inexperienced young men, had been left leaderless. Faced with the responsibility of handling a recognized union of an organization that had some 30,000 direct employees apart from casual labour, the Workers Party group was feeling a little helpless. Though the membership of the union was not very large, its influence was considerable but with the coming of the Defence of India Rules its activities had come to a standstill.

Meanwhile, the activities of the Party were growing in the whole Port/Dock area, particularly in Hyde Road where a large number of factories had come up. A fairly strong union had been formed with the workers of the Brooke Bond factory by Juran Ganguly, a veteran political worker, an erstwhile member of a revolutionary group who, like many others, joined the Communist Party. Brooke Bond, a multinational company, paid its workers a little better than the others. It also had a more educated class of workers, mostly Bengalis; many among them had joined the Party. There were other medium-size engineering units, where also the workers had joined the Red Flag trade unions. The growing influence and activities of the Party and the helplessness of the small group of Workers' Party organizers ultimately resulted in the whole group joining the Communist Party. They were able to convince the party leadership that there was tremendous potential for growth of the union if only some more organizers were made available.

The Party picked me up and drafted me for work in the Port union. The decision was taken by Nripen Chakravarty who was the Provincial Committee member in charge of the Calcutta district. At one meeting of the executive committee, I was appointed General Secretary of the Union with Somnath Lahiri as the President. Indrajit Gupta was elected Vice-President. Later he took over as President but again relinquished the post to accommodate Nepal Bhattacharya when he returned. Fortunately, there were many very able and dedicated cadres from amongst the Port workers, who had joined the Party some years earlier. The Party had been working amongst the Port and Dock workers for quite some time even though party workers had not been able to get a majority in the executive committee of the Port union. Amongst the members and activists of the Party were some outstanding workers with leadership qualities such as Parmananda Shyamal, Sitaram Singh,

Mohammad Amin, Ram Naresh and some others whose names I cannot now recall.

We also had a party group amongst the clerical workers both in the head office and in the various docks and jetties. Among them, Deb Kumar Ganguly, Prasanta Dutta, Himanshu Sinha, Nalini Sen, Debu Bannerjee and Robi Sen were a great asset. Debkumar Ganguly later went on to become General Secretary of the International Transport Workers' Federation with headquarters in Eastern Europe and also one of the Secretaries of the World Federation of Trade Unions (WFTU).

Nripen Chakravarty's decision to draft me to the Port union was a momentous one for me as it marked a turning point in my career in the Party. It was during the nearly six years that I was directly involved in the Port union that I learnt a lot and also matured as a person. This was a very challenging assignment as the Port union was almost a moribund organization when I joined. Reviving it was not easy. The Defence of India Rules (DIR) were in force and the workers were in a somewhat frightened state since many trade union leaders had been arrested or, as in the case of Nepal Bhattacharya, externed from Calcutta.

There was a rival union led by Dr. Maitrayee Bose, a Congress leader. Dr. Bose's union had a fairly good following amongst the Bihari workers, who were generally pro-Congress and were influenced by the propaganda of the Congress leaders that the other union was pro-government and anti-national. Kanti Mehta, too, was associated with the Union for some time.

Despite the odds facing us, our unit was full of enthusiasm and decided to go all out to revive the union. We adopted a two-pronged strategy. Since the union was recognized by the authorities, it took up the grievances of the workers collectively as well as individually and made representations to the management. The then Chairman of the Port Trust was Sir Thomas Elderton, a First World War veteran, who had lost an eye in the war. A hard working, fair and honest administrator, he was willing to listen. If the case was properly presented, he could be convinced that our point was worth considering and would give decisions in our favour. Many corrupt departmental heads or those who were unfair in their dealings with the workers could be forced to revise their decisions.

We had fortnightly meetings with the Chairman, the minutes of which I kept in summary form and sent to him for endorsement. He would generally approve with minor changes occasionally. The company secretary, Suraj Lal Das, who later became Chairman of Stewarts and Lloyds, a Tata group company, was an efficient and strict manager who followed Sir Thomas' policy of listening to the grievances. Where it was possible to redress them, he would do so. With the outbreak of the war the smooth and efficient functioning of the Port became crucial. Since the Party—as part of its People's War line—had decided on a no-strike policy, Sir Thomas was willing to accommodate us in matters where our demands did not run counter to government policies. Usually, these were around minor grievances and we were able to redress them. That helped to establish the credibility of the union leadership and gradually increased workers' confidence in us.

The second prong of our strategy was to go out in small squads to the workers' quarters. Fortunately, the majority of the workers lived in company quarters and so it was possible to approach the various clusters directly. Four or five squads consisting of one outside organizer and one or two worker activists would visit the quarters and try to hold group meetings with them. In the initial stages, many workers were unwilling to listen. Where the rival union had a hold, they would even be hostile and prevent us from holding any meeting or even talking to the workers individually. We persisted though and our squads continued to visit the workers at their quarters.

The other union did not have the cadres to undertake such a programme and were further handicapped by the arrest of many Congress-minded trade union leaders at that time. Their activity was limited to occasionally holding meetings over which Dr. Maitrayee Bose or some other union leader would preside. Our contacts were much wider and deeper and our union had a longer tradition too. Nevertheless, the hold of the unions was confined to a few sections. Many departments, such as the marine department that alone employed about 25 per cent of the workforce, were still outside the purview of union activity.

Gradually our hard work, both at the grass root level and at the negotiating table with top management level, yielded results and more sections rallied around us. The clerical staff still remained outside and was even a bit hostile because of the political prejudice against communists. Our slogan of People's War and the way we lampooned Subhas Chandra Bose, who was the idol of the middle class youth of Bengal, antagonized them. The other union that called itself the National Union continued to have the support of the clerical staff, though that did not mean that they were involved in any trade union activity or were paying members of the National Union.

Since both unions were claiming the support of the majority of workers at one stage, a secret ballot was organized. Boxes of the two unions were put up side by side in all sections and the employees were asked to cast their vote by putting the ballot paper supplied to each worker in one box or the other. This procedure was, however, flawed for two reasons. Instead of only members of the two unions voting, all employees in the section were allowed to cast their votes. Even more importantly, the balloting was given a political colour: and it was presented by the National Union as a contest between the National Congress and the communists. With the prevailing sentiment against the People's War policy the National Union was able to get a fairly large vote. I do not remember if they got a majority but certainly they were almost neck and neck with us. In view of the flawed nature of the voting process, the management decided not to attach any importance to the results of the voting. Both the unions continued to be recognized but the management was aware that the majority of union members were in our union.

Another step taken by us to strengthen the union was to hold annual conferences. They were first held section-wise and then with representatives of all the sections within our union. These conferences were very successful and helped to further consolidate the unity of the workers. The response was, in fact, overwhelming and the obvious reason was that the war-driven inflation was making everyday living a nightmare, especially with wages remaining constant and dearness allowance not being heard of.

A major breakthrough was achieved shortly before the end of the war when the marine section joined the union en masse. The workers of the marine section were all from east Bengal, mainly from Noakhali, Chittagong, Jessore and adjoining districts. Moreover, they were all Muslims and lived together in the Takta Ghat quarters provided to them. There was a tremendous sense of unity amongst them and whatever they did, they did together. The entry of the marine section, strategically the most important, and comprising around 25 per cent of the total work force meant that the primacy of our union was no longer a matter of dispute. The person who emerged as their leader was Bazloo Molla, a born leader, a remarkably good orator and a very intelligent man. He, along with Makhan Chatterjee, one of our organizers of whom I will have more to say later, was responsible for this development.

Yet another incident helped to cement their unity. Port workers were being supplied subsidized rations of rice and wheat and possibly dal at a fairly cheap rate. Depending on where the workers came from they were given rice or wheat. With the price of rice sky-rocketing, the management announced that the marine section workers, all from east Bengal and rice-eaters, would be given a part of their rations in wheat. The moment this announcement was made, there was a lightning strike by the entire marine staff that spread from Budge Budge to Hooghly Point. This indicated their remarkable unity and the wonderful system of communication that they had spontaneously developed. Our union immediately took up the issue. The management withdrew the announcement and within hours the strike was withdrawn and work resumed.

By the time the war ended, our union had been able to win the confidence of almost all sections of workers. Even the clerical staff, seeing that the workers had rallied en masse behind our union, began to join. They too were feeling the pinch of inflation and their measly salaries were not enough even for bare necessities. Thus, as the war ended, the entire mass of workers and clerical staff was like a powder keg, waiting to explode. The explosion came fairly soon and several steps taken by us helped to detonate the keg.

Among the important developments of the time was the lifting of the externment order on Nepal Bhattacharya. However, by the time he came back he had practically no organization to support him; the few cadres who had earlier supported him had crossed over to the Communist Party but the workers had a soft corner for him because of his earlier services and the repression that he had faced. We could easily have refused him entry into the union and any rival union he may have formed would not have been able at that time to mobilize much support. In view of the trends and practices currently in vogue, it is necessary to emphasize that the unity of the workers must be the main objective of any organization that has the welfare of the workers at heart. That was exemplified by our action.

In fact, the party leadership decided, with the full support of the local unit and the workers who were with the Party, that Nepal Bhattacharya would be offered the position of President of the Union and the person holding that post, Indrajit Gupta, who had by this time taken over as the President, would resign in his favour. We also offered to take several persons nominated by him into the executive committee. They were mostly from the clerical staff. The majority in the executive committee were the acknowledged worker leaders of their sections and had been duly elected at our annual and sectional conferences. So our actions did not amount to handing over the union to them. In fact, it increased the prestige of the Party and, by sharing power, we actually achieved hegemony.

I cannot help but point out the sharp contrast to the present efforts that all parties make to capture unions. This concept of capturing unions, capturing institutions, capturing localities, and even booths—which seems to be the strategy of the leadership of all parties—is not only against all norms of democratic functioning but is actually counterproductive since it divides the workers, undermines the leadership of the union, creates resentment and even hatred of the party or group that tries to implement such a strategy.

The impact of our decision was, expectedly, that almost total unity had been achieved and the workers were raring to go. The powder keg was on the point of exploding. At most some 10 per cent outside were part of the Maitrayee Bose-led National Union. The mood of the workers, irrespective of union affiliation, was to struggle to achieve their demand for improvement in wages and allowances. We did not exclude even this 10 per cent when the actual strike call was given. A joint committee was formed for the conduct of the strike with representatives of both the trade unions.

The first signs of the impending explosion had come soon after the end of the war, even before the changes in the union referred to above. Somnath Lahiri was still its President and we had called a meeting at the Mansatala Park. It was a rather small park and we were pleasantly surprised to see that it not only filled up as processions started coming in from various sections, the mass of workers even spilt over to the roads surrounding the park and we had to put up mikes along the roads. This was beyond our expectations and made us understand that the workers were really getting restive. Before proceeding to the next phase of our national movement and of the Communist Party, the trade union movement and my own story, I would like to make some observations on our role in this period.

On the positive side, despite our trying to go against the current, it was during this period that the Party registered a significant growth and emerged as a mass party. This I ascribe to the hardships facing ordinary people as a consequence of the war and the inflation that followed and our party cadres standing by the people, working sincerely and devotedly at the grass root level. They fought to get their grievances redressed to the extent possible, raised the correct slogan of the need for rationing, participated in civil defence activities, even when the Japanese started bombing the city and tried to draw in all sections of the people to our movement and activities.

The constructive work done by our women comrades played a stellar role. They set up work centres, where women from the poorer sections could earn something; they ran gruel kitchens during the famine; prevented girls from being snatched away by flesh traders; and brought about social change by campaigning for the rights of women. These initiatives helped to win support, though the importance of this work was not fully appreciated by the Party. In fact, a large section of the male leaders of the Party sneered at this work as 'Ramakrishna Mission type activity' and considered this as being far removed from revolutionary work.

This reflected an incorrect understanding both of what constituted revolutionary activity and also of the gender bias within the Party. Despite its claim of standing for equality of the sexes unlike the bourgeoisie, at all levels the Party shared the prejudices and attitudes prevalent in our male-dominated society. There were numerous instances. To mention just one: if the husband and the wife were both party members and one wanted to become a whole-timer, it was always the wife who was asked to take up a job and support the husband and the family even if she was as competent, if not more as than her husband. This arrangement was inevitably arrived at because it was not possible to maintain a family on the pittance that was doled out as the party wage. Since only whole-timers could function at the upper levels of the party hierarchy, it also meant that there were very few women at those levels. Other examples will reveal themselves as this story progresses.

Opposing the Quit India call of the Congress and our slogan of People's War were the negative aspects of our movement. The former isolated us from a very large section of nationalist opinion and remains a blot on the Party that it will find difficult to erase. The Second World War was, from the very beginning, against the fascist threat, the seriousness of which was obvious to everyone right from the time of the Franco insurrection and the Civil War in Spain in 1935-36. If we had to give precedence to our world view and if we regarded fascism as the real danger, we should have declared it an anti-fascist war from the very beginning. Harry Pollit, the General Secretary of the Communist Party of Great Britain (CPGB) did, in fact, suggest this course of action and was suspended or marginalized within the Party for his stand. He was, of course, reinstated when, after the attack on the Soviet Union, the Comintern (Communist International) officially accepted the war as a just war.

I do not know whether the top leadership of the Party was aware of the non-aggression pact that Stalin and Hitler had entered into at the beginning of the war in 1939. We had no knowledge of this till much later. Stalin, of course, did what he felt was in the immediate national interest of the USSR, without bothering about ideology. The rest of the communist movement followed the Soviet line: refraining from participating in the war against fascism as long as the Soviet Union was out of it and ignoring national interest when the Soviet Union was attacked. Clearly, the entire communist movement, at least that section being led by the Communist International, had become an appendage of the Soviet Communist Party.

While reminding people constantly of the danger posed by fascism we should have declared, as indeed Gandhiji and others did, that it was not possible for the people of India to participate in the war against fascism as long as the country remained a colony of an imperialist power. Only a national government could rally the people in favour of the war effort. Thus, while not calling it a People's War, which clearly it was not as far as the people of India were concerned, we should have said that even though globally it is a war against the fascist powers, it could only become a People's War for the Indian people when they were freed from the shackles of slavery. We should, therefore, have supported the Quit India slogan of the Congress and participated in the mass movement while trying to differentiate ourselves from those who were carrying on activities such as sabotage, removing the fish plates of the railway lines, hurling bombs and the like.

Without casting aspersions on Subhas Bose and depicting him as a fifth columnist and a fascist stooge, we could even have expressed our disapproval of his policy of trying to liberate the country with foreign military assistance. As it turned out, his successful effort in rallying the Indian prisoners of war and organizing them in the Indian National Army did play a crucial role in the liberation of the country. Significantly, in private, Ajoy Ghosh expressed similar views though he never held a formal discussion in the Party to review this period. This was evidently because he realized that there were sharp differences within the Party on this issue that could have split the Party even earlier than it finally did. E. M. S. Namboodiripad, for instance, told me, when I interviewed him as a journalist much later, that the People's War line was absolutely correct. This interview was published in *The Statesman*.

NINE

Famine and Beyond

The period between the change in the party line (towards the end of 1941) and the next event of historical importance, the transfer of power on 15 August 1947, is replete with developments of enormous significance. Determining the future course of events were such cataclysmic events as the famine of 1943; the trials of the INA leaders and the mass upsurge in favour of their release; the revolt of the naval ratings and the general strikes that took place in their support. These have been recorded and analysed by historians and need not be discussed here except in so far as they affected us and our work.

The famine took a toll of some three million lives, though estimates vary. Amartya Sen's book, *Poverty and Famines: An Essay on Entitlement and Deprivation* (Oxford University Press, 1982), says that the official Famine Enquiry Commission put the figure at 'about 1.5 million' but points out that the 'Commission's own method of calculation does lead to a figure of around three million deaths'. The enormity of the crisis was not immediately apparent to us. Early every morning we awoke to the cries of '*Phan dao, ma, phan.*'. *Phan* is a starchy gruel, which remains after rice is cooked, and is usually drained off. It was this that the starving people were begging for. The situation soon changed for the worse and we stepped out into the roads to find lifeless bodies strewn all over.

The Party blamed the hoarders and black-marketeers squarely for this. Hoarding and black-marketing had indeed taken place and the Ispahanis were among the most prominent names mentioned. There was a Muslim League ministry in office with H. S. Suhrawardy as the Chief Minister. Not surprisingly, some of his cronies got into the rice trade but there were others as well, not connected with the

League. The popular idea is that the initial shortage was caused by the army authorities cornering the bulk of the supplies for the war on the eastern front. Since any criticism of the war effort was taboo, we concentrated on the hoarders.

Amartya Sen's analysis states that it was essentially a rural phenomenon that could perhaps be understood 'in terms of shifting exchange entitlements' (exchange entitlements in terms of entitlement to rice), the worst affected groups being 'fishermen, transport workers, paddy-huskers, agricultural labourers, those in "other productive occupations", craftsmen and non-agricultural labourers, in that order.' Ultimately, it was inflation caused by the war that led to these shifts; there is no doubt that the war was the root cause of the famine.

What is relevant for this account is that during the famine the Party concentrated on critical relief work without criticizing the government. The only example of a struggle of sorts is the one mentioned by Manikuntala Sen in her book in Bengali, *Shediner Katha* (Naba Patra, 1983; Translated and published in English as *In Search of Freedom: An Unfinished Journey*, Stree, 2001). She talks of leading a procession of village women to the Assembly, virtually *gheraoing* it until some truck loads of rice were brought out and distributed amongst the destitute women.

Apart from this, party volunteers, mainly some women activists, helped with keeping in order the queues of women lining up for their quota of rice from the fair price shops that had been opened. More important was their role in saving young girls from the rampant flesh trade. They also ran relief kitchens, where hundreds lined up. I was witness to much of this in the Ballygunje/Gariahat area but it was being organized in other areas of the city too. Famine relief, running gruel kitchens was a feature of activities by party activists and by many others in the rural districts too.

My work involved organizing squads to go from house-to-house collecting relief material, selling party literature and participating in the campaign against hoarding, black marketing and trafficking in women. Initially, when organizing cultural squads among workers

I had inserted into some of Dasratlal's folk songs, lines about the hoarders. It was in this period that the play *Nabanna* (new rice or new harvest) was staged with the 1943 famine as the backdrop. The purpose of this very moving production was to expose the hoarders. Charu Ghosh (a party sympathizer and not a professional actor) played the role of hoarder to perfection. Manikuntala Sen played the old woman and won accolades. So did Zainul Abedin's sketches of the starving that were exhibited all over India and attracted global attention.

Other artists who did excellent work on the famine were Chittaprasad and Somnath Hore. P. C. Joshi, General Secretary of the Party, organized a cultural troupe that toured Punjab and other states to raise funds and food grains. A member of this troupe, Sadhana (daughter of Monoroma Guha, a party activist) sang a song, the opening lines of which were *Bhuka hai Bangal* (Bengal is starving). It not only won her fame but also brought tears to the eyes of listeners and helped bring in liberal donations of food grains from Punjab and some other food surplus states.

Some time in 1943 or 1944, I was informed that I had been selected for a course at the Central Party School to be held at the party headquarters in Bombay. It took me by surprise because I was not aware of any such school. As it turned out, it was just a one-off exercise: this was the first and only time that it was held. I was very pleased to be among the very few selected from Bengal for the Central Party School. There was, however, some heart burning because I was very junior in the Party and senior people had been overlooked.

Much later, in the very late 1950s or early 1960s, some classes were organized by the Party Centre that had by that time shifted to Delhi and I too among others was invited to deliver lectures there occasionally. However, it was very different from the Central School to which I have just referred I was one of the teachers at the Central School and used to go from Calcutta to deliver my lectures.

When I reached Bombay, I found that some of those selected

from other states were not only much older but were at least of the district level. I do not recall everyone from Bengal but I remember that there were a few women comrades among them: Juiphul Bose (who later married Khoka Roy), Kalpana Dutt of Chittagong Armoury Raid fame, Kalyani Bhattacharya, a niece of Biswanath Mukherjee and Nazamunessa Ahmad, daughter of Kutubuddin Ahmad, an old associate of Muzaffar Ahmad.

The teachers were members of the Politbureau and Central Committee including P. C. Joshi himself, Dr Adhikari, Dange, Krishnan, Mohan Kumaramangalam, P. Ramamurti among others. The course lasted for a fortnight or so. Part of the activities was to bring out a journal that would be put up on the wall. It would be a record of the activities in the school and carry a gist of the lectures delivered. I was asked to edit the journal though, being very new and young, the de facto editing was done by P. Ramamurti. The good thing was that I got to know him well during this period and found him to be very sharp and knowledgeable. I met him again during trade union conferences and found that he was a trade union leader with a huge following in Madras and a powerful speaker.

I do not recall the lectures delivered by the various speakers save one remark made by P. C. Joshi. He spoke very fast, his ideas probably running ahead of his words, which sometimes led to a slurring of his words. Sometimes it was difficult to follow him and he had to be asked to repeat what he had said. What was impressive was the confidence and authority with which he spoke. To the extent that we did follow, we understood the drift of the points he made. His remark seemed strange but coming from him, I took it seriously. He was talking about the party journal, *People's War*, explaining how it was designed, the kind of material and news being put in and then said: 'Party members should avoid reading the Marxist classics. Reading them at this time could turn you into Trotskyites. *People's War* will provide all the education needed.' I remember this very clearly because this came as a shock to me. I had fancied myself as a bit of a theoretician and hoped to develop myself by studying the Marxist classics seriously. The Party General Secretary, however, was infallible and whatever he said, especially in a lecture in the Central Party School, had to be adhered to.

This sharp cleavage between theory and practice continues and the gap is even wider in the practice of the communist movement in India today. Instead of facing the reality that the dogmas of an earlier period have no relevance in the changed situation, not only is lip service still paid to concepts that were perhaps very relevant in another age, but any attempt to creatively develop the theory is also dismissed as revisionism. It is no longer treated as a social science but as a religion. It is much like what some of our ancient pandits said about brahmins alone studying the Vedas. The rank and file have only to follow the dictates of the leadership without trying to understand the rationale behind them.

I venture to say that the communist movement in India, while discarding conventional religions, only ended up by adopting Marxism as the new religion. In so doing, the scientific kernel of Marxism as a method of analysing the dynamics of social development and understanding the laws of social evolution has been discarded. Today, with communist parties in power in some of the states it is clear that the Marxist label they sport is only an attempt to exploit its brand equity for themselves. Otherwise it is difficult to differentiate them from all the other parties that participate in the electoral process.

Looking back, it is clear that, from a common sense point of view, Joshi had only stated the obvious in saying that we should refrain from reading the Marxist classics. The situation that India was facing after 1942, especially after the Party had adopted the People's War line, was so different from what Marx had dealt with in nineteenth-century Europe or that Lenin had to face in early twentieth-century Russia that Marxist classics,

> taken literally, were obviously irrelevant. Nevertheless, as long as the Party continued to proclaim that its political line was derived from Marxian ideology, the leadership should have made an effort to show the link between the theory we professed and our practice.

As a person, P. C. Joshi was likeable and friendly. On one occasion, when there was a recess and we were all sitting and chatting, I got up and tried to mimic P. C. Joshi. It was evidently so good that everyone was amused. Just at that moment Joshi came in and asked me to repeat the performance and had a good laugh.

The taboo on reading Marxist literature had an adverse affect on me because I really did not do any serious Marxist reading till much later. It was only during the three years that I spent in jail that I read all the selected works of Marx and Engels, of Lenin and whatever was available of Stalin, even some of Mao. I was also part of a study circle where we were trying to understand the first volume of Marx's *Das Capital.* Krishnapada Ghosh, who later became Labour Minister in West Bengal and Sushital Roychoudhury, who later joined the Naxalites, were among the other members of this circle. I think Subhas Mukherjee, the poet, also attended some of our sessions.

During the course of this programme P. C. Joshi got engaged to Kalpana Dutt. Whether this was officially announced or not I do not remember but we got to know of it and later it became official. The formal registration of the marriage of Mohan Kumaramangalam with Kalyani also took place during this period and was officially announced. I think there was even a mini-celebration with pastry and tea for all the students and teachers.

TEN

Strike Wave; the 'Great Calcutta Killing'

The pent up rage of the working class buffeted by inflation and without any dearness allowance or increase in salaries in the post-war period burst out in a wave of strikes. The tram workers with their strong union and considerable experience of struggles were the first to go on strike. Workers in several industries followed suit. The crest of the wave was reached on 29 July 1946 when, for the first time in the history of Calcutta, there was a total general strike at the call of the All India Trade Union Congress.

This was in support of the Post and Telegraph workers, who had gone on strike for their demands of increased salaries, dearness allowance and other facilities. A unique feature was that even the middle-class employees and supervisory staff, including the Anglo-Indian telephone operators, working in the various exchanges, joined the strike. This was the precursor to the phenomenon of clerical staff, who had hitherto kept aloof from working class movements, getting unionized. This trend continues to this day and unions of bank, insurance, central and state government employees have emerged and not only participated in struggles on their own issues but often also supported movements of workers of other industries.

In the Port we moved carefully. Since it was a recognized union, we did not want to err on any formalities required to preclude the possibility of the strike being declared illegal. A strike notice was served, the union tried its best to settle the dispute through negotiations and conciliation. There was a lengthy exchange of correspondence with the Chairman and, only when there seemed no possibility of settlement, a date for the commencement of the strike was announced. This would have taken place shortly after the war had ended but it had to be postponed because of the outbreak of the August 1946 riots: the Great Calcutta Killing.

A brief reference to the developments that culminated in the riots of August 1946 often referred to as the Great Calcutta Killing and the role that the unions played is in order here. With the end of the war, the freedom struggle took a new turn. The economic struggle of the workers and employees got interlinked with the broader freedom struggle. With the wounds of the 1942 Quit India movement still fresh, the urge for freedom and the determination to achieve it had received a new impetus.

The unprecedented and the spontaneous general strike of 29 July 1946 evidently unnerved not only the Indian government (still controlled by the British) but also the state government, led by the Muslim League with H. S. Suhrawardy as Chief Minister. A shrewd and unscrupulous politician, he was perhaps hoping that in a Pakistan, where East Pakistan's population would form the majority, he might become the Prime Minister or at least an important cabinet minister. The demonstration of Hindu-Muslim solidarity in support of a struggle of a section of the working class boded no good for him or for Jinnah or for the British government. It could blunt the edge of the struggle for the partition of the country.

This was the background of the call for 'direct action' on 16 August given by Jinnah, the leader of the Muslim League. As a part of the day's programme, the Muslim League called on the Muslim workers to go on strike. This posed a serious problem for the trade union movement in the city. In most industries Hindu and Muslim workers worked side by side. True, in some departments there was a preponderance of Hindu workers while Muslims were in a majority in others. A sectarian call for a strike of Muslim workers was a sure recipe for large-scale riots and for clashes within each department and each industry. The leadership of the Muslim League could not have been unaware of this. Indeed, there is little doubt that the whole idea was to disrupt the unity of the working class and to destroy its trade unions. There was, of course, an even more sinister design behind their move: to show that without Partition there could be no peace in the subcontinent. Our immediate concern was to safeguard the unity of the workers and to save our unions.

Our response to the sectarian call for a strike of the Muslim workers was to ask *all* workers to cease work. There would obviously be no work done if all Muslim workers went on strike as the nature of the operations in the Port was such that if one section went on strike the others would not be able to do their part of the work. If the cranes (manned almost entirely by Muslim workers) did not work, workers involved in the loading and unloading of cargo would have to sit idle. This was only one example. If the tugs (also manned mainly by Muslims) did not work, no ship could be brought in or leave the docks. Thus, in asking all workers to stay away, we were not trying to support the disruptive call of the Muslim League but to preserve the unity of the working class.

This tactic did work and even though we were not able to prevent large-scale rioting in various parts of the city, the unity of the workers in the Port and even in other establishments with strong unions remained steadfast. Indeed, it was not just the negative—rioting—that had been avoided, but a positive—feeling of communal harmony—had been engendered. This was even more palpable a few months later during the Port strike when joint squads of Hindu and Muslim workers went out with collection boxes seeking donations from the public in aid of the striking workers.

Official estimates placed the number killed from both communities at some 10,000 within 10 days before the fires could be doused. The embers smouldered much longer; so did sporadic outbreaks and stray incidents. It was only after Gandhiji's fast later in 1947 that a semblance of normalcy returned though the wounds festered as they moulded the psyche of both communities. It was another traumatic experience for me, just about 25 years old then and I aged considerably during these months.

In the prevailing atmosphere, not only in the Port but also in the whole area, everything came to a standstill on the morning of 16 August. A meeting had been called by the Muslim League at the Maidan in front of what was then known as Ochterlony Monument.

We had asked our section leaders to assemble at a point, the union office at Bhukailash Road, and we set off in a procession towards the Maidan. Since the workers were all geared up for our proposed strike, there was a good response to our call and they came with their banners and festoons, marching in a spirited manner. The processionists included Muslim and Hindu workers who had little idea of what was in store.

As usual, when important union processions were organized, I stood at the head, alongside the large festoon bearing the union's name. As we crossed the bridge and approached the Race Course, we felt that there was something odd about the atmosphere. The usual hub and bustle that pervaded the scene of a mass meeting was missing. Instead, there was an eerie silence. As we moved into the Maidan but were still some distance away from the scene of the meeting, we came across dead bodies strewn on the Maidan. We realized that riots had broken out but even then were not able to grasp the magnitude of the unfolding tragedy.

Instinctively, the workers folded up their banners and festoons, quite a few just melted away, probably returning to their quarters. The others continued to march, though in a rather disorderly manner towards the monument. Some of us, the leading union workers and organizers, kept walking if only to figure out what had happened. My mind was in a state of shock as we came to a point from where the speaker's voice could be heard over the mike. The speaker was the Chief Minister, H. S. Suhrawardy himself. He was speaking in Urdu and I could make out a few words in which he spoke of the 'terrible events of the morning'. By now it had become clear that large-scale rioting had broken out in all parts of the city. Without further ado, we headed straight for the union office to prevent the riots from spreading in the Kidderpore area. Indeed, when we returned sometime in the afternoon Kidderpore was still quiet.

Our union office was in the heart of a densely-populated Muslim bustee. The atmosphere was tense but the residents, many of them workers in the local factories and in the port and docks, kept indoors. The lone crusader, probably a militant of the Muslim

League, kept rushing up and down the road, urging the people to come out and fight, without any response till late evening. A prominent leader of the area, also of one of our factory unions, Haroun, stood on guard in front of our union office, taunting back: 'Why do you not go and fight instead of shouting here? We are all staying right here' (*Jao na laro, chillane se kya hoga? Hum yahan thik hain*). Haroun was a stalwart of our Brooke Bond Workers' Union. Looting and arson had, however, started in other areas of Kidderpore. Some 10 or 12 Hindu workers were still at the office; the Muslim workers had no problem returning home in this Muslim area. It would be hazardous for the Hindu workers to venture out. Haroun had guarded us and assured us that no harm would come to us.

In the darkness of the evening, he told us to get ready and follow him. Descending from the rear of the union office, which opened into the bustee, he led us through its narrow winding lanes. With Haroun escorting us we faced no problem; not even hostile stares. There was only shock, astonishment and a touch of fear in their eyes, as we warily made our way. The other end of the slum was not far from the main Diamond Harbour Road. Once we reached there, we were safe. This was neutral territory from where the Hindu workers had no problem making their way to their Hyde Road quarters while I walked back to our commune at Mansatala.

There I found several comrades apprehensively watching the developments and wondering what to do. Indrajit Gupta had also reached the commune by that time. Mansatala was a predominantly Hindu area with a sprinkling of middle-class Muslim families. A Muslim advocate living in the building housing our commune sought our protection; we assured him that he would be safe. We were still trying to figure out how to maintain peace; make a difference in the city wracked by large-scale rioting; at least in our area, a predominantly working class one like Kidderpore. It was fairly late but we took out a peace procession. The few Muslim families in the locality joined us and we set out.

As we got into the main Circular Garden Reach Road, we saw

fires burning on Watgunje Street. We were told that many small goldsmith shops there had been looted and burnt. We could even then see some steel doors of the shops being broken open with heavy hammers and rods, clearly the work of professional criminals. Taking advantage of the situation, they had targeted the shops where the booty would be the most valuable. Our procession was not attacked but further progress was barred by a number of people, including some of those who were engaged in the looting. We were told to go back and we could see that the situation was out of control. The anti-socials had taken over the area and any intervention would have to be by armed police or units of the army.

The administration was clearly not impartial; it had indeed taken the initiative in starting the riots and there was no point in our continuing with the slogan of Hindu Muslim *bhai bhai.* By the next morning the whole of Calcutta was burning: the Great Calcutta Killing was underway. A day or two later, I left the commune to go back to our family residence at Ray Street where one of my brothers lived with his family. Shortly after, the Wanchus, rescued by the army, came to stay with us though we were entirely cut off. There were repeated curfews and it was impossible to venture out.

Ray Street, a middle class and primarily Hindu area in Bhowanipore, was quiet though the tension was palpable. Gradually a semblance of normalcy was achieved though sporadic incidents continued to occur. The government-imposed curfew continued over large parts of the city, making it impossible for ordinary citizens to move about. It was relaxed for short periods to enable people to procure essential supplies but markets were closed. The normal supply of vegetables and cereals was affected because of the unsettled conditions and the curfew. The government arranged to distribute essential commodities to various localities with the help of the local police stations. We had to depend on these supplies, doled out according to the number of heads in each household. Ours now had eight or nine persons with the arrival of the Wanchus. This was the first and hopefully last time when even those belonging to middle class families had to subsist on a government dole, fortunately for a very short period though.

Free movement became possible after some ten days. I walked across to Lee Road, where Indrajit Gupta was staying with his ICS brother, Ranjit Gupta. He told me how he and some others, notably Snehangshu Acharya, had got in touch with the administration and played an active part in rescuing people with the help of the army. It took a great deal of courage and the administration had, in fact, sought the cooperation of the Communist Party. Notwithstanding the bitter relations between the Party and the government, the administration was aware of the Party's secular credentials. Returning to my Kidderpore base, I was very happy to find that the worker unity had been maintained in all establishments with strong unions despite the desperate provocation of communal elements. Many comrades in the Kidderpore commune, who were unable to move out to safe areas, had fought pitched battles with those who had tried to attack the locality. They were able to maintain the mixed character of at least that part of the locality that was in the immediate vicinity of the commune.

Apart from being a traumatising experience, the events of August 1946 taught me many lessons that are worth recounting. There is not even a shadow of doubt that the riots were planned and organized. They were not spontaneous. What had been planned was the lighting of the spark; that it would set off a conflagration of such huge dimensions may not have been foreseen by those who ignited it. There was no fundamental rift between the two communities. Kidderpore was a predominantly Muslim area; the workers in such establishments as the Port, docks and the ships were largely Muslim with the Hindu workers and clerical staff interspersed as a small minority. When we proposed a ceasework of all workers (and not only of the Muslim workers as per the call of the League), there was immediate acceptance both from the Hindus and the Muslims.

Again as we sat in the union office on the evening of that fateful day we saw how the repeated efforts by a lone militant to rouse the Muslim inhabitants of that huge bustee failed. That bustee, it needs to be noted, housed not only organized workers but also the Muslim poor of all descriptions: hawkers, artisans, unemployed and even some anti-social elements. No one responded for hours even after reports of rioting in other parts of Calcutta had reached them, some highly exaggerated. That bore evidence to there being no spontaneous mood in favour of looting and killing. Even when we took the peace march right into where the small jewellery shops were being looted, those breaking open the shops did not attack our procession. They only asked us to go back, saying that it was now too late to talk of peace since rioting had broken out all over Calcutta. Clearly, even the League militants had to be given the incentive of the 'gold' to motivate them to break open the shops.

The point is that even if there is a latent sense of distrust and suspicion between the two communities that does not, by itself, add up to an urge for violence and rioting. It needs much more than a simple spark to set off a conflagration. Even then the vast majority remains a mute spectator while the organized forces take over the dirty work aided by the anti-social elements that are keen to take advantage of the opportunity to loot. Significantly, the unity of the Port and dock workers and of the working class in general in that area continued for long after, as was manifest in the more than three-month long strike of February-May 1947.

The port strike makes for an interesting case study for trade unionists and political scientists if they do ever care to take up such a study. It also constitutes an important landmark in my life's journey, one that helped me to mature both as a trade union leader, as a political activist, and in the development of my personality.

ELEVEN

Lessons from the Port Strike

The port strike has to be studied in the backdrop of the postwar climate of anti-British sentiment and hardship fostered by the spiralling inflation and the oppressive Defence of India Rules. Once the DIR provisions lapsed after the war, the latent unrest of the employees came to the fore: wages and salaries before and during the war were pathetic; the inflation was killing and the sluice gates seemed to have opened, releasing a wave of resentment. A charter of demands had been presented to the Chairman, Port Commissioners but, except for very making minor concessions, he was in no mood to yield.

The Government of India had meanwhile announced the setting up of a Pay Commission to go into the whole question of wages, salaries, allowances and other issues relating to the living standards of government employees. Port employees were not considered employees of the government as the Port Trust was a statutory and, technically, an autonomous body. Our union's contention was that the port employees should be brought on par with other government employees and the award of the Pay Commission should be applicable to them. The Port Commissioners rejected our contention.

A strike notice had been served by our union after the end of the war, on 13 August 1946. The riots forced us to defer the strike but the notice was served again on 21 January 1947, stating that the workers would go on strike from 5 February. In between, there were some efforts by the Chief Labour Commissioner, Government of India, to negotiate a settlement but the Chairman was adamant. Thus began the historic 87-day port strike on

5 February. A notice, as required under the act, had been given. The port management had rejected the conciliation terms offered by the government and the strike was perfectly legal.

Significantly, these circumstances ensured the government's neutrality. This was all the more in evidence as the mood of the country on the eve of the transfer of power was very much against the British government. The Indian National Army trials and the Naval Mutiny bore evidence of the rising tide of revolt in the country and the struggle of the port employees against an adamant British national heading the Port Commissioners gave the strike an anti-imperialist colour. It needs to be emphasized though that neither our union nor the other unions that joined us tried to project the strike as a political struggle. It was strictly based on the memorandum submitted to the port authorities featuring employee grievances.

The strike continued for 87 days during which the management resorted to all kinds of tactics to break it. There were other serious problems as well. The workers were already on subsistence wage; the value of their pay packet had been further eroded during the war. They had nothing to fall back upon when they stopped getting their pay packets after the strike and the union too had insignificant reserves. Its few hundred rupees could not even ensure the day-to-day expenses of running the strike. Providing any relief to the nearly 30,000 port employees sprawled over an area of nearly 80 miles from Budge Budge in the south to Hooghly Point in the north was out of the question. Even more important was the prevailing atmosphere in the city and the country in the aftermath of the Great Calcutta Killing. There was a trail of mistrust and suspicion between the two communities. Riots had broken out in Noakhali and Bihar, home to many port employees. Despite all this and the efforts of the management to break the strike, the workers and employees stayed united and ultimately forced the management to come to a settlement with the union.

The management climbed down and conceded almost every important demand. The main issue, revising emoluments in the light of the Pay Commission report, was settled in favour of the employees. Cases against some worker volunteers were also withdrawn. The strategy adopted by the union to achieve this despite all odds deserves close examination. Step one was to ensure the total unity of all employees. The character of the union had been broad-based earlier, when we made Nepal Bhattacharya president, precluding the possibility of his forming a parallel union. With him as president the overwhelming majority of the employees were behind our union.

There still remained the National Union, originally formed by Suhrawardy, mainly with a section of Muslim workers. Later, the control of the union had passed into the hands of Humayun Kabir with the support of some Congress-minded employees, specially the Bihari workers. Subsequently, Dr. Maitrayee Bose took over its presidentship and was in charge when we called the strike. Even though they represented only a very small section of the workers, we set up a joint committee with the National Union for the conduct of the strike, which was active throughout the strike period. Statements to the press, any negotiations with the government or the port authorities were on behalf of this joint committee. At no stage did we bypass it. At one or two points during the standoff there were indications that some leaders of the National Union were in favour of calling off the strike or at least going in for a settlement short of our main demand. Some worker leaders of the National Union were quite resolute and unity was maintained till the end.

Step two, an important strategic plank, was to ensure contact with the workers and employees at all stages. This was a herculean task, given that the Port sprawled over nearly 80 miles and with large numbers working on tugs, dredgers and other vessels on the river. Also, while the majority of the workers lived in official quarters, the clerical staff was scattered and many lived in the small townships on either bank of the Hooghly River: in Baranagar, Dum Dum, Barrackpore, Belghoria on the east bank and Serampore, Uttarpara, Chandannagar and other places on the west bank. Communicating with them in those days was no mean task.

Shortly after the strike began, we were given a jeep by the very generous Snehangshu Acharya for the period of the strike. There was no driver and I accepted the challenge of driving the vehicle. Even though I had learnt to handle the family car when I was quite young, I had never handled a jeep. Nor had I a driving licence for I had started driving the family car at the age of sixteen, when the minimum age for a licence was eighteen. I had even been summoned once and had to pay a fine, after which I had perforce given up driving.

When the port strike began in February 1947, I was a little over 25, but with little practice after 1941, when I left home. Nevertheless, the jeep was with me 24 hours and very often I had to drive from very early in the morning till very late at night. The rationing of petrol, begun at the start of the war, was still on and getting petrol was a problem. It was available in the black market though for a little over the official price. Even the black market rates were low – around Rs 3 to Rs 4 a gallon. Believe it or not, the supply came regularly from the Watgunje police station! We did not have to go to them; it sent the supplies that were surreptitiously put into the petrol tank of our jeep at a place around Mohan Chand Street in Kidderpore.

We held a series of meetings every day and maintained individual contact with important section leaders. While one group of leaders would be with me in the jeep, other groups would fan out to the various areas where the workers lived and hold meetings there. Makhan Chatterjee concentrated on the marine section, the most vital one from the point of view of the strike. Its workers could practically paralyse the entire port. Almost every night we would sit down with the section leaders to review the situation and to keep them abreast of developments. In turn, they communicated with the workers of their section.

We also sent regular statements to the press, giving details of developments. Not all of them got published but at least one newspaper, the *Amrita Bazar Patrika*, published every one of our statements in full. This played a vital role in helping us to keep in touch with our workers and employees spread over a vast area. Other papers occasionally published stories based on our statements and on information gathered by their reporters. The strike thus aroused general interest and caught the public's attention for the entire period, possibly because it was the first strike after the war, in which some 30,000 workers were involved. There was not only considerable interest but sympathy as well. That became a major factor leading to our success.

We had never imagined that the public support would be so overwhelming. Had it not been so we would have been hard pressed to carry on with practically no reserve fund to fall back upon and the workers in a state of dire penury. The administration probably counted on the strike collapsing once the last pay that workers had drawn was exhausted. Yet the workers carried on for three months without flinching; showing no signs of weakness.

Help came from public donations through the hundreds of collection boxes bearing the seal of our union that were sent out. Worker groups fanned out to different areas in the city and its suburbs; some went far afield to remote areas of Bihar, Orissa, Uttar Pradesh and Madhya Pradesh. Workers who came from these districts carried these collection boxes with them; these not only gave them free passage to their village homes but also enabled them to collect fairly good sums from the passengers on the train and from the people in their villages. Besides, this provided an important medium of publicity for the strike.

One of the most significant features of this collection drive was that within the city our worker squads consisted of both Hindu and Muslim workers. In a city still reeling from the after effects of the riots, it was heartening to see our joint squads, comprising a bearded Muslim with his identity written all over and a Bihari Hindu with his *choti/tiki* (pigtail), being warmly welcomed by people of different localities, given donations and help to raise enough funds to tide over the crisis. There was not a single instance of our joint

Hindu-Muslim squads getting a hostile reception.

We had organized volunteer groups to ensure that blacklegs did not try to break the strike. Picketing is an essential part of any strike organization and requires a large number of volunteers. We were easily able to get them from amongst the workers but, except in the initial stages, picketing was hardly necessary. The structure of the Port is such that picketing would have been difficult if the need for it had arisen. It is not as if there was one large factory and all that had to be done was to set up our picket line in front of the factory gate. Conventional form of picketing would not do so we had groups of volunteers who, with the help of our section leaders, kept a tab on the situation in each section. Whenever we got reports of some demoralization, we rushed to the spot and held meetings that would be addressed not only by the top leaders of the union but also by important worker leaders of the other sections. This kept the morale high at all times.

The feeling of camaraderie between the striking workers and party whole-timers was helped by the fact that they saw for themselves the living conditions in our commune in the heart of Kidderpore. We lived like many workers or worse. In fact, some of them took pity on us, inviting us to their homes for decent meals. Many senior skilled workers in supervisory positions were far better off and would invite us for dinner. The East Bengal workers of the marine section, quite a few of whom came from Noakhali, Chittagong, Jessore, Khulna (now all in Bangladesh), were excellent cooks and particularly hospitable. They would treat us to delicious chicken curry and pulao that was very welcome to us living on a very spartan commune fare.

What about the blacklegs? Fortunately for us, the management was not able to find any blacklegs from amongst the workers. A few attempts were made to recruit employees for which advertisements were put out in the papers. This actually alerted us to what the management was up to and, thanks to the special volunteer squad, ably led by our militant student activist, Mihir Bose, such attempts were easily thwarted. Those who set out in response to the advertisements were chased away. The point is that we had only eight or ten whole-timers to assist us. The Strike Committee, the various supporting organizations and the large number of volunteer groups set up for the purpose were manned by port workers and the employees themselves.

The strike also led to my first arrest and I saw the inside of a police lock-up for the first time. We were holding a small meeting in the area, not far from the Watgunje police station with only 50 to 60 workers present. As we were addressing the meeting the police, who had been standing nearby, suddenly entered the area. This led to a commotion as the workers resented their entry and there was a scuffle. The police resorted to a lathi-charge and arrested some of us who were addressing the meeting. We were in the police lock-up for only a couple of days after which a local lawyer sympathetic to the Party bailed us out. The case dragged on for some months during which we had to attend court occasionally. Ultimately it was withdrawn.

The strike ended in what was clearly a victory for the strikers: our union, the Calcutta Port Trust Employees Association emerged enormously strengthened although we had conceded parity in numbers to the National Union when forming our Strike Committee. After the strike, other forces were reduced to insignificance. We could raise a substantial corpus for the union, a part of which was invested in buying a plot of land with an old bungalow. We renovated and extended it to house the union office and the rest of the fund was invested in banks.

The name of the union was also changed to the Calcutta Port Shramik Union though the registration number remained the same: 10, an indication of its heritage. When the union had been formed in 1920, even before the Indian Trade Union Act had been passed, it was mainly an organization of a few clerical employees with some support in other departments. By the time the strike began, its character had changed, the overwhelming majority of the membership consisted of workers and the clerical staff represented only a small minority.

My mind goes back to those days when I started work amongst these workers in 1943. They seemed to be a totally inert mass, often refusing to listen to us, sometimes even driving us away when we tried to enter their lines. This same mass rallied together, not as an anarchic mob in frenzy but as an organized and disciplined force that patiently bore the pangs of hunger and deprivation for nearly three months. Helping us achieve that momentous change were our young comrades, Makhan Chatterjee and Khiti Burman. There were also our worker leaders, Sitaram Singh, Parmananda Shyamal, Bazloo Molla, Waseq Ali, Mohammad Amin, Ramdeo, Ram Naresh and so many others. I would also like to mention the name of Ram Sundar Singh of the National Union, a Congress-minded worker, bitterly opposed to the communists, who was one of the most resolute supporters of the strike and along with workers of our union, a leader of the traffic department of the port. From amongst the white collar employees we had leaders like Debkumar Ganguly, Himangshu Sinha, Prasanta Dutta, Robi Sen, Debu Bannerjee, Nalini Dutta, Tulsi Baidya, Premangshu Goswami and many others whose names I cannot recall.

People are ready to come together and make sacrifices for a common cause when that cause is genuine and is based on real and felt needs.

Attitudes and mindsets can be changed by patient and persistent work over a fairly long period of time at the grass root level. We could change the mood of the workers from one of apathy and indifference, even hostility, with our small squads of two or three, patiently and regularly meeting the workers in their bustees and 'lines' (the barrack- like quarters where they lived), talking to them one to one or in very small groups, explaining what the situation was and what they could and should do. Going back to them again and again even when they were hostile or when they were completely apathetic ultimately wore away their resistance. They listened when they found that what was being said was in their interest. They were even prepared to act.

When I first started working in the port union—my first experience of working in a recognized union—I was a little taken aback to see that the practice was to start a file of each individual case that any worker brought before the union. This was because the union had been what we called a 'reformist' union. So far, my experience of trade union work had been in holding mass meetings and demonstrations, leading up to strikes. Preparing a charter of demands for presentation to the management and the government was, of course, part of the programme. Beyond that I had never thought that maintaining files of individual cases was of any importance. I saw the significance of this day-to-day routine when I began to work in the port union. This, together with our squad work in the workers' quarters, ultimately helped to change the mood of the workers.

Finally, it is the sincerity and dedication of the organizers and cadres that count. Those who worked as Party wholetimers lived in a 'commune' in Kidderpore, where the workers and employees could see how we lived. When they found that our standard of living was not very different from theirs they realized that we were not out to exploit them but were really trying to help them. On most days, half a duck's egg was what we got with our rice and dal. This made the workers realize that despite our different background we had become virtually members of their family.

The trade union movement has moved away from its original goals though there are a few genuine trade unions left, particularly among the white collar workers. Even they are a dwindling number. Trade unions were meant to be a united platform for all workers in a factory or industry. Today's trade unions are what we called the party 'fractions' within the trade unions. Each party has its own trade union organization and, in many cases, there are different factions within a party, each with its own union.

The absence of this unity has led to the weakening of the trade union movement. Of course there are other factors responsible for the current decline of the trade union movement but the fragmentation of trade unions within each factory and each industry is the main one.

This stems from a trend that I noticed even in the 1940s when I was fully involved in trade union activity. Whenever we discussed this we would say that our main weakness is 'economism'. That meant that we were only concerning ourselves with the economic demands of the workers and not trying to politicize them. It seems to me that the logical conclusion of this trend was that trade unions should become instruments in our hands to further our political agenda. This is precisely what has happened. The result is that we have hardly any genuine trade unions left.

Having participated actively in the trade union movement in the 1940s and watched it at close quarters in later years, I feel that our main deviation—to use the communist terminology—all along has not been economism but a peculiar notion that the Party must capture the union. In practice this means that not only are all other political elements excluded, even workers who are opposed to or critical of our method of functioning are excluded. If we cannot achieve it in an existing union we must split the union, form a union of our own and see that it conforms fully to our 'revolutionary' tactics. This really is a means to ensure that all decisions taken by the Party leadership are carried out through the union.

Without knowing something of the history and geography of his own country, without elementary scientific knowledge, no worker today can really emerge as an effective leader either of a political party or even of his union. He is perforce dependent on outside organizers. It is through them that political parties are able to control the unions. Since many of the important worker leaders were either illiterate or, at best, barely literate, they were unable to function independently. Their ability to participate in decision-making was thus extremely limited and the control and domination of outside Party organizers were inevitable.

This does not apply to the unions of white collar workers that appeared later. In the 1940s, the clerical staff was just beginning to get unionized. Today banks, insurance and even government establishments have powerful unions. Only in the case of white collar workers has it been possible to have effective leaders from amongst the employees and a greater percentage of united unions here. With growing political polarization in the country even these are getting split with the fragments getting linked to the different political groups.

TWELVE

The South-East Asia Youth Conference

The South-East Asia Youth Conference (21-26 February 1948) had evidently been planned and called by the International Communist leadership because the delegates were mostly communists or socialists, close to the communists. A French trade union leader, Jean Latussière, was president and there was Carmel Brickman from England. How a French leader was chosen to preside over a South-East Asia Youth Conference was something that I did not question then. I now see the incongruity. There was a delegation from the Soviet Union with observer status, confirming that the conference was planned by the international communist leadership. In Calcutta, the majority of delegates were communists though there was a Forward Bloc contingent too. I was told that I had been appointed secretary of the Indian delegation. Being fully engaged in trade union work in the Calcutta Port, my sudden selection for this new role surprised me a little but I was quite pleased. It gave me exposure to a new field of activity.

Some resolutions were adopted after discussion mainly against world imperialism, on the need for peace and other issues of a non-controversial nature. I must have participated though I do not remember the subjects on which I spoke. Since this was more or less a communist conference and I was quite familiar with the communist position on different issues by then, I was in my elements at all such conferences, especially those where the proceedings were in English. The conference ended on an unhappy note though because there was a dispute on the composition of the proposed standing committee to carry on the work after the conference was over. The Forward Bloc wanted more seats than were being offered.

I was not privy to the negotiations but Aurobindo Bose was not satisfied with what was happening and kept telling me about it. At one stage he got very agitated and told me that the Forward Bloc's patience was wearing out and he even mentioned that Gopalda was very upset over the whole issue.

Gopal was nicknamed Gopal Patha because he ran a meat shop (*patha* means goat) and had acquired notoriety during the riots. Local Hindus in parts of central Calcutta idolized him because he had defended Hindu localities against Muslim onslaughts. Finally, the negotiations broke down and the Forward Bloc staged a walkout at the open session of the conference that was held at Wellington Square. Later that evening or possibly the next evening, a dinner reception had been organized for the Soviet delegates by Charu Ghosh, a local businessman and a Party sympathizer, at his residence on Dixon Lane in central Calcutta. I was invited to that reception as must have been many other communist delegates.

Suddenly, as the reception was under way, there was a burst of gunfire, quite clearly from a Sten gun. The entrance of the house faced the main road and led into a long corridor that was easily visible from the road. It was through that corridor that the bullets were pumped in. Many of us were in that corridor and tried to rush out of the range of gunfire. Some could not move away fast enough and were injured. One Sushil Mukherjee died on the spot while Bhavamadhav Ghosh, a nephew of Charu Ghosh, succumbed to his injuries later. The assailants disappeared after one burst of gunfire. In Party circles this was believed to be the handiwork of the aforementioned Gopal. The matter was never seriously investigated by the then government and the assailants were not brought to book.

The Soviet delegates were on the first floor, out of range of fire but were very agitated because they realized that possibly they were the targets. I went up and heard them saying that the fascists were after them and must have been among the attackers. They asked to be connected to the Governor and spoke to him, asking for protection. Within a short time a huge posse of police arrived and they were taken away under heavy police escort to Raj Bhavan, where they were possibly staying from the very beginning. They left the very next day and the Conference was abandoned.

I learnt recently from a senior journalist that it was at this conference that the directive of the International Communist leadership was passed on to communist parties of the south-east to go in for militant struggles. Even though the Comintern had been dissolved in 1943, communist parties all over the world still considered directives from the International (read Soviet Party) as binding for them. This sounds quite plausible because it was shortly after this, at the Second Party Congress (28 February to 6 March 1948) that the party line was changed. Ajit Roy, however, believes that there was no such instruction. He had talked to several international communist leaders who said that there was none. He believes that it was possibly an article by Alexei Zhdanov, which appeared in the Soviet Journal, *New Times*, which influenced the Indian and other parties.

THIRTEEN

The Second Party Congress

The developments at the Second Party Congress (28 February to 6 March 1948) lend credibility to the information that the journalist passed on to me. The Party took a turn that was to have far-reaching and, in my view, disastrous consequences. Meanwhile, after the port strike was settled in our favour, I was continuing my activities in the union even as significant and momentous political developments were taking place in the country and overseas. In Britain, a new government headed by the Labour Party had come to power. Unlike the Churchill pledge of never allowing India to leave the British Empire, Prime Minister Atlee had a better appreciation of the reality of the situation. He sensed that it would no longer be possible to hold the country by force. Even though the Quit India movement of 1942 had been crushed, it was clear that the urge for freedom amongst the people was stronger than ever. The formation of the INA by Subhas Chandra Bose had had its impact on the armed forces. The trial of the INA leaders prompted countrywide protests and its lessons were not lost on the Indian soldiers and officers of the army.

The revolt of the naval ratings in Bombay was an ominous portent as far as the British were concerned. They had held India down with a force of some half a million Indian soldiers led by a few thousand British officers. Unlike what happened in 1942, the British government saw clearly that in future uprisings Indian soldiers could not be relied upon to shoot down Indian freedom fighters, no matter what their British officers commanded. So preparations were being made to transfer power to the leaders of the Indian people. However, the nearness of power led to conflicting claims by different communities. Latent animosities, deliberately accentuated by the British government over the years, surfaced and threatened to engulf the whole country in conflagrations of various kinds. Mahatma Gandhi tried his best to quench the spreading fires of communal strife, particularly in Noakhali and Bihar and again in Calcutta and other places. He eventually paid for this with his life as a Hindu fanatic shot him down in cold blood on 30 January 1948 shortly after the transfer of power.

With the release of the Congress leaders (imprisoned after the 1942 Quit India resolution in 1945), the Communist Party became the target of attack by Congress leaders. Branded as traitors and betrayers of the freedom struggle for their opposition to the Quit India movement, they had to run for cover as many of the party offices and cadres were attacked. Internationally, the end of the war saw the beginning of the appropriately termed 'cold war'. This saw the British and the Americans turn against their war time ally, the Soviet Union. The battles were not fought with tanks and planes but with diplomatic and economic weapons. The Soviet Union responded by using all means at its disposal to launch its offensive against the Anglo-American assault. This was the backdrop for the Second Party Congress of the Communist Party of India held at the Mohammad Ali Park in Calcutta.

I was fully engaged in trade union work with the port union. I was also called to address mass meetings of other unions and take classes of worker party members in different industries. By this time I had been elected to the Calcutta District Committee too but my activities were confined to the Kidderpore area where the various factory trade unions were. When the Second Party Congress took place, I was asked to attend the Congress mainly to translate the speeches—almost all of which were in English—into Hindi/Urdu/Bengali for the benefit of the worker delegates. Translations were not made from the dais but in a corner of the pandal erected for the congress where the group of workers was seated. Thus without being a delegate, I was able to attend the Party Congress and to take notes of the proceedings.

Till the opening of the congress, the Party had been led by its

General Secretary P. C. Joshi. This was in line with the pattern of the Soviet Party where the General Secretary was the supreme leader. As far as I am aware this was how most other parties functioned. When I came into contact with the Party in 1939-1940, P. C. Joshi was the General Secretary, having been elected some years earlier. It was not till 1942, after the Party was legalised, that I got to see him face-to-face. I had only seen some of his notes and letters during my underground days in 1941. Again, following the pattern in the Soviet Party, the Party General Secretary was not only the supreme leader, he was in fact idolized and, to use the term that came into vogue later, a personality cult was built around him.

I was always impressed by Joshi's outlook. He had successfully converted the Party into a mass one during the People's War period and had attracted people from all walks of life: writers, film and stage artists, musicians, dancers and teachers. Earlier, the Party's activities and influence had been confined to workers and sections of the peasantry with little penetration into the middle classes except the students. The All India Students Federation (AISF) was, of course, one of the important front organizations where the Party was active. The Progressive (later Anti-Fascist) Writers Association, the IPTA (Indian People's Theatre Association) flourished during the war period and attracted eminent people, quite a few not even in agreement with Party policy.

Given this background, we were in for a bit of a shock when we found that the opening speech at the Party Congress was not made being delivered by the General Secretary, but by Ranadive (BTR). Joshi was not even present on the dais at the inaugural session. During the course of the proceedings it was communicated to us that Joshi was being removed from his position as General Secretary and from the Central Committee because of his reformist line. We were told that it was necessary to adopt a truly revolutionary line. The Telengana struggle was held up as the model. This struggle against the Nizam of Hyderabad, a typical feudal ruler, had developed into an armed conflict with our party cadres taking up guns.

Later, at the open rally on the Maidan, Bankim Mukherjee explaining the party line gave the slogan: 'The Telengana Path Is Our Path'. We listened without being fully aware of the implications of the new line. BTR was elected General Secretary but most of the old Politbureau members were retained. I do not remember all the names but Dr Adhikari, S. A. Dange and S. V. Ghate were the other members. It was possibly at this congress that Bhowani Sen was included in the Politbureau. The implications of the new line became clear soon enough when on 26 March, only a few weeks after the congress, the Party was declared illegal and thousands of activists and leaders were rounded up and put into prison. The Security Act was first used but later it was amended and termed the Preventive Detention Act. The essence of the act was that it permitted detention without trial and this is exactly what happened. I was among those arrested that day and thus began the next three-year phase in my life; behind bars.

The way the congress was conducted showed a number of things. First, it seems to me to have been something of a coup. Even though they said that the General Secretary had been following a reformist line, the sudden coup on the eve of the congress, without giving an inkling to party members, was typical of the way Stalin conducted the affairs of the Party in the Soviet Union. Of course, all this was still hidden from us. Till that time, we firmly believed that the Soviet Party was a perfect model and beyond criticism. We were, therefore, surprised but not shocked when the announcement was made at the Second Party Congress. Never for a moment did we question the decision and I do not remember any member of the Central Committee or the Politbureau—leave aside any ordinary delegate—rising to ask for an explanation or uttering a word of criticism.

I am also convinced today that this coup would not have

been possible had the signal not come from abroad, most likely through the Communist Party of Great Britain, which till that time was our only link with the International Communist movement. Although the Communist International had been formally dissolved in 1943, our Party, as indeed all parties that called themselves communist, only needed a word from the International to change gear at a moment's notice. We had done this in 1941 and we did it again in 1948.

FOURTEEN

Jail, 1948-1951 and the New Party Line

With the new party line, 'The Telengana Path Is Our Path' quite unclear to us, we did not know what we were heading for. Perhaps we were naïve or because the leadership never fully took us into confidence, we continued in our own sphere exactly as we had been doing in the past. Had the Party planned to explain it? One does not know because it was caught unawares by government action. Within weeks after the Second Congress, the Party was declared illegal and its activists all over the country rounded up, starting 26 March 1948.

All this happened within less than a year of the transfer of power in August 1947. Not only were many Indian army commanders still British, even our intelligence service was still pretty much the same. The information about the international communist directive must, therefore, have been transmitted to the Indian government immediately and its action was prompt and efficient. Even the Security Act that we were detained under was more or less the same as the one the British had used to round up our revolutionaries. This chapter of our history has almost been forgotten and I wish to record that this was really a draconian act. The most basic right, the right to a fair trial, was denied and many of us were detained for more than three years. Some, like Muzaffar Ahmad, were jailed for four years without being produced in court even once.

On the eve of this round up, our provincial party headquarters at Dacre's Lane, Calcutta, received information that mass arrests would take place the next morning. We learnt later that an officer of the West Bengal Police had leaked this information to his friend in the Party, who informed the leadership in Dacre's Lane. How they reacted to the information is a mystery and was later enquired into but the report of the enquiry commission was never revealed. From the little that I know, the comrade who passed on the information did not reveal the name of the police officer or his rank for he wanted to protect him and the party leadership probably disregarded it as one of those rumours that occasionally circulate and did not send out a very wide alert. Only a few top leaders were told to take precautions. Those who heeded the warning were saved and were able to continue activities underground.

The Kidderpore commune had not the slightest inkling of what was to come and was taken completely by surprise. All of us in the commune were arrested and, early in the morning of 26 March, I found myself in Lord Sinha Road, the headquarters of the Special Branch of the Calcutta Police. I was reassured when I saw Comrade Muzaffar Ahmad, Kakababu to all of us in the Party, seated there calmly and looking unperturbed. This was my first 'serious' arrest after the experience during the Port strike. This time I knew that it was not going to be a simple affair. At Lord Sinha Road we learnt that the Party had been declared illegal and thousands had been arrested all over the country. We were not questioned and, as far as I remember, no chargesheets were handed over to us at that time. We were only shown our warrant of arrest,mentioning the section of the Security Act under which we were to be detained.

We remained in Lord Sinha Road for some hours and were then shifted to the Presidency Jail in Calcutta. Among the well-known leaders with us were Gopal Haldar, Hiren Mukherjee, Biswanath Mukherjee, Abdul Momin, Shamsul Huda, Ambica Chakravarty, a legendary leader of the 'terrorist' movement, and Subodh Roy of the Chittagong Armoury Raid. There were probably a hundred of us lodged in the Presidency Jail that morning. A few others who were arrested later trickled in gradually. Other communist leaders were taken to Alipore and Dum Dum Jails and many others were initially detained in district jails all over West Bengal.

Many women comrades were also arrested and kept in the women's ward of the Presidency and other prisons. Gita Mukherjee was arrested along with us and lodged in the women's ward of the Presidency Jail. Manikuntala Sen, who was arrested later in Midnapore under rather dramatic circumstances, joined them a little later. After three months, a few of our comrades were released. Surprisingly enough, among them were some important leaders like Biswanath Mukherjee, who promptly went underground and joined other leaders like Somnath Lahiri and Bhowani Sen, who had been able to evade arrest thanks to the warning they had received. Gopal Haldar and Hiren Mukherjee were also probably released at that time. The government did some reshuffling during the next few months and I was shifted along with Kakababu to the Dum Dum Jail before the end of the year. There I remained till my release in April 1951, after the new Constitution of India was adopted on 26 January 1951. As is well known, a Constituent Assembly to draft a Constitution for independent India had been set up as early as December 1946. However in June 1947 the areas that comprised Pakistan were separated and the representatives from those areas formed the Constituent Assembly of Pakistan. The new Constitution that came into force on 26 January enshrined a number of fundamental rights, thanks to which those detained without trial were gradually released in batches. The process was completed only in 1952.

Between March 1948 and April 1951, a little over three years, when I was in jail, some of the most momentous events in the history of the Party took place. For me personally it was a testing time, an experience that could have broken and shattered me but from which I emerged strengthened. We undertook prolonged hunger strikes, once for over 40 days at a stretch; we faced the full onslaught of the armed police. I understood the disastrous implications of the new party line. Yet, and unbelievable as it may sound, I consider this to be one of the most memorable phases of my life during which I matured as an individual and recovered to a large extent my self-confidence.

Writer Subhas Mukherjee, in jail with us almost throughout this period, has described life in the jail in his book, *Hangras*. It is a fictionalized documentary; a truthful record of many events, portraying real characters but under different names. I feature in this book as 'Bansi'. As a writer and poet, Subhas selected events and characters that he found interesting and produced a true picture of our lives in incarceration. I was in close touch with him in jail as he coached me in Bengali to the extent possible under the prevailing conditions. He encouraged me to write and felt that I could become a good writer even in Bengali but I knew that this was not really possible. This period merits an elaborate account not only because of my personal experience but because even from jail we were able to witness the tragedy of a disastrous party line being implemented. It was euphemistically given the name Left-Adventurism, but that would be giving it a semblance of rationality.

In jail, the first issue that confronted us was our status as prisoners. The government had detained us under an act similar to the one used to suppress the 'terrorists' during the freedom movement. The prisoner was not allowed a court appearance to defend himself and could only send a written representation to the authorities. That had no meaning because he could at best deny the charges against him. Under the act the satisfaction of the police was enough and they were not required to furnish any proof. The common charge against all of us was that we were members of a party that had been declared illegal and that we were amassing arms and preparing for an armed insurrection to overthrow the government. There were specific charges against some that were ludicrous and had clearly been framed by persons who had little education. One chargesheet stated that the person was trying to smuggle arms from Mongolia by ship. I do not remember the exact wording but I remember all of us laughing on reading this. Others were only slightly less ridiculous.

Apart from the general charge common to all, I was specifically charged for organizing a strike of the port workers and, incorrectly, also of the tram workers. The port strike was a perfectly legal and peaceful one that had ended in a written agreement signed by the port authorities, the representatives of the Government of India and the unions concerned. It had ended in May 1947 after which the port was completely peaceful. The tram strike was legal too but I had no part in organizing that strike save addressing a tram workers' meeting.

The British, when detaining 'terrorists' without trial had, however, been forced to give them certain facilities: cots, bedsheets, pillows and blankets. The exact specifications were laid down, including the clothes to be provided: either kurtas and dhotis or shirts and trousers. The quantum of food was specified and included fish and meat in reasonable quantities as well as rice and rotis or bread. More importantly, prisoners were allowed newspapers and books of their choice. Certain types of books such as those preaching violence were proscribed however. Further, those who had been working and had families were sanctioned a family allowance so that their families could survive while the earning members were in prison. These rights had been won by the prisoners in the Andamans and other jails after prolonged struggles and hunger strikes during which many lives had been lost. Among those who lost their lives in these struggles was Jatin Das.

We were being given none of the facilities that detenus under the British regime enjoyed. Apart from the food that was at par with what Division II undertrials were given, there were none of the other privileges; not even newspapers and books of our choice. It was clear that sooner or later we would have to start a struggle for these facilities. It was evident that our period of incarceration would be long and books would be essential. Those who had been earning, as employees or as self-employed persons, and had families were concerned about ensuring that their families did not starve.

I was transferred to Dum Dum Jail. So was Kakababu. I do not know what the tactics were but the government evidently wanted to scatter us in different jails though the majority were either in Presidency or in Dum Dum. Sometime in early 1949, we were served with fresh detention orders. Possibly the Security Act had lapsed or there was some legal flaw necessitating this move. One morning, two sheets of paper were dropped into our cells. One was a release order under the Security Act and the other a fresh Detention Order under the new Preventive Detention Act. It made no difference to our status and we realized that we had a long stay ahead. A jail committee was then on our agenda.

I do not remember whether we went in for a formal election for the formation of the Jail Committee. Possibly this was not necessary because Kakababu's decision in this matter was acceptable to all. However, two representatives from each block were elected. The communist detenus were lodged in five blocks and there were ten members in our Jail Committee. I was asked to act as the Secretary of the committee and continued as a member of the Jail Committee till I was released in April 1951. However Mohammad Elias, a worker from one of the engineering factories in Howrah, was asked to take over as Secretary some time towards the end of 1949 or beginning of 1950 but I continued to carry on the correspondence, do all the official work of the committee and take part in the negotiations along with Kakababu, whenever necessary.

We had been able to establish a link with the Party Centre outside shortly after we came to Dum Dum. Kakababu, as a veteran, who had been in and out of jail several times and spent some ten years in jail already, was able to find the necessary contacts among the jail warders to establish this link. They would take our letters to some contact point outside from where they would be collected by a Party courier and delivered to the Party Centre. Letters and circulars from the Centre reached us through the same channel. Our links with the Party Centre were so regular and so fast that very often we got party circulars before they reached the party units in different parts of the state or even within the city. I maintained the correspondence and sent out reports and letters regularly till I was released. I would also pass on letters given to the Jail Committee for onward transmission to the Party Centre outside. Party circulars received by us were circulated through the representatives in each block. Our activities were of three kinds: struggles and hunger strikes; studies and political discussions; sports and entertainment. Everything was important though this account will focus on struggles and hunger strikes.

Once it was obvious that we would have to prepare for the long haul, we planned to organize ourselves and determine what programmes we could take up. Comrades with prior experience told us that it was important to fight for our rights as political prisoners detained without trial. In pre-independent India, the revolutionary prisoners resorted to hunger strikes to wrest certain rights from the government and jail authorities. They also used the time to study political literature seriously and it was as a result of these studies that most of them had turned towards Marxism and formed communist groups within the jail. We decided to follow this example. However, a totally new dimension was added to our activities as fallout of the new party line even for us in jail.

We got an idea of how the new line was being applied outside from comrades who joined us in jail in later months. Most of us having been arrested shortly after the Party Congress had not been able to get any indication of how the new line was to be applied in practice. Some of us had thought that the slogan, 'The Telengana Path Is Our Path', was just a rhetorical statement to indicate that we have to carry on our struggle resolutely. It became clear to us from the circulars and from the accounts of comrades who were arrested later that the Party leadership wanted the slogan to be interpreted literally. In other words, it wanted an armed struggle for liberation to be started immediately both in the rural and in the urban areas.

An armed struggle needed arms and we knew that the Party had none. The know-how for making crude bombs was easily available though and we realized that it was with these bombs that we were supposed to carry on the armed struggle. Reports of demonstrations and meetings where such crude bombs were used when the police came to break up the meetings began to reach us. Choice of weapon apart, we were a little puzzled by the rationale behind this policy. The national government in Delhi was headed by popular leaders who had participated and led the national movement for many years and had spent many years in detention. To imagine that it would be possible to overthrow this government and 'liberate' India seemed a little far-fetched but we kept our reservations to ourselves. Up to this point, disciplined members of the Party did not question the decisions and policies of the top leadership; such was the kind of spirit permeating the ranks of the Party.

In any case, we had no doubt that we would have to start a struggle to win those rights that our revolutionary forebears had wrested from the hands of the authorities after prolonged hunger strikes. So, in the first few months, we formulated our demands as political prisoners detained without trial and planned for the struggle ahead. We staged a token 48-hour hunger strike in January or February 1949 and simultaneously presented a memorandum to the government, listing our demands. The West Bengal Government, headed by Dr. B. C. Roy, appointed a negotiator, one Abani Banerjee, a barrister. After negotiations with him for a few weeks it became clear that the government would not yield to our demands. We, therefore, gave notice of an indefinite hunger strike and went in for it in April.

Our hunger strikes were modelled on the hunger strikes that political prisoners had staged in the Andamans and other jails during the freedom struggle. Today many of the hunger strikes resorted to are looked upon with a lot of scepticism. They are generally short-lived and regarded more as gestures than as serious efforts, though one cannot generalize. Even today many going on hunger strike are inspired by the example set by Mahatma Gandhi; Medha Patkar being a notable one. In our case, there was not the slightest dilution of the classical hunger strike concept. Except water with some lime (*pati lebu*) and salt nothing else was touched.

There was no reaction from the government for the first few days and this attitude might have persisted but for an incident on the streets of Calcutta on 27 April 1949. A women's procession in support of our hunger strike was attacked by the police on Bowbazar Street in central Calcutta. In the ensuing clash, three of our women comrades, Latika Sen, Amiya Dutta and Pratibha Ganguly died in the police firing. There was a wave of resentment throughout the state and it unnerved the government. Abani Banerjee, Dr. B. C. Roy's envoy, rushed to us at the Dum Dum Jail and indicated that the government was keen on a settlement and we started negotiations. It was clear from his demeanour that the deaths had shaken the government. After 15 days of the strike, the government accepted practically all our demands. During these days, there was no attempt to forcibly feed us perhaps because the government and the jail authorities did not expect the strike to be a prolonged affair.

Under the terms of settlement signed by us on behalf of the detenus of Dum Dum Jail and later signed by the representatives of our comrades in Presidency Jail, we would be allowed daily newspapers and books of our choice though the books would have to pass through censors. The agreement made it clear that even political books including Marxist literature would be allowed. We would get all the facilities enjoyed by earlier detenus not only in respect of food and allowance for clothing and other daily necessities but also in respect of allowance for the families of those detained. Relatives and friends would be allowed to visit and meet detenus once a week. Families of detenus would get a family allowance. The major achievement, which had been the sticky point for many months during the negotiations, was the clause that undertrial prisoners arrested in connection with democratic movements including working class and peasant movements would be treated as Division II under trial prisoners. It was agreed that this clause would be included in the Jail Code.

A formal agreement was signed by Kakababu, possibly, me as Secretary of the Jail Committee and by representatives of the state government. We were very particular about inserting the point about undertrials because there were hundreds of political prisoners being brought into jail and kept with the ordinary convicts and treated as Division III undertrials whose living conditions were sub-human. How much is actually implemented today is difficult for me to say;

I have not checked the current Jail Code but I have seen newspaper reports indicating that not all political prisoners are given the treatment that had been assured after our hunger strike. That settlement did much to boost the morale of all the political prisoners. The undertrials lodged in wards facing our blocks were also allowed to mix with us during the day and had to return to their wards in the evening at lock up time; around six in the evening.

Our struggle, up to this point, proceeded on correct lines. It was based on the genuine and realizable demands of the detenus and did not try to go beyond that. We were, however, beginning to feel the heat and the pressure of the struggles going on outside, though we were finding it difficult to appreciate the evolving movement. What was happening outside, in pursuance of the new party line, later rationalized as Left-Adventurism, hardly described the absurd extent to which the Party was pushed by the then leadership. Bits and pieces of what happened have been reported but no serious assessment has been attempted by the Party as a whole.

One event that typified the attitude of the party leadership was the call for a railway strike on 9 March 1949. No attempt was made to ascertain what the workers wanted, what their mood was or even to discuss the issue with the major unions of the railwaymen. The leadership declared that there should be a strike and party cadres were asked to make the preparations for it. Manikuntala Sen has vividly described the way this was attempted and how the party leadership refused to take note of the ground reality when it was pointed out to them. She had been drafted to work in a railway colony and asked to stay underground (incognito) with a worker who was just a vague sympathizer and not a trade union leader. Her efforts to speak in favour of the strike were noticed, she was spotted and arrested. Initially kept in the local Midnapore Jail, the intelligence people were fooled by her acting and thought they had arrested an innocent person. However she was later identified and shifted to the Presidency Jail.

Even when it was clear that not a single worker was in favour of the strike the leadership insisted that the strike would take place and would be total. The whole understanding of the situation was wrong. According to the party leadership, the liberation struggle had started and more and more areas were being liberated. Party cadres had been brainwashed to such an extent that they kept declaring that such and such area had been liberated, when nothing could be further from the truth. Not only in the railways, in practically all our trade unions, absurd strike calls were given, leading to the break-up of the unions and the victimization of hundreds of our workers and employees. All the hard work and sacrifice that had gone into the building of the port union was lost. Our party cadres were thrown out of the union and formed a separate union. The overwhelming majority of the workers and employees remained loyal to their original union. Makhan Chatterjee refused to toe this disastrous line and left the Party and, along with Nepal Bhattacharya, was able to retain control of the union. The same sort of story was repeated in numerous other unions. On the peasant front, the consequences were equally or even more disastrous. In many areas, answering to the call of the Party to attack the jotedars, prosperous farmers and zamindars, even middle peasants with small holdings were attacked and their farms looted. Many lives were lost in the ensuing clashes.

The crusade against reformism did not end there. In a cultural journal of the Party, a Politbureau member, using the name Rabindra Gupta, argued in a long article that Rabindranath Tagore was a reactionary. We were shocked to learn later that the writer was none other than Bhowani Sen and found it hard to believe that he could have penned such a ridiculous piece. Meanwhile, the new line took its toll in the jails too. We were helpless witnesses to these developments. I know Kakababu did not approve of what was happening but, in keeping with the prevailing norms, no one openly protested or differed. Meanwhile, there were comrades in the jail who kept pressurizing us to adopt a more militant line. Accordingly, we would often stage demonstrations and shout slogans. After the April hunger strike our immediate demands had been met and many of us felt that we should concentrate on studying political literature, particularly the Marxist-Leninist classics.

The pressure for a more militant movement came mainly from the Jalpaiguri comrades but also from the Hooghly district comrades. Among them was Sushital Roychoudhury though he was not the most vocal of the lot then. He was one of those with whom I was in close contact in jail and I remember clearly that he was, in fact, one of the more moderate ones. Amongst the Jalpaiguri comrades was the redoubtable Charu Mazumdar who too was not as vocal as some of the others from that district. Subodh Sen, Dilip Chakravarty and some others (whose names I do not remember) were the spokesmen for this group. The group's attitude was never very disruptive however. They were a well-behaved and disciplined lot; members would express their views but were prepared to accept the decisions of the Jail Committee.

Meanwhile reports from outside continued to puzzle us. We were told that Kakdwip had been liberated. Since that area was far from our jail, we could not get first hand reports and tended to accept what we were told. Meanwhile, the railway strike call ended in a fiasco. Reports of actions against comrades who expressed the slightest doubt about any of the decisions of the leadership were reaching us. We knew some of them and found it hard to believe that they were anti-Party. I could see that Kakababu was puzzled and unhappy but did not openly express dissent. Some senior leaders from Howrah, Murshidabad and Birbhum were also clearly not in favour of what was happening but kept quiet.

One day, a comrade who had been recently arrested and detained came up to us. Kakababu's cell was next to mine and this was accepted as the headquarters of the Jail Committee. We knew this comrade well and were rather surprised when he straightaway asked us what plans we had of organizing a jail break. We told him that we had no such plan because the possibility of a mass break out of jail did not appear feasible. He went back to his cell and came back shortly afterwards with a letter that he had addressed to the party leadership outside. He wrote that he had no intention of cooling his heels in prison and suggested that we should try to storm out of jail. He wanted to know what the views of the party leadership were because he did not find the Jail Committee receptive to the idea. We duly forwarded the letter to the comrade outside, tech name Susanta, who had been deputed by the party leadership to maintain contact with us. We felt pretty sure that the leadership would reject the proposal as it was tantamount to asking us all to commit mass suicide.

I do not remember how long it took for a reply to reach us. It was a two-line letter saying that the proposal made by that comrade was correct and should be implemented. It was not signed and only said PB at the end. In other words, this was the decision of the highest organ of the Party, the Politbureau. Since the mail generally came to me, I was the first to open the letter and was shocked to read its contents. I quietly handed over the letter to Kakababu. He read it and did not say a word but I could see that he was as shocked as I was. We decided to keep the letter to ourselves and did not show it even to the other Jail Committee members though we knew that if we had they would have reacted in the same way we did. Fortunately, the comrade who had made the suggestion and sent the letter was released shortly afterwards and that ended the matter. If there had been any doubts earlier of the fact that the leadership outside was completely divorced from the reality this incident made it absolutely clear.

We received a large number of circulars and learnt later that quite a few of them never reached even the party units in the city, not to speak of the districts. One of them was again not only a shock but caused me a lot of anguish personally. The circular dealt with the need to fight reformism within the Party and then suddenly out of the blue there was a reference to Jolly Kaul, the strike-breaker. I scratched my head trying to discover which strike I had broken. I had come to jail after organizing one of the longest and most successful strikes involving nearly 30,000 workers and employees.

Since then I had been in jail. After puzzling over it for a while I discovered what had provoked this comment. When we were in the Presidency Jail, between March and September 1948, one of our leading tram worker comrades had been arrested and brought to the jail. We received word from the jail office that this comrade had started a hunger strike and was being kept in a separate ward. We were asked to go and meet him because the jail authorities were not able to understand why he had gone on hunger strike. I was asked by the Jail Committee of the Presidency Jail to go and talk to him because I knew him well and he was a Hindi-speaking comrade, known as Missirji.

I went and asked him why he had gone on hunger strike but he had no meaningful answer. He said that the Party wanted all comrades to struggle and so he thought he should start a hunger strike when he was arrested. I told him that hunger strike should be a collective decision of us all and there was no point in his individually going on hunger strike. He agreed and the jail authorities sent him to our ward where he broke the hunger strike that had lasted only a few hours. This was the incident. His going on hunger strike individually and on no particular issue except to protest against his arrest made no sense and, in any case, the decision to persuade him to give it up and join us was a collective one. In Presidency Jail, I was not even on the Jail Committee and had been sent on behalf of the committee because I knew the comrade personally. This comrade was released shortly afterwards along with many others and he must have narrated this incident to whoever was the leader of the unit to which he belonged. This must have made its way up to the highest body because the circular I referred to was also signed PB.

I do not remember whether this circular came before or after the June struggle that I will describe presently. I think it came after the struggle, which is why I was all the more hurt. I was also totally convinced that something was terribly wrong somewhere because no sane person could write such a circular. Much later, I learnt that this was exactly the Stalinist technique: punish without adequate proof on the slenderest of evidence, without giving the accused a chance to defend himself. Fortunately, the Party was not in power at that time. Had it been so, instead of a circular there could have been a bullet.

There were other political prisoners, arrested on specific charges and kept in jail as undertrial prisoners and our successful hunger strike meant that we were able to mix with these undertrials for some hours during the day. In the evening, of course, we were locked up in our respective wards or cells. From these undertrial prisoners, many of whom were peasant cadres of the Party, we learnt that the class struggle in the rural areas was being interpreted and directed in such a way that middle peasants were being treated as class enemies and attacked. Sometimes their farms were set on fire and some of these 'class enemies' were even being killed.

The pressure on the jail comrades to launch militant struggles kept on increasing. We were looking for opportunities to launch such a struggle but were not quite sure how to go about it. It needed a spark to ignite the fire and in the absence of that it was difficult to go on the offensive. Manikuntala's account talks of the absurd lengths efforts to start militant struggles could go. They actually locked up their matron in a cell and threw away the keys even though the matron had been going out of her way to help the women comrades in Presidency Jail. For us, the D-Day, as it were, arrived in June. I will try to reproduce what I felt and did by presenting it as an entry in my diary:

'June 1949: We wake up in the morning to sense a rather eerie silence instead of the usual hubbub that pervades the atmosphere as the day dawns in jail. The convicted criminals, assigned to attend to our needs, tell us in hushed tones that something serious had happened in Presidency Jail the previous day but they are not quite sure what because the newspapers carrying the story have been withheld. We rush to the jail office and gherao the jailor. We demand to know why newspapers have not been delivered. The jail officers have no answer. The agreement said newspapers are to be delivered to us every day without censorship; they are neither run nor edited by communists and there was no justification for withholding them. Ultimately they yield and hand over the papers. We learn that there was a clash between the prisoners and the Presidency Jail leading to a vicious lathi-charge on the prisoners and, finally, firing that killed some inmates.

'We call a meeting of the Jail Committee to decide what form our protest should take. It does not take us long to come to a decision. We shall refuse lock-up this evening. We know what is in store if we violate jail discipline and go to the extreme length of refusing to be locked up in our cells after dusk. We also decide on the subsequent steps. The whole thing is to be announced at a general body meeting of all the detenus in the afternoon. Who will address the meeting on behalf of the Jail Committee? It is unanimously decided that I should be given the responsibility.

'I know that I will be asked to do this and am quite prepared for it. What are my feelings? Until the decision is taken there is a measure of excitement coupled with nervousness. Once it is taken, I am perfectly calm and to an extent felt honoured to have been entrusted with the task of communicating our plan of struggle to the general body. The meeting is held. I make a short speech outlining our plan of action: We will refuse lock-up. They will try to force us and will almost certainly bring in the police from outside. They know that a few jail warders would not be able to force the nearly 100 detenus. Moreover, over the long period during which they have been mingling with us, it is unlikely that they will be able to attack us in the manner required to make us accept the orders of the jail authorities. They might and perhaps will bring in armed police. We must be prepared for that. If they try to force us, we will resist. I remember distinctly the words I used: *'Aaamra pratirodh korbo ebong pratirodh jokhon korbo communists der moton korbo Gandhibadi der moton na* (We will resist and when we resist we will do so like communists not like the Gandhites.)' This is greeted with loud applause. I do not know how far it was spontaneous and how far out of a fear that if they did not respond they might be dubbed as reformists.

'We have even earlier drawn up contingency plans because we know that there would be occasions when armed police may be brought in to beat us up. We have decided to defend ourselves with the bricks that we can gather from the road leading to the jail office. There are very few of these as the road is cemented. We could use the bottles that some have for storing water or for medicines. These will not be enough to beat back the armed police and when they break our cordon and enter the area where we are and start firing, we will enter our wards and barricade ourselves and then start an indefinite hunger strike.

'Amongst us is comrade Shivsankar Mitra, who is interested in military strategy and is also a good writer. He has written several jungle books mainly for children but of equal interest to adults and one on guerrilla warfare. Because of his interest in military strategy we have nicknamed him Shivosenko, after the well known Russian general, Timoshenko, who successfully fought against the fascist armies. All the communist detenus are housed in five blocks, each with four floors and each floor with 16 cells. The entrance to the block is through a single wooden gate that opens on to a narrow passage, which forms the verandah in front of the cells. A staircase leads to exactly similar verandahs in front of the cells on each floor. In front of each block is an open courtyard (used as a playground or for walking and exercising). A part of the courtyard is kept for bathing purposes and at the other end are latrines of the old type with pans that are cleaned every day. At night, a similar iron pan is kept in a corner of our cells when we are locked up.

'The tactics worked out by comrade Shivsankar, with help from others, is to use our heavy steel cots in our cells and to take full advantage of the structure of our blocks. If the single wooden gate, the only entrance to our wards, can be blocked, the police force can be kept at bay indefinitely. The wooden gate is locked up in the evening and can easily be opened but if some kind of a barricade can be erected behind the gate, entry would be difficult. Our heavy steel cots can provide just that kind of barricade. Once the dozens of steel cots are massed behind the gate they will form a virtually impregnable defence system. We send a note to the Jail Superintendent informing him of our decision to refuse lock-up that night. He forwards a copy to the higher authorities and I am sure that even Dr. Roy has been informed.

'In the evening, at lock up time, we continue to roam along the road outside our wards. Sometime later, the Jail Super accompanied by some of his officers comes to our ward and starts discussions with us. Kakababu is our spokesman, I sit beside him and one or two of our Jail Committee members are present. The Jail Super appeals to us not to go ahead with our plan. 'If you do so the matter will go out of my hand and higher authorities will directly deal with the situation.' The hint is clear: the warders and staff will have to stand aside and the armed police will be called in and use force. We have nothing to say except to reiterate our stand: our comrades have been killed in Presidency Jail. We cannot but protest. If the authorities want to apply force they are welcome to do so. The discussion goes on for over an hour with both sides reiterating the same thing. It is quite late at night when the Jail Super leaves. There is silence for some time. The iron gate leading to our wards has been closed much earlier. Between this gate and the gate of the jail office is a distance of some 50 yards.

'After a while we find the jail office gate opening. A posse of armed police take up positions in the space between our enclosure and the jail office. We can see even in the darkness that they are armed police, mainly Gorkhas. The battle lines have been drawn. We take up our position just behind the iron gate. Broken pieces of bricks and some broken bottles are our only weapons. Since the police force consists of Gorkhas, I take up my position right in front as I am among the few Hindi-speaking detenus. Alongside me is another Hindi-speaking comrade, Ram Surath Singh. (He had been in the port unit as well and lived with us in the commune. Ram Surath Singh had been a coolie sardar in the docks, originally recruited by the Workers League to which Makhan Chatterjee, Kshiti Burman and some others belonged. This entire group had come over to the Communist Party during the war.)

'Using improvised megaphones made out of old newspapers we start addressing the armed police force facing us. We tell them that we are political prisoners detained without trial, that we are fighting for our rights and that we are on a peaceful protest. We appeal to them not to fire at us. 'You are our brothers', we say. 'You too work for a pittance and are exploited by the government'. We know that this appeal will not prevent them from firing if they receive orders from their commanding officer but nevertheless we try.

'Does our appeal have any impact on them? Apparently it does not. A little before midnight orders are given to the police to advance towards the gate behind which all of us had massed ourselves. They are met with a fusillade of brickbats and broken glass. They retreat. Everything is quiet for a while. Already hoarse with the continuous harangue that we have been delivering interspersed with slogan shouting in which our entire force of detenus join, we resume our appeals but we can see that things are moving towards a climax. The police force takes up positions instead of trying to advance and overpower us. Their rifles are raised and then the firing begins. How many rounds are fired I do not know. The sound is deafening. We see flashes as the bullets came out and then we rush towards our blocks to take cover.

'As has been decided, we quickly bolt the gate that is the only one that allows access to the wards and then, like a well-rehearsed drill, the iron cots come rolling down from the top floor first and then down to the ground floor. A solid steel barricade now blocks the entrance to our wards. The block nearest to where I have been standing is Block No. 4, the first in the row of blocks. After the firing we rush to the nearest block and I go into this block as my own Block, No. 7, is further down. The jail staff now enter the passage where we have been standing and lock up the ward gates from outside. Once inside, we begin to attend to the comrades who have been wounded.

'We have no idea what the position in the other blocks is. Only the next morning we come to know that three comrades, Prabhat Kundu, Sumanta Chakravarty and Mukul Chakravarty have been killed. There are others with injuries that we are able to treat with the little first aid equipment that we have put together. Meanwhile, the police start hammering at the gates in an attempt to enter and to beat us up but find it difficult to penetrate our defences. The police make the most determined effort in the block that I am in, the first in the row. Unable to enter through the gate they scale the wall and stand in the compound facing the cells and start firing tear gas shells at us. We pick up some of them and fling them back at the police force. We have mobilized buckets of water and wash our eyes but the smoke gets difficult to bear and we think that we might have to surrender.

'Suddenly the firing of tear gas shells stops. The police personnel leave the compound and all is quiet. We fear that they will return but they do not. As far as we can make out, they have retired completely and we feel that we have won a victory. The police have not been able to lock us up in our individual cells. The next morning we understand what a heavy price has been paid. Three young lives have been lost. We now send word that since our protest action was for one night only the jail staff could now come in and take away the wounded and the dead. The wounded are treated in the jail hospital.'

The next phase of our movement followed: a hunger strike for 23 days. After 15 days, the authorities started force-feeding. A team of doctors and assistants would enter our cells along with several jail warders, opening them one by one. A tube would be inserted forcibly through the nose and pushed down to the stomach. A gruel, probably consisting of milk, fruit juice and egg, would be poured through the nozzle. One such feed of a few ounces during the whole day was enough to prevent death but not enough to prevent severe debilitation. The health of some had deteriorated considerably before talks were started again through Abani Banerjee. The points of our earlier agreement were reiterated and some loose ends were tied up. Certain clauses that were not being implemented would, the government assured, be implemented and thus ended the second hunger strike.

I forget exactly when and why the third hunger strike took place. It was some time towards the end of 1949 and lasted for 49 days; force-feeding to keep us alive started after 15 days. The strike was, really speaking, a failure because it did not lead to our getting any fresh facilities. In any event, we had no fresh demand to be met and the movement outside had begun to peter out. As far as I remember, some of the earlier facilities were withdrawn. One of these was the access to the open field, where we played football occasionally. So we were confined to the area in front of our blocks and all that we could do by way of exercise was to take a walk on the road facing our blocks and play volleyball in the courtyard adjoining our cells. As we understood later, the second and third hunger strikes were the result of pressure from the Party Centre outside. Finding that the 'movement' outside was beginning to flag the Party Centre tried to whip it up by pressurizing the jail detenus to go on hunger strike hoping that this would give a fillip to the movement.

After the hunger strike ended and normalcy was restored we

start volleyball games. We organized inter-block competitions. I played regularly and was good at the centre, picking up the smashes sent down by opponents. Jamini Saha and Bhowani Choudhury were excellent spikers and their smashes were not easy to pick up. Ganesh Ghosh, who was arrested some time in early 1949 or 1950, was a regular and excellent player, despite his age.

Sometime in January or February 1950 there was an editorial 'For a lasting peace, for a people's democracy' in the journal of the Communist Information Bureau (Cominform). By this time, some of us in jail had begun to have serious misgivings about the policies the Party was pursuing, in particular about the tactics of struggle being followed. How far the Party had strayed from the reality on the ground was evident from the fanciful accounts of our successes being given in party circulars. The editorial let loose the floodgates. Even though the Comintern had been dissolved, and for us the Cominform was as much of an authority as the Comintern had been and its clear criticism of the party line, even though couched in very cautious terms, was enough of an indication. The party leadership had been repeatedly asserting in circulars and documents that the Party in its struggles had to unite only with the poor peasants. The editorial emphasized that in India our effort must be to unite with *all* peasants. This was a clear repudiation of the party line being followed and a rebuff to the party leadership. Cautious and indirect the editorial may have been but the message was clear. The pent-up anger and emotion of the past two years against the disastrous policy burst forth. The period of the Inner Party Struggle (IPS), as it came to be referred to, started in real earnest. For the first time, rank and file comrades started criticizing the leadership and asked not only for a change in the leadership but also for punishment of those responsible.

In jail we started receiving documents that reflected the IPS going on outside. Ajoy Ghosh and Dange had taken over the Centre. In West Bengal, Jyoti Bose and Promode Dasgupta had taken charge of the Provincial Centre. In jail, Muzaffar Ahmad and I along with the majority of jail comrades welcomed the change. I do not remember exactly how Charu Mazumdar reacted; as far as I can recall he just kept quiet. Meanwhile, many comrades had lost their lives in the mindless clashes staged in various parts of the state. In jail too, we had lost several comrades needlessly. Others had been crippled. Many more had lost their jobs, trade unions had been destroyed and, in the rural areas, many comrades had charges of murder and arson against them.

I started copying and circulating documents criticising the old line, mobilizing opinion against it and in favour of a more realistic line. We strongly supported the document circulated by Ajoy Ghosh, Dange and Ghate known as the Three P's Document because of their tech names, Prabhakar, Purushottam and maybe Prakash. We also got to know of a rival platform that had been circulated by the Andhra comrades, who were evidently in favour of emphasis on rural struggles. It was somewhat similar to the Maoist line. We later learnt of a secret visit to Moscow by Ajoy Ghosh and Dange representing one line and Rajeswar Rao and Basavapunniah representing the other point of view. More on that later.

There was more to jail than struggles and volleyball. I did a lot of reading of the Marxist classics but this consisted mainly of the selected works of Marx and Engels, Lenin's selected works and some of the works of Stalin. I was also involved in a study circle for the study of Marx's *Capital.* The other members of our circle were Krishnapada (Kesto) Ghosh, Sushital Roychoudhury and perhaps Subhas Mukherjee. We did not go beyond a few chapters. We also staged *Neel Darpan*, a play by the famous Dinabandhu Mitra in 1860 against the rapacity and exploitation of the British indigo planters, directed by Niranjan Sen, from the Delhi IPTA, who had been arrested in Calcutta. Under his direction the performance was of a fairly high standard despite the severe limitations under which we had to function. Another remarkable event was a magic show organized by Shivsankar Mitra. When we were preparing for this the authorities were scared thinking that under cover of this magic show there may be an attempt to escape! Ultimately, however, they joined in the fun and were highly impressed by the level of our performance.

We also had frequent general body meetings, some at the block level and some covering all the five blocks in which the communist prisoners were being held. Some of these meetings were serious affairs to plan struggles or to review developments. There was a long series by Ganesh Ghosh on the history of the revolutionary movement. Then there were some in a lighter vein where jokes and funny stories were told. Pervez Shahidi, professor of Urdu and Persian Studies in Calcutta University, regaled us with many such stories. The other entertainer was Chimohan Sehanovis.

Indeed, this became one of the most interesting periods of my party life. For the first time I got the opportunity to develop my leadership skills, to regain my self-confidence and to get the feeling that I was getting a chance to be a real revolutionary. I was able to savour in this period some of the romance of being a revolutionary that I missed during my first period of underground life in September 1941-April 1942. The periods of hunger strike were a real challenge that I accepted and met full on and, yes, I have no hesitation in saying, I enjoyed. That I was able to face this ordeal without flinching and with a sense of achievement was a matter of great satisfaction for me. My serious reading when on hunger strike showed me that after a somewhat painful first four or five days, the head becomes absolutely clear and the ability to concentrate is heightened. This needs to be recorded as such prolonged hunger strikes are unlikely to be experienced by people in the future.

Remarkably amidst all this, my family stood by me even though none of them were in Calcutta. They managed to keep track of me and my father even came to see me once. He was well past 70 then and for him to come all the way from Delhi was not easy. Lalitbhai too arranged to send me Rs 30 by money order every month. Since he was in government service his name could not feature as the sender; it was my sister-in-law's name, Roopan. For me, in jail, it was a bonanza as I was able to buy biscuits, chocolates and other savouries, almost all imported, that were available at that time. As far as I remember the only other person receiving money from outside was Charu Mazumdar, who had shares in tea gardens and was occasionally receiving dividends, which were redirected to him in jail.

Finally, I would like to conclude with a tribute to comrade Abdul Halim (Sushanta), who was deputed by the underground provincial centre to keep in touch with the Jail Committee. He possibly also kept in touch with the Presidency and Alipore Jail Committees. Comrade Halim, not only acknowledged and replied to every one of our letters, he also systematically sent us all the party documents. He also wrote personal letters to me and to Kakababu. He never gave any indication of what he thought about the Left-Adventurist line but it was clear that he was no advocate of that line. Without violating Party discipline or going against the party line, he managed to convey his lack of enthusiasm. At the same time his letters were warm and encouraging. They were of great help to me personally in tiding over many a crisis during the three years and more that I spent in jail.

The stay in the jail was marked by remarkable discipline, loyalty and spirit of self-sacrifice and dedication shown by the group of over a hundred communist detenus in the Dum Dum jail during the period beginning the last quarter of 1948 and the first quarter of 1951.

It is necessary to record this in view of the subsequent developments in the Party. That there are circumstances that bring out the best in human beings and those that bring to the surface the worst characteristics is worth noting. The courage and the spirit of endurance shown during the numerous struggles that we waged in various forms, including the most difficult of all, the prolonged hunger strikes, is something that later generations will perhaps find difficult to believe.

Hunger strikes nowadays are looked upon as gimmicks, which they undoubtedly are, since they last only a few hours or at best a whole day and no one really believes that they are genuine. Ours were genuine hunger strikes lasting for weeks and months and yet there were hardly any comrades, I think there were only two or three, who broke the hunger strike. Similarly, the courage and daring shown when we fought pitched battles with the armed police were remarkable.

However, the way the detenus were exploited and repeatedly exposed to the threat of death just to whip up a 'liberation struggle', which had no relation to the reality, is one of the most shameful episodes in the history of the movement. As we learnt later, rank and file comrades outside were treated no better. Whether this line of starting a liberation struggle was formulated at the behest of leaders abroad who had no idea of Indian conditions or whether it was the brainchild of those who had staged the coup at the Second Party Congress is something that will perhaps never be known . . .

Perhaps even more it is an indication of the extent to which members and even sympathizer activists of the Party had been brainwashed with the result that no one openly dared to oppose or even to protest. One can perhaps see a parallel in the blind obedience that religious devotees offer to their gurus to the extent that they indulge in crime or needless violence in the belief that it will further the cause of their religion or ideology.

FIFTEEN

Kakababu

No account of my life is complete without a special tribute to a man who is placed on a pedestal, whose birthdays are ritually celebrated but whose true worth has perhaps never been recognized. My impressions of Muzaffar Ahmad, Kakababu, may differ from those of others, but I believe that they are nearer the truth. Having been close to him ever since I became a Party whole-timer, I lost touch with him after January 1963. It is, of course, possible that he changed completely later on but since he survived only a few years after that, I think it is highly unlikely.

I last saw him on his deathbed in the Kimber Nursing Home in Park Circus; possibly on a Sunday morning. He was not fully conscious and was not able to recognize me but I stood by his bed for some time and observed him. He was in pain and was tossing about but his eyes were closed and he seemed to be trying to bear up with the pain. I was a little surprised to find that he was all alone. There was, at least during the short period that I was there, neither any nurse nor any comrade with him. He died a few days later on 18 December 1973.

Kakababu has said in his memoirs that prior to taking up full time politics he had been debating within himself whether to take up literature or politics. He had been a close associate of Nazrul Islam, one of the great Bengali poets of this period. Nazrul Islam too had a revolutionary bent of mind and Kakababu was influenced by him and I have no doubt that he too influenced the poet. Although he lacked the poetic talent of Nazrul, he was strong willed and totally dedicated to the cause he had espoused. I do not think he was quite suited for the role of a professional politician. There was more of the spirit of a dedicated zealot about him.

When he decided to devote himself to the task of building the communist movement in India, he left his wife and daughter behind and for many years kept no contact with them. Even if he had wanted to, it would not have been possible as he was in prison for many years for his role in the Kanpur (then called Cawnpore) Conspiracy Case, 1924, and later in the Meerut Conspiracy Case, 1929. Most of the early leaders of the Party came from a (terrorist) revolutionary background or from the trade union or student movement. The organization that he first joined was the Muslim Literary Society (Muslim Sahitya Samaj) that indicates that he must have been religious-minded in the beginning.

When, through M. N. Roy who was abroad at that time, he came into contact with the communist movement, he switched allegiance to the new doctrine that he had discovered: communism as preached by the Communist International and its prophet, Stalin. For him it became an article of faith that Moscow was the true Mecca of the worldwide revolutionary movement and Stalin was its only leader. In this he was not very different from many communist leaders. What distinguished him from the others was the fanaticism with which he held on to that faith and his total self-abnegation in pursuing his goal. Neither a great theoretician nor a profound intellectual, his attitude was more like that of a missionary than of a typical party apparatchik. However, he shared with his friend and colleague, Nazrul Islam, a literary talent. Looking back today, while I differ sharply from him in his assessment of Stalin, he was a fine human being and it was the likes of him that first attracted me towards the Party.

Thus, when M. N. Roy, who had initiated him into the communist movement, was expelled by the Communist International, he had no hesitation in dumping him and swearing allegiance to the leaders of the International. Later, when within the Communist Party of the Soviet Union, Khrushchev started the de-Stalinization drive, he denounced him and decided to stand by Stalin. This could be one of the factors behind the fact that the only Communist Party in the world that officially celebrates Stalin's birthday is the CPI(M).

In his personal life he was abstemious and lived a simple life. In jail, even though he was quite frail and already in poor health, he washed his own clothes like all other comrades. Considering his position in the Party and his age he could very well have asked one of the younger comrades to do this or, at least, used the services of one of the convicts whom the jail authorities had deputed to act as helpers to the detenus.

He was soft-spoken and rarely got agitated. It is only when his doctrinaire beliefs were challenged or when disparaging remarks were made about his Leader that he sometimes got angry. Even then he would never shout or use strong words. It was only through his body language that one could see the agony that he was experiencing. During our struggles in prison, he remained cool and calm; there was not a trace of anger in him when he negotiated with the jail authorities on the eve of those struggles. The jail authorities had the highest respect for him and he too never spoke harshly to them.

If our lives in the Dum Dum Jail were not vitiated by the lunacy afflicting the Party outside; if we struggled and fought for our rights, studied and relaxed, played football and volleyball, staged plays and held seminars, it was in a large measure due to the wise leadership that Kakababu exercised throughout. Of course, it would not have been possible had there not been mature leaders from districts all over West Bengal, who stood the rigours of jail life, who fought and struggled in a disciplined way and ensured that the years in jail were usefully spent.

Earlier I had spent some eight or nine months underground in the den; also under the care of Kakababu. I had watched him closely during those months and learnt a lot from him. This learning was not acquired from classes and lectures delivered; he delivered none and, in fact, spoke very little. In jail, I worked closely with him for more than three years, in Presidency and Dum Dum. Later, while preparing for the historic general election of 1952 and many other elections, I worked closely with him, particularly during the bye-election in which we were able to send Sadhan Gupta to Parliament.

Knowing him has been a privilege and sharing my thoughts on him with those who may still be interested is, I feel, a responsibility that I cannot shirk.

He taught me the importance of moderation and abstinence in food habits. In jail we could have rice for both our main meals. Making rotis for such a large number of persons was not a very practical proposition. However, we could have slices of bread for our evening meal if we chose. Kakababu opted for three slices of bread for dinner and, although I was so much younger and in good health, I decided to follow him. I think we were the only two who stuck to this till the end.

From the jail, Kakababu often sent out drafts of circulars to the Provincial Party Centre in Bengal that were evidently intended to be multiplied and sent to Party units all over. They were written in Bengali and I, as the jail correspondent of the Party, had to send the circulars through our secret channel to the Party outside. I was, therefore, the first to read them. They were written in a neat round hand with large lettering. The language was simple and yet readable and even with my poor Bengali I could see that there was some literary merit in them. At the end of one such fairly lengthy circular, he wrote the following words that have stuck in my memory and left a strong impression on me. I do not think I have missed or changed a single word. There were two lines written in the form of a verse a little below the text of his circular. They ran thus:

> *Tomakei shope dilam amar sorbasya,*
> *Tumi bichar korbe hisabe kom holo ki beshi.*
> (To you I offer all that I have,
> It is for you to judge if it adds up to much or little.)

Whom is he addressing as '*tumi*' and '*tomake*'? To me it is obvious and it fits in with his character as I have seen and observed. It is open to others to interpret it as they wish.

SIXTEEN

New Constitution, Freedom, Party Reorganization

I was released in April 1951 and embarked on the next phase of my life. More importantly, it was a new phase for India as a whole. The Constitution adopted by the Constituent Assembly came into force on 26 January 1950, declaring India to be a secular, democratic Republic. The word 'socialist' was added later, and India is now a secular, socialist and democratic Republic. Thanks to the new Constitution the government was forced to order a judicial review of the cases of all those detained without trial. We were asked to make representations to the judicial authority set up for the purpose and explain why we felt our detention was unwarranted.

Accordingly, we sent our representations and the release orders started coming in. (Several detenus were released and I knew that my release could not be far off.) My release order finally came. I collected the few rupees that remained in my account and was told that I would be given my taxi fare for the destination I chose. That presented me with a problem. I had been arrested from the Kidderpore Commune that had since been wound up. The rented family flat had been given up when my brother, Major, the last member of the family staying there, got a job in Delhi. I really had no place to stay.

It may be difficult for those with homes or near relatives in the city to realize what it feels like to emerge from jail after more than three years into the big wide world without a place to stay. Debendra Bijoy Sen (known as Kalachand), who was released along with me, understood my predicament and graciously suggested that I stay at his place. With no better option, I boarded the taxi that he had taken, hoping that I would figure something out en route to his house. I knew that he lived in a hut that had been allotted to him as a refugee from East Bengal. This was at a camp in Ballygunje that had been used by the army during the war and was nothing more than a tin shed. His wife who had also been arrested but released earlier had moved back there with their little child and I knew that we would be cramped for space. Even so the offer was welcome and meant that I would not have to spend the nights on the footpaths of Calcutta. There were friends, acquaintances and some distant relatives, of course, but I wondered whether they would welcome a jailbird, arrested for being a member of a dangerous illegal organization and did not dare to barge in somewhere to be unceremoniously turned out.

Ultimately I plucked up courage and when we came near a shop from where telephone calls could be made I asked the driver to stop for a while so that I could put through a call. It was to a distant relative who had rented the house in which my brother had been staying before he left for Delhi. He had been in the merchant navy and had later joined the pilot service of the Calcutta Port. As such he was in a semi-government organization. If he refused to accept me, I would have to go to the camp. Fortunately, I knew the telephone number since it was the same telephone that my brother had used when he was occupying the house. The lady of the house, Bilas Razdan, answered. I hesitatingly introduced myself and then stated quite bluntly that I had just been released from jail and had nowhere to go. 'Could I stay with them for a few days till I could fix up some other accommodation for myself?' The response was quick. Of course, you can come, she said. I heaved a sigh of relief and thanking the comrade who had brought me so far and so graciously offered to share his little hut with me, I took another taxi and went to the Ray Street flat, once home, though now occupied by a relative.

The point is that in those days it required courage for anyone, particularly one in a senior position in a semi-government organization, to welcome a notorious communist who had just been released after spending more than three years in jail. I shall remain ever grateful to Kailas and Bilas Razdan for having given shelter to me at a time when I was stranded and had nowhere to go. I remember with equal gratitude the offer of Debendra Bijoy Sen, who showed that he had a large heart when he offered to share his one room hut in the refugee camp with me. As chance would have, this comrade became a close relative when I married his wife's sister, Manikuntala Sen. More of that later though.

My father and most of my brothers had meanwhile moved to Delhi though they had individual establishments. My brother Victor, who had also joined the Party and had been working for some years as a whole-timer in the Central office of the Party in Delhi, came over to Calcutta and took me to Delhi where I stayed with another brother of mine; possibly Lalitbhai, who was posted in Delhi then. Victor was possibly staying at Shaktinagar and my father lived with him. My mother was probably living with Majorbhai.

In Delhi, I was first concerned about finding out where Kakababu was. I heard that he had been shifted to a Delhi jail. This had possibly been done so that he could make a personal representation to the judicial authority who was reviewing the cases of detenus. I was not able to meet him but I saw the jail where he had been lodged. It was near Delhi Gate and has since been shifted from there. I suppose it is now known as the Tihar Jail made famous for both its notorious inmates and Kiran Bedi's reforms. I also visited the Party headquarters, at Asaf Ali Road. Kakababu was released a few months later, in early 1952. Since I needed a break after my long spell in jail, Victor suggested that I visit Ramgarh where Lalitbhai was constructing a house. This was my first visit to Ramgarh in the Kumaon hills and the beginning of a love affair with that village in a valley that I have been visiting almost every year since. Ramgarh played an important part in my life and as I write these lines I hope to spend the greater part of my remaining life there. I hope that it will not remain a dream.

Meanwhile, the Central Committee had been reorganized with the sponsors of the two alternative lines (strategies and tactics of the Party). Ajoy Ghosh and S. A. Dange had put up one draft while

Rajeswar Rao and M. Basavapunniah had put up the other. Both agreed that the Ranadive line had been disastrous and hence agreed on the need to change leadership but not on the tactics that the Party should now follow. They had circulated their own documents that were under discussion in the Party and, till a decision had been reached, there was a vacuum at the centre both around the strategy, tactics and the leadership. Fortunately, this was resolved fairly soon. As I learnt later, the four comrades representing the two lines had sent their documents to the Soviet Party leadership and this was followed by a clandestine visit by them to Moscow. There they were kept waiting for a few days after which discussions were started. Finally, Stalin himself met them and delivered the verdict. The outcome came in the form of two documents: one, the party programme representing what was considered the broad long-term strategy. This document was open to the entire Party and to the public. The other was the tactical line for restricted circulation. The main discussion was on the party programme, which was circulated for discussion at the series of party conferences at various levels. The Party was still illegal; partly underground and partly overground.

The first priority was to fill the vacuum at the top for which a Central Party Conference was held. With warrants against many leaders, it had to be a secret conference. Some 60 or 70 delegates from all over India attended. I was one of those who attended from West Bengal. It was at this conference or perhaps a few days before this conference that some of us were briefed by Ajoy Ghosh on what had taken place in Moscow. Apart from being told about the secret visit we were given a detailed exposition on the Party programme by Ajoy Ghosh. I was very impressed by his very lucid presentation. Later, I was asked by the Provincial Organizing Committee (POC) to go round and explain the programme to various units of the Party. My expositions were generally very well received and quite a few Party comrades complimented me on my presentations. The underground Central Party Conference was held in Calcutta. The organizers did an excellent job; the Special (Intelligence) Branch had no clue as to the location or as to how it was camouflaged to escape detection. It remains, I think, a secret till this day.

The Central Party Conference was called thus and not a Party Congress because it had not been preceded by district and state party conferences. Those who attended it were representatives from various states, mostly members of the ad hoc state committees and not elected delegates as such. Thus, while it did have a representative character to the extent possible under the exigencies of the time, it did not have the status of a regular Party Congress. There was little discussion on the new party line after Ajoy Ghosh introduced the new party programme. The word had got round that it bore the imprint of the great Stalin himself and further argument was unnecessary. The new Central Committee was elected with Ajoy Ghosh as the General Secretary and with three other members of the Moscow delegation who were prominent among those included. I do not remember all the names but Jyoti Bose and Bhupesh Gupta were on it from West Bengal.

Those associated with the Ranadive leadership in the 1948-1950 period were not only excluded but a resolution was also adopted barring them from holding any elective post in the Party for various periods, depending on their role in formulating and carrying out the disastrous Left-Adventurist line. All party leaders were also asked to submit self-critical appraisals of their role during that period to their respective party committees. Then came a round of district conferences with mainly two items on the agenda. One was a discussion on the new party programme and the other was the composition of the new district committee. There was, of course, no question of arguing about the basic formulations in the programme.

Given the approval of the International Leadership—read Stalin—the endorsement of the programme was a foregone conclusion. Interestingly enough, the entire debate revolved round one phrase in the programme that stated that the experience of the recent past 'has led' people to the conclusion that the Indian government is subservient to the British imperialists. Some delegates felt that this did not correspond to the reality. Only four years after the transfer of power and only a year after the adoption of the new Constitution by a Constituent Assembly, representing almost all sections of the Indian people, it was not true that the people of India had already come to the conclusion that this government was not really independent but only a stooge of the imperialists. An amendment changing 'has led' to 'is leading' was moved by several delegates, including myself. Surprisingly enough, there were quite a few who felt that neither a comma, nor a full stop of what Stalin had approved could be touched. In the end though, the amendment was accepted: a sign of the changing mores of the Party.

Minor and superficial this amendment may have appeared but considerable significance was attached to it. The Cominform editorial had launched a fierce inner-party struggle. Although the Central Party Conference had put in place a new Central Committee and those who had been implementing the BTR line had been forced to admit their mistake, the factional groupings tended to persist. This was reflected in the party ranks in Calcutta as well. Those opposing the amendment to the 'has led' phrase were not just individual comrades but an organized faction.

The practice in party conferences was for a panel of names to be put up by the outgoing committee for election. It normally got elected either unanimously or, if there was a vote, by majority. Rarely did someone, proposed from the floor, get elected and someone very unpopular lose. In the 1952 District Conference, there was no question of the outgoing district committee putting up a panel because it was discredited and, in any case, had been dissolved. Yet, I recall a panel having been put up though I cannot quite recollect who proposed the names. My name featured in the panel, which was not unexpected because I had been in the District Committee prior to my arrest and since I had spent the entire period in jail I was not identified with the Left-Adventurist line. In fact, I had actively participated in the inner-party struggle against the Ranadive line as soon as the Cominform editorial appeared. Even after my release, I had not only supported the Provincial Organizing Committee

(POC) that had replaced the old Provincial Committee but even been made a member of it.

After the vote, I was surprised to find that both factions supported my name with the result that I was elected by a huge majority. In fact, it was apparent that there had been some discussion probably among a few members of the new POC as well as those belonging to the other faction where it had been agreed that I should take over as the District Secretary. I had assumed that I would be elected a member of the committee but being virtually pushed into taking over as Secretary was entirely unexpected. No one had sounded me before or prepared me for it. All that I had expected after my release from jail when I had been taken into the POC was an active role in the Provincial Committee that would ultimately be formed.

After the announcement of the election results the delegates took it for granted that I would take over as the Secretary even though the District Committee had not met. When the District Committee did meet, I was elected Secretary without any discussion. This marked the beginning of a new chapter in my life as I continued to be re-elected Secretary after every Party Conference for the next 10 years until I resigned from the Party in January 1963.

Looking back on the events of the 1952 conference, some apparently unseen hands had seen to it that I was made District Secretary. I have tried to figure out whose were these hands and what motivated them to do this. My surmise is that the initiative came from Promode Dasgupta (PDG) and he discussed it with Biswanath Mukherjee or some other important member of the opposing faction. The latter probably welcomed it because although known to be a supporter of the new line and strongly critical of the BTR line, I was considered to be organizationally neutral and not a confirmed member of the PDG faction. Why did PDG take this decision? I think there were two reasons: one, I was at that time a strong supporter of the new line and had sided with PDG and Jyoti Bose in the inner party struggle and was certainly a good choice from their point of view.

There was another factor which played a role. Instinctively, PDG must have felt that although a supporter of his political line, I might not be as pliable as he would wish. As such, it was better to pin me down at the district level. If I were to be exclusively at the Provincial Committee level, I might cause problems for him. Whatever the motivation, it was a good thing to have happened to me. I got a unique opportunity to lead what was then probably the biggest district of the Party in India; once again a valuable experience. Moreover, had I remained exclusively at the provincial level, I would have been caught up in the bitter factionalism that developed later.

In Calcutta, I was also fortunate to have as colleagues in the secretariat comrades like Gopal Acharya, Ajit Roy and Biren Roy, who helped me to break away from the clutches of the factionalism that subsequently divided the Party and to steer a neutral and principled course. It also meant that I had to sever all my connections with the trade union movement; in particular with the port union. Whether this was a desirable development or not is another question. For the Party's long-term interests, perhaps it was not. In the prevailing mood at that time though, the primacy of the organization was an axiomatic truth. The working class and all other mass movements had to be subservient to the Party. This was obviously an offshoot of the Stalinist principle of the dictatorship of the Party. Although not articulated in that fashion—the dictatorship of the proletariat was still the official line—by the early 1950s, I think all the parties that accepted the leadership the Soviet Party had become fully inured to the concept of the Party being synonymous with the working class.

As Secretary of the Calcutta district, I was naturally elected to the Provincial Committee as well. Calcutta probably had the largest number of party members but its importance was not based only on that. Calcutta was till then considered as one of the strongest revolutionary bases because of the large number of trade unions led by the Party. The once strong working class base in Bombay had lost much of its importance as the hold of the Party on the trade union movement in Bombay had declined. In Calcutta, apart from the working class, the Party had made inroads among the middle class also which was later reflected in the Assembly elections. Indeed, in the 1950s, the influence of the Party in Calcutta as a whole was very significant. In the 1957 and 1962 general elections, the majority of Calcutta's Assembly and parliamentary seats were won by the Party. As far as the Assembly was concerned, in 1952 the CPI contested 103 seats all over India, won in 46, lost its deposit in three, polled 18,65106 votes or 17.81 per cent of the votes polled and 34.25 per cent of the votes in the constituencies contested. In West Bengal, the Party won 17 seats in the State Assembly and 5 seats in the Lok Sabha plus one, by Sadhan Gupta, in a bye-election held shortly afterwards.

SEVENTEEN

The First General Elections

Even as the Party was debating over the Soviet and Chinese paths, the journey along a totally new path was about to begin, though no one had visualized the shape of things to come. With the Ranadive line discarded as the Left-Adventurist line, two lines emerged. Although couched in different words, the understanding behind one approach was that we must abjure adventurist actions for which the people were not prepared and organize the masses mainly through working class and peasant struggles. When the situation was ripe, we would go in for a revolution on the pattern of the Russian revolution of 1917. The emphasis was on preparing the working class for action in the urban areas, which would then be expected to lead to a wave of peasant struggles.

The other approach also laid stress on organizing the masses but the emphasis was on the peasantry and the rural areas. The advocates of this line visualized that as the struggles grew in intensity, the rural areas would get liberated and lay siege to the urban areas. While the party programme, which was the open document, analysed the situation and characterized the government as a bourgeois-landlord government 'tied to the chariot wheels of the imperialists', the tactical line contained in the document circulated only to selected levels of the party hierarchy, tried to spell out the Indian path to the revolution. It tried to strike a balance between the two approaches but there was no ambiguity around the ultimate objective being to work towards a revolution. The masses led by the Communist Party, acting as the vanguard of the working class, would overthrow the government. In the months and years that followed the adoption of the Stalin approved party programme and tactical line, the course of events took the Party into a totally different direction.

Meanwhile, by early 1952 almost all the communist detenus had been released. A few, against whom warrants remained, had still to wait before those were withdrawn. An important element of the Constitution was the chapter on the fundamental rights that included the right of every adult citizen of India to vote and to stand for election. In accordance with this, the first general elections to the Indian Parliament, the Lok Sabha, and the State Legislative Assemblies were announced and an Election Commission was set up. The Party decided to contest the elections but in doing so, was entering into uncharted territory in a sense. True, it had contested elections earlier, too, both for the municipalities and for the pre-Independence Legislative Councils, but those were based on a very limited franchise. This would be the first election based on adult franchise; voters in each state ran into crores and the electorate of parliamentary constituencies was in lakhs. This was a totally different kettle of fish. Moreover, the new Parliament would be forming the first elected government of independent India.

What was the mood of the Party leadership and ranks at that time? The leadership had just emerged from the jails and from underground. The debates within the Party were still, to put it crudely and in oversimplified terms, between the Soviet and the Chinese paths for a violent overthrow of the bourgeois-landlord government. Elections to the Parliament and the Assemblies were viewed as a minor interlude in the Party's revolutionary struggle for seizure of power in this context.

As a member of the Provincial Committee I could sense the mood of the party leadership in West Bengal. I felt quite excited not because my own perspective was any different from the prevalent mood but because this was something new. It would give me, as the newly-elected Secretary of the Calcutta District Committee, a chance to hone my organizational skills and to get a taste of a totally new sphere of activity. Prior to this, my main activity had been on the trade union front, which was a very different arena and involved activity of a different kind.

The Provincial Party Centre had shifted to 64A Lower Circular

Road (now A. J. C. Bose Road). This was the first floor of a building owned by a Party sympathizer, Karim and his wife, Badshah. It was here that preparations began to be made for the coming general elections. I do not remember whether Promode Dasgupta had shifted to this place by then or whether he was in a nearby flat, which was being run as a party commune.

Nirod Chakravarty, one of the many party cadres who worked selflessly, lived in this party commune. An exceptional person, already advanced in years, he rendered a very valuable service as he had acquired an expertise in preparing the accounts and submitting returns for our unions. Many of our trade unions were run by cadres with little experience in handling the paperwork required for running a registered organization. Just before the last date for submitting the returns, trade union cadres from the various working class localities would queue up before the AITUC office where Nirod Chakravarty would burn the midnight oil to ensure that their returns were in order and submitted in time to the Registrar of Trade Unions.

It was the early 1950s then, he was quite advanced in age and his eyesight was none too good. He had a serious stomach ailment as well but worked for hours without a thought to his personal problems and for a pittance; the party wage of a whole-timer. It was probably only around Rs 50 a month in the early 1950s but was later raised to Rs 60. Of course, the Party paid the rent of the commune but all food and clothing bills had to be met from this wage. Nirod Chakravarty exemplified the spirit of the times as did many others who worked selflessly for the Party in those days.

The District Party office was set up first in Dharamtala Street and later at 80 Lower Circular Road. The latter was a spacious though dilapidated building. It served our purpose because it had a huge hall that was large enough even for the extended District Committee meetings. Another advantage was that it was within walking distance of the Provincial Committee office and I could easily move between the two offices. I spent a lot of time at the PC office as I got totally involved in the challenge facing the Party: a general election. I was aware of the orthodox Leninist position that a bourgeois parliament is no better than a pigsty. I was also aware that Lenin himself had stated that, under certain circumstances and to achieve certain specific objectives, there was nothing wrong in communists standing for and getting elected even to bourgeois parliaments.

I felt, as perhaps did the leadership, that elections were just an opportunity to popularize the Party and that we were merely trying to take advantage of the platform that would be available if we put up candidates for the elections. At the back of our minds was the outlook contained in the secret Tactical Line document referred to earlier: these elections are a passing phase the situation may take a turn again and we may have to go underground or to jail. Little did I realize that the parliamentary path had come to stay and would gradually become the only path to tread. True, there were interludes during which we had to go underground or to jail but these were part and parcel of the parliamentary path, where the opposition is expected to oppose, sometimes vigorously, knowing all the time that this was only to improve future electoral prospects.

Meanwhile, all the technicalities of preparing for the election had to be learnt and gone through. Kakababu was then looking after this part of the work while the other Provincial Committee leaders, in particular Promode Dasgupta, were busy trying to reorganize the Party that had suffered such a serious blow during the disastrous Left-Adventurist period. He was mainly touring the districts outside Calcutta.

Although I was not deputed for election work, I was interested in this work and would be at hand to assist Kakababu, thus witnessing much of the work. One important business was to prepare our election symbol that Kakababu entrusted to Somnath Hore who had been with us in jail. He was a very devoted and loyal member, apart from being a fine artist. The *sickle with sheaves of corn*, which he turned out, was an excellent piece of art that remained the election symbol of the Party until the Party split in 1964. This was not the only casualty of the Party split but it does hurt to see that such a beautiful work of art being overtaken by the CPI(M)'s symbol. True, it continues to be the election symbol of the CPI but the hammer and sickle is the more visible symbol. Although it was entirely Somnath Hore's creation, the fact that Kakababu and I were the first to see and approve it gives me some sort of a feeling of a personal loss.

The next major exercise was to select the candidates for the Lok Sabha as well as the West Bengal Assembly seats and to identify the constituencies where party candidates had a reasonable chance of winning. Various names were being discussed at the local and district levels but there was little discussion as far as Calcutta district was concerned. Calcutta being the centre of West Bengal both politically and culturally, generally it was the Provincial Committee that took the main decisions. I remember very clearly the PC meeting where the final list of candidates for the Parliament and Assembly seats was prepared. No one expected very much from these elections partly, I suppose, because of the experience of the previous election in 1946. Except three, all our candidates had lost by huge margins. In fact, many of our comrades were beaten up and our election offices in most places were vandalized. The atmosphere was very different now and we knew that we would have no difficulty in campaigning. However, the feeling was that our objective was not so much to win many seats as to popularize the Party.

Konsari Haldar, chosen to stand for a parliamentary seat, was still underground. Some others being proposed for Assembly seats were underground or in jail. Ronen Sen was possibly in jail too. The selection of candidates, however, did not pose much of a difficulty. The Provincial Committee proposals were accepted with little or no discussion. There was little scope for me to take part in the discussions; in any event, I was in agreement with the names. In fact, the names of the candidates for some of the important constituencies had been informally discussed and I had participated in these discussions. Thus the names of Hiren Mukherjee, Renu Chakravartty, Kamal Basu, and Konsari Haldar for some of the parliamentary seats had been decided and their formal ratification by the PC was a foregone conclusion.

There was one noteworthy issue that did give rise to some discussion. When the list of Assembly candidates had been finalized and we were on the point of passing onto some other item on the agenda, Manikuntala Sen pointed out that there was not a single woman in the entire list. True, for the Parliament, we had decided to put up Renu Chakravartty but that was more because she was the niece of Dr. B. C. Roy, the Chief Minister of West Bengal, and had a degree from Cambridge that gave her a certain aura, which would clearly be a plus point. That she was a woman comrade was incidental. When this absence of even a single woman in the entire list of about 60 or 70 cleared for the Assembly elections was pointed out, there was a moment of hushed silence. Somebody, I do not remember who, said: 'But, of course, Monidi should stand for the elections.' There was a murmur of assent but then there was the question of finding a constituency for her.

All the constituencies where there was at least some possibility of winning, or even putting up a good fight, had been allotted. Someone suggested that she might be put up for the Kalighat constituency. Kalighat—at the heart of which was the famous Kali temple—was the bedrock of conservatism. The very idea of putting up a communist, and a woman at that, did not make much sense but there was no disagreement over the fact that a list without a single woman comrade would not project the right image for a Party claiming to be socially and politically progressive. It was decided that she should be asked to fight for that seat, even if it be a symbolic fight.

My name was suggested at this meeting and appeared on the list of candidates nominated by the Party. The seat allotted to me was Kidderpore constituency (later renamed Kabitirtha). I was not keen on contesting the election, which in line with the prevailing sentiment, was less important than building up the Party and working to develop its bases in the working class and peasant areas. Also, I was serious about my new assignment as Secretary of the Calcutta district that was still considered to have the most revolutionary potential. Later, when during discussions over seat-sharing with other parties of the

Left Front the seat was claimed by another Party, probably the Forward Bloc, I gave my assent to the seat being handed over to them.

Leaping across time, to a decade later, prior to the 1962 elections when the list of candidates was being finalized, my name was again proposed by the Party for the same seat. I was not present at the meeting at which it was discussed as I was just recovering from an operation and was in bed at home. As per a decision, some members of the Provincial Committee, including Jyoti Bose, came to my residence to communicate this decision and to get my assent to this. I think Jyoti Bose himself knew what my answer would be. I had no hesitation in declining the offer. I distinctly remember what transpired at this meeting and it might be of interest to record what impelled me to do so. One reason was that, as I have mentioned earlier, I had already begun to have doubts about my continuing in the Party. This was so not only for ideological reasons but also because of the way the state leadership was running the Party. Two, I also resented the fact that my name was again being suggested for a State Assembly seat and had all these years never been considered for a parliamentary seat where, with my English and Hindi and my background as a debater, I could really have made a contribution. I, in fact, remember having said that to Jyoti Babu who just kept quiet and left.

To get back to the elections at hand, no one was more surprised than the communists themselves when the election results were announced. Even though small in number, the communists emerged as the largest opposition group in Parliament with 16 seats. In some of the State Assemblies too—West Bengal, Madras, Bihar—they formed the largest single opposition group. There was a whiff of hope during the campaigning. There were indications that these elections were being fought in a very different atmosphere from the one prevailing during the 1946 elections. In some areas, there was quite an upsurge in favour of the communist candidates, despite the Congress' considerable popular support and its added advantage of being the ruling party. Even in the few seats that the Congress lost, it polled a considerable percentage of votes.

The cadres and numerous sympathizers and volunteers worked hard because everyone knew that it would be an uphill task to defeat the formidable Congress candidates with their overwhelming superiority in financial resources and with the election machinery weighted in their favour. They accepted it as a challenge, campaigned more energetically, demonstrated with greater vigour on the streets and attended mass meetings in support of communist candidates in larger numbers. Street plays were scripted and directed by the well-known theatre personality, Utpal Dutt, and played a crucial role in the Party's campaign, at least in Calcutta.

What had brought about this change in popular mindsets? The transfer of power in August 1947 had aroused great expectations among the people. Freedom was expected to bring to an end the misery and poverty of the masses, especially of the poor and the middle classes. Nothing of the sort was in fact taking place. With inflation, the aftermath of the Second World War and the large-scale rioting during and after the transfer of power, the condition of the masses actually worsened. In West Bengal, in particular, the huge influx of refugees from across the border dealt a severe bow to the economy of the state. The rehabilitation of the refugees was not handled efficiently and sympathetically by the central government. There was a perception, not quite unjustified, that much more was done for the refugees from the western parts of Punjab than for those who came from East Bengal. The only people who were seen to be fighting for the rights of the refugees and other poorer sections of the people were the communists. Yet they had been imprisoned in large numbers, their processions had been attacked and many communist workers had laid down their lives in the course of these struggles. The elections were naturally seen by the large sections of the people, particularly workers and middle class employees, as an opportunity to continue the struggle on another plane.

An especially surprising outcome was the election of Manikuntala Sen from the Kalighat constituency. The defeat of the Congress candidate in a contest that had been considered a symbolic one—a Congress victory was considered a foregone conclusion there—was one of the many important upsets of the election that we will examine in a separate chapter. It had a significance beyond what is apparent in the victory of one communist candidate pitted against a formidable opponent and also because it was to have an important bearing on the course of events in my own life. Today, when the question of 33 per cent reservation for women in Parliament and Assemblies is on the agenda, the significance of her stand on the absence of women candidates becomes obvious. The male domination of our society—and this is true not only of Indian society—is so deep-rooted that it will need much more than the efforts of a few women leaders to bring about a change. If there are some who have illusions about the communists being any different, the sooner they shed them the better.

The other significant thing about the selection of candidates was the relative ease with which this exercise was completed at the time of the first General Election. Clearly there were two reasons for this. One was the general lack of confidence in 'winnability' (a word now accepted as part of our election jargon) of the seats. There was an unstated fear that it would not be possible for communists to manage anything more than a token presence in Parliament or Assembly. Since no one wants to lose, there was no great keenness for tickets The second factor was that till that point of time the future of electoral politics was not considered very bright within the Party. It was not a core area of revolutionary activity. Even if the Telengana line had been officially repudiated, the ultimate aim of communists was believed to be seizure of power by an armed revolution, involving the masses.

The relative ease with which many of the important party leaders were able to enter the Parliament and the State Assemblies and the emergence of the communists as the main opposition in the Parliament started the transformation that gradually took place in the thinking of the Party and the attitude of the leaders and members towards elections. Although the party programme and the Tactical

Document still represented the official strategy and tactics, the outcome of the first General Election meant bidding goodbye to the approach of the Tactical Line. It opened out the broad new parliamentary path with all its inevitable consequences.

Looking back at the 1952 elections more than 50 years ago and many general and mid-term elections later, there was so much that was different then. It would be worthwhile to take a detailed look at the manner in which the election was fought in one of the constituencies at that time. I have chosen Kalighat because I observed it closely and because it had a bearing on developments in my own life. Many observations about the way this election was fought would be applicable with some variations to most constituencies where the Party put up candidates in 1952.

How was I able to observe the Kalighat constituency elections more closely than some of the others? I was then Secretary of the Calcutta district and involved in the detailed planning of the campaigns in all the elections being fought in the district, whether for the Parliament or the Assembly. Why then have I chosen Kalighat as a kind of case study? At this time there was only one car that could possibly be considered a party car and it was being used by Jyoti Bose. Some candidates had their own cars or got sympathizers to lend them their cars for the campaign. As the District Secretary I had to monitor the campaigns in the various constituencies of the district and a car was necessary but the district funds did not permit us to buy or even hire one. A friend and a close sympathiser of the Party, Robin Mitter, stepped in and offered to give me an old Standard Herald that was lying unused in his garage. I gladly accepted his offer. I informed Kakababu who was, for all practical purposes, the co-ordinating figure for the elections at the Provincial Committee level. He welcomed the idea. While we were talking about this at the PC office, Ananta Singh, as mentioned earlier, one of the legendary figures of the Chittagong Armoury Raid, was at the office. He offered to get the car thoroughly overhauled and made roadworthy for use in the election campaign at a garage run by his friend. They did a good job and within a few days I found myself driving this

Standard. Had it still been with me, I could have entered it for the vintage car rally.

There was just one problem. Although I was comfortable driving, I did not possess a driving licence. I did not have one when driving the jeep lent to us by Snehangshu Acharya during the three-month port strike. Shortly afterwards, I went to jail and now had a chance to handle a car after nearly four years. Even though driving came easily to me, I could no longer do what I could in 1947, drive without a licence. I applied for one and, again with the help of Ananta Singh, arrangements were made for me to appear for a driving test with the Motor Vehicles Department. I was a little nervous and failed in the first test but appeared for a retest about a month later and passed. I thus became the proud holder of a driving licence in early 1952, which I have been renewing periodically and still hold. All this might appear a little irrelevant to the Kalighat election but is not.

Manikuntala Sen, the only woman party member to be nominated for the Assembly, had been released from detention in 1951. She had been in Presidency Jail while I had spent the major part of my detention in Dum Dum. I had known her before my arrest in 1948; in 1943 I had been saved from being manhandled by her timely intervention. After our release, we were both elected to the PC and got to know each other quite well. The earlier communes had disintegrated while we were in jail and I had taken shelter in one of the PC communes near the Provincial Party office. Manikuntala Sen had, meanwhile, moved to the top floor of the Provincial Party office where Karim and Badshah, the owners of the building which the Party had rented for the PC, were living.

Manikuntala would travel from her Lower Circular Road residence to the Kalighat constituency for campaigning and, after spending the whole day there, return late in the evening. Since I had use of the car and lived near the PC office, Kakababu suggested that I bring back Manikuntala Sen from the Kalighat area to her residence on Lower Circular Road every night when the campaigning ended. While bringing her back from the constituency I would keep abreast of developments in the constituency. As District Secretary, I had to keep regular contact with the local committee and hold general body meetings of party members in the constituency. I met other local committees too to monitor the preparatory work being done in the constituencies where we had candidates. In the case of Kalighat, I had the additional advantage of getting a daily first-hand account from the candidate herself.

In every constituency, we first tried to set up a central constituency office and then to branch out to different parts to set up sub-offices wherever possible. In most places we could get space from Party sympathizers and no rent had to be paid. The sympathizer would himself or herself man the office and see that it was kept open throughout the period of the campaign, especially during early mornings and late into the night because that was when most of the activity took place. In the Kalighat constituency, we were fortunate enough to get a room in the residence of a close sympathizer. In charge of the central election office of the constituency was Amiya Chatterjee, a party member with considerable experience who could handle the accounts as well.

There was no party unit in most areas covered by the Kalighat constituency though there were members attached to different units who resided in the area. Soon after the announcement of Manikuntala's candidature, party members and sympathizers spontaneously started flocking to the central election office of the constituency. With practically no organizational structure in the area, the prospects of our candidate were bleak. Amiya Chatterjee, who was the election agent, told me recently that when they started work no one seriously believed that we had a chance in such a conservative constituency and against a formidable candidate, a well-known professor of law who was practising in the Calcutta High Court. However, after the first few group meetings, particularly after a few mass meetings addressed by Manikuntala Sen, the response was overwhelming. Our campaigners began to feel a little more confident. There is no doubt that as a mass speaker Manikuntala was really extraordinary and it was this ability of hers that made the impossible possible.

Finance is important for every election. In the first election there was hardly any central fund to draw upon. Candidates and the comrades in the constituency were asked to raise funds to run the campaign. Except for some printed posters to popularize the party symbol there was no other help available either from the district or provincial office. Having recently emerged from jail or underground and with some of the comrades and even candidates still underground, there was no question of any central election fund. Apart from posters, the only other central help offered was the services of party leaders for addressing mass meetings in the various constituencies. Since there were few leaders with a popular mass appeal who had to cover constituencies all over West Bengal, not much help on this account was available either.

The candidates and the campaigners had to move on foot and much of the campaigning consisted of door-to-door visits in all parts of the constituency. Few buildings had lifts in the Kalighat constituency and the candidate had often to climb three or four storeys to meet the voters. It was back-breaking work from early morning till late evening with only a break of an hour or so for lunch at some sympathizer's house. Dhriti Kanta Lahiri Choudhury, who belonged to a zamindar family, offered his premises situated at a central place in the constituency for her mid-day meal. He had recently joined the Party. As a woman, Manikuntala Sen had the advantage of being able to enter the homes to meet the women voters during the day but it also meant that she had to continue the door-to-door campaign throughout the day without any break.

Posters too had to be written by hand on old newspapers and pasted on walls and other places by Party volunteers. No paid volunteer was employed in the Kalighat constituency. Lunch packets were provided only on the day of the election by the central office, which was the only expenditure on the volunteers. Many of those who came to work for the Party had to walk long distances to come to where they had been allotted work. No travelling expenses were paid or asked for. Amiya Chatterjee recalled that not even tea was provided. Only chola (gram) and batasas (unrefined sugar candy) were handed out to volunteers who came from great distances and were not able to go home for their meals during the day. It is not surprising, therefore, that the total expenditure on the election campaign was only around Rs 5,000. Amiya Chatterjee maintained strict accounts and there was no concealment or exaggeration or fudging involved. This sum was collected by party members and sympathizers who worked in the constituency and by the candidate herself from her relatives and other personal contacts.

From being an unwinnable constituency, given to a woman only as a token gesture, things changed within the first few days of campaigning. It was clear that this would not be a token fight. The response received was far beyond our expectation. Apart from the feeling of sympathy that had been generated in favour of communists, no doubt because of the repression unleashed against them, Manikuntala's record of sacrifice and suffering attracted people. Her door-to-door campaign, her simplicity and her obvious sincerity touched the hearts of the people. Above all, her ability as a mass speaker was a revelation. Whenever one of her mass meetings was announced, people would come hours before the due time and patiently wait for her to appear. All this turned the tide in her favour and by the time the election was held a mass upsurge was in evidence despite the Congress candidate being a professor in a law college and tipped to become the Law Minister in Dr. B. C. Roy's ministry, if elected. Unlike some other Congress candidates, he had a clean image. It was because of this that despite the groundswell of support for Manikuntala Sen her margin of victory was small, only about 750 votes.

The important thing in Kalighat 1952 was the very insignificant role played by money in the elections. It would be inconceivable, today, for people within the Party and outside to fight an election without paying party workers and volunteers; without the candidate or her election agent having a car; for as low a budget as Rs 5,000;

that too raised locally by the candidate and by the party cadres and volunteers in the area. This had struck me even then and remained embedded in my memory. To make doubly sure, I checked again before writing this with Amiya Chatterjee, who handled the funds for the Kalighat constituency. He confirmed that the figure was correct.

Equally notable was the remarkable enthusiasm unleashed in most of the constituencies where our candidates contested. This was in marked contrast to the picture in the 1946 elections, where our candidates faced hostility, save the three who won: Jyoti Bose from the railway constituency, Ratanlal Brahman from the Tea Gardens constituency and Rupnarayan Roy from Dinajpur. The last named area went to East Pakistan after Partition. Thus there were only two communist members in the West Bengal Assembly after 1947 and until the 1952 elections. What was outstanding was the sincerity, dedication and the willingness to sacrifice for the cause that party workers displayed. Regrettably that spirit has changed to indifference and apathy. Manikuntala has written several pages on her experience in the constituency, which I will not repeat. Readers may like to read her first hand.

EIGHTEEN

The Order Changeth

The first Party Congress had been held in 1943 in Bombay after the legalisation of the Party. P. C. Joshi had emerged as the supreme leader of the Party and was almost being worshipped by its rank and file. There was a dramatic change by the time of the second Party Congress, as we have seen. The Third Party Congress was held in Madurai from December 27, 1953 to January 4, 1954. Manikuntala and I were both delegates to this Party Congress. The understanding that was at the core of the party programme gifted to us by the Soviet Party still defined our outlook. That programme, which had been unanimously adopted at the underground Party Conference held in Calcutta in 1952, was the basis of our slogan of '*Yeh Azadi Jhuta Hai*' (This freedom is a sham). However, doubts were beginning to surface as the contrast between the Programme and the reality was becoming apparent.

An event of significance (the only one) was the presence of Harry Politt, General Secretary of the British Party. We had heard that he was an excellent speaker and his speech at the Congress did indeed impress all of us. However, I do not recall him giving his views on the party programme. After all he knew where it had come from. By the time the next Party Congress took place at Palghat, Kerala, in April 1956 the inner party situation had changed considerably. The draft of the Second Five Year Plan, bearing the imprint of Prasanta Mahalanobis was already before the public. This Plan, prepared after extensive discussions with economists from the western as well as the Soviet and East European countries, had led to rethinking within the Indian communist movement.

After the Twentieth Party Conference of the Soviet Party, there was for some time an atmosphere of *glasnost* within the Party. A section of the Party was not willing to accept the '*Yeh Azadi Jhuta Hai*' line. Industrialization had started with major steel plants, the heavy engineering complex, the Bhakra Nangal Dam and other major projects. Jawaharlal Nehru had worked out the non-alignment policy and had emerged as a major Asian leader at the Bandung Conference with even Chou En-lai referring to him as an elder brother. This section of the Party had begun to work out a new line of interpreting the Congress as a representative of the national bourgeoisie and hence advocating a line of a united front with it. This was more or less the line that Soviet political analysts were also advocating at that time.

The other section was not prepared to accept this and one could see the beginnings of a factional divide in the Party. I attended this Party Congress too as a delegate and so did Manikuntala, whom I had married by this time. It may be of interest to record that both of us went to Puri on a short holiday with Promode Dasgupta and a few others from West Bengal on our way back from the Congress. We stayed at the Puri Hotel.

Delhi with family in 1954. Standing Victor (left) and Jolly (right). Seated from left, Sina Kaul (sister-in-law), S. M. Kaul (father) and Manikuntala.

Mother.

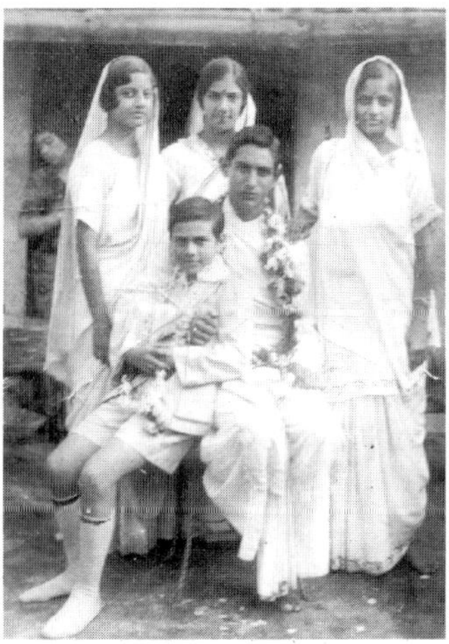

Bak row, my cousins Ladli, Sheila, and Tejan with Suraj Kishen Munshi after his release from jail in 1931.

Photo taken in Delhi after marriage in 1953 by Govind Vidyarthi.

At Lake Club, circa 1979 with the Indian Oxygen (BOC) rowing crew.

Taking notes at a party conference, 1961.

As a party whole-timer, circa 1943.

In Kashmi.r

In Nepal with Anjali Mukherjee and Manikuntala, about 1973.

Our Ramgarh house, now sold to Aurobindo Ashram. Lalit Kaul, Roopen Kaul and Manikuntala.

With Sam Black, leading British public relations expert, and Sanat Lahiri, Calcutta, about 1978.

At the London World PR conference.

At a public relations conference with Jyoti Basu and Anjali Sen, P R Manager, Coal India.

At a seminar with Russi Mody and Biju Patnaik.

At a seminar on Parliamentary Democracy; also to felicitate Somnath Chatterjee on his eightieth birthday.

Sitting on extreme right, most probably, is Kanti Mehta and on extreme left, Mrs. Nihar Mehta.

NINETEEN

Marriage at the Time of Strife

Stalin passed away in March 1953. Given the valiant resistance put up by the Soviet armies leading to the ultimate defeat of the fascists, Stalin was held in great esteem in India and indeed in many other parts of the world. The cold war had already started though and the governments of Britain, USA and many other European countries had begun to spit venom against the Soviet Union. The Indian Parliament, however, paid tributes to him and flags were hoisted half-mast in government buildings throughout the country.

In the Communist Party there was a sense of shock and a feeling of nervousness: what would happen to the world-wide communist movement now that its undisputed leader was no more. We had no inkling of the things to come. Within a few days of the death of Stalin came the startling news: Beria had been shot as a spy! Beria had been one of Stalin's most trusted lieutenants. If he were a spy who had managed to escape undetected all these years, what did it speak of the Soviet system?

We were all a little shocked and puzzled but I do not recall ourselves, in Calcutta, devoting too much attention to it. The Soviet Party had said he was a spy and that was all that mattered. Even earlier, we had been similarly shocked and puzzled when the news was flashed that Marshal Tito had been branded in 1948 spy by the Soviet leadership. It was only later after the famous Khrushchev speech that I began to seriously re-examine my whole attitude towards the Soviet system. On the personal front a momentous event was taking place in my life; one that was to have an abiding and entirely beneficial influence on my life.

Manikuntala and I had come close during the first general election in 1952 and, as a logical culmination of that, we decided to get married. We had taken a decision in 1953 and fixed 8 March as the date for the registration. Just a few days before the proposed nuptials came the news of Stalin's death and we postponed the marriage by a week. The new date was 15 March when the marriage was registered. My family was happy though curiously some sections of the Party reacted rather strangely.

Our family was quite liberal in matters of marriage. My brother, Victor, who was also a member of the Party and working in the central office in Bombay, had married a Maharashtrian girl, Sina Wasoodevv. There had been no adverse reaction within the family. I think one of my brothers, Major, actually attended the marriage in Bombay in 1952. When it was my turn, a year later, one of my brothers did express some reservations about the marriage but, after I wrote to him, he expressed his support. Within the Party the reaction was quite different. When we formally announced our decision to the PC Secretariat, the reception was frosty. There was no valid ground for objecting; we were both adults; we were both party whole-timers; and both unmarried. Why then this coldness? No one said anything though I can think of a couple of reasons for this rather unfavourable reaction.

Traditionally, in revolutionary politics, the concept of the ideal revolutionary was somewhat like that of the ideal *sannyasi*. Such people were supposed to dedicate themselves to the cause and any personal life outside the organization was considered an undesirable distraction. Manikuntala, the dedicated party worker, who had given up her job, become a whole-timer on a nominal wage and sacrificed her whole life for the Party had been one of the strong selling points that had, it was believed, helped her to win the elections. Would it not detract from her winnability in the next election?

What also had upset the West Bengal leadership was that the bride to be was older than the groom. Tradition-bound attitudes probably came in the way of accepting that. While this may have been a deviation from the established pattern, there was nothing unnatural about it. Even within West Bengal there were many well-known precedents for such marriages. Be that as it may, while nothing was openly said, their attitude and body language suggested that in deciding to get married we were harming the Party in some way. Surprisingly though within the district leadership, the reaction was markedly different. My colleagues in the District Committee congratulated me and Manikuntala's colleagues in the women's movement received the news with warmth.

These contrasting attitudes became even clearer on the day of the marriage. Our financial condition was such that there was no question of holding any kind of a reception. We had approached P. K. Roy, a marriage registrar related to Dr. B. C. Roy, who was known to us. He readily came and registered the marriage at Fern Road where Manikuntala's relatives lived and where we had decided to register. He also refused to accept any fee for his services. We did want to invite a few people for tea and serve some snacks but were wondering how to defray the expenses. My friend Amal Bose stepped in and volunteered to bear the expenses of the frugal fare that we decided to serve. I remember serving a mishthi or sweetmeat, a savoury, samosa, some chanachur and a cup of tea.

Muzaffar Ahmad came on behalf of the Provincial Committee and was one of the witnesses to the marriage. Niranjan Sen, who had Barisal connections with Manikuntala's family, had agreed to come but I do not remember if he did finally turn up. Geeta Mullick, a close friend came, signed as one of the witnesses. Suhasini Ganguly (Putudi), one of those who had been with the revolutionaries and was a close friend of my wife, was the third witness. More than a dozen comrades from the District Committee attended. Quite a few comrades from the women's movement brought gifts: plain handloom saris, since the bride wore nothing else.

This record is important because it indicates the conservative attitude of some of our top leaders. Manikuntala was not only a member of the PC, one of the leading figures of the women's movement, which she could well claim to have pioneered, but also Deputy Leader of the Communist Group in the Legislative

Assembly. Yet this was the turnout at the wedding! As for apprehensions that the marriage would spoil her image, it is worth recalling that she was elected again from the same constituency in 1957 and we shall see how in a later chapter.

My father and one of my brothers had, between them, sent me some Rs 600, which was all the capital I had for the marriage ceremony. I bought a Kashmiri embroidered woollen shawl for my wife and had a cotton suit tailored for myself with this. For us it was quite a grand trousseau.

TWENTY

The Tram Movement

The tram movement was an extremely important one and was the precursor of many mass movements that spanned the 1950s. The issue was the one pice increase in tram fares. The first class tram fare had been four pice—this was before the naya paisa came into vogue—and the tramway company proposed to raise the fare to five. The second-class fare would correspondingly be raised from three to four pice. (Four pice equalled one anna and 16 annas equalled Rs 1 under the old system.) The Communist Party decided to oppose the fare increase and started a mass movement on the issue. A joint committee was set up with all the other Left parties. The Calcutta Tramways Company was still British-owned and the movement took on an anti-imperialist colour on the one hand and an anti-Congress movement on the other, as the fare increase was supported by the Congress government of West Bengal.

The Party, heading the movement, said that the British company was trying to fleece the people to increase its profits and this should be resisted. With the other Left parties joining, the movement took on a mass character within a short time. We asked the people through press statements and through mass meetings not to pay the increased fare and the people responded. They offered to pay the old fare which the tram conductors had been instructed by the company not to accept. So everyone enjoyed a free ride. Hordes of young men started boarding the trams when they realized that free rides could be had by just refusing to pay the increased fare. At this stage the government stepped in by arresting those refusing to pay the new fares. This altered the complexion of the movement. The anger of the people turned against the government and several trams and government buses were burnt. A general strike was called, which turned into a mass *hartal.*

There was one very significant development though. At a late-night meeting on the eve of the strike day, the executive committee of the tram workers union decided not to go on strike. The Party had taken it for granted that the union would respond to its call but it did not. There were several party members in the executive committee of the union, including some members of the District Committee. They too did not oppose the decision to ignore the strike call. We were stunned when this news reached the district and provincial offices. As secretary of the District Committee, I had been actively campaigning for the success of the strike and the news that the one organization, which was the strongest base of the Party, had refused to fall in line with the Party decision came as a severe blow. Without wasting any time and after consulting those members of the District and Provincial Committees who were available, I and some District Committee members decided to approach the tram workers directly and ask them to reverse the decision.

We spent the whole night going round the tram messes from one end of the city to the other exhorting the workers to ignore the union executive's decision and to go on strike. We found that the workers were in no mood to listen and, even though they did not say so to our face, we found that our exhortation was not having any effect. Indeed, the next day while there was a total shut down in Calcutta, trams came out as usual. However, there were hardly any passengers. This phenomenon, I will discuss presently. For the time being, given the successful bandh, the movement continued with even greater vigour. A new form of protest was devised by people of many localities. After dusk the lights were put out and no police vans were permitted into the area.

There was a tense atmosphere in the whole city. At a public meeting called in support of the movement, journalists who had come to cover the event were beaten up by the police. The next day almost all the newspapers ran banner headlines on the incident and fiery editorials condemned the police action. The government realized that it was time to retreat. A face-saving formula was devised. A fact-finding commission was set up to go into the question of the fare revision. That the commission would not favour the hike in fares was obvious. The movement was withdrawn and the climb down by the government was hailed as a victory of the people.

Somewhere midway during the movement I was arrested. The manner in which the arrest was carried out indicated the panic in the ranks of the police. We were then staying in a flat in Shyamananda Road, Bhowanipore. Since we could not afford to rent an entire flat by ourselves, we shared it with a Gujarati family. I went out every morning to the Lansdowne Market to buy our requirements for the day. On the day of the arrest, as I walked up to the market, I noticed a person casually reading the newspaper in front of a bustee beside the road. I should have realized the significance of this but though I did suspect this person to be a Special (Intelligence) Branch inspector, I thought that he was on routine duty because of the ongoing movement.

When returning from the market with my bag of vegetables and provisions, I was surrounded by several plainclothes men led by the newspaper reader, whom I now recognized. He was the same person who had arrested us on the morning of 28 March 1948, when the Party had been declared illegal. He told me politely that I was under arrest and asked me to get into the police van that had by now drawn alongside. It had evidently been lying in wait in a lane nearby. I told them that I would go but I wanted to deposit my bag at home so that my wife could cook the meals. They told me that the bag would be delivered to her and I was forced to get into the van and driven to 14 Lord Sinha Road, the Special Branch office and from there to Dum Dum Jail. I found leaders of the Left movement, including Jyoti Bose, Jatin Chakravarty of the RSP, Subodh Banerjee of the SUCI and many others, already there. In jail, we continued to receive reports of the movement outside and were encouraged to see that the government was totally on the defensive.

With the setting up of the commission, those who had been detained were released. Surprisingly, my own release came much later than that of Jyoti Bose and others who were members of the Legislative Assembly. I had spent a little over six weeks or so before I was released. Notably, these arrests too were under the Security Act with no provision for a trial. Even after the new Constitution had come into force and many fundamental rights enshrined, detention without trial posed no problem for the authorities. Notably also, at that time, in 1953, there were no terrorist groups operating within India or across the border. It was thus a case of sheer violation of fundamental rights. The tram movement had, meanwhile, set the trend for other mass movements over a number of issues that I will describe in the next chapter.

TWENTY-ONE

The 1950s Food and Other Movements

There were numerous issues plaguing the people and the tram movement laid the tracks for a series of movements throughout the decade. Since the issues at hand were very real the response to them was tremendous. There were several factors beyond those on which the movements were based that influenced the outcome. There was, of course, the effect of the Partition and the influx of refugees; at least five million fled East Pakistan between 1947 and 1950-1951. Most of them were Hindus who were subjected to or feared persecution. There may not have been an authentic record of the number killed; the numbers dead may not have been as large as those in the west but many were killed and the properties of many more were forcibly seized. The economy was reeling under such an influx and, save a few very rich zamindars, most had to leave their belongings and property behind and trek across the border. The nature of the eastern Partition was different. In the west it was tremendously violent: an orgy of killing, rape, abduction of women, mutilation, unspeakable horrors that took place very rapidly. In the east the displacement carried on for years, persecution and violence forcing people to become refugees. Many women were abducted; many men and women were killed. The long duration made it appear as if the displacement and loss would not come to an end.

The refugees had nothing but the clothes on their backs and bitterness in their hearts. Most did not have friends or relatives to provide them with shelter in West Bengal. They were housed in temporary camps and given a subsistence dole. Many squatted on vacant land in the suburbs of Calcutta and other towns in West

Bengal. This huge mass of refugees seething with discontent further stoked the fires of discontent among the people of West Bengal. For them, Independence had not brought the promised rewards. Instead, there was a severe food shortage as food production could not keep pace with the rising population. The poor peasants and agricultural labourers were the hardest hit. No wonder they rallied in large numbers to the call given by the Left parties. Apart from the food movement and the struggles by the refugees for proper rehabilitation, there was another important issue: the plight of the teachers.

Teachers were among the most poorly paid in the state and, indeed, all over India. Primary schoolteachers got only Rs 200 or less a month and secondary school level salaries were hardly better. Even college teachers and university lecturers received much less than what unskilled workers received in factories. This reflected the low priority for education in the thinking of the government of the day, both at the state and central levels. A movement was waiting to happen.

I do not remember what triggered off the 1954 schoolteachers strike in West Bengal but it was a strike with a difference. The teachers decided to squat in front of Raj Bhavan, the Governor's official residence. There was a round-the-clock relay squatting and the place became a kind of pilgrimage centre. Delegations came from different sections of the workers and of the community, carrying food packets, refreshments and even cash donations to help the movement. Once again the government completely misjudged the popular mood and the resolve of the strikers. It chose repression to scare the teachers and break the strike. Almost all the leading teachers of the movement were arrested, which only strengthened their resolve and drew greater public sympathy and support.

Learning from the experience of the earlier movement, we decided to send some of the key organizers underground, including myself. This ensured that the movement did not fizzle out and the various activities that had been planned to keep the movement alive were kept going. This time, while I was able to avoid arrest by going underground, Manikuntala was arrested. This was hardly unexpected as she was very closely associated with this movement and visited the squatting teachers every day. A general strike called as part of this movement was a huge success. The government had to climb down and the process of revising pay scales of all levels of teachers was set in motion. Although, compared to the salaries of government officials and company executives, salaries of all teachers, college and university teachers included, were still far lower, some measure of respectability was achieved. When the movement was called off, all the leaders of the teacher's movement were released. Surprisingly enough Manikuntala continued to be detained. Snehangshu Acharya asked Dr. B. C. Roy why she was still in jail when the movement had been withdrawn and all the teacher leaders had been released. Dr Roy is believed to have said that she needed to be taught a lesson for her 'unseemly behaviour' in the Assembly.

He was referring to an incident that occurred during the tram movement. While the subject was being discussed and speakers from the opposition were talking of the police repression and holding Kalipada Mukherjee, the Home Minister, responsible, the minister stayed unmoved with a smile of smug satisfaction on his face. Provoked by this, Manikuntala took off her slipper and flung it at Kalipada Mukherjee. The slipper landed harmlessly in no man's land but the incident created a sensation and was front page news the next day in quite the same manner as the shoe flung at George Bush was headlined and, later, the one flung at P. Chidambaran. Manikuntala had set the precedent!

Food scarcity intensified from the mid-1950s and prices increased. The years 1955-1959 found poor peasants seriously affected all over rural Bengal; not even the urban poor were spared. A succession of inadequate monsoons combined with low productivity in the countryside had led to severe shortages. The country was importing food from the USA and others mainly through the PL 480 programme. Another movement was inevitable and a committee: '*Durbhikha O Mulya Bridhi Pratirodh Committee*' (Committee for fighting famine and rising prices) was set up.

The main crop in West Bengal (*aman*) is harvested in December-January. The rice produced lasted for a few months and by May-June a large section of the peasantry had no food left. The new hybrid varieties of wheat and rice that produced the Green Revolution had not been developed and there was an acute annual food shortage till the next crop was harvested. This provided the backdrop to our food movement. It took the form of rallies and meetings all over the state. It was generally followed by a large central rally at the foot of what used to be the Ochterlony Monument, now named Shaheed Minar or Martyr's Column. The issues were genuine and the response to our calls for mass rallies, strikes and satyagraha was fairly wide.

Unable to find a solution to the problem and vexed by the intensifying response to the movement, the government used the only weapon it was familiar with: repression. This repression was absolutely brutal. In 1959, a peaceful rally of peasants, men and women from the rural areas was subjected to a lathi charge that killed a large number of them. That so many could be bludgeoned to death in the heart of the city does not speak well of the kind of democracy that prevails in our country. The exact number was never tabulated but some newspaper reports suggested that as many as 59 persons were killed in police firing and the lathi charges in August-September 1959. Some estimates put the number bludgeoned to death on 31 August 1959 at eighty (Progoti on the internet).

The tragedy of these deaths apart, there was a subtle change in mind-sets during the food movement. The revolutionary posturing and phraseology were still there but the practice was quite different because somewhere there was an eye on the ballot box. The success achieved in the first general election had whetted the appetite of the party leadership for the loaves and fishes of office. Though power, even at the state level, was still a long way off, the limited opportunities that membership of municipalities, State Assemblies and the Parliament had opened up were being eagerly sought after. The era of Parliamentarianism had begun and I use the term in the pejorative sense used by Lenin.

TWENTY-TWO

The Twentieth Party Congress of the CPSU

The Twentieth Congress of the Communist Party of the Soviet Union took place in 1956. In a way, it marked the beginning of the end of the Soviet Union, though the final break up was still more than three decades away. The resolutions adopted at the Congress and the subsequent events indicated for the first time that the monolith was beginning to crack up. The concepts of peaceful coexistence between the two systems and of a peaceful transition to socialism, propounded by the leadership of the Soviet Party for the first time, marked a decisive break with the Stalinist outlook. Along with that came the personal attack on Stalin that opened up a can of worms. This was, of course, not presented at the open Congress. It was some time later that Khrushchev's speech on Stalin, delivered at a secret meeting of leaders of some parties that attended the Soviet Congress, leaked out. It was made public by the *New York Times*.

The objective of Soviet society remained what it had been before the Congress: 'satisfaction of the increasing wants of the people'. It was declared that the Soviets would catch up with the western economies within a very short time. Truth to tell, there was not much of a difference between the objectives of the Soviet state and those of the capitalist states of the West. To build a consumer society that would be similar to the western model but with slightly different methods: through state ownership of the means of production, the implications of which we will examine in my concluding chapter.

Meanwhile, the de-Stalinization drive was to have far-reaching repercussions in the Soviet Party, in the Party in India, and in other communist parties the world over. Its effects on the Indian Party can be discussed from several angles. First: the theoretical concepts of peaceful coexistence and the peaceful transition to socialism. Prior to this phenomenon, unquestioned acceptance of all that came from the Soviet Party was the norm. After these formulations, there appeared a sharp division in the Indian Party. One section totally opposed these concepts, decrying them as revisionism at its worst. This feeling was strengthened with some Soviet journals, considered authoritative mouthpieces of the Soviet Party, advocating a united front with the Indian National Congress, which was then the ruling Party not only at the Centre but in practically all the states.

Thus began a schism in the Party, which led to the formation of two well-organized factions: one advocating the National Front line, which meant a joint front between the communists and the Congress. The other faction rallied round the slogan of the Democratic Front, which meant a front of Left and other democratic parties opposed to the Congress. For me too it was a turning point from being a blind follower of the party line, as laid down internationally by the Soviet Party and, nationally, by the top leadership of the Indian Party, I began to think for myself. To that extent, it was a great liberating influence. It also marked a sharp division in the Party and the clear emergence of two factions. Alongside was the emerging rift between the communist parties of China and the Soviet Union that probably started much earlier with the victory of the revolution in China. Even while the struggle against the Japanese was going on there was simultaneously an ongoing conflict between the Chinese communists led by Mao and the Kuomintang led by Chiang Kai-shek. The emissaries of the Communist International had, till the last, been advocating a united front with the Kuomintang. Mao preferred to follow his own course and ultimately triumphed. Chiang Kai-shek and the remnants of the Kuomintang armies fled to Taiwan. After the victory of the Chinese communists in October 1949 Mao must clearly have felt that he could now take over the leadership of the world communist movement. He was in no mood to accept Stalin as his leader.

The Party in India was unaware that the megalomania seizing Stalin had assumed a particularly acute form after the Second World War but Mao evidently was not. Not much is known of what transpired when the two leaders met shortly after the victory of the Chinese Revolution in October 1949 but it is possible that even in that meeting the two sensed that they would emerge as rivals competing for world leadership rather than as comrades in arms. With the death of Stalin, who was succeeded by mediocre leaders, Mao saw no reason not to take over the mantle of world leadership. The road was now clear for him.

This was to have a great import for the Party in India, sowing the seeds for the many splits that followed. First came the formation of the CPI(M) and then the further splits with the emergence of the CPI(ML), which further split into numerous Maoist groups. Personally, it first aligned me with those who were advocating a Democratic Front and later put me on a course that ended up in my formal resignation from the Party. A series of party conferences was held, beginning from the district to the state level. Each conference debated the National versus a Democratic Front issue. For me, these district-and state-level conferences were important as I was one of the main spokesmen for the Democratic Front line. I had taken my position with the Democratic Front primarily because it was clearly different from the Soviet line that was egging us on to a joint front with the Congress.

Having broken the chains that mentally bound us to the Soviet Party, there was a thrill in following a course directly opposed to what they were advocating. Perhaps an even more important factor was that our day-to-day experience, one of struggles and confrontation with the Congress, made it difficult, if not impossible, for us to think of a joint front with that party. The entire raison d'être of our existence would be lost and for me the ideological position was important. Factionalism has its own logic though and very soon the ideological divide had begun to take organizational shape. Even at the state level, two distinct party centres had begun to emerge. Two other factors strengthened the barriers dividing the two factions that take us back a little to the 1948-1950 period of the Left-Adventurist line.

That misadventure had done great harm to the front organizations of the Party and broken up the various party units at all levels. When that line was repudiated by the International leadership through the Cominform editorial, new committees were set up, first on an ad hoc basis and later through conferences at various levels. Disciplinary action was taken against those leaders who had been identified with the Left-Adventurist line. They were debarred from standing for elections and hence their exclusion from the elected committees at all levels was ensured. Many of them were leaders of proven ability and considerable experience. They had realized their mistakes and had submitted their self-criticism as was asked of them. Among them were Bhowani Sen, Somnath Lahiri and Indrajit Gupta. Indrajit Gupta, who had always concentrated on trade union work, went back to his trade unions but Bhowani Sen, a member of the Politbureau during the Left-Adventurist period, and Somnath Lahiri, member of the Central Committee, were completely sidelined when the reorganization began in 1951 after the release from jail. The disciplinary action, barring them from standing for election for one year, had to run its course because they had to be held accountable for the damage done.

From behind the bars we had seen the absurdity of the line that saw so many workers lose their jobs, others maimed for life and yet others killed. The majority of the party members were seething with indignation. The point, however, was that even after the one-year period was over, factional considerations prevented the rehabilitation of these otherwise valuable comrades. For sometime they were deliberately prevented by devious means from being placed in positions of responsibility. It was natural under these circumstances for them to try to find a niche for themselves from where they could operate and put pressure on the other faction. As individuals, they stood little chance of either getting elected to party committees at various levels or getting the party nomination for contesting the Assembly or parliamentary elections. Factionalism became a regular feature of party life from this point of time. Although the difference was projected as one of policy—National Front versus Democratic Front—the personal factor was no less important. In course of time, different individuals became identified with different factions and the struggle for policies got intertwined with the struggle between personalities.

Each faction tried to capture as many committees as possible but the odds in West Bengal were against the National Front faction since the majority of the ranks were definitely against that line. In the party conferences, the arguments for the National Front line were basically of two kinds. The communist movement has always stood for internationalism and the Soviet Party had, since the 1917 Revolution, been the leader of the international communist movement. Any attempt to defy the line advocated by the Soviet Party would amount to a betrayal of our international solidarity. The second set of arguments was on the lines that right reaction was gathering strength and if the Left and the centrists, represented by the Congress, did not unite we would be handing over the country to the reactionary forces.

The Marxist principle of uniting with the national bourgeoisie to complete the still unfinished anti-feudal democratic revolution was also cited. On the other side, the advocates of the Democratic Front deflected the charge of being anti-international by stating that a ruling party had to maintain government-to-government relations and it is part of international diplomacy to support or even praise bourgeois governments of developing countries so that they remained part of the anti-imperialist front. Second and the more potent argument was to cite the day-to-day experience of all communist cadres, who had to face repression at the hands of the Congress government, when conducting popular struggles for food or employment or trade union rights and for other issues facing the people. When abstract theory was pitted against the reality it was obvious which side would win.

I was the main speaker for the Democratic Front line at the Calcutta District Conference held when this debate was going on and Somnath Lahiri was the speaker for the other line. The National Front line was, as expected, rejected by the conference and it was supported by only one-third of the delegates. I would like to mention here that even though the feelings were strong on both sides the debate was conducted without any great bitterness. Till this point neither faction seemed to have visualized the possibility of a split. Things changed within a few years.

According to the principles of party organization, with the adoption of the majority resolution the whole debate should have ended and the minority should have accepted and carried out the party line without any reservation. The majority should also have treated the whole issue as a closed chapter and treated the leaders of the minority group on par with those in their own group. This did not happen. It only marked the consolidation of the two factions and each side was sharpening the swords for the next round as it were.

Meanwhile, perturbed by the developments in the Soviet Party, the Calcutta District Committee organized a series of discussion meetings. If memory serves, apart from the DC members, local committee secretaries and some others were also invited. Free and frank discussions were held and everyone was permitted to air his or her views. This would have been unthinkable some years earlier and it was an indication of the spirit of *glasnost* that had been unleashed by the Twentieth Congress. No definite conclusion was reached but there was general agreement that there should be more scope for expression of dissenting views and that the cult of personality should be avoided. I do not know if any other unit in the Party in India held discussions on such a scale on this issue. This did not lead to any decisive break with the pattern of functioning of the Party though there was a little more openness and slightly greater emphasis on the democratic part of the democratic centralism principle. That was short-lived though. Momentous events within the country and elsewhere in China and the Soviet Union brought about a totally new situation. In the Soviet Union, with the ousting of Khrushchev, the Soviet Party gradually reverted to the Stalinist style of functioning until many years later, when Gorbachev tried to bring about drastic changes.

As I look back on these events, I realize that even though I was shocked and shaken by the revelations in Khrushchev's secret report, I was not bold enough to take the decisive step that I should have taken and that I ultimately did take some six years later. I had joined the Communist Party in pursuit of an ideal, the building of a new society, Sidney and Beatrice Webb termed it a new civilisation in which the evils of the capitalist system would disappear and, more importantly, a new and better human being would evolve. The Twentieth Congress and all that happened there removed the blinkers that had prevented us from seeing the reality. However, so deeply inured were we to the dogmas that had been part of our mental make-up that we refused to understand the full implications of what we were seeing. It is something like bandages being removed after an eye surgery; as the light comes flooding in, the patient instinctively closes his eyes because he is unable bear it. I still felt that with Stalin gone and his mistakes and aberrations being noted, the Soviet Party would emerge cleansed and strengthened. In other words, our faith in the ultimate infallibility of the Soviet Party received a jolt but still remained unshaken. Yet, the seeds of doubt had been planted and, as events unfolded, they bore fruit and helped to uproot the hold of dogmas.

It is also necessary to appreciate that our whole life had got so deeply linked to the Party that the thought of making a break and starting on a clean slate just did not arise. I was still the District Secretary, a very large number of party members had reposed faith in me and there was a sense of responsibility towards them and the thousands who had made enormous sacrifices to be in and serve the Party and the people. Till that time, 1956, most party members were still fully convinced that they were working for a cause that would lead to a better society, a socialist society. Manikuntala was still an MLA and, even though she did not express it, she too must have felt that she could not abandon those who had reposed faith in her.

There was also the very mundane question of how the two of us could survive as we had nothing to fall back upon. There was no bank balance, no property and no dividends coming in. My father was still alive but had only a small pension from his years in government service with which he made both ends meet. It was only by living by turn with one or the other of my brothers that he could manage. My brothers, except the eldest who was abroad, were in service; one in a government department and the others in private sector organizations on salaries that were just enough for them to maintain their families.

Even so, the shock administered by the Khrushchev report made me question whether all that I was doing made sense. My work as a party organizer was not giving me any great satisfaction. Yet I was not able to consciously consider the possibility of leaving the Party. I am sure that subconsciously such thoughts existed. The sheer weight of inertia kept me going.

TWENTY-THREE

The Kerala Experience

The second General Elections held in 1957 brought in the unexpected. The communists won a majority in Kerala and formed a government! It was headed by the veteran communist leader, E. M. S. Namboodiripad. This created history; never before had the communists been able to win a majority through elections and form a government. The result was even more surprising because the elections were held in the framework of, what in Marxist terms was a bourgeois constitution. Under that, the powers in the hands of a state government are extremely limited, with the central government not only having most of the financial powers but also the authority to dismiss a state government. I do not know whether the question of accepting office under these circumstances was seriously debated within the Party either at the central or at the Kerala state level. As far as I am aware, it was taken for granted that if the Party mustered a majority, even with the help of allies, it would form the government. Whether this squared with the orthodox Marxist standpoint about communists staying away from the bourgeois parliaments or not was not even seriously considered.

In fact, on the eve of the 1957 General Election, the slogan of forming an alternative government was raised even in West Bengal. However, the communists were far short of a majority when the results were declared. The District Committee engaged in serious discussions as to whether it was right for us to speak of an alternative government. There was one view that raising this slogan scared away one section of voters who would have been happy to see the communists improving their position as an opposition but were not yet prepared to accept them as a ruling party.

In 1957, when elections were being held in the newly formed Andhra state, there was wide expectation in the Party that the communists would get a majority in the assembly and form a government. Not only did this not happen it was almost a clean sweep for the Congress. The lesson that should have been drawn from this was that the Party was greatly isolated from the masses and was unable to feel the pulse of the people. So far removed was it from reality that shortly before the elections there were functions where the Andhra Party leader and one of its founders, Sundarayya, known for his integrity and his almost Gandhian lifestyle, was felicitated as the future Chief Minister.

To resume the account of the Kerala experience, the Centre could not stomach the installation of a communist government in the state. From the very first day, efforts began to be made to dislodge it. In 1957, Jawaharlal Nehru was still the Prime Minister and the Congress enjoyed an absolute majority at the Centre and in practically all the states. Indira Gandhi had been appointed President of the Congress Party. The events that followed revealed the hollowness of the claim that the Constitution had given the country a federal structure. Article 356 of the Constitution empowered the ruling party at the Centre to dismiss any elected state government at its discretion as long as it could get this act ratified in both houses of Parliament. As long as the Congress commanded this majority, this article was used to dismiss state governments not to its liking on numerous occasions. Subsequently too, when non-Congress parties, either singly or as a coalition came to power at the Centre, this article was used to dismiss state governments on one pretext or the other.

The details of the events leading to the dismissal of the Kerala government are not important here. The main issue on which a state-wide mass movement was whipped up by all the forces opposed to the government was its education policy. The state government felt that it had a right to follow its own education policy but this was used as an excuse to dismiss it, invoking Article 356 of the Constitution for the purpose.

In Calcutta, the Party organized a massive demonstration protesting against the dismissal of the Kerala state government even while it enjoyed a majority in the state legislature. This demonstration could not reverse the course of events in Kerala or in New Delhi but I have no doubt that this added to the many other factors that were leading to the isolation of the Congress Party from the politically-conscious sections in West Bengal. Since the communists were in the forefront of this anti-Centre and anti-Congress movement, it was only natural that it was helping the Communist Party to extend its base in the state. While that is one side of the story, it is necessary to take a look at the Party's role in Kerala once it came to power. However short-lived it may have been, quite a number of policy decisions taken by the government set the trend for future communist governments when they came to power later in Kerala or in West Bengal.

In certain areas such as implementation of land reforms and education, efforts were made to take some measures in the interests of the peasants and the common people. Other measures surprised me and others within the Party who still swore by the classical tenets of Marxism. An agreement was signed with a Birla company under the terms of which quite a few concessions were given to them to start an industrial unit in the state. In another incident, when a section of postal workers were preparing to go on strike the government took strong measures to prevent them from doing so. These actions came as a shock to me and I remember having a heated discussion with Bhupesh Gupta, who stayed in our flat—which was, in fact, run as a party commune—on these issues. How could a communist government grant concessions to a Birla company? How could a communist government take action against a workers' movement? He could provide no satisfactory answers but all these questions were pushed into the background by the wave of indignation that swept all over, following the undemocratic action of the Central government in dismissing a duly elected state government. Looking back on these events, I realize that implicit in the measures taken by the communist government in Kerala was an understanding that has been at the basis of subsequent policies pursued by the communists whenever they have been able to come to power in any state.

This understanding has never been made explicit but has existed as a determining factor in all decisions that have been or are still being taken. Clearly the reality now is that the possibility of a peaceful change through the ballot is accepted. That much is obvious from the functioning of communist governments. Since the posturing with the old slogans continues, the result is that the divide between theory and practice widens by the day.

The reason why no attempt has been made to make this explicit is that it is difficult to reconcile it with Marxist theory as has been laid down in the writings of Marx, Engels and Lenin. The possibility of getting a majority in an election conducted under a bourgeois constitution and of forming a government at the state level with limited powers in a situation where the main levers of power are in the hands of a non-communist government at the Centre was something that had never been visualized before by Marxist theoreticians. In India, when faced with this situation, ad hoc responses were made. The only way these can be defined is to use the very flexible and fashionable term: pragmatism. The failure to come to grips with this problem, to try to understand all its implications and ramifications and to work out a policy framework has been one of the biggest failures of the communist movement in India. This is a failure for which it will have to pay a heavy price. Some of the consequences of this failure are evident both in Kerala and in West Bengal.

TWENTY-FOUR

Money Matters

As we have seen, the transformation in the Party had started even before the success in Kerala thanks to two factors. One was the Twentieth Congress of the Communist Party of the Soviet Union where the concepts of a peaceful transition to socialism and of peaceful coexistence between the capitalist and communist systems were advanced. Even though a section of the Party vehemently opposed these concepts, these clearly had an impact on the thinking of the Party leadership. The other was the taste of power that the Party began to get the moment it successfully entered the Parliament, the Assemblies and the municipal corporations. Initially, the pay and allowances of even members of Parliament were relatively low but compared to what the Party paid its wholetimers they were princely. In addition, the perks and the power, however limited, were like a heady wine that brought about, a little imperceptibly at first and later quite patently, a change in attitudes, lifestyles and the policies and practices of the Party. That the Party emerged as the largest opposition in the Lok Sabha and in some of the Assemblies contributed in a large measure to this transformation, opening out a new perspective for it.

Gradually the focus of Party activity shifted from the trade union and peasant movements to elections. The organizational structure of the Party too began to reflect this change. In many places Party units were based on constituency configurations. The discussions at Party meetings concentrated more on election prospects, selection of candidates, alliances and fronts to improve the chances of improving the Party's position in the Parliament and Assemblies rather than on strengthening its working class base or over struggles on issues affecting the peasants and landless labourers. As far as I remember, only once in a PC meeting did someone raise the point about too much time being spent on discussions on elections and too little on the trade union front. The latter was left entirely to the trade union comrades to handle. No one openly controverted the opinion; it was too patent a fact but the matter was brushed aside. The focus of the Party's activity and of its concern continued to be the elections.

Since votes had to be collected from all classes, all communities and strata of the population, it was not possible to antagonize anyone. In the rural areas, particularly, it was impossible to champion the cause of landless workers, the poorest and most oppressed as it would alienate not only the rich but even the middle peasantry. The two together formed the bulk of the rural vote bank. Class conflict was now interpreted as Congress-Communist conflict.

Elections need money; over time the amount of money involved grew larger. Since winning elections was the prime consideration, the source of the funds ceased to matter. Moreover, once the polarization between Congress and Communists had taken shape, aspirants in West Bengal, began to realize that the only chance of getting into the Assembly or the Parliament was to get either a Congress or a communist ticket. This gave rise to two kinds of aspirants for the Party nomination. Those among Party sympathizers and members who had put in a substantial sum of their own into the Party's election kitty had a better chance of getting the Party nomination. Others with nothing in common with Party ideology but nursing ambitions of getting into Parliament turned to the communists when they failed to get a Congress nomination or did not want it, particularly if they could back up their efforts with their purse.

One such successful aspirant was Biren Roy of Behala. Owner of extensive tracts of land in that area and known as a rich zamindar, he began approaching the Party in the mid-1950s. He first sent out feelers to the Party through Bankim Mukerjee, the Party's well known mass leader and mass speaker. I recollect that the Party leadership warned Bankim Mukerjee to steer clear of him. A few weeks later, Biren Roy did succeed in meeting the top leadership. It was not a formal meeting. Two of our top PC leaders were at the house of one very affluent comrade. So was Biren Roy. I happened to drop in at that time but was ignored since I was the only a district leader and my place in the PC was only as a representative of the Calcutta DC. I found that a deal had been struck to officially support him as an independent candidate for the Lok Sabha and Biren Roy appeared quite jubilant. He would make a substantial contribution to the PC's central election fund and pay a share of the expenses incurred on his behalf in each Assembly constituency within that parliamentary constituency.

Later, the Calcutta DC was informed that Biren Roy would be supported by the Party for the parliamentary seat in South Calcutta. We were also informed that each of the Party's Assembly candidates in that parliamentary constituency would receive a sum of money towards the expenses of the campaign for Biren Roy. Since Biren Roy had no election machinery of his own, he depended entirely on the party machinery in the various assembly constituencies that formed part of his parliamentary constituency. There was considerable resentment in the party ranks as it was obvious that Biren Roy had been given the seat only because of his money power.

His behaviour too was resented. Manmohan Banerjee, secretary of the local committee in that area told me that on one occasion, when on a round of the assembly constituencies, Biren Roy stopped at one of our party election offices where our comrades were hard at work writing posters. Getting down from his car and looking approvingly at them, he flung a Rs 10 note, asking them to have tea. The local committee secretary told me very proudly that they flung the note back to him and told him that our party comrades did not work for money. This incident showed the mood in the party ranks at that time.

This is only one aspect of the transformation taking place in the approach of the party leadership. The other aspect was the change in the lifestyle and behaviour of party comrades at different levels but mainly at the top level. With Party whole-timers in Calcutta getting Rs 60 a month—even less in the districts—the gulf between whole-timers and those who were elected to the assemblies or the central Parliament had widened. Apart from the status and the power that such elected positions entailed, the monetary benefits they brought was an added reason for the intensifying scramble for getting tickets for the Municipalities, Assembly or Parliament. Even election to the municipal corporations was a much sought after prize. Initially, municipal councillors were not paid any salaries but the opportunities for making money were far greater in the municipalities. Gradually, the vices that we had been attributing to the bourgeois parties began to visit the Communist Party.

In West Bengal the party mandate was that whole-time members who were elected to the legislatures should deposit their salary with their District or Provincial Party Centres and draw only their party wage. Those who had been in any of the professions, teachers, lawyers, doctors were supposed to pay a percentage of their earnings as a levy to their respective party units. In the early stages, this was adhered to by most members but gradually more and more members defaulted on one plea or the other. Thus the gulf between MPs, MLAs, municipal councillors and the others kept widening.

Despite the money being collected from the levy on members and from the contribution from MLAs and MPs, the Party's financial position in West Bengal was quite precarious. Apart from the wages for whole-timers and the rent and other expenses for maintaining the modest infrastructure, a fairly huge drain on the finances was on account of the Party's daily paper, *Swadhinata*. Since no advertisements were received or sought, even though the number of copies printed was not large, the paper was incurring heavy losses. Yet it was difficult to think of running the Party without the paper that served as a party organizer and educator. At one stage the Provincial Committee wanted to close down the daily paper and switch to a weekly tabloid. It dropped the idea when there was a virtual vote of no confidence against the party leadership at a meeting of the general body of members of the Calcutta district. This indicated the confrontational trend gradually emerging between the Calcutta District Committee and the Provincial Committee. This was in addition to the factional divide that was evident. The Party's monolithic structure was beginning to weaken and while the formal split was far off, the cracks were showing. Another factor prompting this was the fact that the editorial board of the daily paper was dominated by comrades who were not fully in agreement with the policy and line of the dominant faction that controlled the Provincial Committee. And yet the paper was formally an organ of the West Bengal Party and organizationally accountable to the PC.

Money was also taking toll on another important sphere of the Party organization: the wage structure. In the early days, the wage structure was devised when membership was limited and the Party had to function underground or work under conditions of semi-legality, under constant threat of imprisonment. Those who worked whole time had to depend entirely on what the Party was able to pay. If this meant hardship and semi-starvation, they were ready to face it. Sometimes, the families of such comrades helped but for those who came from poor families or those not sympathetic to the Party, a kind of asceticism was the only course open. With legality and under conditions where a section of comrades were successfully entering the municipal corporations, the Assemblies and the Parliament, the wage structure was losing all rationality. The minimal increase had little relation to reality.

When I entered the Party in 1941, the monthly wage was Rs 30. We lived in communes and it was somehow possible to manage by pooling the wages of all the commune members. With galloping inflation during and after the Second World War, the wage structure ceased to have any meaning even though it gradually increased. When I left the Party in January 1963, my wage had increased to Rs 60. Manikuntala received another Rs 25 because she was an MLA and had to nurse her constituency. The rent of our flat was paid by the Party, as it was a commune. Two other comrades were members of the commune: Bhupesh Gupta and Dinesh Roy. Bhupesh Gupta was a member of the Rajya Sabha and lived mostly in the government accommodation allotted to him in Delhi but stayed with us when in Calcutta. He paid the meal charges for his period of stay in the city. Dinesh Roy contributed the major portion of his wage as a party whole-timer for the board provided to him. It may sound unbelievable but we actually lived on this till the late 1950s. My wife managed so well that we could even entertain comrades and friends occasionally. With inflation spiralling out of control, however, it became very difficult to manage and whole-timers felt the pinch all over the state.

By the mid-1950s, the Party's wage structure had become absolutely unrealistic. Yet, not only was there no attempt to address this problem seriously, a policy of drift was actually adopted. This had serious repercussions in many ways. Finding it impossible to manage on the party wage, members found a way out by leaning on sympathizers. Some helped out of a sincere love for the Party, expecting nothing in return but others clearly did this on a quid pro quo basis. With a nomination from the Party amounting to a sure road to the municipal corporation or the Assembly or even the Parliament, supporting a particular comrade or group of comrades was an investment that many shrewd and ambitious aspirants were not averse to making. Turning a blind eye to the phenomenon of party cadres seeking financial support from 'sympathizers' meant that the Party had begun to slide down the inclined slope to corruption. That became a widespread party feature over time.

Another fall out of this phenomenon was that the working class and peasant cadres, who could neither draw upon family resources nor on friends and sympathizers from the relatively more affluent sections of society, were marginalized and even squeezed out. The Party of the proletariat was turning into one of the middle and upper middle class cadres and supporters, whose one interest was either to enter the municipalities or the legislatures or to seek favours of one kind or the other by helping party cadres to get into these institutions. The Party continued to swear by the mantra of working class leadership but everything it did ensured that the few working class cadres we had would have no role to play in decision-making, even if they were retained as members of district or the state committees for cosmetic reasons.

This I can say on the basis of my experience in the West Bengal party. But even though slightly different methods might have been used to tackle the problem of party finances in other states the end result was the same everywhere. The story of Nasarulla, a working class cadre in our District Committee, otherwise a worker at the Garden Reach establishment of the Calcutta Electric Supply Corporation is worth recounting. He had leadership qualities and commanded considerable support among the workers in that establishment. I do not remember the exact circumstances under which he lost his job; possibly it was in that mad 1948-1950 period. He was made a whole-timer and later elected to the DC. At every committee meeting, no matter what the topic under discussion—it could have been one of the many struggles that we were waging at that time: tram fare, famine and food scarcity, teachers' wages or the elections, Nasarulla would begin by muttering a few words relating to the subject under discussion, mostly supporting someone or the other who had expressed his views, but ultimately coming round to the one thing that was uppermost in his mind. He was just not being able to survive with his family on his wage nor did he have any of the resources that other DC members from middle class backgrounds had.

Once he talked of his wife berating him because, unlike other workers in the locality, he had not been able to give her a new sari for Id. We were touched by his very moving account but had more urgent matters to attend to. As far as I remember, we dismissed it as one of the many problems that the Party faced but for which there was no solution. The majority of committee did not feel the need to spend time on this issue because they did not feel the pinch that Nasarulla did. For my wife and me, this was becoming a serious problem though. My own family was away from Calcutta, in Delhi and in any case, I did not want to scrounge on them. I had voluntarily left home to work for the revolution and there was no question of turning to the family just because we were finding it difficult to make ends meet. My wife's family was mostly in what was then East Pakistan or had migrated to West Bengal but all of them were in dire straits. In fact, even with her limited resources, Manikuntala had to extend a helping hand to them and devote a fair amount of time in trying to tackle their problems.

The other option of taking the help of sympathizers did not appeal to us either. Instinctively we knew that this was a slippery path that could lead to our dependence on them. Temperamentally, both of us were not made out for depending on charity despite our shrunken resources, though we had to survive and needed at least two square meals a day. That was when an opportunity opened out for me sometime in 1957 or 1958. I was offered a part-time teaching job in a leave vacancy in South Point School. Uma Sehanovis, a teacher, who was among those who really built up that school, took leave to attend a Peace Conference in Europe and suggested to the authorities that I be given a part-time assignment to fill up the gap. The Principal, Satikanta Guha, readily agreed to do so. I opted for a time slot that would not interfere with my work as DC Secretary: 2 p.m. to 4 p.m., the time usually set aside for rest. We normally worked from about 8 a.m. to 1 p.m. and then from about 5 p.m. till late evening, depending on the programme for the day. When we had a party or a mass meeting to attend, we would only return home by 10 p.m. or even later, depending on how far the meeting place was from our residence. Naturally, we had to cover the distance by bus, tram or by train if we had to go to a nearby district and that took time.

The afternoons were supposed to be rest periods. I accepted the part-time school job and started work as a teacher. At the end of the month, I was thrilled to receive a packet of a little over Rs200 that represented a princely sum for us. I had hoped that I would carry on and thus solve our financial problem. The principal was keen to give me a long-term assignment even after Uma returned as he was pleased with my performance during the six weeks or so but my luck ran out pretty soon. When members of the District Committees and of the units lower down came to know that the District Secretary had taken up a job there was a hue and cry. Bridging the gap between income and expenditure by doing honest work was not acceptable but a blind eye was being turned to the unsavoury methods adopted by some.

By this time I had become a member of the National Council of the Party and got to meet comrades from other states and also got an idea of the functioning of the Central Secretariat. Ajoy Ghosh was now the Secretary and the organizational structure of the Party had been changed. After the Left-Adventurist period of 1947-1950, the Politbureau had been abolished and in its place was the Central Secretariat. Branches replaced cells as the primary units of the Party. The small District Committees, with no more than seven members, were expanded and could have up to 101 members. Similarly, at the apex the National Council had 101 members, though there was a smaller body, the Central Executive with about 21 members. The Central Secretariat had seven members based at the party headquarters in Delhi.

When I had to attend the National Council meetings, I sometimes had to fend for myself to find the money to meet the expenses of travel. Travel was, of course, by ordinary sleeper class but even that was more than what one could afford on our party wage. The District Committee was generally able to provide the fare from point to point but nothing more. Surprisingly, many members from other states seemed to be quite comfortable as far as money was concerned. Instead of availing of the hospitality provided for members by the host committee they would dine out at some of the better restaurants. On one or two occasions, I had carried some magazines published by local organizations in West Bengal and I was surprised that they were lapped up in minutes by members from other states. I had thought that the prices were too steep and had expressed my doubts to the comrades who had given me the magazines about their sale prospects. I realized that I could have sold many more. It was obvious from the way some of these comrades moved about and functioned that their lifestyles were very different from those of whole-timers in our state.

Once I wanted to raise the issue of whole-timers wages and the financial problems facing us in the National Council. In Calcutta our sources of finance were two: we imposed a levy on employed and earning Party members. It was on a graded scale with those earning below a certain level being exempt, the levy percentage going up with increased incomes. It was not more than three or four per cent for any level. There was also the contribution from our MLAs and MPs. Elected whole-timers were supposed to donate their salary to the Party and continued to receive the whole-timer's wage. Those who were not whole-timers were expected to pay the levy on their earnings but many MPs and MLAs were defaulting on their payments.

Others too, particularly professionals with what were then considered very high income levels, were refusing to pay their levies at the stipulated rates. We thought that it was unfair that party members doing far more important jobs and holding senior posts had to try to survive on what was clearly less than a living wage while those elected, thanks to the efforts of the Party, should live in relative comfort. That is why I wanted to raise this issue and see whether a uniform code of conduct and some sort of a uniform wage structure could be worked out for the entire country.

At my insistence this issue was included in the agenda of one of the National Council meetings. I was looking forward to the discussion. When the time came for this item on the agenda, I found that most of the members of the National Council were away. When I rose to speak, there were a lot of empty chairs. Even those who were present had a bored look and seemed as if they were being forced to listen to some sort of a cranky idea. After I had made my brief submission none other than the redoubtable A. K. Gopalan, a legendary figure in Kerala politics, rose to express his views on the subject.

He presented a very vivid and moving picture of what it meant to be an MP. He explained that when in Delhi there were, at any point of time, between 10 to 20 people from his constituency who parked themselves in his MP bungalow and had to be housed and fed for as long as the session lasted. Most of them had come with problems and with questions that had to be raised on the floor of the house by the MP or had to be sorted out by the MP with one or the other ministry of the central government. In other words, there were on legitimate business and not just casual visitors out to have a good time in Delhi. He had to put up with them if he had to retain his seat. In his home state too, the picture would not be very different. In fact, the number of people who stayed at his house would be much larger, not to speak of the hundreds who thronged the place just to have a darshan of their leader.

He explained that the MP's salary that he got was a mere pittance compared to the huge expenditure that he was incurring in exercise of his responsibilities as an MP. Obviously, he was being able to meet this expenditure only with the help of donations that he was regularly receiving as a leader who was not only extremely popular but commanded respect from all sections of the people; even from the Congress of which he had once been an important leader.

Gopalan's speech opened my eyes to the reality of what it meant to be an MP and what costs were involved if the MP had to retain his popularity and seek re-election. I realized that it was not possible to pursue the parliamentary path in a bourgeois democracy with the mind-set and the organizational structure of a secret and illegal revolutionary party. Yet that was precisely what we were trying to do. As far as discussion on the agenda was concerned, there was nothing further on the subject and as other items came up for discussion many National Council members who had gone out gradually trooped back. As far as I was concerned, we were back to square one. The discussions at the National Council had shown that no serious attempt to address the problem would be forthcoming. However, the fact that I had put this on the agenda of the National Council made some top leaders aware of our plight and Ranadive (BTR) made some proposals to me that somewhat eased the situation.

I was told that I could occasionally contribute articles to the theoretical journal of the Party that was being edited by BTR himself.

For each article I would be paid Rs 200. I did start contributing articles. I do not remember all that I wrote but one was on the refugee problem in West Bengal. I pointed out the differences in the situation faced by refugees in West Bengal as compared to those faced by the refugees from West Punjab and referred to the consequences of this for the economics and politics of the state. I think, I wrote some articles for the Party's weekly journal as well. In addition, I was invited to deliver lectures at the Central Party School that had been started in Delhi and was paid my fare to and fro and an honorarium; I do not remember how much. Besides, I did some translations, one major project being translating Rahul Sankritayan's book on Central Asia from Hindi into English. It is an important historical work and I enjoyed doing it. A recent edition of this book mentions my contribution as translator as did the earlier edition. This took care of our problems for a short while but once the clashes with the Chinese started, all that come to an end

Although we were not facing the reality and continued to mouth revolutionary slogans, the Party had by the mid-1950s become a petit-bourgeois Party not very different from some others that we condemned as bourgeois parties. One look at the composition of the National Council of the Party of the proletariat was enough to show that the working class and peasant element had completely disappeared. This was reflected in the sort of issues that came up for discussion. They were either on abstruse formulations regarding the character of the state or on whether we should go in for a National Front or a Democratic Front or on the question of electoral alliance and election tactics. Issues pertaining to the working class and peasant movement hardly ever came up.

The assumption was that such issues were for those comrades still working on these fronts at the state or district levels to discuss or sort out. The National Council had more important matters to attend to such as whether the central government was a big bourgeois-led government or a bourgeois-landlord led government or a government led by the national bourgeoisie. Whether our revolution was to be a bourgeois democratic revolution or a revolution to bring in a people's democracy!

There was also the lifestyle of some members of the National Council from other states. Some had landed interests in rural areas and came with big purses. Others with apparently no such family property seemed to be quite prosperous too. At the Party Centre, the General Secretary had a heart problem and made frequent trips to Moscow for his treatment and for discussions with the Party leadership there. This was understandable but that others around him too were seen to be in and out of Moscow, seemed odd to us and was the subject of comment in party ranks. Comrade Dange, of course, was a class apart and would never stay with party comrades when he visited different cities for party conferences or council meetings. A room in one of the top hotels of the city was booked for him. We were told that as President of the World Federation of Trade Unions, he received a huge salary and everything was above board as far as his lifestyle was concerned. There was no reasonable explanation for the lifestyles of some others though.

Clearly an elite class had begun to spring up both at the state and central levels, elite not in the sense of intellectual or moral level but purely in the sense of their lifestyle and their capacity to spend. The phenomenon of lavish wedding feasts when sons or daughters of some of these leaders were married had begun to surface. Not that it was anywhere near what the Jayalalithas and Laloo Yadavs of today have been doing but in terms of the near-starvation wages at which most of the Party whole-timers had to work, it was not expected of a Party dedicated to the cause of building a communist society.

What were the sources of party finance when the Party was not in power in any of the states? Apart from the levy on the income of party members, the overwhelming majority of whom at this time were either blue or white collar workers, there were the substantial donations given by some rich party members and sympathizers. Some with fairly large landed property donated the whole of it to the Party as E. M. S. Namboodiripad and Sundarayya are believed to have done. Others like Snehangshu Acharya made substantial financial contributions to the Party from time to time, apart from the regular support they gave to selected leaders such as Jyoti Bose.

What about Soviet money? There was support in kind such as free hospital and rest house treatment in Moscow or in other seaside resorts in the USSR for sick comrades. Later, after communist regimes were established in East Europe, similar facilities were provided by the other countries in that region. It was also generally believed that a fair amount of financial support came in the form of Soviet books and publications, the major part of the sale proceeds of which remained with the Party. There are reasons to believe that assistance in other forms was made available on certain occasions. After all since we were all part of one international movement there was no harm in one party in a position to do so helping another which was in need!

What seemed unfair was that in a Party aiming for a classless society—where each would contribute according to his ability and get according to his needs—there was a wide gap between the lifestyle of a few at one end and the overwhelming majority at the other end. I am talking about the whole-time cadres and leaders of the Party only; not of members and sympathizers who were employed or in the professions or in business. It is obvious that in the kind of society that we now have, there are and there will continue to be wide disparities between one section of the people and another. The lifestyles of those party members who work at senior levels in large companies or as well-established professionals are not expected to be the same as those of workers on the shop floor or of workers or peasants in rural areas. Surely, however, there should not be two standards for whole-time cadres whom we designate as professional revolutionaries and who are considered to be comrades in arms.

Even if the exigencies of work necessitated certain facilities and perks such as cars, air travel and an infrastructure for the kind of functions that had to be performed by those at the top levels of the Party hierarchy, surely there could be no justification for such a wide difference between the lifestyle of the leaders and the ranks. By the mid-1950s, it was almost as if they belonged to two different classes and the disparities widened. Those who had accumulated enough to have substantial bank balances, property in the form of large tracts of farmland or urban property tended to develop a petit bourgeois mentality. This was particularly so because their income was being derived not from labour either as blue or white collar workers engaged in a productive enterprise in a rural or urban setting. How ironic that those who swore by the infallibility of Marxism ignored one of the cardinal principles of Marxian thought. Their economic status affected their thinking and planning. Once the Party had tasted power in Kerala, the strategy and tactics were entirely geared to repeating this experience in other states and again in Kerala. Surprisingly, no efforts were made to draw the lessons of the Kerala experience.

Existing Marxist literature prescribed that communists should not participate in bourgeois parliaments—'pigsties' was the label given to them—except for short periods in exceptional circumstances. If the situation necessitated a change, it should have been acknowledged. By formulating a strategy for the changed situation and placing it in the context of Marxist theory, a creative development of Marxian thought could have been achieved. No such effort was made. While dogmatic assertions regarding the validity of all that Marx, Engels, Lenin and Stalin had said continued to be made, the practice had no relation to theory. As in other parties, the gap between profession and practice continued to widen with repercussions in many areas as we will shortly see.

TWENTY-FIVE

Of Worker Cadres

One of the cardinal principles of the communist movement is that of working class hegemony. The working class is the vanguard of the revolution and even though the term 'dictatorship of the proletariat' later went out of fashion, the whole idea was that socialism had to be built under the firm leadership of the working class. This was what we were taught and what we were striving to achieve. It was with this in mind that communists concentrated in the early days on the working class movement.

This was also the motivating spirit when, on emerging from the underground in April 1942, I told the party leadership that I would like to work on the trade union front. This was what I began to do and continued right up to 1948. I devoted my entire time to the trade union movement and met some outstanding characters from among the working class cadres. I worked closely with some when I was directly involved in the trade union movement. As possibly the only Hindi-speaking DC member, I was asked to take classes for these worker cadres or even to act as translator and to interpret the proceedings of party conferences for them. Many of them merit special attention because at least some have been all but forgotten. If ever the history of the Party were to be written, they are unlikely to find a place. Given their contribution, they could have risen to leading positions in the party hierarchy but were never given the opportunity. Had that happened, the course of events in later years might have been very different. I am of course referring here only to some of those whom I personally knew and interacted with in Bengal. I have no doubt that there were many in other states and I only hope that those who have written or will be writing about the history of the communist movement in those states will see to it that they are not forgotten.

To begin with the worker cadres that I worked with in the Calcutta Port, Parmananda Shyamal was a crane driver. When I first met him, this comrade from Orissa was probably in his late forties or early fifties. He was intelligent, mature and respected by his fellow workers. He had known and worked with some earlier communist leaders who had been active in the port trade union before I came on the scene in 1943. He had attended classes organized by them and had a better understanding of Marxist theory and practice than many trade union leaders introduced from outside. More importantly, he knew how the Port worked, the function of the various departments and the links between them. I learnt a lot from him as I was fairly new to the trade union movement while he had a lot of experience of earlier struggles. Although not a great orator he, in his quiet way, could impress and influence those around him. His personal life and conduct were exemplary. Given the opportunity he would undoubtedly have been an asset not only to the district leadership but even at higher levels.

As we worked in the Port area, we would roam around it from early morning to late evening. Returning to our commune for lunch would have meant a waste of time. So we often had lunch at the house of some worker or the other. I had an arrangement to have my midday meal at Parmananda Shyamal's place on a fairly regular basis. This not only saved time and helped me to remain close to him and other workers in the area but also ensured a more nutritious and wholesome meal than I would have got at the commune.

Sitaram Singh, porter in the jetty section of the Calcutta Port, was also an experienced person, in touch with the Party before I arrived on the scene. He was from the Azamgarh district of Uttar Pradesh, a born leader and a fiery speaker who had influence over workers of most other departments, apart from his own. He was very different from the introvert Parmananda. Sitaram was flamboyant and outgoing; fond of drinks but rarely losing control. Crates of Scotch, lowered from the hold of the ship sometimes fell and half broken bottles were scattered on the jetty. Many workers helped themselves to it for it would be a shame to allow premium Scotch to go to waste! Minor vices apart, Sitaram was a great asset to the union because of his leadership qualities and his oration without which we could hardly have brought about the sea change; turning a moribund organization into a united militant mass organization of the workers in a few years.

Bazloo Molla was one of the most interesting of our union leaders. He worked in the marine section of the Port, probably in one of the tugs. He came from Jessore, now in Bangladesh and was the unquestioned leader of the entire marine section. When I came to work at the Port in 1943, this section was entirely manned, as I have said earlier, by East Bengal Muslim workers from the districts of Jessore, Faridpur, Noakhali and Chittagong. In the beginning, they had kept aloof from the union but were gradually won over. When they did join, it was all together; several thousands of them. The credit for bringing them in goes mainly to Makhan Chatterjee but he was fortunate in roping in Bazloo Molla, their natural leader, that made it easy to bring them all in at one go. They were among the most reliable members of our union. Unlike the other two worker leaders though, he was neither a party member nor did he have any political leanings. Like many other trade union leaders, it was a natural and instinctive sense of working class solidarity that made him emerge as an important functionary of our trade union.

Bazloo Molla was an excellent speaker and could hold audiences spellbound. His moment of glory was on 29 July 1946, the first general strike called by the trade unions in support of the postal workers' strike. The Maidan meeting held that day was attended by many thousands and although there were many veteran trade union leaders on the dais, it was Bazloo Molla who won the loudest applause. This was remarkable in so far as this was Bazloo Molla's first experience in addressing a mass meeting outside the Port where the audience was not his fellow workers but workers from all over and a fairly large section of the middle class too. That he was speaking in his mother tongue, Bengali, helped him strike an instant rapport with the middle class members of the audience. That he could rise above the narrow limits of his union and strike a responsive chord with a mass of such heterogeneous people showed his maturity and his skills as a speaker. His speech emphasized the need for Hindu-Muslim unity and working class solidarity and was in tune with the anti-imperialist sentiment of the vast Maidan audience. I have no idea what happened to Bazloo Molla after I left the Port. Post-Partition, the entire mass of East Bengal workers moved to East Pakistan and was replaced by others. I have no doubt though that if he had been properly looked after and had received the right kind of training, he would have become a mature trade union leader capable of participating in the decision-making process of our committees.

Ram Sundar Singh was a Congress minded worker who belonged to the National Union of Port Trust Workers led by Dr. Maitrayee Bose. We had formed a joint strike committee to ensure total unity in favour of the strike. Nevertheless, during the long strike there were vacillations among some sections of the workers but these natural leaders proved steadfast till the last, overcoming the vacillations of those who found it tough to carry on and were almost on the point of giving up. Ram Sundar Singh was one of those who made sure that unity was maintained till the end and that the weak and timid sections were kept in check. He was intelligent and an excellent speaker. That an understanding of the need for united working class struggles comes naturally to those who participate in these struggles is clear from the example of workers like Ram Sundar Singh.

Not only was he not a party member, he was quite an anti-communist at the time of the strike. Yet he proved to be one of the bedrocks of the movement. He had no hesitation in accepting our leadership despite his political differences. As far as the national movement was concerned, he considered that the role of the communists in opposing the 1942 movement was a betrayal of the national interest but he accepted that as far as the working class struggle was concerned, it was necessary to work with and even under the leadership of the communists.

Ram Naresh, another worker from Uttar Pradesh worked in the traffic department that handled the railway wagon movement within the Port. I think his duty was to man one of the cabins that monitored and controlled the train movements. Possibly in his late forties when I started working, he was quite mature, intelligent though his academic attainments were limited and that possibly hampered his performance. He was not a good speaker at large meetings but had leadership qualities. He had become a party member, with an understanding of the party line that he could explain to his fellow workers. There were others like Ram Deo, also a party member and one of the leaders of the traffic department.

The loco, comprising engine drivers of freight carrying trains, was manned by Muslim workers from Bihar and Uttar Pradesh. We had some fine cadres sympathetic to the Party and very loyal to the Union. Unfortunately, except for Mohammad Amin, an engine driver, I cannot recall their names. There were some excellent cadres from among the clerical staff too: Himangshu Sinha, Tulsli Baidya, Robi Sen, Nalini Dutta and, of course, Debkumar Ganguly who later matured, and as mentioned earlier, became one of the important leaders of the World Federation of Trade Unions. One needs to belabour the point that a party of the working classes should have developed these exceptional cadres by educating and training them to play a leadership role. The logical culmination of neglecting worker education is that today there is not a single member of the working-class cadre in the top leadership and, as far as I am aware, not even at the state-level leadership.

Because of our strong union in the Calcutta Tramways, we had a fairly large number of worker cadres who had joined the Party. I knew many of them well because even though I was not involved in the day-to-day work of the tram union, I took their classes and later, as District Secretary, I oversaw the party units to which they belonged. Chatur Ali, who worked in the Nonapuker workshop of the Tramway Company, became a DC member later. Zaheer and Missirji were either drivers or conductors. Zaheer, in particular, was extremely intelligent and given the right education, opportunity and responsibilities would have been an asset to the Party. There was also Kali Banerjee who had a political background. He had been with the Socialists before joining the Party.

Then there was Mohammad Elias, a skilled welder at the Guest Keen Williams factory, who rose to a fairly high level in the Party. He worked hard to improve himself and got elected to Parliament from a Howrah district constituency. He was in jail with us throughout the three years that I was incarcerated and at one stage became the secretary of the Jail Committee. In jail, he appeared for and passed the Matriculation examinations. He learnt to speak English even though he was not always grammatical but he epitomized the potential in the worker cadres around the Party.

Two other names come to mind: Rahman, a worker in the Bhartia Iron and Steel Company, a whole-timer when I joined the cell in that area, extremely intelligent with leadership qualities but poorly educated. That prevented his rise in the Party. Sarcastically he would say that he too belonged to a high caste; only he was a *kata* brahmin (as a Muslim he was circumcised). I lost touch with him when I shifted to the port union in the Kidderpore area. Later, in the 1970s, after I had left the Party, a comrade from the Ballygunje area, who had left the Party too, told me that Rahman had cancer and that they were raising funds for his treatment. I contributed whatever I could and Rahman himself or his younger brother would come to me sometimes to collect the money. I learnt of his death from his younger brother after some months.

From amongst the bidi workers too we had some good cadres—Ershad, for one—who may not have been party members but were close to the Party. I remember having attended a *mushaira* or perhaps a *kavi sammelan* arranged by them in the Rajabazar area and I was impressed by the quality of the lyrics. Two lines recited by one of them are still fresh in my mind.

> *'Nirdhan hona pap hai bhai,*
> *Nirdhan ka bhagwan bhi naahin.'*
> (It is a sin to be poor/Even God seems to have deserted the poor.)

Since the communist movement began in the mid-1920s on the premise that the Communist Party represents the vanguard of the working class, it was natural that the Party concentrated on the working class movement. It was also natural that quite a few working class cadres emerged. I have only talked of a few with whom I came in direct touch. There were many others in the rest of the country particularly in Bombay and Madras and regrettably we let them languish for want of education.

The course that we did organize for them—in Bengal the responsibility was mostly given to me—only sought to explain the elements of Marxism. We did tell them something about the Soviet Union, the November revolution and the class struggle as the moving force in history but made no effort to improve their general knowledge and give them some basic and elementary ideas about the history and geography of the country and the world. We did not ensure that they had some acquaintance with the politics and economics of the country and did nothing to instil in them a scientific outlook. Without such basic knowledge it is not possible for anyone to really understand the developments taking place in the world today and to take part in the decision-making process.

During the Left-Adventurist period, efforts were made to artificially foist worker cadres into different level committees. The West Bengal PC was disbanded, Ismail became the Secretary and a few other worker cadres were added. Haridas Malakar, a worker who had been active in the Usha Engineering Works was one of them. Ismail was not really a worker but he had identified himself with the working class and was one of the most effective trade union leaders that the Party ever had. I later heard—I was in jail during this entire period—that it was really the assistant, Subhas Sinchan Roy, assigned to help him write circulars and reports, who was functioning as the de facto PC Secretary. He would, on behalf of Ismail, only carry out the directives of the Party Centre, the Politbureau, which was the only decision-making authority during this period. There was not a single worker in the Party Centre, the Politbureau. The proletarianization of the Party was just an eyewash and it was being run as a completely centralized organization with what in Marxist terminology could be called petit bourgeois party cadres.

TWENTY-SIX

Heading for a Split: The Extraordinary Congress at Amritsar

The Democratic Front line got a boost with the dismissal of the communist ministry in Kerala and anti-Congress sentiments gained ground even though the signals from the Soviet Party were strongly in favour of an alliance with the Congress. Thus the National Front line also had its supporters. The theoretical justification for this was provided by the concept of the need for a united front with the national bourgeoisie in a country where the bourgeois democratic revolution had to be completed.

The proceedings of the Twentieth Party Congress of the Soviet Union and the revelations of the Khrushchev report on Stalin also had their impact on the Party. There was *glasnost* in the air for some time and we, in the Calcutta DC, started publishing a bulletin; an open forum for different points of view. This was something unique because I am not aware of such a thing being tried out anywhere else. It did not last long as by 1959 the shadow of the impending conflict with China was looming large. Moreover, even though it was meant to be a forum for free discussion, a considerable polarization between the two main factions had taken place and the contributions represented the standpoints of the two factions with little by way of original thinking reflected.

While the CPSU's Twentieth Party Congress and the revelations of the secret Khrushchev report had shaken me up considerably and had, indeed, created a factional divide in the Party, both factions had realized that something had gone wrong somewhere with regards to practice and theory. Old habits persisted though and there was no real break from the earlier mind-set. The only change was that as the rift between the Chinese and the Soviet parties became obvious; one faction relied on the Soviet Party and the other on the Chinese.

The Amritsar Party Congress, held in April, 6-13, 1958, shortly after the de-Stalinization drive had begun in the Soviet Union, was impacted by it. As was only to be expected, the old debate that started after the Twentieth Party Congress was revived. While the point of view that an alliance with the Congress was necessary to fight the threat of right reaction was strongly put forward by those advocating the National Front line, those opposing it argued that right reaction was gaining ground because of the anti-people policies of the Congress and hence the main fight had to be against these policies. Ajoy Ghosh, keen on ensuring that the two factions stayed together within the Party, took a centrist line. Mohit Sen has summed up the stand taken by him well in his autobiography. 'He, Ajoy Ghosh, said that there had to be a simultaneous struggle against the Congress because of its anti-people policies and against Right reaction because it was both anti-people and anti-national. It was worse than the Congress but if the Congress was not checked by the CPI, it would run away with the masses who were discontented with the Congress.'

Some amendments to the party programme were taken up. Amendments were usually initiated by members of the Secretariat but I plucked up courage to move an amendment of my own. Taking note of one point of criticism against Stalin, that he had equated himself with the Party and thus had been able to exercise complete control, severely curtailing the democratic functioning of the Party, I moved an amendment to the party programme, which said that in a socialist India there would be scope for more than one party; in other words it would be a pluralistic society. I had moved the amendment more to provoke a discussion on the issue, without quite expecting it to be adopted because at that time it was quite a heretical concept. In fact, when I got up and spoke for a few minutes in favour of the amendment not many people were listening.

To my surprise, Mohan Kumaramangalam, who was till then a

member of the CPI's Central Committee, got up and delivered a passionate speech in favour of the amendment. This created a bit of a stir and some of the top leaders began to take notice and one member of the National Council, I do not remember who, argued that parties that favoured a return to capitalism could not be permitted. I added a clause to my amendment to the effect that other parties would be permitted to function as long as they abided by the constitution of socialist India. The resolution as amended was put to vote. I noticed that some of the top leaders of the Party including the then secretary, Ajoy Ghosh, were still not paying much attention and were taken by surprise when a vote was called for. There were a few hands raised against but the majority voted in favour.

Promode Dasgupta who was sitting beside me voted in favour. Ajoy Ghosh and some other members of the Secretariat did not vote. It seemed from his body language that Ajoy Ghosh did not take this whole debate seriously at all. Much later after I had left the Party, I happened to look at a copy of the party programme. I did not find this amendment anywhere. Recently I asked a friend to check again and he confirmed that in the proceedings of the Amritsar Party Congress there is no reference to this amendment and the discussion on it though it was passed and had been seconded by as important a person as Mohan Kumaramanagalam who, till then, was considered to be among the top leaders of the Party. However it appears that what was incorporated was the right of opposition or dissent provided it did not violate the constitution of socialist India. In other words, this would mean that individuals could express different views but they could not organize themselves into separate political parties to contest elections and strive to come into power. I understand that it was only in this diluted form that the amendment was incorporated. The rule of one party as the only party to be allowed to function was too sacrosanct to be meddled with!

At the Party Congresses, apart from the political resolutions on the international situation and on some current national issues, there were sometimes resolutions on social issues. At one Congress, possibly at Amritsar, someone had referred to the practice of dowry and moved a resolution that party members must insist that the practice of dowry be stopped in their own families. A lot of discussion went on behind the stage and ultimately the comrade who had moved the resolution was persuaded to withdraw it. We were told that it was not considered a very practicable proposition!

The story of my amendment that disappeared gives an idea of the prevailing atmosphere in the Party. Even after Khrushchev's revelations, there did not seem to be any serious soul-searching. One faction felt that Khrushchev was trying to settle personal scores and doing a lot of harm to the Party. The CPI(M) that still celebrates Stalin's birthday and pays tributes to him does not try to make an objective and critical assessment of his role. The other faction was prepared to go along with the explanation given by the Soviet Party, blaming it on a personality cult. My impression is that they too go to the other extreme and either avoid the subject altogether or more or less echo the subjective and one-sided appraisal of western historians. That there was need to change the basic monolithic structure of the Party by making it more democratic was not seriously considered at all. The catch word—democratic centralism—was considered a sufficient safeguard to ensure inner party democracy. On this point there has never been much difference between the two communist parties –.CPI and CPI(M).

The factional outlook got reflected in the organization in interesting ways. I was inducted into the Provincial Committee secretariat, shortly after my election as Secretary, Calcutta District Committee, in 1952. The Calcutta district was especially important not only because it had the largest number of party members but, being the capital of the state, all important movements, political or cultural, had their centre in Calcutta. My induction into the PC Secretariat was, therefore, quite natural. Very often meetings of the two secretariats were held at the same time and I was not always able to attend PC Secretariat meetings. I usually walked across from the DC office to the PC office after the DC Secretariat meeting to check if any decision of significance had been taken. It was only when my presence was considered essential for any reason that I was asked to attend the PC Secretariat meeting and the DC Secretariat meeting was deferred to another date.

This arrangement worked for sometime but at a certain point of time, perhaps in the mid-1950s, I felt that combining the two functions was becoming difficult. I expressed a desire to be relieved of my position as member of the PC Secretariat. Promode Dasgupta took me aside and whispered that I should continue, otherwise there would be pressure to take Somnath Lahiri in my place. I was hesitant but I did not insist on quitting the Provincial Committee Secretariat. I was after all still a supporter of the Democratic Front line though post-Twentieth Party Congress I had already begun to distance myself from the factional groupings in the Party. Shortly after this—I do not remember the year—I was dropped from the PC Secretariat. Since I had asked for it earlier, I welcomed it. I realized that to do justice to the responsibility imposed on me as DC Secretary, I needed to concentrate on this task and this needed me to relinquish my position in the PC Secretariat.

The interesting part of this episode is that later, some time in 1959 or 1960, when I expressed a desire to relinquish the DC Secretary's post and devote myself completely to work in the PC Secretariat the move was opposed vehemently at a meeting of the District Executive at which PC Secretariat members were present. As far as the DC was concerned we had a very good team in the DC Secretariat consisting of Biren Roy, Ajit Roy, Gopal Acharya, Krishnapada Ghosh and Ramen Banerjee. Biren Roy could very well have taken over as in fact he did for some time after I left the Party. However, after the formal split Biren Roy, Ajit Roy and Gopal Acharya refused to join either party and formed a Centrist group of their own. I had no doubt even then—it is even clearer today—that the opposition to the move was deliberately organized not because of any concern for the smooth functioning of the DC but because the PC Secretariat members knew that I was not going to be a yes man in the Secretariat. They were not prepared to take on someone not a fully committed member of their faction.

Manikuntala's *Sediner Katha* described another incident that showed how factional considerations influenced party decisions:

> In 1958, when I was truly agitated by what was happening to the Party, I was selected to be a delegate at the Amritsar Party Congress. Every time it was I who was selected from the women members. I did not particularly approve of this. I thought Pankaj Acharya could be sent in my place this time. She was the head of the Mahila Samiti and, after all, we went to the Party Congress in order to learn something. Thus it was appropriate to select someone from the workers of the samiti too. But the party leaders stated that this was not possible. 'If you do not wish to go, it will not be difficult to find a delegate.' I realized that what was at stake was my vote. Even if one vote was cast for the other side, there would be fear of this side losing. However, there was a great deal of objection against a comrade who would voice a different view. I was extremely angry and said, 'I won't go.' But what effect did my views have on the way things were. The behaviour of the leaders of the other faction was no different either.

Ironically, Pankaj Acharya, who was rejected because her loyalty was suspect, later became one of the most trusted members of the CPI(M) and even, when this incident took place, her support to the Democratic Front line was not in question. It was only that her husband Gopal Acharya, also a supporter of the line, had distanced himself organizationally from the faction and so an element of doubt had crept into the minds of the faction leaders that, when it came to a crunch, she may not vote along with them.

The incident, mentioned by Manikuntala, also reveals the extent of the patriarchal mind set in the Party. In one Party Congress after another, when there were as many as 50 plus delegates from West Bengal, the number of women delegates was few; far below the 33 per cent reservation being demanded for women in Parliament and the Assemblies. At most, there were only three or four. As far as I know, the situation has not changed much since.

Clearly, the division in the Party was not based on policy but on the leadership of both groups seeking to consolidate their factions by making sure that only those who were personally loyal to the leaders held key positions in their respective organizations. I refer to 'respective organizations' although it was still a single Party because the two factions had begun to prepare for a sort of showdown by setting up their own Party centres, their own organizational machinery and their own communications network. This became clear at the Vijayawada Congress in 1961.

Indeed, as early as 1958, the outlines of the division that was to take place later were already visible. In the West Bengal Party, there was the dominant faction led by Promode Dasgupta and the opposition faction of Biswanath Mukherjee. Bhowani Sen and Somnath Lahiri were not factionally inclined but had perforce to align with this faction because of the determined effort of the dominant faction to marginalize them. There was also the non-aligned centrist group consisting of Ajit Roy, Biren Roy, Gopal Acharya, Subodh Dasgupta and many others to which, at this time, Manikuntala Sen and I belonged.

At the central level things were a little different. Ajoy Ghosh was the General Secretary who tried to steer a middle course and did succeed till his death in preventing a formal split in the Party. The 'Left' group was in a minority in the National Council and, if memory serves, also in the Central Executive. The organizational structure of the Party consisted of a Secretariat, an Executive Committee and a National Council. At the state level it was the same, with a Provincial Council taking the place of the national body. After the split, the CPI(M) reverted to the old structure of a Politbureau and a Central Committee.

Ajoy Ghosh's own inclination was clearly in favour of the National Front line though he was careful till the end of avoiding any direct link with either faction. He made frequent visits to Moscow on account of his ill health and was in touch with CPSU representatives. Since they were clearly in favour of the CPI having an alliance with the Congress in India, it is easy to understand Ajoy Ghosh's predilection for that line. However, the CPSU was also against any split in the Party and hence the need for Ajoy Ghosh to try to strike a balance between the two positions.

What was going on in my own mind at this time, 1958? The seeds of the decision that I took four years later had begun to germinate between the Twentieth Congress of the CPSU and the Amritsar Congress of the CPI. That the Soviet Union and the society that had been built up there was no El Dorado was clear. I had begun to ask myself: 'What am I doing here? In what way is the work I am doing connected with the goal I had set out to achieve: building a better world?' Alongside these nagging questions in my mind was this whole game of one-upmanship being played by the two party factions. In fact, I was already looking at it with a feeling of disgust as I distanced myself from either faction even without seriously thinking of leaving the Party. I felt that I was drifting aimlessly and all that I was doing was leading to nowhere. I had a kind of premonition that something was going to happen soon that would help me to decide what I should do. Very soon it did happen: the conflict with China

The period of blind loyalty was over. This period of party history is being deliberately suppressed and efforts are being made to see that the post-1970s recruits to the Party, who now probably form the majority, revert to the same sense of blind loyalty. I doubt whether this effort can or will ever succeed.

TWENTY-SEVEN

Conflict of the Giants

The growing rift between the communist parties of the Soviet Union and China was gradually spilling out into the open since the late 1950s. The Stalin and Mao differences, evident after the final victory of the Chinese communists in 1949 and clear at the meeting of the two leaders, were taking a toll. What transpired in the Stalin-Mao meeting was not known though and in India, we hailed it as a great event. The meeting of the two giants could lead to only one outcome—the victory of the socialist revolution all over the world!

As historians of the communist movement have revealed, the Communist International (read Soviet Party) had, during the years of war against the Japanese, advised Mao to come to an agreement with the Kuomintang but had been rebuffed. Even earlier, the Chinese communists had rejected the advice of the Communist International on the line to be followed in pursuit of their goal of bringing about a successful revolution. Mao worked out his own strategy that depended on the peasantry and the liberation army recruited from the countryside rather than the proletariat which, in any case, was far too small to be a significant force in China. Actually Mao was deeply suspicious of Stalin who probably expected China to accept the hegemony of the Soviet Party and of Stalin himself. He had no intention of submitting to the leadership of Stalin and had his own roadmap for making China a great power and of taking over the leadership of the world-wide Communist movement.

After Stalin's death in 1953, Mao remained the only leader to have successfully staged a revolution and that too in the world's most populated country. Khrushchev's line of peaceful coexistence with the capitalist world and his theory of the possibility of a peaceful transition to socialism were considered a reformist deviation by the person who had declared that 'all power flows out of the barrel of a gun'. The differences between the two leaders were to have the most severe repercussions on India and the Communist Party here. Indeed, within a few years, the impact of the conflict of the two giants began to be felt all over the world.

The border between India and China had not been clearly defined when India was part of the British empire and China was ruled by the Kuomintang. Evidently the Indian government had its own ideas about where the border stood that did not tally with those of the government of the People's Republic of China. The seeds of a potential conflict lay within these two different perceptions. The question of Tibet was also one that could trigger off conflict. The British considered Tibet to be an independent country but one within their sphere of influence. In 1904, a British military expedition led by Francis Younghusband had forced Tibet to open its doors to trade with Britain and prevented other foreign powers having commercial relations with it. However, since the eighteenth century, China claimed suzerainty but was too weak and too busy dealing with the inroads the British and the Japanese imperialists were making to be able to effectively exercise its suzerainty.

Shortly after the liberation of China in 1949 there was the Bandung Conference in Indonesia of the Asian countries attended by both Nehru and Chou En-lai. The two probably met for the first time and it was here that the non-aligned movement took shape. Mao and Chou En-lai's priority was, it seems, to consolidate their power and to secure their borders. Dalai Lama himself, given the choice would definitely have preferred autonomy under the Indian Union than under the People's Republic of China. In the years that followed, Chinese leaders proved to be diplomatically far shrewder than India's Nehru and Krishna Menon, the Defence Minister. The two felt that ideologically a communist country would have a much broader view and would not be swayed by narrow chauvinistic considerations. They realized their mistake too late.

Chou En-lai cosied up to Nehru and the *Hindi Chini bhai bhai* slogan emerged, giving rise to expectations of a long period of close friendship and cooperation. Completely disarmed by the charms of Chou En-lai, Nehru signed on the dotted line as far as Tibet was concerned. No attempt was made to get any commitment from China regarding Kashmir or the border. Nehru evidently took it for granted that after his gesture regarding Tibet he would be given a free hand in delineating the unmarked and undefined India-Tibet, India-China border. This proved a costly mistake.

The rest, of course, is history. The Indian army started setting up posts on the border and found the Chinese too setting up their posts, some in advance of India's. Again there was the mistaken impression that India's attempt to demarcate the border, according to its own perception, would not be challenged and would in any case not lead to any full-fledged military response. Nehru asked the Indian army to 'throw them out'. The result was that after certain initial border clashes, the Chinese army swooped down on India in October 1962 and advanced as far as Tezpur in Assam. The Indian army was caught entirely unawares and had to beat a hasty retreat before the advancing Chinese troops. On 21 November, the Chinese forces withdrew as suddenly as they had come in.

These events mark a kind of turning point in the post-Independence history of India. Nehru was devastated and there is no reason to doubt that the debacle suffered by India hastened his death in May 1964, in less than two years. The opposition demanded Krishna Menon's head and Nehru had no option but to yield. Krishna Menon resigned. It was from this point that the fortunes of the Congress Party began to decline and, by 1967, for the first time non-Congress governments came to power in many states. More important for these memoirs is the effect these events had on the Party and on me personally.

Our access to information was extremely poor in those days and the iron curtain was a reality for us. We were, therefore, late in understanding these developments in the communist world, especially in respect of the relations between the two communist giants. Ajoy Ghosh, S. A. Dange, Bhupesh Gupta and others, who practically had a hot line to Moscow, must have known but were secretive about the whole thing. They probably thought that it would blow over and did not want to expose us to the widening rift. International affairs were, after all, the prerogative of a few at the top and it was not considered necessary to take even members of the National Council into confidence. Bhupesh Gupta lived in at our commune, in the next room, but we had no idea of what was happening.

Ajoy Ghosh had told us that they had received an assurance from the Chinese Party that, though they did not accept the McMahon Line as the border between the two countries because it was drawn by the imperialists, they would not cross the Line. Mohit Sen in his autobiography has given a more detailed account of the abortive efforts made by the Indian communist leaders to persuade the Chinese Party to change their aggressive stand. They paid no heed, crossing the Line and going beyond. The first major clash between the Indian and Chinese border patrols took place on October 29, 1959 in Ladakh. Nine Indian military police personnel were killed. Feelings in India ran high and jingoistic sentiments were roused by all the political elements in the country, barring the communists.

Dange started issuing statements condemning the Chinese government for violating our borders. He, of course, knew by this time that the Soviet Party did not approve of the Chinese stand on the border issue and this probably encouraged him to go public with his condemnation. We, in the Party in Calcutta, felt that Dange was going against the international communist leadership as a whole, something akin to a blasphemy in those days. There were very heated discussions at a meeting of the Calcutta District Council on the subject. Comrades belonging to both factions were united in condemning Dange, and some were almost hysterical. A meeting of the National Council was due to take place shortly after and I was to attend as a member of the National Council.

The District Council unanimously adopted a resolution

condemning Dange and asked me to see that the National Council was apprised of our sentiments and wanted action taken against him. Usually, I would arrive for the National Council meeting just a day before the meeting or even on the day itself unless I had a specific mission. This time I had to lobby to get a resolution of the nature we had adopted in the District Council discussed and passed by the national body and it was necessary for me to reach a couple of days earlier. So I was asked to go by air instead of taking a train. I had travelled by air once or twice earlier; once to Darjeeling, paying Rs 40 for the ticket. I had taken the Dakota that flew between Dum Dum and Bagdogra in the early 1950s. Going to Delhi by air was quite an experience. The plane was possibly a Viscount and the fare was around Rs 300. The meeting was to be held in Meerut but we had been asked to assemble in Delhi from where we would be taken by bus.

On arrival in Meerut, where we were put up in some hostel, I found the situation very different from what I had expected. There was a kind of hush-hush atmosphere with the top leaders confabulating among themselves behind closed doors. No one was in a mood to listen to me. I did manage to convey the message to a few of the top leaders, probably Bhupesh Gupta, the only one to whom I had easy access. No one seemed interested. The word had already gone round that the communists were not condemning the Chinese. Demonstrations were taking place in many places all over India. In Meerut too there were rumours that there would be demonstrations against us and the meeting might be disrupted. The meeting began but other items in the agenda were taken up. On the second day or on the night of the first day there was a flurry of activity and we woke up to hear rumours that the Party might be declared illegal or there might be large-scale arrests of communist leaders. Again, nothing was formally communicated to us.

We learnt that some leaders, as far as I remember, Jyoti Bose and Bhupesh Gupta, had rushed to Delhi to find out what the government was planning to do. They had contacts with senior Congress leaders (was it Ashoke Sen?) and were expected to get the correct information. They returned later and we came to know that no such action was imminent. So the meeting was convened again but no serious discussions took place. A resolution was adopted urging that the border dispute between India and China should be settled through peaceful negotiations, which was the prevailing view from the moment the border clashes started. We were still in the dark about the rift between the Soviet and Chinese parties.

It was probably in 1960 or 1961 that documents pertaining to the on-going debate between the two parties reached us and we learnt of the serious differences between them. Strong indications notwithstanding, we found it difficult to believe that rather than side with a communist country, the Soviet Party would actually support a bourgeois government. An article in the *Mainstream* reveals how the world came to know that in the developing conflict between India and China, the Soviet Party was not, in fact, supporting its communist brother but its Indian friend.

The following extract from the article 'Masood Ali Khan—Tribute' by Arun Kumar Mahanty will be of interest. 'Masood broke several stories with international significance. It was he who broke the story of the Soviet position on the Chinese aggression on India at a time when the entire world was breaking its neck over what would be Moscow's possible reaction to the event. For Moscow, China was a comrade and India was a friend . . . It was Masood who broke the astounding story to the rest of the world. He happened to be in a close get-together where the Soviet leader Khrushchev was present. Masood asked him a pointed question on the Chinese attack. In his characteristic humour the Russian leader said: 'If a comrade attacks a friend, our sympathy would obviously be with the friend.' This clear position came to be known to us only sometime after the Chinese attack in October 1962.

Until the events of October-December 1962, the official position of the Indian Party was that the border conflict should be resolved peacefully through dialogue. In the Calcutta district, we shared this view though I had sleepless nights dreading that the conflict would take a more serious turn. The worst scenario even at that time for us was of many more clashes such as the one in Ladakh, leading to the death of nine Indian soldiers. The expectation was that the matter would be resolved through negotiations; neither anyone in the Party nor evidently did Nehru believe that the Chinese army would march into India.

Once the widening ideological rift between the Soviet and Chinese parties was known, the factional strife within the Party in India intensified. In West Bengal, particularly since the Twentieth Party Congress, the dominant party leadership considered that Khrushchev and the Soviet Party were taking an out-and-out reformist line and there was great sympathy for Stalin. When it was known that the Chinese Party was against the Soviet line, this section of the Party felt vindicated and its sympathies veered towards the Chinese.

How close it came to the Chinese Party is difficult to say. Harekrishna Konar, who visited Vietnam and China, met me shortly afterwards and told me of his discussions with the Chinese leaders that had greatly impressed him. I found it difficult to appreciate the Chinese point of view as I had already begun to have doubts about the Chinese intentions but I was willing to listen to him and he too was prepared to confide in me because he knew that, as far as the line of anti-Congressism was concerned, I was more in agreement with the line of the Promode Dasgupta (PDG)-Konar faction which in West Bengal was the dominant faction than the other. Meanwhile, we suddenly found that a flat bed rotary printing machine had arrived and been installed in the office of our daily paper, *Swadhinata*. It did appear a little strange that just when the whole country was seething with indignation at the killing of Indian soldiers by Chinese army patrols on the borders, a Chinese machine had been installed.

It needs to be pointed out that with our daily paper running into huge losses as a result of the outdated system of printing, a rotary machine was just the thing that could help to ease the situation. We did not specifically ask how this had happened nor were we told but we took it for granted that it was a gift from one communist party to another. It was therefore a great shock and a sense of disbelief when later we were told that the machine had been paid for by Biren Roy, the same person to whom a parliamentary seat had been 'sold'. I will speak about that part of the story a little later. Another development that deserved more attention than it received was that just at this time an account was opened in the Bank of China. Again no questions were asked but it is an indication of the total lack of transparency in the functioning of a party which was functioning legally and participating full heartedly in the parliamentary process.

Till the final, full-scale attack of October-November 1962, I had not taken a clear position on the issue. I felt, along with the overwhelming majority in our District Committee, that the problem would be resolved and the *India China bhai bhai* spirit would be revived. It was only after the October 1962 invasion and after it became clear that the two communist giants were taking up directly opposite positions on the developing situation in India that I woke up and understood that not proletarian internationalism but narrow national interests were motivating the Chinese.

The next significant event was the Vijayawada Congress held in the summer of 1961. This was a very tense period for both of us. Manikuntala has described how, ever faithful to the party line, even when she disagreed with it, she valiantly campaigned in the districts. I quote from her book:

> 'It was the Party's misfortune that it was entrusted with the responsibility to propagate that the fault lay with India not with China. I too was included in the campaign and there was no end to my worries.'

She goes on to describe the experience that she had in trying to hold public meetings on the issue and gives details of how she faced people's ire in a number of places. There is a particularly moving description of a meeting in Balurghat in Dinajpur where, despite a mike being denied to her and despite the very hostile atmosphere, she managed to speak and was able to persuade the people to give her a patient hearing.

Despite all that was happening, we held on to the belief that this was a temporary aberration that would ultimately be resolved peacefully. It was unthinkable that a communist country would escalate the border clashes into a full-fledged attack on India with thousands of troops and heavy armour. Yet, that is exactly what had happened with disastrous consequences for the country and for me.

TWENTY-EIGHT

India-China Relations: The Vijayawada Congress

The Vijayawada Congress was held in the summer of 1961 under the shadow of the India-China border skirmishes. Most resolutions were on non-controversial issues and adopted without any discussion. The dramatic events took place during the closing hours of the Congress which was attended by a very large and high-powered Soviet delegation, headed by no less a person than Mikhail Suslov. An important member of Stalin's Politburo, Suslov had managed to retain his position even after Khrushchev took over as the General Secretary. The Soviet Party was aware of the virtual split in the Party in India and wanted to assert itself, given the growing rift between the Chinese and Soviet parties. The Chinese Party had begun its drive to take over the leadership of the world communist movement and was posing a challenge to the Soviets. The Soviet Party was anxious to ensure that a major party such as the one in India sided with it rather than with the Chinese.

After Stalin, the Soviet Party had no leader to compare with Mao, whose prestige among the parties of the developing countries was particularly high. Aware of this and knowing that the Chinese Party had been able to influence sections of the Indian Party, particularly in the states where the Party was strong — West Bengal, Tripura, Kerala, Andhra Pradesh—the Soviet Party was keen to ensure that the Indian Party continued in the Soviet camp. Ajoy Ghosh was still the General Secretary and his pro-Soviet views were well known to the Soviet party leaders. However, he took great care to see that the views of the other section were accommodated as far as possible in party resolutions. The Soviet Party's hopes of preventing a split in the Indian Party were not baseless.

Another important event during the Party Congress was the announcement by Suslov of the successful launch of the Soviet cosmonaut, Yuri Gagarin, into space. Significantly, the Soviet Party used the Vijayawada Congress forum of the Indian Party to break the news of the successful launch of the first manned spacecraft to the world. This event was intended to boost the image of the Soviet Union already engaged in a cold war with the United States. The fact that it was in India, at the Congress of the Indian Party, that the news was broken, was expected to show the importance the CPSU attached to the Indian Party. Thus it was a two-edged weapon; aimed against the United States and at the Chinese Party. As the leader in world space technology, it should be the Soviet Union that the developing countries should turn to, rather than to China (still relatively undeveloped) was the message that the Soviets intended to convey.

Within the Indian Party the factional divide was too far gone for such gestures to have any effect. This became clear at the closing session of the Congress at which the election of the National Council and other central bodies such as the Control Commission was to take place. The general practice was for the outgoing National Council to propose a panel of names that was normally accepted. Sometimes one or two names were proposed from the floor of the house but such names were rarely accepted. It was only at the lower level conferences that there were instances of someone nominated from outside the panel being elected, where there was a better chance of an 'outsider' being sufficiently well known to get enough votes to beat someone on the panel. At the highest level, it was difficult for someone outside the panel to get elected, as delegates from different states would not know the person. At the Vijayawada Congress, things took a very different turn.

The panel was presented very late at night, after Ajoy Ghosh, who had a serious heart problem, had retired for the night. Many, including myself, who were not aligned to any faction, had thought the delay was only due to the top leadership being busy with other things. It was only later that we realized that many rounds of negotiations had taken place without any unanimity being achieved. This became clear when after the panel was placed before the delegates, one by one some, whose names were on the panel, marched up to the dais and, without any explanation, withdrew their names. We thought this was due to some personal reasons but it became clear to us that this was a concerted move. The first few withdrawals were by lesser known persons but ultimately some of the top leaders including leading members of the 'Left' faction in West Bengal withdrew their names. When BTR too came up to do the same, the message was clear. If proper representation to the Left panel was not given in the National Council they would stay out. This was an indication that a split was in the offing. While this charade was going on, there was a grim foreboding in the conference and no one quite knew what all this was leading to. Whatever it was it did not bode any good for the future of the Party.

The Soviet leadership that had been watching the proceedings understood what was happening and sent word to Ajoy Ghosh who hastily got out of bed. Another round of negotiations followed where Suslov and other Soviet leaders played a part and a compromise was reached with the National Council being enlarged to admit many members of the Left faction. For the time being the split had been averted but many of us knew that this patchwork would not last. Earlier in 1951, differences could be resolved because the Soviet Party was till then the undisputed arbiter to which all factions owed allegiance. Even in 1933, when the Party had been on the verge of a split, a letter jointly sent, clearly at the instance of the Comintern, on behalf of three parties had helped to avert the crisis.

The situation in 1961 was clearly very different with the Chinese Party now increasingly asserting itself as the leader of the world communist movement. With the death of Stalin and the de-Stalinization drive carried on by a section of the Soviet Party, the prestige of the Soviet Party had reached its nadir while Mao's was at its zenith, thanks to his successful leadership of the Chinese revolution. The Chinese experience seemed more relevant to the developing countries. There was also no doubt that the Chinese Party was pro-actively trying to wrest the leadership of the world communist movement from the Soviet Party.

With the skirmishes on the sensitive India-China border and the Chinese Party realizing that sympathy for the Tibetan revolt was strong in India, Mao was clearly desperate to get the support of the Indian communists. To achieve this he was not relying on ideological propaganda alone. I am not aware of the methods being used to win the support of Party units in other states but in West Bengal its moves were quite obvious; *Swadhinata's* brand new rotary printing machine was just one of them. Indeed, till this time there was tremendous admiration in the Party in India as a whole for Mao and the Chinese Party that had been able to stage a successful revolution against such odds. They had not only to fight a civil war against the Kuomintang but also to defeat the Japanese army that had occupied large parts of China. The border clashes had surprised and pained the people but there was still hope of a peaceful resolution as the Party met for the Vijayawada Congress. There was a lull in the events between the Ladakh incursions of 1959, in which many Indian soldiers were killed, till the events in 1962, when the Chinese army marched into India.

As I look back on these events I realize how they were leading to a denouement almost like a Greek tragedy. The great October Revolution, which had inspired such hopes and expectations of the beginning of a new stage in the history of social evolution, was being betrayed. A generation, dazzled by the glamour of the American lifestyle, where the satisfaction of ever-increasing wants was the only goal, had forgotten the sacrifices and the sufferings of the people of Russia and the proclaimed goal of the Revolution to build a new civilisation, a more advanced society and men and women of a different mould.

TWENTY-NINE

The Chinese Attack

In October 1962, the nightmare became a reality as Chinese troops swooped down on India through Arunachal Pradesh and marched right up to Tezpur in Assam. Caught unawares and unprepared, the Indian army on the border was overwhelmed and had to retreat, preparing to take a stand in Tezpur. Then, as suddenly and unexpectedly as they had entered, the Chinese returned to the position they had occupied earlier. These few weeks shook India and changed the face of Indian politics; perhaps for ever.

Several million words have appeared in print, in books and newspaper articles, on the whole episode. Where exactly was and is the border between the two countries? Was Nehru right in asking the Indian army to throw the Chinese out? Is the McMahon Line valid? If it is, through which territories does it run? A host of such questions have been and are being discussed ad nauseam. The border question continues to be the subject of talks between the experts of the two countries! This narrative is more concerned over the effects of these events on India, on the communist movement in India and on me.

First, it struck a death blow to the whole concept of communist internationalism. Even if the Chinese communists were convinced that their stand on the border question was correct, was a full-scale army operation necessary to assert their right? Today the Chinese are eloquent on the need to settle all border issues, not only between India and China but between all countries through peaceful dialogue. Even if they felt that India was wrong in setting up posts on a disputed border, should their action not have been defensive rather than an all-out offensive? They had already taken action in Ladakh; it is not as if they were being pushed back.

More importantly, did they not think of the consequences of this on the Indian democratic movement and on the communist movement? Their action paved the way for the advance of the reactionary right wing forces in India and proved a major setback for the communist movement. The fillip given to the reactionary forces helped them to overcome their isolation and to gradually enter the mainstream of Indian politics.

Finally, it led to a split in the international communist movement. So far there had only been polemical exchanges between Chinese and Soviet parties.. Now it was no longer a matter of differences of opinion but a complete break in fraternal relations that was replaced by hostility. Later there were even armed clashes between the forces of the two countries on their borders. The logical consequence of this was a split in communist parties all over the world; a split that far from ending has only led to further splintering of the communist movement.

Initially, I was too stunned to believe the reports of the Chinese offensive. Once I realized that it was a major offensive, I knew what my stand should be. There was no hesitation: the attack had to be condemned as unwarranted and a violation of the norms that a country should follow towards another country with which it had the friendliest of relations. The action of the Chinese Party was a repudiation of all principles of international relations but the District Committee was split. Despite earlier differences in outlook, there had been agreement on the need for a peaceful resolution of the border conflict. Now one section not only refused to condemn the Chinese aggression; it was vociferously laying the blame on the Indian government.

Shortly after, a National Council meeting was held in Delhi. I had made it a point to attend all National Council meetings and was there for this as well. It turned out to be a historic one as it marked the beginning of the end of the united communist movement. Dange who had been elected chairman of the Indian Party after the death of Ajoy Ghosh, moved a one line resolution condemning the Chinese attack. The atmosphere was bitter. Instead of a principled discussion on the issue, a lot of time was taken up on charges against S. A. Dange who was accused of being a spy. It was alleged that the archives had revealed that he had signed a bond to secure his release. There was practically no discussion and there were calls for a vote. A majority, including myself, voted in favour of the resolution moved by Dange and a minority representing about a third of the members present voted against. The resolution was carried. The meeting dispersed with members of the two sides hurling epithets against each other.

The government was closely following the developments within the Party. It was aware of the sharp differences and the bitterness amounting to virtual hostility between the two factions and was quick to take advantage of the situation to further widen the division. The differences had percolated right down to the ranks and the factions made no attempt to hide them. Heated exchanges would take place not only within the Party units but on the streets, in work places, in school and college campuses. It was not difficult for the Intelligence wing to know which party member was on which side. It decided to strike.

Public anger had been roused against those who refused to condemn the Chinese and it was deliberately fanned by jingoistic elements. The government knew that arrests of those belonging to the Left faction would not evoke the same kind of protest that had been provoked when the government had arrested those who had led the popular movements of the 1950s. One night, well past midnight, the police knocked at the doors of our flat. It was not entirely unexpected. There were only two of us there. Bhupesh Gupta was in Delhi and, in any case, he was not identified with the Left faction. The only other member of our household, Dinesh Roy, had left our flat a few days earlier, anticipating the arrest. Earlier rounds of arrests in the 1950s had not spared any prominent leader. This time, too, we thought that there would be wholesale arrests of all in leading positions in the Party. The police had worked out a different strategy. They had decided to pick out members of the Left faction and to spare the others. The police hardly made any attempt to search. They only wanted to know where the other member of our household was. We told them that we were not aware of where he was. They left without taking us. They came back a number of times enquiring about him and on getting the same reply they left.

Leaders of the Left faction were picked up in large numbers. Of course the police were not always right in their guesses. For instance, Dr. Ghani who was definitely not with the Left, was also arrested but released shortly after when they understood they had made a mistake. The police knew that this would only exacerbate the bitterness between the two factions, especially as they took good care to spread the canard that the list of those belonging to the Left faction had been supplied by members of the 'Right' faction. I got to know much later that some of those arrested were even told my name as the person who had supplied the list of the Left members to them! This was the normal tactic of the police of which all party members should have been aware but the pity is that quite a few believed in the canard that was being spread. This Left and Right nomenclature was partly the coinage of the media but it was the Left faction that called the other 'rightists' and by default the other faction naturally came to be called the Left faction.

With Jyoti Bose, Promode Dasgupta and others under arrest, the remaining members of the Executive Committee of the Provincial Council met and elected Biswanath Mukherjee as acting Secretary of the PC and a sort of Secretariat was constituted with Bhowani Sen, Somnath Lahiri and myself as the other members. The events that followed ultimately prompted me to submit my resignation from the Party.

THIRTY

Severing Party Links

The arrest of practically all the leading members of the 'Left' group created a totally new situation. The Provincial Council Secretariat, the main driving force, the steering committee of the Party, as it were, had been virtually removed at one stroke by the police action. The main task of the Secretariat constituted by the remaining members of the Provincial Executive was to ensure that the Party continued its normal activities. Of these, *Swadhinata,* the party organ was the most visible and we felt that we had to ensure its survival. Of its staff, some had been picked up but there were enough to keep it going. The main problem was finance for this loss-making paper. With the arrests, even the little that earlier came in was not forthcoming.

Apart from the organizational and financial problems, the selective arrest of one section of the Party created a very awkward situation for those who had now assumed responsibility for running the Party. In West Bengal and in Calcutta the Party was completely divided on the issue of the Chinese attack. While the large-scale arrests of the leaders prevented those at the lower levels of the Party, who supported the line of the arrested leaders, from being very vocal, there was an attitude of non-cooperation with the new leadership.

Biswanath Mukherjee, the new Secretary had very little contact with the party organization in Calcutta. His base was in the (as it was now called) Midnapore district where he had built up a strong party structure. Somnath Lahiri was, of course, fully competent to run the party paper but was of little help with raising funds. Members and sympathizers who could and did contribute large amounts to the Party were all directly under the Provincial Council,

Snehangshu Acharya included. Their contributions had been going to the PC directly. The Calcutta District Council, of which I was the Secretary, depended entirely on small collections and the levy paid by those party members who were employed in offices or factories. This was barely enough to pay the wages of whole-timers directly under the Calcutta DC. I was the only one among the members of the newly-formed PC Secretariat who had some contact with those members and sympathizers who made major contributions to the PC. The onus for contacting them and raising funds to keep the Party organization and the paper running thus largely fell on me.

We kept *Swadhinata* running for some time against all odds when suddenly some people came with a court order one day for sealing the printing machine for failure to clear the loan taken for the purchase of the machine. This was the first time that we learnt that a loan had been taken to purchase the machine. As mentioned earlier, it was Biren Roy, then a Rajya Sabha member elected with the help of the Party, who was supposed to have given the loan.

Biswanath Mukherjee—for reasons of health or because he was just accustomed to doing so—worked mostly from his residence. He came to the party office for formal meetings. Members of his faction reported to him at his residence where they were given instructions on the basis of which they carried out their assignments. It was a kind of inner core within the main factional group that the media had christened the Rightist faction.

I was in an awkward situation. Contrary to what some newspaper reporters said, I had, till the actual Chinese attack, been politically aligned with the Left faction though I had been very critical of their organizational methods and had for this reason become their *bête noire*. Things changed dramatically after the Chinese attack. I just could not accept the proposition of some of our Left leaders that a communist country could not be guilty of aggression. An armed attack by the regular army of a country, entering deep into another's territory, could be nothing but an aggression, no matter what the provocation. If ideology had to be considered, the issue should have been resolved through dialogue and discussion. After all, the region where the skirmishes were taking place was uncharted territory and did not deserve the kind of response that came from China. The fact that China was supposed to be a communist country made the attack even more reprehensible since it should have taken into consideration the impact of their action on the communist and democratic movement in India.

The Chinese attack gave the jingoists and the fascistic elements in the country an upper hand. It took them some time to come to power but without doubt these events gave them a chance to malign not only the Left but even Left of Centre forces represented by Nehru and Krishna Menon. The damage done to the entire democratic movement was immense. As for the communist movement, the Chinese aggression was the last straw that led to a split. It brought about a new alignment within the Party. The refusal of the Left section to call a spade a spade and its blind faith in the infallibility of the Chinese Communist Party made it impossible for me and others who had till then been siding with the Left to support their stand.

Earlier the differences in the Party had been based on attitude towards the Congress with the 'Right' section calling for a National Front with the Congress and the Left opposing the idea and asking for consolidation of the Left forces. They did add that we should ally with the democratic forces apart from the Left but ruled out the possibility of alliance with the Congress. After the Chinese attack, the dividing line between the two sections of the Party was the attitude towards the attack: those who condemned the aggression and those who refused to call it aggression. A new alignment based on the new situation had arisen. The National Council meeting in Delhi where Dange's resolution condemning the Chinese attack on India was passed by a large majority made two things clear to me: that the Party was clearly headed for a split and that dogmatic beliefs rather than rationality had become the basis on which the policies were being framed and decisions taken.

My mind was already in a state of turmoil following the Khrushchev report on Stalin and his misdeeds. The explanation, that 'the cult of personality' was responsible for it all, did not and could not satisfy me. Surely there was something very seriously wrong with the organizational principles of a party that could allow a one-man dictatorship to arise and continue for three decades during which the dictator could physically eliminate almost all his colleagues. Reports, which there was no reason to disbelieve, indicated that the atmosphere created was such that even after the death of Stalin his colleagues were terrified of his corpse.

Khrushchev could speak out his mind only three years after Stalin's death. Till then, the world and the international communist movement had been kept completely in the dark about all that had happened. There was no smooth succession either with Lavrenti Beria shot as an imperialist spy and Georgy Malenkov, another trusted aide of Stalin, shunted off to run a generating station. How could rational beings swallow all that? The Calcutta District Committee did have a round of discussions where many of these questions were frankly raised but no conclusions were reached; individual members expressed their own understanding of the issues and there was a wide divergence of views.

Then as the de-Stalinization drive in the Soviet Union came to a halt with the ouster of Khrushchev—again in some sort of a coup—the Party in India was back to business trying to win elections and carrying on factional struggles. No attempt was made at the higher levels of the Party to understand the implications of the Soviet developments or draw lessons from them. The half-hearted attempt by some of us to start a discussion on the issue through an amendment to the party programme at the Amritsar Congress received cold and contemptuous treatment. Even the adopted amendment was quietly ignored and never incorporated in the programme that was finally published. The polemics between the Chinese and Soviet parties and the accusatory nature of the debate, knocked out the concept of proletarian internationalism. No one attempted to understand how such a phenomenon could take place. For one section, the Chinese Party was the new infallible leader. For the other the Soviet Party, having corrected some of the mistakes one of its leaders had made, continued to be the only leader of the world communist movement.

I had, as a 19-year-old young lad, full of idealism, decided to give up everything and dedicate myself wholeheartedly to the Party, believing that it was the only instrument that could bring about a better world. Deeply moved by the glowing tributes of objective and neutral observers (Sidney and Beatrice Webb, the Fabian socialists) that a new civilisation was arising in the Soviet Union, I dedicated myself to the task of building such a society in India too. From the day the Khrushchev report came into our hands, it became clear that it was indeed what he had stated and not something cooked up by the bourgeois press. I had begun to realize that the Soviet Union was not the harbinger of change, the citadel of a new civilisation that we had imagined. This was hardly the better world for which I had dedicated my life, undergoing such sufferings and sacrificing so much.

Even as this question was haunting me, it was not easy to make a break from the only life that I had lived ever since I came out of college. It was almost like thinking of suicide because that is how the break appeared to me then. So I kept debating with myself about the right course to take as the Party environment worsened. Following the Vijayawada Congress in 1961, there were two Party Centres, each with its own line and, it may be said, its own ideology. There were differences within the factions too and neither of them was totally homogeneous. In fact, it is hardly correct to say that the differences were ideological or even tactical. The clash of personalities and the ego factor had much to do with it. The elections to Parliament, the Assemblies and the municipal corporations meant many aspirants for party tickets and already the tussle for the party nomination was a regular feature before every election. All this lent weight to my growing sense of disquiet and the desire to quit.

The revolutionary spirit of the 1940s where members and leaders were prepared to make sacrifices, including the supreme one, had disappeared. This spirit was so much in evidence when I was arrested in March 1948, along with thousands of other party functionaries and even remote sympathizers. I had felt happy and proud to be going through the ordeals and travails of a revolutionary life. By the last quarter of 1962, the atmosphere was different even though the kind of corruption that seeped into the Party after 1977, when it came to power in West Bengal, had not become a part of party life. There were, however, enough indications that it was beginning to go downhill; with many of the features that we condemned in bourgeois parties. Even more galling was to find erstwhile comrades regarding one another as enemies. Manikuntala's book has described in moving words the anguish that she felt when she found that women comrades, who till the other day had worked together and fought shoulder to shoulder against the greatest odds including imprisonment and lathi charges and bullets, were hurling accusations against one another. My own feelings were not very different.

Things came to a head one evening in December 1962. A general body meeting of members of the Calcutta Party had been called at the Muslim Institute Hall. Dange, the Party's Chairman and Namboodiripad, the General Secretary (after the death of Ajoy Ghosh) were both to address it. Namboodiripad spoke first and was given a patient hearing. Dange then got up to speak but was shouted down. A large section of the Party members present had evidently come prepared and the decision had clearly been taken earlier. It was no spontaneous outburst because it started the moment he rose to speak and before he had uttered even one word. Many years earlier the Party had used similar tactics to disrupt the meeting organized by Dr Shyama Prasad Mookherjee against the Hindu Code Bill. Party members were asked to come well before the scheduled time of the meeting and take their positions in different areas of the hall. When Dr Mookerjee's supporters arrived, the hall was almost half full. It was only after Dr Mookerjee and the other speakers had taken their positions on the dais and were about to speak that the shouting started. The meeting was successfully disrupted and the organizers had to beat a hasty retreat through the back door. This was in retaliation against a similar technique used by the Hindu Sabha earlier to disrupt a party meeting. It was a measure of the estrangement between the two party factions that the tactic used against what was considered a right wing reactionary party was used to disrupt a meeting of party members called formally by the District Committee and to prevent a speaker who was till then the Chairman of the Party.

Any modicum of doubt in my mind that the Party was going to split was removed. Since the meeting had broken up in a pandemonium, I went back to the District Party office and found groups of members arguing, shouting even exchanging blows. My mind was made up: the time had come for me to quit. I also saw no future for a Party that could refuse to see the reality. I do not recall the date when this meeting took place; possibly it was sometime in the second half of December 1962. My resignation letter to the Secretary of the Provincial Committee was dated 21 January 1963. I have retained a copy of the letter that I reproduce in full. It was written at a moment of deep anguish and despair and when reading it today, 40 years and more since the day I wrote it, I feel again the agony I felt at that time.

TEXT OF THE RESIGNATION LETTER

To
The Secretary
Provincial Committee

Dear Comrade,
I am hereby resigning my membership of the Communist Party of India.

After having spent the major part of my life as a whole-time worker of the Party a few words are perhaps necessary.

Ever since a situation developed in which a neighbouring Communist country began to behave in a manner which weakens the democratic and progressive forces in the country and brings grist to the mill of the reactionaries, I have been considering whether the Communist Party in our country could have much of a role to play while this situation lasts.

It is encouraging, of course, to find that the majority of the Communist Parties in the world do not see eye to eye with the Communist Party of China on this and many other international issues and consider their views to be wrong and harmful, nevertheless there are no indications that the Chinese Party has seen its mistake or is inclined to correct itself. This has given rise to a number of fundamental questions and doubts in my mind.

In spite of these questions and doubts, I was continuing to work in the Party, hoping that, in course of time, through experience and as a result of the process of discussions now going on in the international communist movement, I would find the answers that I was seeking to my questions.

But if now I have decided to submit my resignation it is because of the inner Party situation that has developed in our Party, especially in West Bengal. There is now a virtual split in the Party and it is not difficult to see that the Party, crippled as it is in the peculiar situation facing the country, is likely to be completely paralysed for a considerable period of time as a result of the bitter internal strife that has started and is likely to grow in the days to come. This is a prospect at the very thought of which I feel repelled but I do not see any hope that it will be possible to avoid it or that it will be short-lived.

I remain as interested as ever in the cause of democracy, socialism and peace for which I had been working so long but I do not feel confident that by remaining in the Party I shall be able to further that cause.

Fraternally yours,

Jolly Mohan Kaul
Calcutta, 21st January 1963

After submitting the resignation I found that it was not being taken seriously either by my colleagues in the District Committee to whom I had given a copy of the letter or by the members of the Provincial Committee: Bhowani Sen, Somnath Lahiri, Biswanath Mukherjee and others. They thought it was some kind of an impulsive reaction to the events on the day of the general body meeting of Calcutta Party members. I saw that if I continue to stay in Calcutta the pressure on me would mount and my life would be made difficult. My mind was clear that I had taken the right decision and I was determined to stick to it. Under the circumstances I thought the best course for me would be to leave Calcutta and I left for Delhi, alone.

I had no idea as to what I was going to do. My instinct was to get away from Calcutta and since I had nowhere else to go I chose to take refuge with the family. I went to Victor first as he was closest to me and had himself been in the Party. He had not formally resigned but had just dropped out after his marriage to Sina and the birth of their twin sons. They were themselves not in very comfortable circumstances but both Sina and Victor had jobs. Sina had joined the Cottage Industries Emporium and Victor had joined a fan company, Kassels, with the help of Majorbhai, who was in a senior position in that company. Their salaries were meagre but they managed.

Even in Delhi I was under pressure as my leaving Calcutta and coming away to Delhi suddenly had been noted in the press. Different interpretations were being given. None of the reports referred to my resignation because the Party in Calcutta too thought that it was an impulsive decision, taken in a huff and that I would soon be persuaded to return. Naturally, they did not reveal to the press that I had submitted my resignation. Just about this time another member of the DC Secretariat, Biren Roy, visited Delhi and met me. He told me about the reports in the press, including one in a Bengali paper, suggesting that it was because I was disgusted with the 'rightists' that I had decided to distance myself from them and gone away to Delhi. By implication, it suggested that I was actually close to the

Left, that is the group that had opposed the resolution condemning China.

I realized that there were totally wrong interpretations of my act, that the party leaders in Calcutta were not making public my resignation letter and that I had to make my position clear to the public. So I put out a press statement to a Delhi *Statesman* reporter, who was known to me. I had seen a report published in the Delhi *Statesman* which had stated that I had come to Delhi to 'sulk in my tent'. I rang up the reporter and told him that I wanted to give a statement. He agreed to accept my statement dictated over telephone. The report published in the Delhi *Statesman* on 16 February 1963, gave almost the entire text of my statement:

> JOLLY KAUL RESIGNS FROM C.P.I
> (From our Special Correspondent)
>
> New Delhi Feb. 15. – Mr. Jolly M. Kaul, a member of the National Council of the Communist Party of India and Secretary of the Calcutta District Committee, has resigned from the party.
>
> Announcing his resignation, Mr Kaul in a press statement explains that for some time past, in fact ever since the revelations made at the 20th Congress of the CPSU came to light, he has been perturbed by certain questions and doubts about some of the theoretical and organizational postulates of the communist movement.
>
> Recently, Mr Kaul says, after the open and unabashed Chinese aggression against India with all its disastrous consequences for the socialist and democratic movement in India my doubts have been further strengthened. The philosophy of the inevitability of war and the callous disregard for human life that find their grossest expression in some of the preachings and practice of the Chinese communists can have the most serious effects on the whole of mankind.
>
> Although it is an encouraging fact that other healthier trends

are asserting themselves in the world communist movement, these do not to my mind go far enough and tend to compromise with the dogmatic trends which still remain quite powerful and are having their repercussions on the world communist movement including the CPI.

While I still remain interested in the future of socialism and democracy in India, my thinking has led me to submit my resignation from the CPI, which I sent some time towards the end of January last. (End of press report)

The *Hindusthan Standard* of Calcutta also published the statement almost in full with some additional comments of their own on the same date. The statement was given in some of the Bengali papers in Calcutta as well.

Shortly after I had come to Delhi, Bhowani Sen and Somnath Lahiri had come and met me. I cannot now recall whether this was before my press statement or after; probably a little before. They asked me to withdraw my resignation and return to Calcutta. Bhowani Sen said that if financial difficulties had induced me to resign, they could help me to solve my problems. We were, indeed, in dire financial straits. I have referred earlier to how it had become virtually impossible for Manikuntala and myself to survive on our meagre salaries. After the arrest of many Provincial Council Secretariat members, Sailen Dasgupta, in charge of the PC finances from whom my wife drew her salary, bluntly told me that it was not possible any longer to pay her salary as with the arrest of the leaders funds had dried up. Unlike me who, although a member of the PC and of the National Council, drew my salary from the District funds, she was a member of the PC, in charge of its women's unit and drew her salary from there. The curt refusal of the PC cashier to pay her salary was like a death blow as it meant that even the little that we had would no longer be forthcoming.

I told the two that although our financial problems were real they were not the main reason for my resignation and that I would not withdraw it. The two leaders were shocked but understood that my decision was irrevocable. Somnath Lahiri was angry and said to Bhowani Sen in my presence: 'Then we must denounce him and issue a public statement.' I had been prepared for this but even such a threat did not make me relent. Bhowani Sen who, unlike Somnath Lahiri, had not looked angry only rather sorry, quietly said '*Na, thaak* (No, let it be).'

Despite this incident both these leaders continued to maintain the best of relations with me. I met them occasionally and they were always warm and cordial towards me. Later, in the 1980s, Somnath Lahiri, who like me was a tenant at a government housing estate, worked closely with me to organize a movement that we were forced to launch against a proposal by the government to change our status. The proposal was to term us as 'licencees' instead of tenants who would have to renew the licence every year. This would have been disastrous for the tenants who would have been at the mercy of some bureaucrat in Writers' Buildings. It would have made our position absolutely insecure. Somnath Lahiri was unwell but maintained regular contact with me over the telephone and suggested the strategy to be followed to defeat the move.

Whether the proposal to turn the tenants into 'licencees' emanated from the Minister in Charge, Jatin Chakravarty, or the Secretary of the ministry, Murshed, an IAS officer, was not known. It appears that it was the latter. Since this was a major issue affecting a few thousand tenants of government housing estates all over Bengal, we launched a movement that drew all the tenants together; organizing a convention where even Congress MLAs were present. I had also reported the matter to Sunanda K. Datta-Ray, then editor of the *Statesman* and a good friend of ours. He prepared a news report and had cross-checked details with Murshed when he found that Murshed was hellbent on pushing this measure through the Assembly. I was then working as editor of *Capital* and had a press card for free entry to the Ministers' wing of the Writers' Buildings, the secretariat that housed most of the ministries.

I went right in and waited for the Chief Minister, Jyoti Bose. The moment he came up the lift and started walking towards his chamber, I went up to him and said I wanted to discuss an urgent matter with him. He invited me to come up to his room. Meanwhile, Krishnapada Ghosh, then the Labour Minister, also a tenant in our housing complex, had come into the room and I explained the position to Jyoti babu. I must mention here that when Manikuntala had applied to Dr. Roy for the flat, Jyoti babu, leader of the opposition then, had supported our effort and was familiar with the circumstances in which these housing estates had been set up.

The Chief Minister expressed surprise at the move and said that he would do what was necessary to help. Evidently it had not been brought up before the Cabinet at all, which strengthens my suspicion that this was a brainwave of Murshed. In any case, even though Murshed was still asserting to Sunanda that nothing would prevent the passage of the Bill in the Assembly, by the same afternoon the Bill was withdrawn. The Chief Minister had kept his word and it was from the *Statesman* that I learnt that the Bill had been withdrawn. The news story that Sunanda Datta-Ray had prepared was dropped.

To return to the story of my resignation, while I knew that I had taken the right decision I was also aware that I was taking a plunge into uncertain waters. At the age of 19, while I was still a university student, I quit everything, gave up studies and joined the revolutionary movement where normal life would not be possible. In a sense, my decision to resign was as drastic and as hazardous a step as the one I had taken some 25 years ago when I decided to join the Party, then illegal with many of its leaders in jail and others underground. Yet there was a vast difference in my feelings then from what I was experiencing now.

The teenager's trepidation and apprehension as he stood on the threshold of joining the communist movement was true but there was the countervailing feeling of excitement, a sense of adventure. I had overcome my fears and had plucked up the courage to embark on what I realized would be a hazardous yet glorious journey to build a new and better world. I knew that suffering, imprisonment and even death possibly awaited me but there was the feeling of elation that I would be creating history.

When I left the Party, I felt that my life was ending. I might manage to exist for some more years but it would be a living death without any goal, without any purpose, with just one aim, survival. A sense of defeat, of sorrow at a dream that lay shattered. I was, however, only 41 years of age and life did not end. I had many more interesting experiences and continued to learn many lessons from life. I found that one can keep on learning, keep on trying to make a contribution to the betterment of society till the very end; at least till one's faculties are still functioning. This intermission between the two acts in my life's drama provided me with the opportunity to reflect on the changing political perspective that had so influenced its denouement.

The war that started in 1939 brought about the first major change in the situation. The Soviet Union began to take up positions that could hardly be justified from the proletarian internationalism perspective: the attack on Finland, for instance. It was justified as a measure of self-defence against the mounting threat of fascism. Then there was the Soviet Pact with Hitler of which we were not aware at that time. This too could be, and I suppose was justified by the communists, as a piece of realpolitik. The Anglo-American imperialists wanted to turn Hitler against the Soviets, so Stalin turned him against the British and their allies. This did not work in the end because Hitler double-crossed Stalin and turned against the Soviets. All this perhaps makes sense if politics is considered from the narrow, nationalist point of view and the Machiavellian tactics are employed.

Although I did not see things as clearly then as I see now, I was clear about one thing. Our earlier stand on the Quit India Movement and our subsequent stand refusing to characterize the Chinese attack as aggression was absolutely wrong and isolated us from the masses of India. I realized that there was no future for the communist movement in India with this kind of a mind-set. What was being passed off as proletarian internationalism was nothing but subservience, in the one case, to the Soviets considered by us to be the citadel of the progressive forces of the world. In the other case, it was to the Chinese, who were now considered the true upholders of the communist cause and support to whom was considered more important than defence of our own country. By this time the Soviets had come to be regarded as revisionist or even as 'social imperialists'. The utter irrationality of the stand that was being taken by the Party left me with no alternative but to completely disassociate myself from it.

I was amused by the different interpretations being given to my resignation. I was aware that I was accused of being a revisionist and reformist; I learnt that some party members were convinced that I was acting as a police informer. Later, my wife came across a comment in Professor Hiren Mukherjee's book in Bengali, *Tori hote teer,* that it was the lure of a bourgeois life that prompted me to resign from the Party. My wife pointed it out to me for it had pained her tremendously. There was no question of a bourgeois life, for a few years after I left the Party both of us had to survive by living on the charity of my brothers, some of whom were not too well off themselves. We lived a far, far more austere life than many party leaders and struggled to make ends meet. It was this that shattered my wife's health to such an extent that much later, when I was able to afford better treatment for her, it was too late. Her end came sooner than it should have.

There was yet another story in circulation about why I had resigned: that I had been assaulted at the district office after the crucial general body meeting. Though there was a clash between the two factions at the district Party office, it was a relatively mild affair compared to the things taking place now. In any case, no one said or did anything to me. My only regret was that I had to stand by and see it all happen and that nothing that I could do or say at that stage would help. This strengthened my conviction that I had no role to play and that it would be best for me to sever my links with the Party.

Looking back on my years in the Party, I have no feeling of regret, no sense of years wasted, no anguish because of what might have been. Yes, I could have sat for the ICS and perhaps succeeded. The very thought appals me. No, I am glad that I saw life, saw the reality, helped to change things for the better in certain spheres. It is because of this that I was able to unshackle the chains of dogmatism, to keep an open mind and to move on to a better and deeper understanding of the reality.

In the late 30s and the early 40s of the twentieth century, the analysis of the world political scene being made in the books that I read at that time, R. P. Dutt's *India Today* and his *World Politics*, John Reed's *Ten Days That Shook the World* and Edgar Snow's *Red Star Over China*, Bernard Shaw's *Intelligent Women's Guide to Socialism* seemed to make more sense than books by other writers. Prior to 1942, there was also the communist literature I was able to get such as *The Proletarian Path* by Ajoy Ghosh. The lengthening shadow of fascism was at that time the most important phenomenon and the consistent stand of the communists against that naturally attracted all those who were imbued with some kind of idealism towards the Party.

THIRTY-ONE

The Struggle for Survival

Leaving the Party was a monumental move for a couple that had been engrossed with it for more than two decades. When I left the Party in January 1963, I earned a whole-timer's wage of Rs 60. Manikuntala got the same plus an extra allowance of Rs 25 and deposited the entire MLA's salary with the Party. We had zero reserves to fall back upon and now neither was getting any wage. I wanted to take up a job but the going was difficult for a plain graduate. Even a schoolteacher's job demanded a BEd or a BT degree and I had no technical qualification of any sort. There was also the legacy of my background as a trade union worker and a Communist Party functionary; a serious disqualification from the employer's perspective. Finding a job was more difficult than I had expected. Yet, the question of making both ends meet was the least of the problems that we were facing.

Our commitment had been total over the two decades and more and as we served the Party wholeheartedly, we had never visualized a future outside it. The trauma of quitting shattered both of us mentally. Manikuntala's agony was worse because, at least, I had my brothers to turn to. Even if not affluent, they could look after both of us for sometime till we found our feet. Manikuntala's relatives were all refugees and struggling for survival. Given these circumstances, I instinctively turned first to Victor, who as a whole-timer had experienced the horrors of the period of Left-Adventurism.

In 1953, Victor had married another communist worker, Sina Wasoodevv. They both worked for the Central Party organ of which Victor was for some time the editor and Sina the design artist. In

1954, after the birth of their twin sons, they found it impossible to continue as whole-timers and took up jobs, even though it meant starting at the bottom of the ladder on very meagre salaries. As mentioned earlier, Sina found work in the Cottage Industries Emporium while Victor found employment in a fan manufacturing company with the help of Majorbhai, who was in a senior position in that company. They were both in Delhi. I turned to Victor knowing that he would appreciate our plight and would not turn us away. I went alone to test the waters and, finding both Victor and Sina sympathetic and willing to help, I asked Manikuntala to join me. This she did a couple of months later. Fortunately, my other brothers, Lalitbhai and Majorbhai were also in Delhi and just as hospitable.

Having decided to park myself in Delhi for the time being—possibly, permanently—I started looking for a job. Journalism was apparently the only avenue open for me. Our friend Bhupesh Gupta, who was to play an important part in the events that unfolded post-resignation, was trying to help. Bhupesh Gupta was able to get me some offers from business houses that were financially good but the job profile made them unacceptable. I kept trying to find a niche in the field of journalism. The profession demanded no degree, my honours degree was good enough, but my lack of experience was a stumbling block. I also realized that an ability to write correct English was not enough; reporting for a newspaper or a news agency had its own rules and techniques.

Apart from my lack of experience as a reporter, my past as a communist activist made it virtually impossible for me to try to approach any newspaper or journal run on commercial lines by business houses. *Patriot* and *Link* claimed to be progressive papers and I tried my luck there with Aruna Asaf Ali, who knew me. I had been deputed by the Party to accompany her when she had come to West Bengal to campaign for its candidates in the 1957 general elections. While she received me cordially and was very sympathetic she did not want to appoint me on the editorial side; she would rather consider me for the business side: for collecting advertisements. Even this was said rather casually for even she must have realized that I would not be an effective space seller. Her suggestion may have been prompted by the need to stave off my request for an editorial job that she did not want to give me. I had no inclination to take up the job of a salesman for any product; I was temperamentally totally unsuited for such work.

I turned to Nikhil Chakravartty who proved to be my saviour. He and I had worked very closely in the 1940s. He had joined the Party in England and on returning to India had joined the History Department of Calcutta University as a teacher. He was among the guiding spirits behind the Youth Cultural Institute, which we started in 1940 when the Party was illegal. Between January and April 1963, I had started meeting people for jobs in Delhi and had contacted him too. He first tried to help me to get into *Patriot* or *Link* but, finding that they were not very receptive, he offered me a job in one of the organizations that he was running: the *India Press Agency* (IPA). This was a news agency that mainly supplied political news to newspapers and to some of the embassies, particularly the East European embassies. He also edited *Mainstream*, a weekly journal. Although the salary was small—Rs 300 a month—it was kind of a lifeline for me. I gratefully accepted his offer and started to contribute articles to some papers as well. Although payments in those days were small, I earned, on an average, an extra Rs 150 to Rs 200, apart from my IPA salary.

Of particular importance in my career then was *Seminar*, run by Romesh Thapar for whom I did regular book reviews and occasional articles. The payments were small but it was a prestigious journal and I valued being able to contribute to it. With Romesh's help, I also tried to become a regular contributor to the *Economic and Political Weekly*, though I did not get the position of a correspondent with the journal. The sample piece that I wrote for Sachin Choudhuri was not good enough and the editor returned it with a very kind note pointing out its shortcomings. Years later, the *EPW* did publish some of my pieces but, by then, I had realized how inadequate my initial piece was for a journal of *EPW*'s standing. It was this setback that strengthened my resolve to become an economic journalist and along with the experience that I later gathered working with Indian Oxygen, I was able to successfully take over as editor of *Capital*, in the 1980s.

It was disappointing to be let down by Aruna Asaf Ali but I learnt from my friend, O. P. Sangal (a former party member whom I had known), who was in a senior position in *Patriot*, that *Patriot* and *Link* were supported by the Soviets. Appointing anyone who had resigned from the Party and given a statement critical of the Soviet Party would be sacrilegious. Sangal and others were, however, good enough to assign a regular column to me, publishing my pieces under the byline, 'Our Correspondent'. This was another learning experience for me. The bourgeois press would not have me because I had been a communist. The Left pro-communist press would not take me because I had resigned from the Communist Party! I am however grateful to Sangal and also to Viswanath, editor of *Link* for the opportunity they gave me to work as a freelance columnist for *Patriot* and *Link*. I was assigned the task of doing a column for both papers on Pakistan which I was able to do after studying the Pakistan papers that were available in the Sapru House Library.

I would have been left stranded had not Nikhil Chakravartty decided to take me on. He was probably still a party member and could have played safe and refused to take me but he rose above such sectarian considerations. He had an independent mind as was revealed when he defied his Party and took a stand against the Emergency, even though the CPI supported Indira Gandhi's decision. He had remained with the CPI after the split and had not gone over to the CPI(M). It was this independence that added to his stature and until his death he remained the doyen of Indian journalists, a highly respected figure. *Mainstream*, now being run by his son, Sumit, is among the few journals of the independent Left.

Apart from my work for the IPA, I contributed to *Mainstream* as long as I was in Delhi. My articles were against the dogmatic trends in the communist movement; the complete lack of democracy; the absence of freedom for one to act or think for oneself, which were a part of the conditions of membership of the communist party. These ideas are commonly talked about even within the Left movement today but were absolutely heretical in those days. Yet *Mainstream* published them regularly.

Life continued in this vein in Delhi for a little less than two years, 1963 and 1964, working for IPA, contributing regularly to *Mainstream, Seminar* and occasionally to some other papers, including articles that I wrote for a paper started by Krishna Menon and a weekly column to the *Patriot* and *Link* on conditions in Pakistan. Of great help to me throughout this period in Delhi, were Balraj Mehta and O. P. Sabherwal of IPA, Sangal and Vishvanath, of the *Patriot* and *Link* group of papers, apart from Nikhil Chakravartty, from all of whom I received my first lessons in journalism. Life as a journalist provided interesting glimpses into many aspects of human psychology and of life in the political world.

While working for the IPA, the Gujarat government invited a group of journalists to visit the state to see its development projects and I was deputed by IPA to represent the organization. It was quite a memorable experience as I saw almost all the Gujarat districts and also made friends with some journalists. I have lost touch with most of them but have maintained regular contact with Sunanda Datta-Ray, who was then a reporter but later became the editor of the *Statesman*. My friendship with him has been a rewarding one and I hope that he has benefited from it too.

Meanwhile, in Delhi, I moved from Victor's place to Lalitbhai's in Motibagh, where I got to use his car occasionally. Had it not been for the combined hospitality of my brothers, it would not have been possible for us to make the transition from being party whole-timers. Despite the lack of money, we had a pleasant time. Manikuntala was a perfect housewife and we hosted many family get-togethers where her cooking was savoured by all. Nevertheless, moving from one brother's place to another's meant a nomadic life and we decided to live on our own. We hired the *barsati* (an attic, a terrace room meant to be a shelter from rain) from Mohammad Elias, my one-time jail mate, and at that time a CPI M.P, who was ready to oblige with the accommodation. After a few weeks there, we found the place unsuitable. We also talked to Bhupesh about shifting to his place but the arrangement would not suit us. Bhupesh wanted Manikuntala, in particular, to run the household but we felt that it would be too much for her, given her state of health. Bhupesh's place was like an open house; many casual visitors came and stayed for days. It was then that our thoughts turned to Calcutta again; even though it would mean going job-hunting again.

Calcutta would be more affordable and we knew doctors who would look after Manikuntala in her fast-deteriorating state of health for free. In Delhi we would have to pay through our nose. I would still need a job though. We had the Karaya Road flat, where the rent was low. I thought that I would be able to get a schoolteacher's job and somehow make both ends meet. Meanwhile, I would try to survive with the help of some freelance writing. Manikuntala went first to start her treatment and I followed. She stayed with her nephew and nieces in Fern Road as our flat had been given to Bhupesh Gupta's brother when we went to Delhi. This arrangement had become necessary as I was not in a position even to pay the meagre Rs 77 rent. Manikuntala had a difficult time at Fern Road because while her niece and nephew could just about manage to provide board and lodging they were in no position to arrange for her treatment. With doctors such as Dr. Narayan Roy, Dr. Ghani and Dr. Santi Neogi (Rajeswar Neogi's brother) continuing to be sympathetic to us, particularly to Manikuntala, her treatment did start but, as we realized much later, a correct diagnosis came when it was too late.

Any hopes of finding a job at South Point School, where I had worked for about six weeks on a leave vacancy, were soon shattered. The principal had then told me that he would be happy to have me back any time but when I returned towards the end of 1964, the situation in the school had changed. The group of teachers led by Uma, who had really built the school, had fallen out with the principal, Satikanta Guha, and had left. Sometime later, they started another school, Patha Bhavan, which continues to be one of the good schools in Calcutta. Satikanta Guha was polite but cold when I approached him, saying that with my background I should try some other vocation that could pay more. This was a polite way of rejecting me; not entirely surprising given my closeness to Uma and the group that had left.

Again it was Nikhil Chakravartty who provided a solution, allowing me to be an IPA correspondent—though they had one and did not really need an extra person—till I found something suitable. I gladly accepted this because he protected the salary that I had been drawing in Delhi. In Delhi, however, I had the support of the family and regular writing assignments from *Patriot* and *Link*. Calcutta was even more difficult because we had to pay the rent besides incurring the expenses on Manikuntala's treatment and on running the household. Nevertheless the stint as a journalist in Calcutta was interesting and another learning experience. In Delhi, I mainly did desk work, subbing; here I covered political events such as the Congress sessions, one of which was held in Durgapur. I stayed there in a tent put up for the journalists and sent despatches through press telegrams. I did a reasonably good job even without any great sources in the Congress that correspondents generally had to be able to get exclusive stories. I was also sent to Cuttack to cover a students' movement there. I interviewed the Orissa Chief Minister as well as the student leaders and sent despatches to Delhi, giving both sides of the story.

Even so, I was desperate for a regular job with a decent income. That I found only towards the end of 1967. For nearly three years after our return from Delhi in 1964, it was a struggle for survival on my IPA salary and some writing assignments. Manikuntala too had to take up a teaching job offered to her by our friend, Anjali Mukherjee, who though never a member of the Party was active in the women's movement. She ran a school for infants at her residence; not a high-faluting Montessori school, such as have mushroomed all over today, but a modest one. The salary that she could offer was very meagre but Manikuntala accepted it despite her ill health. She also took up some tutions that enabled us to pull through the crisis. I wish to gratefully acknowledge this gesture of the late Anjali Mukherjee. She and her husband, Bimal Mukherjee, were good friends, who introduced us to Santiniketan, where they had a beautiful house.

The secret to managing on such a small income was frugal living. We took no financial help from friends in Calcutta or relatives in Delhi even though they would have willingly helped. We did get free service from Dr. Ghani, Dr. Narayan Roy and Dr. Santi Neogi though. Rajeswar Neogi, a member of the Party—CPI after the split—continued to offer the free clinical services of his pathological laboratory and even supplied free medicines from his chemist shop, People's Pharmacy. Without this help, Manikuntala would probably have succumbed to her ailments even earlier than she did.

As the saying goes when the night is darkest the dawn is near. Help was at hand through the medium of another friend, who too had been in the Party and had left after his bitter experience in the Left-Adventurist period. Prasanta Sanyal, who had been instrumental in bringing me into the Party, was now fairly well placed as the public relations head of a British company (Indian Oxygen, part of the world-wide BOC). He had very innovative ideas about the practice of PR and was looking for someone who could help him with IOL's many publications. He asked me to write some pieces for his journals and paid me well. As he passed on more and more work to me, I was able to emerge from the crisis and raise my head above the water even though this was still only freelance work. I had not yet found a stable job.

Prasanta saw my desperation and began to think of solutions. This set in motion a chain of events. As head of his department, he could recommend to the management that there was need to recruit someone to look after the publications. On his own, he could only recommend someone for a clerical post in the department. The procedure for recruitment to management posts was different. He, therefore, proposed to the management that I be taken for the job and sent my biodata, only mentioning my journalistic experience. He had thought that the required approval from top management would only be a formality as there had never been any problem about his recommendations being accepted. The formal approval had to come from the head of personnel, a certain Mr Bonnerjee.

Mr Bonnerjee had, however, known that I had been an active worker of the Party and had been involved in the trade union movement. Instead of according his approval, he passed on Prasanta's recommendation to the managing director with a note of his own giving my past as a trade union leader and an activist of the Communist Party and strongly objecting to this proposal. The Managing Director, Amiya Kumar Sen, who was incidentally the first Indian to hold the post, summoned Prasanta and expressed his annoyance with him for having concealed my communist past. Prasanta was actually accused of trying to smuggle a communist into the organization. He realized what he was up against; the not unnatural prejudice of the personnel director and the MD against a former communist. He told me that there was nothing that he could do and that I should look for a job elsewhere. I was, of course, disappointed but not surprised. I knew that my past would continue to haunt me wherever I went and that I had to find a way of surviving despite this.

I started exploring other options since my freelance work was not yielding much and my finances were in an alarming state. I had left my studies in the university after completing one year of post-graduate studies and thought that it might be a good idea to try to get a Masters degree in English literature. It would be relatively easier for me than to take up any other subject. I would, of course, have to appear as a non-collegiate candidate. I could then try for a teaching job in a college. First I had to get hold of the details of my earlier records of the 1940 examination and I turned to my old college, St Xavier's. I had serious doubts as to whether the old records would be available after a lapse of a quarter of a century. In any case I decided to try. Some of the old teachers were still there. They recognized me and welcomed me cordially, agreeing that I should sit for the Master's examination. I met Fr. Schepers, my former history teacher, now the Prefect, and told him about my plans. I requested him to try to find out my old records so that I could apply to the university to appear as a private candidate. I had thought that he would need a considerable amount of time to hunt for records almost a quarter of a century old. But, even as I was talking with him, he had been moving one of his hands along some files on the rack beside him. In a flash he fished out the 1940 file and, lo and behold, all the details pertaining to the examination that I had appeared in were before me. This was a remarkable exhibition of the efficiency and the filing system of the Jesuit teachers of the college. So I set to work preparing for the examination that was only a few months away.

Meanwhile the struggle to make both ends meet continued. The prospect of getting a Master's degree and with its help a teacher's job was still a long way off and search for work that could bring immediate returns continued. I had friends in Clarion Advertising, who knew of my problem and were on the look out for something that would take care of my needs. Subroto Sengupta, my old school and party mate, who left along with many others in 1951-1952, was the chief executive of Clarion. He told me that a large company was celebrating its fiftieth anniversary and would need a lot of articles to be written and even some booklets prepared. Clarion would need the help of freelancers and pay much better than newspapers did. Taking up this work would, however, mean that I would have to give up the idea of appearing for the examination, which was due in a couple of months. I decided that a bird in hand was worth two in the bush and opted for the Clarion proposal.

After Prasanta's effort to get me an assistant's job in IOL failed, I had, more or less resigned myself to the prospect of continuing to eke out an existence by doing freelance work with newspapers or advertising agencies. Nevertheless, the thought that I would never have a secure job and would always lead a hand-to-mouth existence was daunting. Just when I had given up all hope, there was a dramatic turn in the situation. This time, Bhupesh Gupta turned up trumps. Bhupesh who continued to be sympathetic and helpful even after I had quit the Party, would come and stay with us at Karaya Road.

He heard from us the whole story of the fiasco about my nearly landing the IOL job, thanks to Prasanta, and losing it because some top people in the company had refused to accept that a one-time communist revolutionary could be trusted to work as a regular employee of a British company. We were actually letting out steam and not expecting Bhupesh to help. Help he did and how!

Bhupesh Gupta was a member of the Rajya Sabha and along with him in the Rajya Sabha was N. Dandekar, representing the Swatantra Party. Although a communist, Bhupesh was respected by all parties as a man of integrity: a quality becoming rare among politicians. He was one of the most active and effective members of Parliament. So was Dandekar, an active and serious member of the Rajya Sabha. The two, although on opposite ends of the political spectrum, were not just on talking terms with each other but were friends. Dandekar happened to be the Chairman of the Indian Oxygen board at that time. Evidently, Bhupesh told him about how the company had rejected me for no other reason but my communist past even though I was no longer in the movement and was eminently suited for the job. Dandekar took a serious view of this and discussed the matter with the managing director, Amiya Sen. What transpired at the meeting between A. K. Sen and Dandekar, we did not get to know but some time after this Prasanta was summoned by Mr Sen and asked to continue to give me work on a freelance basis. He was told that they were reviewing the situation. They wanted to try me out and see whether I really measured up to the description that Prasanta had given of me. They evidently had no complaints with the first major responsibility that they gave me: a writing assignment on a technical subject pertaining to the industry.

Meanwhile, Prasanta submitted his resignation, something that he had planned to do, as he had accepted a job to work as the London correspondent of the *Times of India*. By this time the company had got an idea of what I could do and I was immediately asked to join in Prasanta's position as head of the department of public relations, although at a lower salary. That marked the beginning of a new stage in my life's journey.

THIRTY-TWO

The Corporate World

My fears that my efforts to contribute to improving the rather sorry state of affairs in the world had ended in failure with my resignation from the Communist Party were unfounded. It was my stint in the corporate world that showed me that no matter where one is, one can find avenues of making a contribution, however modest, towards making the world a better place. Today, I can say that my education would have been incomplete without the corporate world experience. Thanks to the nearly fifteen years that I spent in Indian Oxygen Limited/BOC, I gained an understanding of the way companies work, the problems they face and the strategies they adopt. I also understood a little better how human beings behave in environments very different from the ones I had been familiar with. Of course, I had to understand different environments myself; particularly the business environment.

My disappointment over the article rejected by the *Economic and Political Weekly* had stayed with me. Only after entering the corporate world did I realize that what I had done was to try to fit business policies into a Marxist straitjacket and, in doing so, had used a lot of Marxist jargon but not made any meaningful comments on the subject I was writing on. The work assigned to me in Indian Oxygen involved scanning the media for news items that could have an impact on the company, favourable or unfavourable. In doing so, I was able to see how certain decisions of the government created difficulties for companies such as IOL while others helped. This was between 1967 November, when I joined IOL, and December 1981, when I retired.

This was also the period when the Central government under Indira Gandhi took a Left turn. Foreign companies were pressurized to reduce their foreign holding to below 40 per cent. The forced divesting of foreign holdings in Indian operations to lower than 40 per cent meant that a lot of blue chip equity was available in the Indian stock market marking the emergence of the equity cult even among the middle class. There was a lot of good scrip for investing in.

There was also the question of government clearance for expansion by companies in areas where they had 30 per cent or more of the market share. Even in other areas, licences to expand were not easily given to foreign companies as the emphasis was on import substitution rather than on export promotion. One could easily see that these policies were adversely affecting the company. Even though proposals for new projects were not within my sphere of operation, I was interested in the developments in this vertical. With growth in its core businesses effectively choked as a result of the restrictions, IOL was desperately looking for projects in other areas to expand. Its UK-based parent, BOC, had proposed a project that eminently suited the criteria laid down by the government for expansion in new areas. It was export-oriented, linked to an agricultural product that would have helped the farmers and, although not really labour-intensive, would have provided at least a few hundred jobs. It took nearly two years to prepare the project. Then negotiations with the government went on for over a year. When everything seemed to have been finalized, there arose another hitch and some fresh objections were raised by one of the bureaucrats. Market conditions changed meanwhile and the proposal was finally withdrawn.

In the light of developments that took place in the 1990s, I can see how the logic of capitalist development inevitably leads to the market economy and the kind of liberalization that has come about. One cannot build socialism within the framework of a capitalist structure and while I will discuss this in detail, it is enough to state here that my stint in the corporate world helped me to understand the way the economy works in the present environment. Noting my interest in studying the economic environment, the company also gave me the responsibility of setting up the economics department of the company and looking after it.

Since the top management of IOL was active in the Bengal Chamber of Commerce and in the Indian Engineering Association, which evolved into the CII, I was able to interact with important business leaders of the time. I had achieved an understanding of business concerns, which enabled me to function effectively as the editor of *Capital* after my retirement from IOL. I had also achieved a certain command over the art of public relations, then in its infancy in the country. Paradoxical though it may sound, my background in the communist movement and my acquaintance with Marxist theory contributed considerably to the success that I achieved both in developing the discipline of public relations in India and in making progress as a management executive in the company.

Although the compulsions of sheer survival led me to look for a job in the corporate world and I found myself in a multinational company, my outlook had not changed. My resignation letter had stated clearly that I was still interested in the future of socialism and democracy in India and that I was leaving the Party because I felt that it was following the wrong road altogether. Thus, even when working for the corporate world, I was trying to see to what extent it was possible to broaden the outlook of the company that I was working for and to make them appreciate that profits could not be the sole raison d'être of the existence of a company.

Studying the works of the pioneers of public relations in the United States such as Edward Bernays, I realized that they too had tried to give a new direction to corporate policies at a time business was under attack after the Great Depression of the 1929-1933 period. They had talked of the concept of the *Social Responsibility of Business* and were taking that concept forward to its logical conclusion. Some public relations practitioners had even in the United States and Europe persuaded their companies to take up projects that were in the public interest even if they had no direct bearing on the business of the company.

This enabled me to give public relations in IOL a direction that the pioneers of the profession in the USA had advocated and which, I felt, was eminently suited to the situation that the corporate world was facing in India in the 1950s and 1960s. Keeping this concept in mind, I was able to persuade my Managing Director, Amiya Sen, and later Keith Hartley, who succeeded him, to sponsor several programmes that created something of a sensation in corporate circles at that time. We started bringing out a *Statistical Outline of India;* we published a selection of the speeches of Martin Luther King Jr after his assassination. We adopted a fairly extensive programme on the occasion of the Gandhi Centenary. This included some village development projects and sponsorship of a folk song troupe led by the well-known Nirmalendu Choudhury to the Gandhi Centenary exhibition held in Delhi in 1969.

Later, on the completion of twenty-five years of Indian Independence, we brought out a book giving the history of this period. I was impressed by Keith Hartley's complete approval of the project. He read and cleared the entire manuscript despite its inevitable criticism of the British rule in India. In addition, we brought out a quarterly journal—*The Changing Scene*—which was a review of the economic and political developments during the quarter. The journal was aimed at journalists and parliamentarians and I was glad to find that some members of Parliament and journalists found it useful for their work.

Another very significant IOL's PR initiative was a fairly large book titled *West Bengal: An Analytical Study*. This was part of the PR exercise for Amiya K. Sen, when he took over as the President of the Bengal Chamber of Commerce and Industry in 1970. It was a significant publication and made a contribution to the planning for the rejuvenation of West Bengal that was just beginning. Ajit Roy had made a major contribution to all these publications with his remarkable capacity of presenting fact-based material. He could even point out management shortcomings while making the publication acceptable to top managements in the corporate world. Ajit Roy, who had been with the Indian Statistical Institute, had a good understanding of both Marxist economics and the classical economics that was the basis of the prevailing business environment.

When we were working on *West Bengal: An Analytical Study*, which was to be published by the Bengal Chamber, I had to interact with the secretary of the Chamber, then an Englishman, Mr Paris. He was rather sceptical of the whole project, though he could not reject something sponsored by the chamber President. A. K. Sen had complete confidence in me and told Paris that he could take a look at the manuscript before it was sent for publication. Paris went through the manuscript very carefully and was effusive in his praise. He had never expected that we would be able to prepare such an excellent analytical study.

Even after A. K. Sen's term in the Bengal Chamber ended I continued to maintain contact with the Chamber top brass. Madan Ghosh took over as the secretary and became not only a personal friend but also a very firm supporter of the kind of PR that I was advocating. The Bengal Chamber was at that time representative of the professionally managed companies; multinationals then were being run in India by professional managers, many of whom I met. Some were not only good managers but were also good human beings. The names of T.D. Sinha of Indian Aluminium and Mudalier of ICI come to mind. There was, of course Bhasker Mitter, who had been in school with me and who had, I was told, had been close to the group of Indian students in the UK, Jyoti Bose, Mohan Kumaramangalam, Krishnan and Snehangshu Acharya, among others. Some were either members of or sympathizers of the British Communist Party (CPGB).

Within IOL, I came into close contact with both the middle and top management. Amiya Sen was not only a very successful managing director but a Brahmo of the old school, upright and honest to a fault. He was so punctilious that when returning home, if the office car in which he was travelling had to make a slight detour to meet a personal friend or relative on the way, he would ask the driver to note down the mileage covered in the detour and make sure that it was charged to his personal account.

There was also Dr. Sasadhar Chakravarty who had joined as company secretary but retired as the deputy managing director. He and his wife, Eileen, were both shining examples of integrity and right conduct. They both became personal friends and our relations with them continued even after both of us retired. Eileen had belonged to the Quaker fraternity and both of them radiated peace and goodwill. He was only about a year older than I was but died a few years ago and his wife went back to England. They had no children. She still writes to Kamal Sanyal (Prasanta Sanyal's wife) from England and says that she misses India and feels lonely even though she is living close to her sister's family. I met her on her recent visit to India and learnt that she is involved in social work in England.

This realization that a capitalist is not necessarily a crook and a worker is not necessarily a proletarian hero came to me during the course of these experiences. I have had the unique opportunity of acquiring first hand experience of the working people, their qualities, their problems, their weaknesses and their strengths and again working with people who are on the other side of the fence, the managers and captains of industry. My understanding and knowledge of the plus and minus points of the class of people that we would lump together as capitalist was further deepened when I worked as editor of *Capital.* It is because of the experience I had in the trade union movement and later in the corporate world that I was able to appreciate Gandhiji's thoughts on the subject.

Experience of another sort I acquired during the course of my work in and for the Public Relations Society of India. When I took up the job in Indian Oxygen I had very little idea of what PR was about. I had worked on a free lance basis in the PR department while Prasanta was there. This had, of course, helped me to see the work being done in the department. I had also realized that this was a new field in India on which very little literature was available, unlike advertising, which had been around for a few decades and had an even longer history in Europe and the United States. Circumstances propelled me to take over the responsibility of PR in a company, which really needed PR at that time.

The government's leftist stance meant that the Monopolies and Restrictive Practices Commission was imposing all kinds of restrictions on increasing market share. For a company like Indian Oxygen, which had a fairly large share of the market, the going was quite tough. My political background helped me to size up the situation fairly early, but I was not aware of the strategies that needed to be adopted to counter it. I started looking at the books on the subject but they were all written by British or American writers and were meant for the kind of environment that prevailed in those countries.

Apart from trying to work out how the PR practices that were described in those books could be applied to Indian conditions, I thought it was necessary to exchange notes with PR practitioners in Calcutta, working in other companies. I looked around to see if there existed any professional body that could help me to meet and interact with other PR people. I found that some attempt had been made and a PR Circle had been set up but it was not very active. I got busy on the job of building an organization that would enable me to interact with fellow professionals. Fortunately, an All India Public Relations Conference was being organized in Delhi, and I began to participate in the preparations. Meanwhile, I began contacting those who had been active in the PR Circle. Among them were Dulu (Surya Sengupta), Shankar Mitra, Mahesh Varma, Bhababuti Roy and others whom I cannot readily recall.

The first All India PR Conference was to be held in Delhi in April 1968, shortly after I joined IOL. I was keen to participate and was encouraged to do so by both A. K. Sen and Keith Hartley. At this conference I met PR practitioners working for companies in other parts of India but particularly those in Bombay where the Public Relations Society of India (PRSI) was first formed. It was from this conference that my involvement with the PRSI started. In fact, at this conference itself I was on the committee along with

Harish Raja and Anand Akerkar, who had studied Public Relations in USA, to revise the Constitution of the PRSI. Within a few years I had become Chairman of the Calcutta Chapter and in little over ten years after this conference I was elected President of the all India body.

Earlier in 1976 my book *Public Relations in India* was published. It was the first comprehensive book on PR suited for the Indian environment and it was and perhaps still is being prescribed as one of the textbooks for students of PR, journalism and communication in several institutions. Apart from other benefits that I derived from this activity, I was able to form friendships that have stood me in good stead over the years. Radha Prasad Gupta and his wife Moni, Dulu Sengupta and his wife Kajal, Jayanta Chatterjee and his wife Mallika, Adity Shyam (now Dua), Shanker Mitra, Sanat Lahiri and his wife Sheila, Tapan Sinha of Hindustan Motors and his wife, Bhababuti Roy, Anjali Sen, Rita and Kishore Bhimani, Rita's parents, P. N. Mukherjee and Tajudi, Rusi and Zarin Gimi are some of the names that occur to me right now. Unfortunately, some of them are no more; others, I meet occasionally. I lost touch with the many more that I met outside Calcutta once I left the profession. My PR work field involved meeting journalists and I got to know some all over India and many in Calcutta. Alas, many of them too are no more.

As head of Indian Oxygen's PR, I visited different parts of the country and went abroad many times. Within the country, I needed to visit all the branches, from Ahmedabad to Bangalore. As an active functionary of the PRSI, I was also able to visit the different states where we had chapters or where our annual conferences were held. I joined IOL in November 1967 and got an invitation to visit the British headquarters of the company in 1975. I had not gone abroad earlier—not even as a senior functionary of the Communist Party—and I was fairly excited over the prospect.

Strangely, I had not been to Moscow or any of the East European countries even though after the mid-1950s, when relations with the Soviet Union had become quite cordial and not only the top leaders but hundreds of party members and even sympathizers were visiting the Soviet Union and the East European countries. Organizations such as the Friends of the Soviet Union or FSU (later Indo-Soviet Cultural Relations/ISCUS), All India Peace Council, our youth and student organizations, our women's organizations were all sending delegations to the Soviet Union or to the East European countries and also to China.

I too was invited on more than one occasion to attend seminars and once even to attend a conference of the Communist Party of the Soviet Union as a delegate from the Party in India. Surprisingly, even though I applied for a passport each time there was no response from the government and since each time the application was for a specific event, when the date of that event had passed the application just lapsed. I was quite mystified by this. Was I an even more dangerous communist than any of the top leaders of the Party in the politbureau or the Central Secretariat, I kept asking myself. It was not that my application was not pursued. Bhupesh Gupta, who was a Rajya Sabha member and highly respected in government circles, did try to follow up with the passport office and even with the External Affairs Ministry. Every time there was just complete silence. There was no refusal as such because if they had done so they would have to give some reason that they evidently did not wish to. The file was being quietly buried every time.

Given this background, I was a little apprehensive when I received the invitation from BOC to visit their headquarters, an invitation obviously prompted by the IOL management. Having crossed all the hurdles in the way and now working as an executive in a multinational company, I did not really anticipate much difficulty. To play safe, I applied well before the date of my departure and to prevent any bureaucratic obstruction I got my application endorsed by the Commissioner of Police, Ranjit Gupta, a contemporary in our university days. Even so there was no response from the Passport office and I was worried. I met the Regional Passport Officer who told me that my file had been sent to Delhi. This seemed quite ominous and I decided that I must find someone who could make enquiries on my behalf in Delhi. Fortunately a friend, Dilip Mukherjee, who had been close to the Party at one time and was now a senior journalist and who had access to the top bureaucrats in the External Affairs Ministry, agreed to make the enquiries and follow up the application. He was finally able to persuade the ministry to instruct the Passport Officer to issue the passport. It arrived only a few days before my date of departure. It would have been disastrous if it had not been issued.

I was naturally keen to know what had held it up so long. It may sound ridiculous but apparently some remarks, patently absurd and totally false, had been noted on the file concerning me. Although I had had earlier experience of how the IB deliberately told lies and sent up false reports to spite someone who might have created problems for them, I thought this was the limit. I realized that my not having gone to Moscow and other countries in East Europe within the Soviet orbit proved good for me in the end. Had I been a regular visitor to the Soviet Union and the other East European countries, I might have been thoroughly spoilt under their influence as some of our other party comrades had been. I know of a few cases where regular visits proved a corrupting influence that changed the personality and the character of the comrades.

To continue with the main story, I visited several countries while working for IOL. The first was in 1975 when BOC invited me to its Hammersmith House headquarters. It was during this visit that I met Alan Eden Green, head of their PR. I found in him a kindred soul who had been connected with the socialist movement in his youth. He was one of the finest human beings I have met. I do not know if he still alive; he was much older than I and would be in his nineties if he is. It was during this visit that I got an opportunity to visit Nairobi, capital of Kenya in Africa where an IPRA meeting was being held. Alan was also attending this meeting and it was thanks to him that I got an opportunity to visit the Tsavo National Park and spend a night at one of the forest lodges. From the balcony of that lodge I had a ring-side view of animals that kept coming to the water hole that was just a few yards away. One of my most unforgettable experiences was what I saw that night from the balcony. The behaviour of the two elephant families that visited the watering hole helped me to appreciate how close certain animals are to human beings in their emotions and behaviour. I wrote about this in one of the souvenirs of the Calcutta Club when I was asked to contribute a piece.

There were many principles that the pioneers of public relations in the United States had emphasized. Major developments in the field of PR took place in the USA during and after the Great Depression that began in the late 1920s and continued till the mid-1930s. The image of business had taken a beating because of the unethical practices of many business barons. Writers like Upton Sinclair had exposed many such companies in his books and public indignation was high. With thousands of people turning paupers overnight, socialist ideas were gaining ground. It was in this background that the concept of Social Responsibility of Business evolved. It meant that business should not think only of profits; it had to give back to society what it had acquired from it by way of an environment in which it was possible for business to grow and prosper. Taking note also of the damage done to PR by tricksters and cheats who called themselves PR practitioners, the pioneers of public relations also attached much weight to ethics and many of the definitions of public relations clearly stated that PR should be based on truth and on facts. To introduce some order and discipline in the field of public relations, the International Public Relations Association had drawn up a code of ethics adherence to which was compulsory for those desirous of becoming members of that body.

PR in India was still in a formative stage when I joined and those of us who played a role in establishing the profession on a sound footing tried their best to ensure that ethical standards were adhered to. We also laid great stress on training and standardization of curricula for training programmes. The first courses were run in make shift halls and hotel rooms. Since then considerable advances have taken place and many institutions such as the Bharatiya Vidya

Bhavan, the Institute of Mass Communication in Delhi, St. Xavier's in Bombay and many others have established diploma and even degree courses in PR and a number of books have been published in India. Earlier, we had to rely on American and British publications. Several books have followed my pioneering venture. My book went into three editions and a fourth is under preparation, though I am not sure that it will see the light of day before my departure from the world.

Apart from writing the book on public relations, I was fortunate enough to get an opportunity to teach in some of the institutes running PR courses. Among these was the Bhavan's Institute of Communication and Management, which was one of the earliest to offer such a course. I was associated as a teacher for many years both in the Salt Lake and later at its Bhowanipore branch. I also taught at the Indian Institute of Modern Management for some time and was once invited to deliver lectures at the Indian Institute of Management, Joka.

Journalism had, however, been my preferred vocation and an opportunity to re-enter that field presented itself when I got an offer to take over as the editor of *Capital*, a prestigious economic journal, after my retirement. I received this interesting offer even before I retired from IOL. Started by the British managing agency houses, *Capital* represented their interests and was, till Independence, virtually the economic think tank of the British government in India. After the British left and the managing agency houses changed hands or closed down, the journal was in the doldrums. It was put up for sale but found no takers from among the established newspapers. Finally, Praful Goradia, the erstwhile marketing director of Duncan's, a G. P. Goenka group company, now doing independent business, was able to buy it. I ended up becoming its editor after retiring from IOL. It was like going back to the first love of my working life; back to journalism.

THIRTY-THREE

Back to Journalism

The circumstances in which the offer of editorship was made to me need recounting. A friend from my rowing days in college and the university, Manish Sarkar, had retired as advertising manager of *Deccan Herald* and was looking for some post-retirement work in the same line. He met me and said that *Capital* needed someone to handle its space selling and requested me to put in a word to Bidyut Sarkar, the editor, which I did. Bidyut had once been with the *Times of India* and was the first editor of *Capital* after Praful Goradia took it over. Manish became the advertising manager of *Capital* and, subsequently, its general manager.

I had renewed my friendship with Manish when I had started rowing after joining IOL and become a member of Lake Club, in which Manish, a champion oarsman, was actively involved. When I was due to retire, he introduced me to the proprietor of *Capital*. I was not aware then that this introduction was intended to give Goradia an opportunity to check me out for a future editorship of *Capital*. He had probably interviewed others, who had either turned him down or had not been found suitable. Shortly after I had met him, Manish came to me with a formal offer to join *Capital* after I retired. He said that Goradia was willing to wait.

The terms were not too attractive but since I would be getting my retirement benefits along with a small pension, I accepted the offer because it helped me to return to a field that I had been very keen on. *Capital*, a business journal, would not give me the same opportunities as a news agency would but I welcomed it because I was confident that of being able to live up to the challenge of being an economic journalist. I still had to address that rankling sense of rejection from Sachin Chaudhuri. I think I did succeed and some editorials and articles that I wrote for *Capital* would have passed muster in any economic journal in the country.

The roughly five-year stint with *Capital* was another interesting phase and even when I had formally opted out from its editorship, I virtually did all that I had been doing earlier. It was during this period that I got to know Aditi Roy Ghatak, Indrani Kar, Tirtha Roy, Sankar Ray, Aditi's friend Jhumu, and much later, even younger friends such as Suman Layak and Sukanti Ghosh and also Radha Prasad and Moni Gupta's daughters, Gargi and Uttara, with whom I am still in contact and whom I count as close friends. Aditi, in particular, has been very close and today even my relatives count her as one of the family.

Even though I had met top leaders of industry while in IOL, it was during my *Capital* days that I met almost everyone who mattered in West Bengal. We tried to carry out an informal readership survey with captains of industry with a view to making improvements in *Capital*. I had framed several questions and talked to quite a few managers, some of them middle-ranking managers but some in fairly senior positions as managing directors and chairmen of companies. Few went in for serious reading and there were virtually no worthwhile suggestions as to what the content of business journals such as ours should be. I suppose they relied on consultants and think tanks to advise them. Nor did companies undertake original research; not even to update their own technology, which is why they had to go in for foreign collaboration or for foreign equity participation to be spoon-fed for product development and for marketing. The picture has changed after the onset of globalization and many Indian companies are doing research and even acquiring major foreign companies. At that time, there were virtually no worthwhile suggestions as to what the content of business journals such as ours should be. One fairly senior manager jokingly said 'pornography'. This was just a joke but he did not make any other suggestion at all!

At *Capital* too, our whole team realized that the proprietor was not prepared to put in any serious investment to make our magazine competitive with the emerging business glossies. He either did not have faith in the future of the magazine or in the team that was running it; possibly both. He closed down the magazine just when it was beginning to almost break even, in its ninety-ninth year of publication. We had two persons in our team with outstanding talent—Aditi Roy Ghatak and Indrani Kar—both of whom made good and rose to fairly high positions.

There was one experience that made a deep impression on me. Since *Capital* had once been the only economic journal greatly relied upon by the expatriate business community, it was entrusted with the task of preparing the cost of living index for white collar workers. On the basis of the figures that it provided to the Bengal Chamber of Commerce and Industry, the dearness allowance was calculated and paid out to the clerical staff of the various BCCI-affiliated companies. When I took over as the editor, I looked into the file on this subject and found a lot of correspondence between earlier editors of the journal and the Bengal Chamber. The basket on the basis of which the index was drawn up had been prepared some fifty or sixty years earlier. The formula for preparing the index was also not very clear. Earlier editors, including the British editors, such as Tyson, had been pressing for a fresh survey, a revised basket and a revised formula for determining the index. The BCCI turned it down fearing that such revision would mean a further rise in the index for paying enhanced dearness allowance that the BCCI members were in no mood to pay.

It was clear to me that the *Capital*'s cost of living index needed to be updated and I wrote a strong letter to the BCCI secretary, repeating what some of my predecessors had said. I suggested updating the basis of the calculation with a fresh survey. While not formally disagreeing with our contention, the chamber wanted the status quo and the exercise of preparing the Index on the earlier basis continued. Meanwhile, the trade unions of the organizations concerned felt that the index did not fully reflect the increase in the cost of living index and started an agitation on this issue.

One day, a group of employees staged a demonstration in front of the building where *Capital* was located and started shouting slogans. I again contacted the Bengal Chamber and told the secretary that a decision on a fresh survey needed to be taken on an urgent basis but there was still no response. A few days later, another demonstration was staged right in front of our office; it was a virtual gherao and slogans were shouted denouncing *Capital* for its 'index'. They alleged that the index was depriving thousands of employees of their just dues. I went up to those who were demonstrating and asked them to come and talk to us rather than *gherao* the organization.

When they came in I asked them what they wanted. They said that they wanted to know the basket of commodities on the basis of which the index was being prepared. We had no difficulty in giving this information because the basket, even though somewhat out of date, covered 90 per cent of the essential requirements of the employees. We also used the latest price quotations from the market by deputing someone to get the actual prices from the retailers. I supplied them with the information and they went away shouting that they had won a great victory. The result of all this and our own pressure on the chamber was that shortly after this the government and the chamber decided to shift to the Cost of Living Index being prepared by the Simla bureau of the government. My impression is that the employees actually lost out on this as the *Capital* index had been more favourable to the employees. My colleagues and I welcomed the decision as this matter was becoming a source of embarrassment for the journal and for me personally. I did not want to be seen as someone who was depriving employees of their dues even though that was not the case.

I continued with *Capital* for some more time but as editorial consultant. I opted for the change because, for one, I was not happy with the setup there, particularly the way the proprietor was trying to run the journal. More importantly, Manikuntala's health was deteriorating. She needed constant attention and leaving her in the care of nurses or ayahs was not enough. I informed the management that I would not be able to keep regular hours but could do some work at home. I continued to write the editorials and some columns such as the 'Ditcher's Diary'. Others also contributed to that Diary, which maintained the fairly high standards that earlier editors had set for it.

Yet another experience gave me a foretaste of things to come in the business world. My name had been suggested to Goradia by my friend Manish Sarkar, whom I had helped to get into *Capital* by putting in a word to Bidyut Sarkar. Bidyut was an excellent writer and had a fine grasp of the business scene and there was no reason why he should not have been continued as editor. I learnt later that the proprietor decided to get rid of Bidyut Sarkar probably because he was too expensive and the paper was continuing to run at a loss under him.

In the interregnum, between the dismissal of Bidyut Sarkar and my taking over, the editorial work had been carried on by Sankar Ray, who had been taken as Assistant Editor and paid much less. Sankar was first class as a correspondent, very well-informed and an excellent news man though his writing style may have been old worldly for the emerging readership. Sometimes, he would tend to forget that the journal was meant to be more the voice of the management than one of criticism. He made the cardinal error of taking on the tea industry, with which the management's interests were intimately linked. Howsoever fair—or unfair—his position may have been, Goradia was clearly upset. After appointing me as editor, he felt that he could dispense with the assistant editor and sought my help. He asked me what I thought of Sankar Roy, expecting that I would take the hint and say that he could be dispensed with. He did not get this answer for me and found other excuses to ask him to go. Fortunately, Sankar found a better paying job and continues to be a journalist to this day.

It was then Manish's turn to be sacked because he was getting on in years and the owners saw that Aditi and others, who were being paid a pittance, could handle both the editorial and the revenue-earning work quite competently. There can be no human face for capitalism. It has its own logic: human life is expendable for profits. This was not the first occasion that I had this experience of people being ruthless and inhuman to achieve their objectives. I found this in the Party as well.

Yet another experience provided an insight into the type of senior managers that are in demand in the corporate world. Since recruiting agencies played an important role in the selection of managers, I interviewed one that specialized in recruiting managers for board level positions. The managing director of the head-hunting firm reiterated that they took on recruiting assignments for top management positions only and gave a long account of how they went about it, the qualities that they looked for in managers and so on. I duly noted all that down and was about to leave when it struck me that he had omitted the one quality that I had expected him to mention. I had already spent too much time and was not keen to prolong my stay but on my way out I casually asked him, 'What about integrity?', feeling that this was probably a superfluous question since this was one thing that they must be taking for granted. To my surprise he answered: 'Not at all. As long as the person meets the objectives set for him in terms of profits, et cetera, we are not bothered about how he does that.' I saw how backdated I was in asking such a foolish question. It is taken for granted that ethics and integrity are not constraints for top managers in many concerns. This is possibly why there is so much enforced focus on corporate governance and corporate social responsibility today, though to what effect, I am not totally clear. The global meltdown has laid bare the repulsive actions of some of the most revered names in global business as millions of families have been wiped out; their life-savings gone, without any prospect of jobs or any other means of sustenance.

To refer to an interesting experience of the 1980s though, I had heard reports of a managing director of a multinational company having indulged in such malpractices. I happened to visit the company headquarters and found the place plastered with accusatory posters.

This was unusual because never had the top managers of the company been accused of such wrongdoing. Knowing that false accusations are often made, I chose not to give much credence to these posters. Sometime later I met a chartered accountant who had been with the company and who had first brought this matter to light. I learnt later that he had been dismissed. I had not known him earlier but when I met him he told me the whole story. He had been recruited in England and posted in the finance department of the Indian company in a fairly senior position. He discovered the many practices through which company funds were being siphoned off and had complained to the top management of the parent company but got no response from them. In fact, the response was that his services were terminated. Clearly the Indian and overseas management were hand in glove and the whistle blower was unwelcome.

There is yet another story establishing ethics to be old-fashioned. Conferences of advertising and public relations practitioners are held at regular intervals. Some of them give prizes to the best case study. A panel of judges is set up to select a winner. I was invited to be a member of one such panel with two very eminent persons, highly respected veterans in the profession. We sifted through the material entered for the competition and short-listed some three of four entries. After discussion, we narrowed down the choice to one. We all agreed that from the professional competence and skill in dealing with the problem perspectives, it was the best. One of the judges, however, pointed out that though the PR agency had succeeded in getting his client's point of view accepted, one should also look at the ethical aspect of the case.

The case was around a consignment of imported butter that had been brought in by a company amidst allegations that it had come from a radiation-affected area where there was a leakage from a nuclear reactor. While some 'experts' had cleared the consignment and declared it safe as the level of radiation to which it had been exposed was very low, there had been some agitation against it from environmental groups. They insisted that it was unsafe and should be scrapped. One of the panellists thought that this aspect needed to be discussed and I talked to the third panellist, regarded as the most eminent person in the panel. The minute he heard the word 'ethics' he laughed and brushed aside the whole idea. He did not think it worth any discussion at all and said that the selection we had made should stand. So it did.

I am not for a moment suggesting that the member who took this view was advocating or condoning unethical behaviour. His integrity was above questioning. The conclusion to be drawn from this episode is that in evaluating a case study, the only issue before the panel of judges should be how skilfully and effectively the tools available to the professional have been used. To that extent the panel's decision was the only one that could have been taken. What is necessarily missed out is the broader perspective of the possible impact of a PR exercise on society as a whole. There is usually no place for the ethical in most corporate exercises.

This becomes all the more clear when one considers the advertising scene. When evaluating the relative merits of different advertising campaigns, the criterion naturally has to be whether it helps to sell the product or the service. Earlier, an advertising campaign for a brand of cigarettes or of liquor could be rated good if it led to increased sales of the brand. That cigarette smoking is bad for health and should not be the subject of an advertising campaign at all was ignored. Even today, as far as professionalism in advertising is concerned, many such questions are ignored by the majority.

When I was on the executive committee of the Indian Society of Advertisers and for a year or so the Secretary of the Regional Council, we tried to emphasize standards and codes for regulating advertising. An Advertising Council to oversee the advertising had been formed or at least was proposed to be formed. I have noticed an advertisement that indicates that the Advertising Council (the name may have changed to Advertising Standards Council) is still alive. I do not remember the exact wording of the message but I think it said that the public could draw the ASC's notice to any advertisement that it considered misleading. It did not suggest that attention could be drawn to unethical advertising. I can see the ASC's difficulty: ethics is a very subjective matter.

In a consumer society, where the creation of wants is the very basis of the entire economy, anything that creates desire and motivates people to buy a product or use a service would be considered ethical. However, even if one limits oneself to the question of whether an advertisement is misleading, there is little indication that the Advertising Council is making any effort to weed out the misleading ones. The case of surrogate advertising that became popular once restrictions were placed on cigarette and liquor advertising is a case in point. Liquor and tobacco companies have since created other lifestyle brands with the same name and are perpetuating the brand through surrogate advertising and are getting away with it.

Capital gave me an opportunity to get acquainted with some top leaders of industry. I had good relations with the Bengal Chamber on whose Public Relations Committee I served ever since my IOL days and was, of course, friends with Madan Ghosh, the BCCI's first Indian Secretary. He was not only intelligent and perspicacious but, unlike many in top management, had a better understanding of the political and economic situation. He could also appreciate the labour point of view even if, as the position he held demanded, he chose to disagree with it.

Among interesting interviews was my experience with interviewing members of the Birla family when we did a cover story on the Birla empire in *Capital.* We proposed the feature to B. K. Birla who readily responded and asked his senior executives to give us all possible help. We interviewed many of the Birlas but the major inputs were provided by B. K. Birla himself. He invited me to visit Pilani along with some other journalists from Delhi. The correspondent of the *Financial Times* was amongst them and we travelled to Pilani on their private Dakota. It was a small plane that accommodated no more than 12 persons. B. K. Birla travelled with us. I gathered that it was the practice to take journalists regularly for their annual function in Pilani where, apart from their own company meetings, they invited some distinguished person to give a lecture in an open public meeting. On this occasion, Dr. Karan Singh was the speaker and he gave a discourse on the Gita. Karan Singh is an excellent speaker and I was very impressed with his speech. We stayed at the Birla guest house in Pilani and had our meals together. The fare was quite frugal—dal, roti, rice and two vegetable dishes—but was served in what were possibly silver thalis.

I had interacted with many other industry leaders, particularly in West Bengal, and contrasted the experience with my mind-set as a trade union movement when we regarded every capitalist as a villain and idolized every worker. My experience in the trade union field and later with management has shown that there are some fine human beings amongst industrialists and top management people just as there were those who were ruthless in their search for profits. I have also come across some fine cadres in the working class movement who could and should have risen to top positions in the movement. They did not because, as I have pointed out earlier, we neglected education and training that could have made them outstanding leaders. There are also corruption and vices of all kinds, not only in the ranks of the mass of workers but also among some trade union functionaries. This was not so evident in the early days when the workers and the trade union movement were struggling for survival. The deterioration has begun with the living standards of the workers improving in the organized sector and as the trade union movement has been able to consolidate itself and gain recognition both from government and from industry.

While in *Capital,* I interviewed Chief Minister Jyoti Bose in the early 1980s. He readily gave the interview and we published the full text of the interview with his photograph in the background of Writers' Buildings on our cover. He said nothing very new and, to that extent, it was a somewhat boring session. I did ask him a question regarding corruption, signs of which were becoming apparent even though this was only the second term of the Left Front Ministry and of his Chief Ministership. He gave a routine answer that indicated that he was not prepared to take it very seriously.

Some years after I had left *Capital* and was doing some freelance work for the *Statesman*, I tried to interview him again on behalf of the paper. I rang up Writers' Buildings and asked to speak to him. My call was passed on to his press adviser, who knew me—I have forgotten his name now—and seemed confident that he would be able to get me a date for the interview. He was probably not aware that at that time the Chief Minister was annoyed with the *Statesman* and when I rang up the Press Secretary again he said that the CM had not agreed to give a date. I thought he was busy but I soon realized that it he was not prepared to give an interview to the *Statesman*. Fair enough, but I had expected him to speak to me on the telephone and tell me so himself. Surprisingly, a year or so later, he did give an interview to the *Statesman* but to another correspondent. In this interview too he made no notable announcement or expressed any view beyond what he had done earlier.

I also interviewed E. M. S. Namboodiripad, then the General Secretary of the CPI(M), sometime in 1984 or 1985. The interview was published in the *Statesman*. The only significant thing that he said was about the role of the Party in the 1942 movement. He fully justified the Party's stand in opposing the movement, citing the danger of fascism as the justification for its stand. Even while he was expressing this view, in West Bengal, the Party was eulogizing Subhas Chandra Bose and observing his birthday!

THIRTY-FOUR

Manikuntala and I

I have a feeling that there was an unseen hand that was from the beginning trying to bring us together. As mentioned earlier, I first went underground in September 1941. In the den were two women comrades whose identities I did not know. Nor did they know mine. One of them turned out to be the wife of Sudhi Pradhan, a comrade who, as mentioned earlier, has written a history of the Left cultural movement. The other, then Bela Chatterjee, subsequently married Somnath Lahiri. I was once talking to Beladi in the den—I forget her tech name—and the topic of women comrades in the Party came up. Beladi mentioned a few names but when she started talking about Monidi her expression changed completely. I could see that the person she was referring to was highly respected; to whom one looked up with awe. The impression remained in my mind: Monidi was someone special.

Shortly after I emerged from the underground in April 1942, I saw her face-to-face when working on the trade union front. I had returned to our home in Bhowanipore and the nearest working class area was in Bondel. The easiest way to go to this working class area, then known as Talbagan, was to cross the railway line at Ballygunje Station. I would come to Ballygunje from Bhowanipore and make my way across the railway line to the factory area.

Manikuntala lived at Fern Road (Ballygunje) with her nephews and nieces, who were refugees from what was then East Pakistan, now Bangladesh. I do not know which party unit she was attached to but she mainly worked on the women's front and the Mahila Atma Rakhsha Samiti (Women's Self-Defence Organization). This had been established by her along with Renu Chakravartty and other women comrades of whom I can only recollect the name of Bani Dasgupta and Santi Sarkar. Since Manikuntala lived in the Ballygunje area, much of her work was connected with famine relief there. In addition to my work in the trade unions, I occasionally participated in the activities in Ballygunje proper and would see her. I do not recall meeting her or talking to her then though I remembered Beladi's glowing face when she talked of her. I said to myself when I first saw her: 'Oh! So this is the Monidi about whom I had heard so much.'

The unseen hand soon brought her into my life again when she had me saved from being beaten up badly during the first anniversary of the Quit India Movement. Even then, I did not meet her or try to know her better. Within a few months of that incident, I was moved far from Ballygunje, to the Kidderpore area to deal with the Port Trust union. Given the distance between the nature of our activities and our areas of work, I had no occasion to meet her, though I did catch a glimpse of her on one or two occasions. I went to see the play, *Nabanna,* which created history as it was on a contemporary issue for the first time and dealt with the great famine of 1943, in which she played the role of the old woman to perfection. Her make-up was so good that not even her mother recognized her. Her acting too was superb and was commented upon in some press reviews. Her other commitments prevented her from acting in this play after one or two performances. I remember seeing the play only once and getting a glimpse of her from afar, not being amongst the few who sat in the front rows.

The unseen hand was at work after another five years, bringing us close, even though we were physically far apart. On 26 March 1948, the Party was declared illegal. In a midnight swoop, thousands of party leaders and activists all over India were arrested. I was first lodged in the Presidency Jail but was shifted to the Dum Dum Jail later where I was Secretary of the Jail Committee. Early in 1949, Manikuntala had been arrested and, after being kept in the Midnapore Jail for sometime, she was brought to the Presidency Jail (Female

Ward) where most of the leading women party members had been detained.

As the senior-most amongst them, Manikuntala was the spokesperson for the women detenus in Presidency Jail. Abani Banerjee, B. C. Roy's emissary, maintained contact between the prisoners in all the jails and the Chief Minister. This was a wise move as quick decisions were often needed and going through the bureaucracy, or the then Home Minister, Kalipada Mukherjee, would have been a fruitless exercise. It was known that Dr. Roy's ministry was a one-man show with Dr. Roy himself in charge of all the ministries and the only person who could and did take decisions.

Since the senior-most communist leader in West Bengal, Muzaffar Ahmad, was in Dum Dum, it became the main centre for negotiations. I had been able to bring in my typewriter; a Hermes portable, which Princebhai had brought for me from Switzerland shortly after I had left college. I used it all these years, till the computers came and it became junk. (Not too long ago, I sold it to a *raddiwala* for Rs 100.) I had permission from the jail authorities to bring the typewriter and had set up a regular office in my cell. As Jail Committee Secretary, I drafted letters that had to be sent to the government. While all matters were discussed in the Jail Committee, of which many senior district leaders were members, the day-to-day work was carried on by me in consultation with Kakababu, as he was universally known. Abani Banerjee gave us the gist of the discussions that he had had with the communist prisoners in the Presidency Jail and with the women comrades who had a Jail Committee of their own with Manikuntala as the spokesperson. Similarly, he reported to the Presidency Jail women detenus the discussions held with us. Abani Banerjee told me that he had told Manikuntala that he was impressed by the way I functioned, drafting our memoranda, our charter of demands and other letters. In effect, Manikuntala and I were getting regular reports of each other through Abani Banerjee. The thought of destiny or the unseen hand uniting us in the bonds of matrimony never occurred to me at that time though. We had hardly seen each other; only heard about each other.

After the adoption of the new Constitution in 1950 and our release, Manikuntala, a member of the Provincial Committee before her arrest, automatically became a member of the POC (Provincial Organizing Committee) set up as soon as the Party could function legally. I too was co-opted as a member of this body after my release. Earlier, I had only been a member of the Calcutta District Committee. Kakababu was still in jail and released only a year later, in early 1952. Jyoti Bose probably became the PC Secretary after the formal PC Conference held towards the end of 1951 or early 1952. Promode Dasgupta, Bhupesh Gupta, Niranjan Sen, Benoy Chowdhury and Harekrishna Konar were among the other names that I recall.

The PC headquarters, as mentioned earlier, were on the first floor of a house owned by a Karim and Badshah, who were related to Mansur Habibullah and Sahedullah, both important members of the Party's Burdwan District Committee. The top floor was occupied by the owners and, for some time after our release, a part of the house had been used as a commune. Later, the entire first floor was made available for the PC office except for one small room where Promode Dasgupta continued to stay. He still lived there when I left the Party. Manikuntala had decided to stay with Badshah and Karim to be near the PC office. I also stayed in the commune in the PC office for a while but later shifted to another nearby commune. With Manikuntala and myself both becoming PC members, we met frequently and got to know each other better. Then came the elections.

March 1952 was the date set for the first General Election based on adult franchise and hence an historic event for which much preparation was needed. A party symbol had to be prepared, candidates had to be selected, polling agents had to be enrolled and trained; the Representation of the People Act had to be studied. Not many members were available in the PC office at that time. Having emerged from underground or jails, they had gone to the districts and Kakababu was holding the fort. I, being nearest at hand, assisted him.

The reader knows the story of Manikuntala's nomination for the Kalighat constituency and her victory. What is important here is that this election brought me into even closer and more frequent contact with her. I was chauffeuring her back home after her day's campaign in the old Standard Herald. Till that time the Party did not have a car and even the PC members moved about on buses and trams. Manikuntala had to leave for her constituency quite early in the morning, after breakfast and returned late at night; usually around 9.30 or 10 p.m. Returning to Lower Circular Road alone at that time of the night from Kalighat was a problem since there was no direct bus or tram route from there to our PC office. In any case, hardly any buses plied at that time of the night. Since I too returned around 9 or 9.30 p.m. from the DC office—I was Secretary of the Calcutta D.C. by then—I think it was Kakababu who suggested that I pick her up from the Kalighat election office and drop her back. This practice continued till the election and for some time after. During these trips we got to understand each other better; I found that there was much that we had in common and much that I could learn from her.

An interesting interlude to this is the feedback that I got from a friend a few weeks ago (May 2009). He had been a very young party sympathizer and was an active campaigner for Manikuntala in the Kalighat constituency in 1957. When we were having an *adda* session and the issue of the circumstances leading to my marriage cropped up this friend remarked: 'Your marriage to Monidi did cause problems for us; there were all kinds of rumours. One of them was that she had married her driver!' We laughed and I said to myself: well, there was a great deal of truth in this. From this point of time her role in the shaping of my life has been enormous. In fact, I owe to her most of what I am today. Her strength of character, her fearlessness, her capacity for renunciation, her patience and the resilience she was capable of have helped us to overcome many crises in our lives.

First, was our marriage itself: the opposition from a section of the leadership was such that anyone else would have wilted under it. There was nothing that anyone could say against it; we were both whole-timers; both unmarried; not even divorcees. True, she was 10 years older, which is not such a big difference. In any case, it was no one else's business except our own. In our patriarchal society, if the man marries a woman young enough to be his daughter or even his granddaughter, no one gives it a second thought.

As far as our two families were concerned, Manikuntala's parents had passed away. More than half her family was still in East Pakistan. Her nephews and nieces in Calcutta attended our marriage, held at 11B Fern Road, which had been a commune and was later occupied by her nephews and nieces. Most of my family was in Delhi and though no one could come to Calcutta, everyone sent letters of congratulations, blessings and good wishes, apart from a contribution towards the expenses. Despite the attitude of her PC colleagues, Manikuntala stayed perfectly calm and composed and set about making our one-room home on Shyamananda Road, Bhowanipore, comfortable. This was a three-roomed flat rented by a Gujarati family who were sympathetic to the Party. They sublet a room to us and we had gratefully accepted their offer. A gas stove in one corner of the room was the kitchen and a steel almirah in another corner was the dressing room. The toilet was shared with the Gujarati family. I remain friends with the family, though a part of it has settled in the United States. Manikuntala combined her party work, the women's movement and the household so well that she earned a name for herself in all the spheres in which she was active. When one of my brothers came on a business trip to Calcutta, she invited him to dinner and served three varieties of fish, some of which he had never tasted before even though he was a well-travelled man. With marriage, not just a new chapter had begun in my life; it was more like beginning a new life.

Some years ago, when I completed the eighty-fifth year of my life, some friends decided to hold a function to celebrate the event. They wanted a brief biographical sketch from me and I sent them a page long note. I had written that whatever I achieved after marriage I owed to Manikuntala. My friend rang up to check whether I meant it, and I said that I meant every word. Evidently, he still thought it was a piece of rhetoric because he omitted it when sending out the sketch, along with the invitation card, asking people to join the function. Over the next few pages I intend showing the kind of person she was. The more I look back on this period of my life—1953 to 1987—the more I realize how much I owe to her.

There was turmoil in the Party after the death of Stalin in March 1953. That was also the month and year when I began my life with Manikuntala. As long as Stalin was alive, we were naïve enough to believe that all was well with the Soviet Union. Since all communist parties till that time revolved like satellites around the sun—Stalin and the Soviet Union—we were sailing along merrily. Borrowing, from Browning, we would say to ourselves: 'Stalin's in the Kremlin,/ All's right with the world'. His death rocked the boat as shock after shock began to hit us without anyone asking pertinent questions. No one in the Party challenged the official explanation for Beria being shot dead: that he paid the price for being an imperialist spy but it definitely set me thinking that something was wrong somewhere. I do not know if our Central Committee or the top party leadership discussed the implications of the developments but it is highly unlikely that their significance was discussed.

To come back to the story of my life, the going was difficult with a combined monthly income of Rs 145. I cannot recollect whether the Party was paying the rent of the room that we had taken. I think the rent was around Rs 30 but even that was difficult to pay from our meagre kitty. We had a gas connection—not the cylinder gas that was still to come but the town gas—supplied by the Oriental Gas Company. We had been gifted an Ic Mic Cooker by Ananta Singh that I consider to be one of the most wonderful inventions of the twentieth century. For us it was a boon for we had to leave the house for our respective areas of work: mine at the District Party office and Manikuntala's to her Mahila Samity office, or to the PC office, quite early. On days that the Assembly was in session, she had to be at Assembly by 10.30 or so and left at about 9 in the morning. I left at about 8 as our DC Secretariat met at 8.30 every morning.

I would go to the Lansdowne market by 7 a.m. to buy fish and vegetables. By 8.30, Manikuntala had peeled and cut everything and put it in the IC Mic Cooker. Whoever left later lit the stove at the bottom of the cooker. When we came back, around 1.30 or 2 in the afternoon, everything had been cooked. We just had to open the lid and eat piping hot food. The cost of the charcoal was just a few rupees a kg. So our fuel costs were negligible and we got good, healthy and tasty food with very little effort.

Alas, neither the Ic Mic Cooker is available now nor is charcoal easily to be found. On a visit to the small industries institute in Wardha, I found that they had re-invented the Ic Mic Cooker with a better finish (the outer container was of brass instead of the tin one that we were using) but were not producing it on a commercial scale. There were no takers for the sample that they made. In any case, even if they made one especially for me, to bring it to Calcutta would be cumbersome and even I did, where would I find the charcoal? Till a few years ago, when people still smoked the hookah, charcoal was, I believe, available but now the hookah is only a museum piece, though I learn that there are modern day hookah bars in metropolitan cities that are frequented by the jet set. The cigarette, the biri, the pan masala with zarda and the khaini have otherwise taken its place. So we spend hours on cooking even with the help of pressure cookers and hundreds of rupees for fuel. Even at over Rs 360 a cylinder, there is stress and tension whenever a new cylinder is required. Our gas dealer finds it more lucrative to sell the cylinder in the black to hotels or auto drivers.

Thanks to the Ic Mic Cooker and to the wonderful person named Manikuntala, who managed *ghare* and *baire* (home and away), on next to nothing, we were able to survive on our meagre party wage. I even put on weight because, prior to marriage, I had been eating at one party commune or another or at wayside restaurants, where one ate what one could afford. That could perhaps fill one's belly but provided little nutrition. In Kidderpore, where I worked among the port workers, one could get a sheekh kabab and a paratha for eight annas and that was lunch or dinner depending on which time of the day one happened to drop in.

Meanwhile, the wartime inflation spilt over into the 1950s. Food shortages became the norm, particularly in Bengal, and even though the famine of 1943 did not recur, food scarcity was endemic in the rural areas. P.L. 480 prevented the starvation deaths but could not stave off hunger and malnutrition. Full marks to Manikuntala for being able to manage in the midst of it all; not even taking money from 'sympathizers' that was a common enough practice for others. There was often a hidden quid pro quo attached to the help that sympathizers rendered. That I did not succumb to this temptation is perhaps more due to the fact that no one ever tried to tempt me because I never had the power and the authority to nominate persons to the Assemblies or Parliament.

Manikuntala not only managed to keep both of us in good shape but even helped her family. She could hardly help with money but used her contacts as an MLA to get them admitted into hospitals, or to get them cheap accommodation to stay in. To do this, she had to spend a lot of time and had to bear the cost of travel on their behalf. One of her nephews got TB and she managed to get him admitted to a sanatorium in the Midnapore district and often made trips there to monitor his progress. She has described in her book how on one occasion she was stranded somewhere in a remote village with the last bus having gone. A life of great hardship had, however, taken a toll on her own life. She started getting a slow fever occasionally, which no doctor had so far been able to diagnose. It is in this background that one can appreciate the greatness of Manikuntala. She had managed our lives so well; all my relatives developed a strong affection, even admiration, for her. She had no expensive habits; so simple and frugal was her lifestyle that no one felt that she was a burden.

As soon as I started earning after leaving the Party and we got our own establishment in Delhi briefly, she invited my brothers and their families to lunch or dinner and cooked meals that they relished. How she could do that on so meagre an income, without any help in a city like Delhi, is again a marvel. Whether in Calcutta or in Delhi, she dressed in a simple white handloom sari with a narrow border. The saris were washed and ironed at home, though I did help out in view of her failing health. It was mainly because of her health that I had to decide to return to Calcutta. Although I was making some progress as a journalist, I could not afford the cost of her treatment in Delhi, where we did not know any doctor whom we could consult without having to pay a substantial fee. Manikuntala, therefore, decided to leave in August/September 1964 for Calcutta and stay at Fern Road and get herself treated by doctors like Dr. Narayan Roy, Dr. Shanti Neogy and Dr. Ghani. They treated her for free and even gave free medicines. The People's Clinic owned by the Neogy brothers conducted free pathological tests not only for us but for all party whole-timers who sought their services. Rajeswar Neogy told me that even Jyoti Bose and Snehangshu Acharya sometimes used the services of this clinic. Dr. Neogy did suggest tuberculosis but Dr. Narayan Roy, on whom we relied more, was categorical that it was not the case. He treated her for *E coli*, for the continuous slow fever that was gradually weakening her. Despite this she worked at the kindergarten school on a salary of Rs 200.

My job with IOL in 1967 changed all that and it was in this period that my debt to her increased manifold. Since I was now able to breathe easy after years of deprivation, I was tempted to change my lifestyle. I could have gone overboard and lost my way had it not been for her restraining influence. In fact, I very nearly did so and I am grateful for her patience and help. I have seen how the values of people change totally after a change in their financial status. I keep telling people that by abandoning Marxism, the CPI(M) in West Bengal has proved the validity of the Marxian principle that the economic/financial status of a person conditions his ideas.

Today, the CPI(M) has become the mouthpiece of the business class and the policies of their leaders are being influenced by the fact that they are no longer poor; many are reportedly quite wealthy. As had happened in the Soviet Union, the Party in India—with its huge appendage of a stratum of the population now growing rich through political patronage becoming a new class—the Party's interests are now getting linked up with those of the business class. The poor, who constituted the constituency of the Party at one time, are being oppressed and harassed, even shot down when their protests become too militant; all in the name of 'industrialization', which is supposed to be synonymous with 'progress'.

To get back to Manikuntala's restraining influence that prevented me from going astray, I would be departing from the truth if I did not mention there was much about my lifestyle that she did not approve of. Since I had to entertain company executives or journalists, sometimes at home, I kept a few bottles of liquor in a small cupboard in the house. It was hardly a bar; but a mini-bar of sorts that she did not approve of. Nevertheless, she tolerated it. I took dancing lessons from a professional dance teacher whose name and address I got from an advertisement in the newspapers. I never became very proficient at it but, at Advertising Club and PRSI conferences and parties, I did dance with some of our lady colleagues. That too was not to her liking but she digested it. I had to go out on frequent tours when she was left alone and felt neglected but bore it silently. When I look back on this period from a situation where today I too live alone and often feel lonely, I realize how she must have suffered.

During all the years that I was working in the corporate office of an MNC her own lifestyle did not change one bit. She kept herself away from the social life that I had to become part of but she ensured that our standard of living at home did not change very much from what it had been when we were whole-timers. Most of the entertaining that I had to do was confined to the clubs that I had to join and, occasionally, at home when she would do the cooking. If I am in a fairly comfortable situation as far as my needs go and can afford to do voluntary work practically whole time, without any honorarium or salary, it is because of the spartan lifestyle she got me accustomed to. After her death, I have further simplified my lifestyle. Earlier, we had a little fish every day. Now I have become a vegetarian and am, of course, a teetotaller.

Above all else, it is to her that I owe the complete turn my life took shortly before her death. I found God again; the God that I had abandoned and even reviled for the greater part of my life came back to me again through her. Having been brought up in a Catholic school run by Jesuit priests, I had not been irreligious in my early years. At home too, though my father was never particular about visiting temples—in the many years in Calcutta we had never been inside the Kali temple in Kalighat—we were believers. Indeed, reading my father's diaries, extracts of which I have published in a book for private circulation within the family—I saw that he had a deep and abiding faith in God and often quoted those words from the Lord's prayer, 'Thy will be done'. These words helped him overcome many of life's crises. I had also read the Gita many times when in school. All that had had to be driven out of my mind.

So strong was the hold of the 'religion-is-the-opium-of-the-people-dogma' that on my own I would probably never have been able to change. It was she who asked me to read the Vivekananda-Ramakrishna literature and to visit Mayavati in the Kumaon hills, which finally broke down the wall that was preventing me from seeing the truth. I realized that religion, particularly religion as it was practised and interpreted by vested interests, was not the same thing as spirituality. It is Vivekananda and none else who uttered the strongest indictment of the fanaticism of the bigots who, in the name of religion, have exploited the people and even shed the blood of innocents to achieve their ends.

I realize too, today, that even when I shouted the loudest against religion it was the spiritual feeling, innate in every person, which motivated me to live a life of hardship and suffering; that enabled me to make one sacrifice after another; even to risk my life for a cause in which I believed. My conception of God is not that of a venerable old man with a long white beard somewhere above the clouds but of an intelligent cosmic consciousness that is all pervasive.

Beyond that, it is not possible to describe or understand this reality.

To take up another aspect of Manikuntala's life and its influence on me, my Indian Oxygen days were a period of relative affluence in our lives. I call it relative because what I was getting was nothing much, even in terms of the value of the rupee in those days. There were strict restrictions on management salaries right up to the 1980s, when I retired. Even our managing director got not much more than Rs 10,000 and executive salaries were much lower; so were the perks. With a conventional wife this would have hardly been enough to make both ends meet. Manikuntala was neither interested in clothes—except the bare minimum needed to cover herself—nor in jewellery of any sort and practically had no expenses. Her medical expenses, which became fairly heavy at the later stages of her life, were paid for by the company. This helped us to save in two ways. My wife was a 'low maintenance' lady unlike many others who demanded that their husbands lavish wealth on them. She was moreover someone who insisted that I be thrifty; she kept me on a leash. We never went out to expensive restaurants for meals even on occasions like birthdays or marriage anniversaries. If I had to entertain for professional purposes, I could use the small expense account that I was entitled to and I never exceeded that. I could thus have as much as 20 per cent of my salary deducted to be credited to my Company Provident Fund account. The company did not pay more than 8 per cent but the whole amount accumulated and was exempt from income tax. Our lifestyle continued to be nearly as spartan as it was when we were struggling in the Party, though we ate a little better at home. This has enabled me to have enough for a comfortable life after retirement.

It is not easy to switch lifestyles even if one can afford it. In my case, having given up fish and meat, the two most expensive items of food, and not being either a smoker or a consumer of hard drinks, I do not currently consume very much more than I did as a party whole-timer. I can now occasionally afford to buy books or to entertain friends. I had bought a second-hand car after retirement. I gave up the car shortly after Manikuntala's death in 1987. I used a bicycle for going to the club in the morning for my daily exercise, which attracted a lot of attention. This was not only because I was cycling after the age of sixty when people often find it difficult to walk without a stick but also because cycling is considered a poor man's mode of transport and, in Bengal at least, even lower middle class people would rather go in a bus than cycle. The only luxury that I still indulge in is the continued membership of two clubs. In one, I used to row. In the other, I swim and use the library. Once in a while I take out friends or relatives to the club for a meal. Drinks, except nimbu pani, are a strict no no.

I started a PPF account shortly before my retirement and till recently only added to it; never taking money out. During the last two or three years I have taken out small amounts; once to buy the flat I am in and on another occasion to invest in the Senior Citizen's Scheme. My PPF account that has grown is being kept for emergencies and will be donated after my death.

To go back to Manikuntala, the antibiotics that she was being treated with since the 1950s made her feel slightly better once in a while but the problem would recur. During the Party days she was under tremendous work pressure. Her's was no desk job but involved moving from place to place, from district to district in West Bengal and delivering speeches. As one of the Party's best speakers and one of the best known leaders, she was in great demand all over. Also, living conditions of the comrades in whose houses she was put up in the 1950s were not always very comfortable. Sometimes she had to put up with peasant comrades who often did not have enough to eat themselves. She had to move around in third class compartments or crowded buses. All this had taken a further toll on her health.

After the 1957 elections, Jyoti Babu suggested that we go to Darjeeling for a brief holiday. Kamal Basu (later Mayor of Calcutta), who had been elected to the Lok Sabha came from a wealthy family with a house in Darjeeling, which he had offered to make available to Jyoti Babu and his family for his holiday. We badly needed a rest and readily agreed. Jyoti Babu suggested that we take our domestic help along as we would have to run the kitchen ourselves. In those days the Farakka had to be crossed by steamer. This meant that we had to leave our train compartments at one end and board another train at the other end. While we travelled by train, third class, the Basus travelled first class. At that time we thought nothing of the difference in our travelling status: it strikes me today as odd because after all, we were both Party whole-timers and Jyoti Babu was not being financed by his family. It was generally believed that Snehangshu helped him whenever needed. None the less, we enjoyed the stay in Darjeeling with Manikuntala running the household, Mrs. Basu not being much of a housekeeper. She found it difficult even to handle Chandan and her husband had to help her deal with their son too.

During her visits to the districts, Manikuntala had to undertake strenuous tasks sometimes that she should not have been permitted to do at her age and in her state of health. There were serious floods in north Bengal and she was asked to go to Cooch Behar, large parts of which were flooded. There was no question of holding mass meetings in those conditions. The comrades there asked her to wade through the flooded waters for quite a long distance. She spent hours wading through waist deep water along with the local party leaders just to impress upon the people of the area that the Party was with them in their crisis and shared their problems. Such things did help the Party to build a firm base in the district but it ruined Manikuntala's health.

It is such sufferings and sacrifices made by hundreds of party workers that laid the foundations of the success that the Party achieved in the 1960s and 1970s. Do the party workers and leaders of the present generation care to remember that? I weep when I see the turn the Party has taken today. The goodwill earned in those days, the love that the peasants and workers had for the Party, have been steadily eroded by the overbearing attitude of the present generation of leaders and their volte-face from being champions of the poor, the workers and the peasants, to becoming protectors and promoters of the interests of the richer sections of society.

Between 1967 and 1981, we were in a position to afford better treatment for Manikuntala. She was not only treated by senior doctors, I was also able to admit her in good nursing homes but even there a correct diagnosis eluded us. Her condition deteriorated further and it was only in 1985 that she was correctly diagnosed. A young doctor in our complex, Dr. Srikumar Mukherji, who was more a friend than a doctor to us, recommended a senior physician, Dr. Pal. He suggested some very elaborate tests that showed that she was suffering from tubercular kidneys. We tried to treat her with the anti-tuberculosis drugs prescribed by the doctors but she could not tolerate them and her condition got worse. As a desperate measure, she was admitted into a nursing home to see if they could devise some method of getting her to tolerate the anti-TB medicines. Nothing worked and the doctors gave up. So we brought her back home and tried homeopathic and ayurvedic treatment. It was clear by now that the end was approaching.

In spite of her ill health and her other preoccupations, which included looking after the household, she found the energy to write her much acclaimed autobiography. She had begun writing in the late 1970s and it was finally published on 1 August 1982 as *Shediner Katha.* Later, an English translation *(In Search of Freedom: An Unfinished Journey)* along with a brief biographical sketch and a foreword by the well known historian, Professor Tapan Raychaudhuri, was published in January 2001. This too has attracted the attention of historians and readers not only within the country but also abroad.

Even earlier, a research scholar from Denmark had held a series of interviews with her and published a monograph on women in the Tebhaga struggle. This was a long and very militant struggle waged in 1947 by the peasants in different parts of undivided Bengal for their rightful—two-thirds—share of the crop. Earlier share-croppers were being forced to hand over half the crop or even more to the landowners as they sometimes had to pay back in kind debts incurred for hiring inputs for cultivation. Despite the brutal repression unleashed in an attempt to crush the movement, women were in the forefront of the battle and Manikuntala went round the districts helping in the organization of the struggle and providing support. The struggle was successful and the government had to pass legislation ensuring that the peasants received their rightful share of the crop.

Since the early 1980s, Manikuntala had begun to develop an interest in spiritual literature, thanks to her friend Prabhati Ghosh, who had taken *diksha* (initiation into spiritual life) from the then President of the Ramkrishna Math and Mission. She somewhat hesitatingly passed on some of the books she was reading to me. She was uncertain whether I would be interested in reading them, given my background as an atheist. I too had begun to find by this time that while Dialectical Materialism seeks to explain some of the transitory phenomena of the world, it did not provide an answer to many fundamental questions that arise in the human mind.

Although I had heard of Vivekananda even as a child, I had never had the opportunity or the curiosity to read his books or even to read books about him. I now read Romain Rolland's biography of Vivekananda and Ramakrishna and then went on to read some of the works of Vivekananda and that remarkable work of Mahendra Gupta: *Sri Sri Ramakrishna Kathamrita* (the English translation is *The Gospel of Sri Ramakrishna*). These books opened my eyes and lifted a veil, as it were, suggesting the answers to many questions in my mind, questions that have been in the minds of all human beings ever since the emergence of *homo sapiens* on our planet. Manikuntala suggested that I visit Mayavati, the Advaita Ashrama in the Himalayas that Vivekananda established shortly before his demise.

Having read books about it, which Manikuntala had been reading, I too developed an interest in the place. I was at that time working for *Capital.* I sent a letter to Mayavati informing them of my impending visit and seeking their permission to stay there but set out before getting any reply. As I was travelling, I was a little apprehensive because I had not received confirmation that accommodation had been booked for me. I was not even sure whether my letter had reached them. I prayed that I would be able to stay there and, when I reached, I found that my prayers had been answered. Swami Ananayananda, whom I had never met and who did not know me, received me with open arms when I landed up, even though my letter had not reached. He had only received an earlier letter in which I had merely spoken about the possibility of my coming. That visit to Mayavati and the reception I got was a kind of turning point in my life.

Meanwhile Manikuntala's health continued to deteriorate and she, too, wanted to take diksha. We first approached Swami Lokeswarananda, then the Secretary of the Ramkrishna Mission Institute of Culture. She went to him and he talked very sympathetically with her but told her that only the President Maharaj and the Vice President Maharaj were authorized to initiate devotees. Belur Math, where the President Maharaj stayed was too far. So we turned to Swami Bhuteshananda, Vice President, who was at the Kakurgachi Ashram, nearer our home. Usually only devotees recommended by regular visitors on whom the swamis can rely are initiated. Seeing her worsening condition and her anxiety to take diksha before the end came, I went and pleaded that her last wish be acceded to.

The convention was that those seeking initiation had to come to the ashram. Exceptions had never been made but Manikuntala was in no state to leave the house. I met the Swami and told him of our predicament and requested him to consider the special circumstances and come to our residence for the purpose of her initiation. He told me that he would consider the matter and let me know in a few days. When I met him a few days later, he said he would come but would decide whether he would actually initiate her after talking to her. Accordingly, a date was fixed, and one day in February 1987, I drove up to the Jogudyan Ashram in my old Fiat and picked up the swami and another monk, who would assist him.

Swami Bhuteshananda sat beside me as I drove down to our house on Karaya Road with the other swami on the rear seat. At home, he wanted a few minutes with her alone. So Manikuntala got out of bed and was brought into the sitting room where we left her with him. After a few minutes, we were all summoned and the initiation ceremony was performed. Those few minutes had convinced the swami that her desire for initiation was genuine and she was fit and ready for it. I was told that this was a unique gesture on the part of Swami Bhuteshananda; he had never made such an exception before. Nor has it been made any time after as far as I am aware.

Manikuntala's condition continued to deteriorate but she was at peace. On 11 September, the same year, she passed away.

THIRTY-FIVE

Ramgarh: Village in a Valley

If Manikuntala influenced my life from the early 1940s to the late 1980s, Ramgarh did so from the early 1950s and continues to do so. What and where is Ramgarh and why do I love it so much? It is just a small village in a valley amidst the Kumaon hills about 30 or 35 kms from Nainital town, at an elevation of 5,000 feet. It has not attracted many tourists or settlers from the plains. Evidently its charm has not worked the same magic on others as it has on me and some others in our family.

I have watched this village change and grow. Thankfully, it has not grown very much but change it certainly has; not as much as some of our cities and towns or even many of our villages, though. It is beginning to be very different from what it was but even today, it is a place where I love to go if only for a for a few days and I still dream that before I leave this world finally—which cannot be very far off—I will have a place to stay there and to look at the mountains around and breathe the still pure air and walk the still solitary paths through the forests.

I first visited Ramgarh in 1951, shortly after my release from jail. I think the first visit was along with my sister-in-law Roopan and my father. We travelled up to Lucknow and took the metre gauge to Kathgodam. We got down at Haldwani, one station before Kathgodam, because all buses started from Haldwani and it was better to board the bus at its starting point. The bus wound its way past Jeulikote, the centre for bee hives and honey. As the bus proceeded, little urchins came up with leaf plates full of strawberries that tasted delicious. The bus did not proceed beyond the hill crest known as Malla (Upper) Ramgarh. From there we had to trek down a very steep footpath that led to Talla (lower, i.e., the valley) Ramgarh, which is what we were headed for. Right through the valley raced a roaring torrent to mingle with other streams and then perhaps carry on its long journey to the sea. We were not bothered about where it went and never asked. It was enough for us that it ran just a few yards from where our house was being built. How on earth did my brother choose that spot to build a house in this remote village?

Ramgarh must have been, even till the early years of the last century, part of Jim Corbett territory where the man-eaters of Kumaon freely roamed. There are no man-eaters now but an occasional leopard still snoops down from the forests around to snatch away a dog or a calf or even an adult cow or buffalo. Lalitbhai was building this house in this remote village and we were all very proud of it because this was the first house that any one in the family had built; my father had little left after giving his sons a good education. Lalitbhai had married Roopan Bakaya, a girl, from a Kashmiri Pandit family in Lahore in 1945. She had an uncle by the name of Rajendra Nath Muttoo, who had been in the army and retired early to set up house in Talla Ramgarh. He was a remarkable man who cleared the forest and set up an apple orchard on the land acquired by him. Apart from growing apples and other fruit, such as apricots, peaches, plums and walnuts, he became one of the country's greatest experts on bee-keeping. His work in that sphere earned him the respect of the world bee-keepers' community and he was asked to take over the editorship of the *World Bee-Keepers' Journal*, a responsibility that he carried out with devotion and seriousness till his death in the 1960s.

It was a plot of land from his orchard that Muttooji gifted to his niece Roopan Bakaya (Kaul) after her marriage to my brother. Lalitbhai bought a little more land adjoining that plot and it was on a part of that land that he started building his house. It was named *Sadasukh* by my father; an appropriate name that meant 'eternal happiness' but the name had significance as well. One of our illustrious ancestors of a few generations ago was a 'Sadasukh Kaul'.

My father plucked that name out of the family tree and bestowed it on the house. The family records said that this ancestor had earned a name for himself in the community.

The construction started in 1948, as a plaque on the supporting wall below the house still proclaims. I first visited it in 1951, shortly after my release from jail in April that year. I fell in love with the place from the moment I saw it. It was calm and serene, the fresh mountain air soothing the nerves frayed after the battles of the previous years. The river, running below just a few yards away from where the house stood, dashed against huge boulders that must have been carried down in the distant past, when the stream came cascading from the mountain tops in torrential fury. One could see the froth and foam from a distance as it raced down, creating little waterfalls on the way. The valley created by the river is surrounded by high mountains on either side. Cultivation was on terraces gouged out of the mountain side in some places but mostly on the level ground created by the shifting stream that made the land suitable for farming.

Our house was only half-built then but we were proud of it. As I have said, it was the first family property, our own house. So far we had all lived in rented flats in Simla, in Calcutta and elsewhere. Additions were made to it gradually to make it more comfortable and livable but it was only completed when my brother decided a few years after retirement to shift from Delhi and live there permanently, instead of just coming for occasional visits. This was in the late 1970s or early 1980s. The house has meant a lot to me and the family. This was the one place where Manikuntala and I could come for a holiday and we did this regularly till she became too weak to travel. Friends and relatives who often compliment me on my good health today do not know that I owe it mostly to Ramgarh. Whenever I felt the need for a change or seemed to be sinking under the strain of work, I rushed to Ramgarh. Even before Lalitbhai moved to the place full time, we could go there and the family that provided the domestic help looked after us and made us feel at home. It was Ramgarh that I used as the base camp for my regular trekking expeditions, almost every year, from the 1970s till the late 1980s.

Ramgarh has changed and is changing; changing for the worse with 'development' taking place, thankfully at a very slow pace. When we started going there in the early 1950's, we had to trek down a rough and stony footpath that sloped sharply all the way from Malla (Upper) Ramgarh. It was a sheer descent of about a thousand feet from Malla to Talla (Lower) Ramgarh and one needed stout knees to bear the strain of the trek down to the valley. We were young and enjoyed every bit of it.

How green was the valley! On the other, the western side, of the river was a thick forest through which one could climb up to Mukteshwar, where the famous Veterinary Research Institute had been set up. It was an eight-mile trek through the forest with hardly any footpath. One had to crawl on all fours clutching shrubs and the roots of trees at many places. I actually did the trek some time in the early 1950s with Muttoo Sahab's son. It was an exhilarating experience. The cool breeze whistling through the pine forest was a tonic that made one forget fatigue. Since there was no transport except horses and mules, there was no question of pollution of any sort. It was a health resort superior to all the conventional resorts in crowded towns like Simla, Mussoorie, Nainital and such hill stations.

Of course, if one was looking even for basic amenities such as electricity, there was nothing like it at Ramgarh in those days. Kerosene lamps sufficed to keep the darkness at bay. There was no bank any where within miles and no post office in the real sense of the term. One could buy a postcard or a stamp from the *halwai* or sweet maker, who made jalebies in a small shop on the northern side of the village. A predominantly upper caste village, most people owned at least some land on which they had set up orchards. The largest orchards belonged to Mantriji's family (a farmer named Dewan Singh who was the secretary of the Arya Samaj; *mantri* is the Hindi word for secretary, also for minister).

The Sri Aurobindo Ashram of Pondicherry also had a fairly large orchard with the picturesque name, Mountain Paradise. Most likely it was the Mother who had thought of this name. There were other farmers too; they produced potatoes and some wheat and pulses apart from fruit. The secret of their relative prosperity was the abundance of water from the mountain springs, which were a perennial source of water for irrigation and drinking. Some springs were reputed to be virtual elixirs that could match the best mineral waters anywhere in the world. Ramgarh also had artisans: carpenters, masons, cobblers, who constituted a very small percentage of the population.

One of the founders of the village was Shri Narayan Swami, a sadhu of the Arya Samaj movement, who had set up the Narayan Swami Ashram. The post office, now a regular one, is named after Narayan Swami as is the high school founded by him; one of the earliest in the region. It has now been taken over by the government and has grown into an intermediate college. It is thanks to this school/college that there is over 90 per cent literacy in Ramgarh with girls constituting the majority of the student community. Standing before the first floor window of our house, it was a refreshing site to see girls and boys in their blue uniform walking past the house to the school, just a kilometre away.

The people have been friendly and, when we first went there in the early 1950s, theft and crime were unknown. We never needed to lock our houses. All we had to do was to close the windows and doors securely and trust God and the people. The trust was never betrayed. I may be exaggerating but to me at that time this was indeed a bit of *Ram Rajya*. Then 'development' started taking place! It was in the 1970s that the motor road from Malla to Talla Ramgarh was built. The three-four kilometre trekking trail was virtually abandoned and a 9-km motor road for cars, jeeps, buses, trucks, motorcycles came up. At first it only came up to the Talla Ramgarh Post Office but, within a few years, it was extended right past Ramgarh to Nathuakhan, Hartola and beyond to Almora. Progress indeed!

How convenient to drive down from Haldwani or Kathgodam straight to our abode of 'eternal happiness'. Progress and development did not end with the laying of motorable roads. By the 1980s, video parlours had started not very openly but furtively in dark rooms in secluded corners. Television came too but the location of Talla Ramgarh in a valley girdled by hills all round prevents easy access to TV programmes. Only those who could afford their own dish antennas could watch television programmes but with Direct to Home available, many more homes are going in for TV.

Yet more 'progress' was in store. A licensed Indian-Made Foreign Liquor shop has been opened and it is no longer very safe to walk along the road late in the evening. Till the 1980s I remember going out after dinner with Lalitbhai and my sister-in-law to watch the Ramlila. We used to return after midnight wearing thick woollens and wrapped in blankets greeted with *namaskars* all the way to our house. Alas, one must make some sacrifices for 'progress'! A part of 'progress' and 'development' is, of course, crime.

I know of at least one murder that took place some time in the 1990s just a kilometre from our house on the road to the Jhuthia village, perhaps for the first time. The police had to be called from Bhowali, some 15 or 16 kms away, to investigate. Like many villages in India, Ramgarh never had any police station or even any police *chowki,* outpost, to investigate. It is the *patwari,* the only government official in the village, who carries out the dual function of maintaining law and order and keeping land records. In fact, he is the arbiter of land disputes to whom initially all villagers go with their grievances. Only if they still feel aggrieved, do they go to the district court, which may be many miles away and which only the more affluent can afford to visit. Even then it is the testimony of the *patwari* which plays a decisive role. The *patwari* continues to fulfil these functions and mercifully there is still no police post either in Malla or Talla Ramgarh. There is not much need for one either, as crime is still the exception rather than the rule. To that extent Ramgarh is still a backward village. The *patwari* is a familiar and often much feared person in most backward Indian villages in Uttar Pradesh. and perhaps also in other parts of north India and figures in many Hindi novels.

There are two persons in Ramgarh, both devotees of the Aurobindo Ashram, who have become personal friends. Although from very different backgrounds, they have been able to strike the right chord in me. One of them, Kurban Hussain, comes from a relatively affluent Gujarati Muslim family that runs a small business in Pune. Exactly when and how he was attracted to Sri Aurobindo's philosophy I have never thought it necessary to ask. I think it was some time in the late 50s or early 60s of the last century that I first met him. He was already managing the next door Madhuban Orchard and we often walked across to Madhuban or he came over to Sadasukh. I had just started going for long treks at that time and with his wide knowledge and experience of the region his guidance and advice was extremely helpful. Later, he took a fairly advanced course in homeopathy and I still use some medicines that he prescribed. I have even been able to help others who have had similar ailments.

The other person is Manish Rai, a young man born and brought up in Pondicherry, who took charge of the Tapogiri Ashram, a unit of the Sri Aurobindo Ashram, some time in the 1990s. A wildlife enthusiast and a nature lover, he began to transform the place, which had gone to seed as a result of neglect over the years, from the moment he took over. His training in nature and wildlife studies in the Pondicherry educational institutions enables him to catch snakes with ease. He has asked the villagers not to kill snakes but to contact him whenever they sight one. He rushes to the spot on getting the information and brings the snake over for observation and study after which it is released in the jungles some distance away from human habitation. Apart from this trait, which has earned the admiration of all, he has a genial and affable temperament that endears him to all who know him. It is in Tapogiri that I usually stay when I go to Ramgarh now.

The Ramgarh of the 1950s no longer exists. The Ramgarh stream has virtually dried up. When we started going there in the 1950s the water of the stream was so clear and pure that Manikuntala and I would walk down to the river with all the clothes that had to be washed, sit on a boulder, dip the clothes in the river water and applying just a little bit of Sunlight soap—detergents had still not arrived—and beat the clothes gently on the boulder and lo and behold the clothes were clean. Then we put them out to dry in the sun on the string stretched out on the verandah and by the evening they were dry and crisp. Today, except during and immediately after the rains, there is hardly any water and even during the rains the water is often muddy and hardly fit for washing. The spring from which we drew our drinking water has dried up and we now depend on the erratic government piped water supply, though there still are still some springs with crystal clear water where people go for their supply of drinking water.

As with many other experiences, my visits to Ramgarh have been a learning one for me. Born and brought up in an urban atmosphere, I would have known little of what villages were like had it not been for Ramgarh. It is, of course, not a very typical village but the changes there have enabled me to understand a lot of what is happening in rural India. I love Ramgarh, warts and all, and cannot think of missing my annual trip to that place.

Our house was sold off after the death of my brother in 1999 but the Sri Aurobindo Ashram authorities, who have bought it, are kind enough to permit us to spend some time there provided it is not being used for their summer camps, which it often is. Otherwise I stay with Manish at the Tapogiri Ashram. Even though neglected for some years, it is beautiful and despite the living conditions not being as comfortable as they were in our house, I am grateful to the management for permitting me to stay there. It is through Ramgarh and the different units of Sri Aurobindo Ashram in that village that I developed my interest in Sri Aurobindo's philosophy and started visiting Pondicherry.

Even when we stayed in our own house, Sadasukh, in Ramgarh we would spend a considerable amount of time in the Tapogiri Ashram. It was founded in the twenties of the last century by Dr. Indra Sen, a professor in Delhi University, who had become a devotee of Sri Aurobindo. It is at a height of about 500 feet from the main road and is at different levels of the hill side on the eastern side of the river. He, along with his younger brother, Arjun Dev, built a few rooms using the stones found in the valley and developed an orchard surrounding it. Gradually the number of rooms grew. When I first went there, Pramod Tripathi, a retired officer of the Press Information Bureau was in charge. A very dedicated devotee he would take classes on Sri Aurobindo's philosophy that were often followed by kirtan sessions. Another regular visitor to the ashram was Dr B. S. Sharma, a retired professor of Delhi University who had been head of the department of African Studies. He had spent many years in African countries and in Mauritius as a teacher in the universities there. He had earlier been a freedom fighter who had participated in the Quit India movement and had taken shelter in Ramgarh when there was a warrant of arrest against him. I learnt from him that Girilal Jain, later editor of the *Times of India*, had been with him in Ramgarh for similar reasons.

Dr Sharma and Tripathiji got me interested in Sri Aurobindo's philosophy and inspired me to visit Pondicherry. The Pondicherry ashram guest houses are unique institutions where one can get clean accommodation for a very small sum and food coupons that enable one to take three meals, breakfast, lunch and dinner for Rs 20 only. I have been impressed by the atmosphere in the ashram and benefited enormously from their collective meditation sessions that are really a source of inspiration.

THIRTY-SIX

Adrift on the Open Sea

After I left *Capital*—towards the end of 1985 or early 1986—I was again adrift without a regular source of income, apart from my meagre pension and the interest on my savings. I was keen on doing freelance work and Sunanda Datta-Ray, the editor of the *Statesman,* whom I had known since my days with IPA in Delhi in 1963-1964, encouraged me to write. I started writing articles for the *Statesman* and also doing book reviews. Shortly after this, Aditi joined the *Statesman* as assistant editor in charge of their business page. Aditi suggested that I do a regular column for the business page based on an analysis of chairmen's statements at annual general meetings. The column was called 'Through the Corporate Looking Glass'. Other freelance work came my way, from some corporate houses, including Indian Oxygen for whom I did a corporate history.

In between, I worked on a very interesting project, a socio-economic survey of the Andaman and Nicobar Islands, as part of a team. I visited the islands thrice. In the first visit, I covered Port Blair; in the second, I did a survey on the Car Nicobar Island. That visit was most educative because of the totally different conditions there. My third visit was as faculty for a Public Relations course organised by Adity Shyam. All this kept me busy till the 1990s. It was around this time that I decided to do voluntary work, without any honorarium or monetary compensation. I was prompted by what, for want of a better term, can be called my 'inner voice' and volunteered to work with the Gandhi Labour Foundation in Puri.

Prior to this, I went through what was a relatively low point in my life, a period of depression triggered off by several factors. I had hoped that I would spend a large part of the last years of my life at our house in Ramgarh. My sister-in-law was keen to sell it and ultimately did so. Her sons and I failed to dissuade her. This was a blow to my dreams. Perhaps an even bigger factor was the absence of work. Even though it did not take up all my time, the freelance work that I did as a journalist for *Statesman* and some corporate houses kept me fairly busy. Several changes in the political environment of the country and in the *Statesman* brought to an end the work that I had been doing for the paper.

In the beginning of the 1990s, the Soviet Union collapsed and brought about the end of the cold war. It also saw the emergence of a unipolar world. Socialism became a dirty word and in its place came the new ideology of globalization and the market economy. Although the proponents of globalization and the market claim to be against all ideologies, in reality theirs is a very distinct ideology, with all its dogmas and rigid ideas, which underpins the drive that has successfully drawn the entire world into the globalization net. With the collapse of the Soviet Union and the only other major 'communist' country, China, taking to the capitalist road and integrating itself with the globalized system, the world and the media lost interest in Communist/Marxist ideology. As far as they were and are concerned, it had been cast into the dustbin of history.

Since I mainly wrote for the *Statesman* on subjects pertaining to the communist movement, past or present, this had a special import for me. For instance, I had written articles on Liberation Theology, a term coined to depict the thinking and activities of Catholic priests who embraced Marxist ideas and participated along with communists and socialists and other radical groups in the struggle against the dictatorships in some South American countries. This was a very interesting development that did not leave India untouched. I had also done reviews of books which described the research that some American universities were doing on Marxian ideology. With the media convinced that Marxist/communist/socialist ideology and movement were dead and not worth wasting newsprint on, my writing was of no interest to them. Just about this time the owners of the *Statesman* decided that they did not need an editor and Sunanda Datta-Ray, who had taken a year's sabbatical, was not allowed to join. Aditi also left the *Statesman* sometime later.

I could, of course, have continued freelancing with other papers and journals. Some did ask me to write but on issues I had no interest in. I could also have taken up writing offers for corporate houses but I turned them down for the same reason. The upshot of it all was that after a lifetime of intense activity of one sort or the other, I suddenly found that I had nothing to do. My blood pressure, which has always been low, dropped further and made physical activity difficult. Whether this brought on the depression or whether it was the depression that led to the sharp drop in pressure is difficult to say. Obviously, the two are interlinked.

I was looking for meaningful voluntary work and tried at to associate myself with the National Alliance of People's Movements (NAPM). The late Dr. Ajit Narain Bose, president of the local chapter, was a close friend and at my suggestion they started a paper. I had hoped that I would get involved with it but those put in charge of it did not need my assistance. Other baneful influences on my life included the loss that I suffered because of the crash in Unit Trust's Unit 64. This by itself would not have mattered had it not been for the fact that I was not able to find any worthwhile outlet for my mental and physical energy.

The depression was not very severe but for a while I had to take anti-depressants. The doctor, who attends to me and is a personal friend, happens to have specialized in psychiatry. Even though I was reluctant in the beginning, I accepted his suggestion. I was able to dispense with them when I resumed my rowing and cycling. Earlier, when my blood pressure dropped to an abnormally low level, I had been advised to stop rowing, my main physical activity. While working in Indian Oxygen, I used the company car to go to the Lakes. On retirement, I decided to cycle as I had done throughout my school and college life. It was the most natural thing for me to do. For many though, it was a subject of comment. Friends complimented me on my boldness and said that my action was a source of inspiration for them. Apparently, some who had been or still were close to the Communist Party also took note of it and contrasted my lifestyle with those who were now at the helm of affairs in the Party. On the advice of my physiotherapist, I also resumed rowing.

Every experience was an opportunity to learn; every event has lessons to impart. This five-year stretch taught me that work is necessary for survival; not work in the derived sense of something that generates a cash income. I am referring to work in the literal sense of the body and the mind having some specific activity in hand. This may seem obvious but is not the general perception of many for whom work is a drudgery that becomes necessary to earn a living. The moment there is enough money to make work unnecessary, the best thing to do is to avoid work like the plague and take it easy. I found that one of the severest punishments that can be meted out to a person is to deprive him of the chance to do any meaningful work. Solitary confinement in a cell without any books to read is a recognized form of torture that breaks down the spirit of the toughest of persons.

Bernard Shaw's aphorism comes to mind. Twisting the oft-repeated saying: 'Drink is the curse of the working classes', he said: 'Work is the curse of the drinking classes.' All over the world there is a class of moneyed people that spends its time going to parties, philandering, drinking, travelling from one resort to another; all in pursuit of fun or having a good time. Even among the middle and working classes in India, the concept of the good life is often one where people do not have to do any meaningful, productive work for society. They dream of the luxury of just spending their years idling away the hours, spending as much time as possible in bed.

In contrast I would like to quote Kahlil Gibran who writes:

> Then a ploughman said, Speak to us of Work.'
> And he answered saying,
> You work that you may keep pace with the earth and the soul of the earth.
> For to be idle is to become a stranger unto the seasons, and to

step out of life's procession that marches in majesty and proud submission towards the infinite.

When you work you are a flute through whose heart the whispering of the hour turns to music.

Which of you would be a reed, dumb and silent, when all else sings together in unison.

Always you have been told that work is a curse and labour a misfortune.

But I say to you that when you work you fulfil a part of earth's furthest dream assigned to you when the dream was born,

And in keeping yourself with labour you are in truth loving life,

And to love life through labour is to be intimate with life's inmost secret.

From Kahlil Gibran, *The Prophet,* courtesy the Gibran National Committee, Bsharry, Lebanon.

THIRTY-SEVEN

Kanti Mehta's Gandhi Labour Foundation

Towards the end of November or early in December 2002, out of the blue a letter arrived by ordinary post. I glanced at the end to see who the writer was. It was signed Kanti Mehta. The letter addressed me in familiar terms: 'My dear Jolly'. The name Kanti Mehta was not unknown to me. I recollected hearing the name often during the 1940s, when I was active in the trade union movement. Our comrades in the Electric Supply trade union spoke of him as an adversary because ours was a rival union. Later, while working amongst the Calcutta Port workers, I heard his name as a colleague of Dr. Maitrayee Bose who led the National Union of port employees, a rival union to ours.

Why was a person, against whom we had fought bitterly, addressing me in such familiar terms? I was even more surprised when I read the letter. He told me that he was aware of my activities and even knew that I had acquired an interest in spiritual matters. This was something that was not even known to my close circle of friends. I was even more puzzled when I read this. Reading on I learnt that he had established an organization in Puri known as the Gandhi Labour Foundation (GLF) and that he would be happy if I could speak at one of their programmes.

I would normally be wary of such invitations. Turning to my diary of that period I find that I wrote as follows: 'I have not mentioned here that I received a letter a few days ago from Kanti Mehta who is now running an organization called the Gandhi Labour Foundation. He has invited me to speak at one of their programmes. I have agreed to do so partly because this programme is somewhere near Puri and partly because I was keen to meet

Kanti and take a look at this organization that he is running. Whether this visit will just be a one-off affair or lead to my getting involved with their organization depends on my experience during this visit in January.'

It did not take me even a minute to respond to the letter. There was an email address and I wrote back that I would be interested in visiting his organization. From the diary entry it may be noted that even in that initial letter I had a premonition that it would lead to something more than a one-off visit. A few days later there is another significant entry:

> '5 Jan 03: A memorable day from many points of view. In the morning Kanti Mehta came over. I had never really met him earlier but very likely seen him from afar because very often his meetings and ours were held within a few yards of each other. Those had taken place at least 50 years earlier but even then I had no difficulty in recognizing him. That could have been because I had already started corresponding with him ever since he wrote to me about a month ago. He looked somewhat frail. I heard him talk about the work he had been doing and I was quite impressed. It seems I am being drawn into the work of the organization he has set up. Am I being too hasty in thinking this way? I definitely must proceed more slowly and cautiously. In any case, I have decided to pay an exploratory trip to his institute where I will get a chance to see things for myself. It is only then that I will be able to decide my future course of action. I have already committed myself to Tapogiri and then there are my commitments in Calcutta. After this, can I take on anything else? If so what do I cut out or where do I scale down my activities? Again a dilemma seems to be confronting me but I am sure I will be able to sort out things after visiting the place. I will, of course, keep on seeking guidance and I am sure I will be able to decipher the message when it comes.

The message did come loud and clear. I did get involved in the activities of GLF to such an extent that within two or three years I was considered an indispensable part of the organization and virtually Kanti Mehta's alter ego. Hard as it might be to believe, it is a fact that I found within a few months of my arrival in Puri that, despite having come from such disparate backgrounds and traversing paths that were far removed from each other, our views on almost all issues, national and international, were almost identical. For him to come to Gandhi might seem natural since he had a Congress background. However his *Gandhivichar* (the thoughts or philosophy of Gandhi) was very different from what the mass of Congressmen and even Congress leaders believed then and believe now. For them Gandhi is an icon to be worshipped and projected as a kind of a brand though his ideas and his message are of no relevance in the present situation. *Gandhigiri* has, in recent times, been popularized by Bollywood, through a film called *Munnabhai Lage Raho*. The bulk of the Congressmen today were probably not around in the pre-Independence period. Kanti Mehta, however, fully accepted the relevance of Gandhi. As his autobiography reveals, he had accepted it in the days of the freedom struggle in which he had actively participated and he continued to live the life of a Gandhian. His autobiography has now been published and I hope it gets a wide readership. He too had been an agnostic, had been influenced by Marxism and still held the view that much of it was valid but did not consider it an alternative religion or an infallible truth for all time to come. He has mentioned in his autobiography that in the ILO debates he often found himself on the same side as the representatives of the Soviet bloc to the extent that he was told by a European delegate that the American participating in a debate had on one occasion whispered the question: 'Is that guy a communist?'

What is important for the purposes of my autobiography is that he understood me fully and gave me full scope to use my creative faculties. He gave me full charge of the English journal and though for technical reasons—and because of my own unwillingness to be designated editor—my name was not printed as the editor, he did make me the de facto editor. On the title page I was referred to as the consulting editor. He gave me full authority to buy any book that I wanted for the library and I was able to buy and read many books I might never have been able to do otherwise. When the *World Social Forum* was held in Bombay, he insisted that I go and paid the airfare and the registration fee. My visit to Mumbai for the *World Social Forum* was and will remain a memorable event. It gave me a glimpse of the current global efforts to search for a better system and to create a new world. It was after this visit that I felt that I was not alone but part of a world-wide movement searching for what I have been seeking all my life.

An important part of the GLF agenda was the *Working Together* annual meet where top management and leaders of the trade unions of Tata Steel and associate companies discussed problems of mutual interest. Usually, an important dignitary either from the corporate or the academic world was invited to give the keynote address. On one occasion, Kantibhai invited me to deliver the keynote address. I accepted the invitation and the address was circulated while I spoke extempore on the main points of my speech. The speech has been printed in the proceedings of the meet that was brought out later.

I also shared his views on the problems plaguing the trade union movement. I had left the field over half a century ago, while he was still in close touch and I learnt a lot from him about the developments that had been and were still taking place. His long experience in the trade union movement had convinced him that without the right kind of education, mere increase in salaries and other emoluments would not benefit the workers: hence his passion for providing education. He set up an Institute for Miners and Metal Workers Education, which evolved into the Gandhi Labour Foundation. This gave him the greatest satisfaction and remains his lasting contribution to the cause of the working class. It was built up gradually over a period of time with the help of the workers themselves and some of his colleagues and well wishers. When I went in January 2003, it was already a vibrant organization holding regular educational programmes for workers. The motto of the institute attracted me immensely: A Better Worker, a Better Citizen and a Better Human being.' The education imparted was on the lines suggested by Swami Vivekananda while being attuned to contemporary needs.

Kanti Mehta's vision is expressed best in his own words and I quote:

> 'My feeling had been that my mission was to carry on educational work. Thus when I submitted my resignation as General Secretary of Intuc it was with a sense of relief that at last I would be able to concentrate entirely on what I felt was my mission.
>
> 'I was all the more keen on doing this because I had seen how values were deteriorating and corruption was seeping into almost all levels of society. Speaking of the mining industry with which I had been intimately associated all these years, I had seen the various phases of the movement. When I had just started work in the forties, there had virtually been no proper trade union movement. I have already described how some organisations that called themselves trade unions functioned on the basis of pure muscle power. Mafia raj was prevalent and one had to be prepared for the worst whenever one stepped out to work in the mining areas. However, after years of struggle and thanks to the tribunals and wage boards, which the government had to set up as a result of the pressure of our movement, the condition of the workers gradually started improving. Trade unions, in the proper sense of the term, began to be built and as a result of our efforts the Indian National Mineworkers' Federation became a strong and powerful organisation, supported by the majority of the workers.
>
> 'However as wage levels increased, workers attitudes began to change. I think when they were very poor and were struggling for a minimum wage, they had a greater feeling of solidarity, a better appreciation of the need for unity and struggle to achieve

their goals. Later, as their pay packets improved from 30 to 100 and gradually to 2000 and kept increasing steadily, they became more self-centred. Preserving their relatively higher standard of living became more important. Indeed, as they moved into higher income brackets they wanted more and more. The feeling for other weaker sections of society began to fade; they were not able to see that they themselves were becoming a privileged force. They were no longer the proletariat for whom Marx had given the slogan 'You have nothing to lose but your chains'. Gandhi had himself warned that if the workers, in their fight against the Capitalists, go beyond meeting their needs and develop ambitions of becoming Capitalists themselves they will forfeit the goodwill of society and be looked upon as just another privileged section of society.

'It is interesting to take note of what happened when the big upsurge of students took place in France in the mid- sixties. It was really a very big wave and took all the forms of a classical insurrection such as took place in Russia in 1917 with, of course, one big difference. The students had appealed to the workers to join them but the French working class did not respond—the 'vanguard' was not even willing to play a rearguard role and so the forces of the establishment rallied and gradually the wave receded leaving a trail of bitterness and disillusionment in a whole generation of youth. The impact of this has been felt all over the world and I think it is very clearly visible in India.

'The reason for the fragmentation that has taken place in the trade union movement is that the workers have, by and large, lost their radical outlook and are not able to look beyond more money and more privileges. The perspective is not one of struggle but of exerting pressure to get more. Trade unions are relying on using the leverage of political parties to gain their ends rather than on their own unity and the strength of their organization. This is one of the factors that has led to the fragmentation as political parties, whose sole objective now is to win the electoral battle by hook or by crook, by fair means or foul, are very eager to take the help of the organized workers to come to power. Having a trade union wing on the support of which they can count certainly comes in handy for the Party at election time.

'The other and perhaps even more important factor that has led to the growth of factions within trade unions is the greed for the assets of the union and the power that comes with control of the union. It is not surprising that the process of fragmentation continues so that even in a union affiliated to one central organisation, there are several factions, which ultimately results in each faction forming its own union. The deterioration in values and the corruption that has permeated to other sections of society has not left the workers untouched.

'The adoption since 1989-90 of what is called the New Economic Policy the basic elements of which are 'Liberalisation, Privatisation and Globalisation' has further worsened the situation as far as the poorer sections of the population are concerned. The opening up of the country's markets to foreign imports by a drastic reduction in the import duties and the desperate appeals to foreign Capital to invest in the country has further widened the gap between the rich and the poor within the country. Although it is claimed that this will help our country and other developing countries who pursue similar policies to come up to the level of the developed world, the latest Human Development Report of the United Nations has estimated that India will, even if it continues to grow at its present rate, take till the year 2106 or a hundred years to catch up with the developed world.

'It is not only that the wealth produced in the poor countries is distributed unevenly within these countries but a disproportionate part of it goes out of these countries to investors of the industrialised countries. For example, for every pound sterling the rich countries invested in the poor countries during the sixties, two pounds were repatriated to the rich countries as profits on earlier investments.

'The widening gap of economic disparities is slowly leading to economic imperialism, which is a more subtle type of exploitation than political imperialism. This is being reflected in many aspects of international relations. The suggestion of Mr Lawrence E. Summers, when he was Chief Economist of the World Bank, in a memo to some of his colleagues, to encourage more shifting of dirty industries to the Third World and his contention that "the economic logic of dumping a load of toxic waste in the lowest wage country is impeccable", is one such example.

'Today one looks back at the other impeccable logic of Gandhiji who on the eve of Independence pleaded with Jawaharlal Nehru not to be taken in by the glamour and the seeming prosperity of the West based as it was on the exploitation of the colonies and of the less-developed countries. He wanted India to go in for a self-reliant, decentralized economy, based on the development of the villages rather than on the reckless urbanisation that was a feature of western 'civilisation'. Had we heeded his advice, today we would not be caught in the trap of the imperialism-led 'globalisation' with a debt of over a hundred and thirty billion dollars and one that is growing every day.

'Unfortunately, before the dialogue that had been started between him and Nehru could be concluded, widespread communal disorders broke out and further discussion was not possible. After Gandhiji's assassination on the 30 January 1948, Pandit Nehru did try to the best of his ability to keep the ideal of self-reliance in view but his approach was different. Being enamoured of centralised planning the approach was that of development from above, from one centre. There was development from above in industry and agriculture, education and health care and even the technological development was from the top. The result was that there was lop-sided development in the country.

'There are indications that this lop-sided development had begun to lead some re-thinking in the mind of Pandit Nehru. This is reflected in a statement he made in 1963 a few months before he died. One thing that distresses me very greatly is that, although I am convinced that the great majority of our population have bettered their economic conditions a little, with more calories and more clothes, yet there is a good number of people in India who have not profited by planning, and whose poverty is abysmal and most painful. I begin to think more and more of Mahatma Gandhi's approach. It is odd that I am mentioning his name in this connection. I am entirely an admirer of the modern machine, and I want the best machinery and the best technique but taking things as they are in India, however rapidly we advance towards the machine age and we will do so—the fact remains that a large number of our people are not touched by it and will not be for a considerable time.

'That Jawaharlal Nehru was desperately seeking for some method to remedy the situation is clear from his statement. One does not know whether he would have been successful in finding a way to revert to the approach that had been suggested by Gandhiji but he died soon after, in May 1964. The governments that followed continued with the centralised planning approach while the people, especially the affluent and even a section of the not-so affluent middle class, continued to demand that we should try to catch up with the West and adopt the materialistic culture prevalent there. As a result of heavy imports of luxury items, sophisticated machinery and defence equipment without a corresponding increase in exports the country came to the end of the precipice. The rescue operations were based on heavy borrowing from the International Monetary Fund and the World Bank. Later, we started going in for commercial borrowing with even higher rates of interest and on more onerous repayment terms.

'The question before us is whether the New Economic Policy will lead to the elimination of poverty and unemployment or whether some basic changes in our thinking and approach are required for solving these problems. For this purpose it will be necessary for us to consider what kind of society we want and how to attain it.

'Do we want an acquisitive society in which the jungle law of survival of the fittest prevails or one in which the culture of contentment will be cultivated? Gandhiji's epoch-making dictum that "there is enough in the world for everyone's need but not for any one's greed" should remind us that there are limits to growth. The chaos and anarchy that we see around us arise from the fact that man's baser instinct to grab whatever he can for himself has had free play and even gained respectability. Under the slogan of "survival of the fittest", we have made competition our instrument of progress. History has shown that cooperation and not competition is the key to survival. It is the bee and the ant and not the dinosaur that have survived the passage of time.

'Do we want a society in which economic growth takes place at the cost of conservation of nature and arable land? Or do we want a society in which "wealth accumulates and men decay"? Gandhiji said the goal of economic progress should be "human happiness combined with full mental and moral development". Can this be achieved by sacrificing social justice at the altar of economic growth?

'On technological development Gandhiji had once expressed his fears about" the head moving faster than the heart. Martin Luther King, Jr, echoes the same sentiment when he said "Our scientific power has outrun our spiritual power. We have guided missiles and misguided men." Gandhiji wanted production by the masses instead of mass production. He was against man being the slave of machines. He wanted man to be restored to his proper place in the scheme of things and production to be geared to the well-being of man instead of men being used as expendable material to increase a production. Where money and mechanism rule, said Gandhiji, "Capital exploits the labour of a few to multiply itself, but the sum total of the labour of the crores, wisely utilised automatically increases the wealth of the crores. He wanted labour to be so used that production should be a source of life, joy and freedom, instead of any one of these being sacrificed to production and all to money values. Therein lay the key to democracy.

'It is true that if Gandhiji's approach is accepted the people may have less of the gaudy goods of life—"the toys of civilisation"—but they will live in close contact with nature and enjoy abundance of fresh wholesome food which they could obtain by their own labour and sunshine, fresh air and aesthetic delights which nature freely provides but which today are not even available to the wealthiest of people. Work will not be the antithesis of life but a means of realizing the full content of life—a thing of beauty and a joy for ever. There will be no poverty of essentials though many non-essentials which are considered luxuries but most of which are harmful may not be available. The needs of the many will not be sacrificed to cater to the privileges of the few or for the "abstraction" called "national prosperity" or "progress".

'In advancing to his ideal society, I still venture to think that the workers have a great role to play. But for that the various shortcomings and weaknesses that have crept into the trade union movement will have to be eradicated and the ego and self-interest of a few will have to give place to a united movement.'

I have quoted at length from his autobiography because his views coincide with mine. During the nearly five years during which I interacted with him for hours on a regular basis, I think I learnt a lot from him and I venture to think that I too had an influence on him. My own role in the Gandhi Labour Foundation was to take classes for workers along with other faculty members. The subject I chose was globilization and its impact. I tried to present what I thought should be the Gandhian approach on the subject. I was helped a lot by the articles published by Professor Amlan Datta and some others who held similar views. As far as our critique of globalization was concerned, there was much in common with the Left critique though our views on the alternative social system differ very widely from theirs. Even in the matter of the critique, the Left viewpoint lacks credibility because their practice is very much in sync with the capitalist viewpoint. In fact, I think the Left is entirely under the influence of the Chinese communists and, when it comes to practice in West Bengal and Kerala in particular, it is trying to follow the Chinese model in toto. Since the conditions, political, social and economic, are vastly different, it is not succeeding. It is not likely to succeed in future as far as one can see.

A sea change in the situation occurred on 20 October 2007. I usually visit Ramgarh in October and was on the Ranikhet Express that night when, at around 3 o'clock my mobile phone started ringing. I woke up but did not answer. I thought it was one of those messages sent by the Telecom organization or some marketing organization. The ringing persisted and since I was awake, I answered. It was a call from GLF Puri informing me that Kantibhai had passed away. Although he was in his eighty-seventh year and suffering from several ailments, he was active till the last. In fact, we were planning a big national seminar on the issue of Culture of Peace and Non-Violence where we were hoping to bring on one platform all the Gandhian organizations and even those who did not call themselves Gandhian but were carrying on non-violent struggles and movements.

I had been actively involved in the preparations along with him and all the circulars and other literature that was needed had been prepared by me. I too had hoped, as he had, that this would be a turning point in the democratic movement and make a major impact on the national scene. The news came as a major shock and I changed my plans of going to the hills and headed straight for Delhi and from there to Puri. I was not in time for the cremation. I reached the day after. The shock disoriented me completely and brought on all the depression and other ailments that had been plaguing me. The immediate problem facing GLF was whether to go ahead with the seminar or not. I had assumed that with the demise of Kanti Mehta the seminar would be abandoned or at least postponed indefinitely. However, on arrival in Puri I found that they had already taken a decision to go ahead with the seminar. Their logic was simple: since Kaul Sahab had been involved from the very beginning with the planning of the seminar he would be able to handle it. I had no option but to agree.

They had overlooked the fact that in two areas, essential for the success of the seminar, my ability to contribute was nil. The first was to raise funds. We had estimated that a budget of around Rs 5 lakhs would be required. Kantibhai with his contacts was confident of raising more than that amount. On my own, I would not be able to collect a single rupee. The second requirement was to ensure the participation of the key figures in all the Gandhian organizations spread across India and even abroad. Kantibhai knew almost all of them personally and a telephone call from him would be enough to secure their participation provided their fare, to and from, was paid for. I had been involved in the Gandhian movement only for a few years and, with the exception of four or five important personalities, I knew no one.

We did have the seminar that turned out to be a little better than I had feared, thanks largely to the participation of Professor Amlan Datta as the keynote speaker, Justice (Retd) C. S. Dharmadhikari and a few other Gandhians but fell very much short of what had been planned. This experience made me feel that without Kantibhai there was not very much that I could do on my own and I began to wonder whether my continuation in the organization would serve any useful purpose. In any case, I was finding it difficult to cope with the shock of Kantibhai's death. My general health had deteriorated with advancing years. As these lines are being written I must record with regret that I decided to withdraw from the organization and end my stint with GLF, though I might still visit the place occasionally. A little over five years ago, my inner voice had told me that I should respond to the invitation extended to me by Kanti Mehta. It is the same voice that told me that I ought to retire and move on to the next chapter of my life story that would undoubtedly be the last. My association with Kantibhai has been a rich learning experience for me. As I came to know him intimately and heard him narrate his experiences, I was able to appreciate how he had, throughout his life, tried to mould himself on Gandhian lines and had boldly tried to correct and refashion the trade union movement.

I was sixty when I retired from Indian Oxygen, towards the end of 1981 and keen to work because I needed to earn and, with all my faculties in fine trim, I could carry on much longer. After I retired from *Capital*, some five years later, I had begun to feel that I needed to call it quits and to prepare for the end that, I felt, could not be too far off. That did not happen. When I left the Gandhi Labour Foundation in October 2008, I was already in my 88th year. I felt that I had to complete my memoirs that I had started writing some years earlier because the time for my retirement had finally come. After all, our own Indian tradition lays down the different phases of life quite clearly and prescribes *sanyas* (a retreat to a monastic life) for the last phase of one's life. That is how I hope it will be though I have a lurking fear that it may not actually turn out to be so. As the saying goes, man proposes and God disposes.

A few words about the somewhat dramatic transformations that have taken place in my life. From a lover of literature and poetry—Tagore's *Gitanjali* in an English translation had influenced me tremendously both for its spiritual and its poetic content—to that of a card-holding hard-line communist living in workers' slums or party communes, proclaiming atheism and Dialectical Materialism; moving on from there to the other side of the fence, entry into the corporate world as an executive of a multinational company, roaming the corridors and banquet halls of five-star hotels and elite clubs; and not long after, initiation into spiritual life through the Ramkrishna Math and Mission and through Pondicherry and Sri Aurobindo's philosophy; then some years as a Gandhian activist in the Gandhi Labour Foundation and, finally, to the last phase (will it really be the last?). The transition from one phase to another has been smooth. I have never felt these changes as sudden breaks. The force of circumstances, my own experience, and my own understanding of the developing situation has led to the different stages. The books and the literature suited for each phase have automatically come to me and, along with this theoretical background, the actual practice has deepened my understanding and helped me to develop my own philosophy of life as I have gone along. Human beings are not very different, whatever the class they belong to. In whichever sphere of activity I have been involved with, I have found the same strengths and weaknesses, the same vices and virtues, the same hopes, the same despair, the same success stories and failures.

Today in the phase that I have perhaps over-optimistically referred to as sanyas, I am not altogether inactive nor am I just reading spiritual books. I am trying to catch up on my reading that had been neglected all these years. Fundamentalists of all brands do not want their cadres to read anything except the prescribed texts relating to their own ideologies. Having shaken off the shackles, my current areas of interest are: literature, fiction, philosophy, the cultural heritage of India and recent developments in science, written for the general reader. Despite my unwillingness I am also often drawn to seminars or discussion groups on current political issues.

Since I now live alone, friends often sympathize with me and wonder how I cope with my loneliness. I do feel lonely sometimes but there is no reason why I should feel so. I have very good neighbours in Kaustav Chakravarty and his family and others with whom I am in regular contact and whose help and protection are always available. The office bearers of our Apartment Owners' Association are also quite helpful, even though my closest companion in the building, Nripen Chakravarty, passed away in April 2009.

Ours was a very closely-knit family but, as the youngest of six brothers, I am the only one who survives. However, I have nephews and nieces, many of them in Delhi, some in Kolkata but some abroad in Canada and the United States. With those abroad, I keep occasional contact by email. With those in Delhi, I am in close touch thanks to the telephone and email but also through visits at least once, sometimes twice a year. While these are occasions when I can relax and unwind, my interaction with them helps me keep abreast of the thought processes of a different generation that is no longer very young. Some have retired, others are on the verge of it, and yet no one is on a very different wavelength from mine. Rummy and Sudhir Dar, Anoop and Divya, Naveen and Gita, Ranjan and Rekha, Sanju and Anita, all very talented and eminent in their own fields, are among those members of our family whose company and hospitality I enjoy and benefit from.

I am particularly grateful to three families in Kolkata whom I look upon as my guardians. Without their support I would not have been able to survive in an environment that is markedly unfriendly to senior citizens living alone. My niece, Vini and her husband, Prem Shivpuri, Rana (Dipankar) Sengupta, my wife's nephew, and Jhuma and, of course, Aditi Roy Ghatak, a person of outstanding talent and ability, whom I look upon as my daughter.

I am loosely associated with some organizations and groups. The West Bengal Federation of United Nations Associations (Webfuna)—the moving figure of which has been my friend Sitaram Sharma—has been holding seminars and conferences on various issues ranging from human rights, peace, reform of the UN charter, in many of which I have participated. It organizes student debates when I am sometimes asked to be on the panel of judges. When I was more actively involved with the Webfuna, I had occasion to interact with its President, H. A. Halim, Speaker of the West Bengal Assembly and a prominent leader of the CPI(M). I also participate in discussions and *adda* sessions at Santosh Bhattacharya's house. Santosh, a former party activist, later economist and Vice-Chancellor of Calcutta University, is a good friend. Our views coincide on certain issues but on others we do not always see eye to eye. Another friend, Subhas Roy, who tells me that he has at one time been associated with the Trotskyites, a Foreign Exchange and Management Consultant, also invites me to occasional discussions at his residence, where retired intellectuals from various disciplines participate.

I am privileged to be a member of an informal group the moving spirit of which is my very good friend Kamal, former communist and wife of Prasanta Sanyal. Prasanta, who was among my very close friends and benefactors, is no more. He had been active in the student and communist movements and later became Managing Director of the Clarion advertising agency. Some of the other members of this informal group are Mayadi (Sen) now in her nineties, Gopa Burman, wife of writer Ashish Burman, Radha Ghosal, Lipi Ghatak and Anjali Sen, a contemporary of our university years and later a colleague in the public relations profession. I would also like to refer here to Kamal's daughters, Babli and Gulan, both outstanding individuals, who have made a mark for themselves. I have learnt a lot and benefited from my association with them. I also enjoy the morning tea sessions that I occasionally have with Sunanda Datta-Ray, now a well-known columnist whom I first met in Delhi in 1964.

Amongst my former comrades, I was in touch with only a few after I left the Party. Most of them are no more. 'They are all gone into the world of light/And I alone sit lingering here'. I meet a few occasionally, among them, Ajit Roy, one of the most erudite and perspicacious Marxist scholars of the day; Prabhat (who passed away recently) and Bani Dasgupta, the only one left of the intrepid band of communists who built up the women's movement in the 1940s and 1950s along with Manikuntala Sen. They were vibrant actors in my life's stage; they enhanced the quality of the drama; inspired me to achieve greater heights and supported me when my spirits seemed to flag.

THIRTY-EIGHT

Whither Better World?

From the time I arrived in the world, muling and puking in the ayah's arms, at 20 minutes past seven on 22 September 1921, my life has been a series of phases over nearly nine decades. This is possibly so for most people; what distinguishes mine is the dramatic manner in which I plunged into every one of them, never sparing even myself. I look back in amazement at the way the prospective ICS became a diehard communist; how that communist turned to be a communications expert for a multinational; and then again, how the MNC spokesperson immersed himself in a world of Vivekananda and then Gandhian philosophy. The common thread, throughout the vicissitudes of the changing circumstances, was my keenness to learn, to broaden my understanding and never to lose sight of the objective of trying to contribute to the betterment of society.

Many questions have been asked of me; questions that different people have answered differently. I have my own set of conclusions on these issues:

1. How did the mighty Soviet Union—with its sphere of influence extending from Czechoslovakia in the west to Vladivostok on the east, from Murmansk in the north to Tashkent in the south, with a nuclear arsenal that could have destroyed the planet many times over, collapse within a few days, like a house of cards?

The answer is not merely of academic interest. In a proper understanding of this question lies the clue to an understanding of many other vexed issues that face us not only in India but the world over. Some years before he passed away, Abani Lahiri, a veteran leader of the undivided CPI, whom I held in high regard, dropped in at my flat on one of his visits to Calcutta. We chatted for a while and before leaving he suggested that I do research on this subject. He promised to discuss it when he visited the city next. I would have loved to hear his views and share mine with him. Unfortunately, the second round of discussion never took place. He passed away shortly afterwards. Regrettably, none of the various wings of the communist movement have tried to come to grips with this question. An open debate on the factors that led to this collapse would have helped them and all others interested in a more humane and just social order.

2. Why has the communist movement in India not been able to expand outside its three bases in West Bengal, Kerala and Tripura? It had been operating in other parts of India and was a fairly important political force in states such as Bihar and Andhra. Today, it has to ride piggy back on regional parties to register its presence in the State Assemblies. Indeed, in many other countries too, Italy and France in Europe and Indonesia in Asia, for instance, where the communist parties were once a major force, they have been marginalized.

Four or five years ago, in one of the exchanges between civil society groups in India and Pakistan, I met some members of a Pakistani delegation to India, who had leftist leanings. They asked me precisely this question. In the very brief time at our disposal, we were not able to get beyond a perfunctory exchange of views. It did reveal though that, not only within India but, elsewhere too, people sympathetic to the communist ideology wonder why the communist movement in India has been unable to expand outside its few bases.

3. Capitalist democracy, the dominant model in Western and also in Eastern Europe, has its defects but is there an alternative? Although the Francis Fukuyama thesis of the End of History does not have many takers today even in the United States, most

> political scientists in the West and many even in Third World countries believe that no other viable political system can or will emerge in the foreseeable future. In the West and even in India, socialism has become a dirty word. Even a communist Chief Minister states that his brief is to build *Capitalism* and not socialism. Is this a reality that we have to accept or is there an alternative, not just utopian but realisable?

On this issue we held a series of discussions at our flat on Karaya Road. Dr. Ajit Narain Bose, Sunil Sen Sharma, a geologist, close to the RSP and an intellectual of note, Anil Biswas, also a geologist and environmentalist, Subhas Roy, Nibedita Roy, a young social activist and some others whose names I cannot recall were part of what we called a kind of study circle. We had hoped that at the end of these discussions we would be able to bring out a book setting down our conclusions. However even though some common points did emerge from our discussions, some of which are part of what I have put down in this chapter we could not proceed after Sunil Sen Sharma suddenly died, Dr. Ajit Narain Bose joined the West Bengal Planning Commission and could not spare time. He too is no more now.

The three issues are not entirely disparate I would like to deal with them all together as they are ultimately interlinked.

I The Collapse of the Soviet Union

There is one view that the onus for the collapse of the Soviet Union rests squarely on Gorbachev who subverted the Soviet system from within by trying to foist *glasnost* and *perestroika* in a hurry. The proponents of this view say that this was an attempt to introduce a western political system not suited to the Soviet Union. Shortly after the break up of the Soviet Union, I had occasion to visit Minsk, the capital city of Belarus, where I met the Secretary of the Belarus Communist Party. To my surprise, I found that even at that time the Party seemed very much in control in that country. When I mentioned Gorbachev's name he flared up and said he should be put in jail.

Not much credence can be given to the view holding a single individual responsible in the light of what happened after the coup when, for a brief, period the hard-line group within the Communist Party of the Soviet Union took control of the country. If the people and the army had rallied in support, Yeltsin could not have ousted them within days as he managed to do. There can be no denying that the people were not willing to see a restoration of the rule of the Communist Party. So what were the factors that made the people turn away from the Party and the system that had been in force till the late 1980s?

In 1982, before the break up of the Soviet Union, I was invited as a journalist to visit the country. Apart from visiting Moscow and Leningrad, I had an opportunity to visit some of the important towns in Siberia: Abakan, Shusenskaye and Novosibirsk, where large development projects, including a 6,000 MW hydro-electric power plant, were coming up. As the editor of *Capital*, I was interested in the economic developments there and had opted to visit Siberia because I had heard of its vast reserves of oil, gas and minerals. On my return from the trip I did some research at the Gorky Sadan library and wrote a book: *Siberia and the Soviet Economy*. I also consulted a western authority, Alec Nove, whose book *An Economic History of the USSR*, gives a wealth of information on the development process in the Soviet Union. The growth rate of the Soviet economy had been very impressive throughout but there were some reasons why the Soviet Union lagged far behind the West European economies.

One: it had been devastated by the civil war immediately after the Revolution. Although it has been referred to as a civil war, it was actually an attempt by the imperialist powers to overthrow the government. Two: there was the Nazi invasion, which dealt a very severe blow to the economy as the German army had penetrated deep into Russia, as far as Stalingrad, where it was finally defeated and forced to turn back. Three: the arms race during the cold war severely strained the resources of the country. In tying to keep pace with the growing military might of the USA and the Nato forces, the Soviet Union, with its relatively lesser economic muscle, was forced to divert its efforts from economic development to bolstering up its war machine.

The point is that it was not that the Soviet economy had collapsed and the Soviet Union broke up on that account. Indeed, even western sources have admitted that there was almost total employment in the country and starvation and hunger had been eliminated though agricultural production had not kept pace with the growth in industrial production. To that extent, the condition of the Soviet people had improved compared to what it had been in the Tsarist period. Under the Tsars, as many as 34 years in the eighteenth century and 40 years in the nineteenth had been years of famine.

Whatever may have been the extenuating factors, there is no doubt that the standard of living of the Soviet people, and of those in its sphere of influence in Eastern Europe, was much lower than those obtaining in the developed West. The contrast between East and West Germany was so marked that repeated attempts were made to scale the Berlin Wall and to cross over to the West. No one knows how many were shot down in such attempts. The radio, the telephone and, by the 1970s and 1980s, television had made the Iron Curtain irrelevant. It was this glaring contrast between the living standards of the two worlds, the one in Western Europe and the other in the eastern part that the people in the Soviet led countries refused to accept. And when the opportunity came they broke free.

Again, Russian claims of having a classless society rang hollow with the people seeing for themselves how the new elite class had emerged: the communists. The lifestyle of this elite group was not very different from that of the western elite. When Djilas wrote *The New Class*, he and other communist leaders of Yugoslavia, not excluding the legendary anti-fascist fighter, Marshal Tito, were denounced as imperialists but the Soviet people knew the reality.

The East European countries: Poland, Romania, Bulgaria and Czechoslovakia had communist regimes but these were foisted on the people after the Soviet army marched in following the retreating Nazi army. The nature of these undemocratic and unpopular regimes was exposed when popular revolts in Hungary and Czechoslovakia were crushed with the help of Soviet tanks and troops. Naturally, they were the first to collapse the moment Gorbachev loosened the steel grip of the administration. Clearly the situation was rife for a change. Had Gorbachev not ushered in *glasnost* and *perestroika,* some other communist leader would undoubtedly have or else there may have been a far more bloody revolution to affect the change.

Certainly the Russians are not living in paradise today. The introduction of the capitalist system has brought with it the entire range of ills inevitable in capitalist society. Widening disparity between the different sections of society, crime, violence, drugs and corporate frauds are rampant. The rejection of the system prevailing in the Soviet Union by the vast majority of the people showed that it did not create the kind of society that had been hoped for by Marx, Engels or Lenin. The promise of the Revolution was: All power to the Soviets: Land to the peasants: Peace. While the Soviets were established, power was usurped by the Party; within it, power was usurped by the General Secretary. Instead of the dictatorship of the proletariat, it was the dictatorship of the Party, which no longer represented the working class. Instead of land being given to the peasants, it was taken over by the state in the name of collectivisation. Instead of peace, the forcible acquisition of the land led to a kind of civil war between the state and the peasantry. Sholokhov's *Quiet flows the Don* chronicled the tragedy that unfolded on a massive scale when the collectivisation drive was going on. Some have described the system that prevailed as 'state capitalism' and not socialism.

Charles Bettelheim, a French Marxist economist, goes further and calls it 'party capitalism'. In his monumental work *Class Struggles in the USSR* he states: 'The present work stands opposed to this thesis ("failure of socialism"), since it reveals that the USSR and the other countries who had declared that they had "built socialism" had not accomplished any of the radical social transformations which could have permitted them to break away from this specific form of state capitalism which I have described as "party capitalism".' To sustain that system emerged a rigid form of dictatorship—certainly not the dictatorship of the proletariat—but an oppressive dictatorship of the Bolshevik Party led till 1953 by the Stalinist leadership. Despite a few abortive efforts in subsequent years, succeeding leaderships only replicated the system.

The bottom line was that notwithstanding the severe strain on the Soviet economy caused by the civil war and the Nazi occupation and again by the arms race during the cold war, there was enough for the basic needs of the people. However, the system that ensured this was not based on the support of the people and could be sustained only by a coercive dictatorship. It was the discontent over the wide difference in the living conditions in the Soviet Union and the western countries on the one hand and the disparity in the life styles of the top communist brass and the ordinary Soviet masses on the other that led to the break-up of the Soviet Union. One is reminded of Gandhi's words of wisdom, which bears repetition: 'There is enough in this world for everyone's need but not for everyone's greed.' The lure of the riches of the West beckoned the people who looked with greed at what lay on the other side of the fence. It is not that they were unaware of the inequity of the capitalist system but the temptation provided by the possibility of becoming rich prevailed.

This explains why the communist leaderships of China and in Vietnam, too, having fought bitterly to overthrow the imperialists and Capitalists, took to the capitalist path. A consumer society cannot but be a capitalist society. In any society, where the motivating factor is greed, the only system that will emerge is what we see in countries all over the world that are caught in the tentacles of the present form of globalization.

No matter what it is called, any system the objective of which is not just to meet the basic needs but to pander to people's greater wants and desires that are limitless cannot but be capitalist in nature. In that system alone can at least some people become extremely rich and have their desires for the good things (read luxuries) fulfilled. Not that it satisfies them. Millionaires yearn to become billionaires and even then their thirst is not quenched, never mind that their billions are made at the expense of millions of people who remain in dire poverty.

Capitalism had from its very inception been an exploitative system that increased the divide between the haves and have-nots. The industrial revolution accelerated the process. Post the Second World War, capitalism acquired several other characteristics. Technological changes and an enormous increase in the military and financial powers of what are now known as the G8 countries, have enabled them to get hold of the oil, the coal and the other mineral resources of the world and thus dominate the less developed countries. Globalization is only another name for the new world empire, much larger than any in previous history, at the head of which is of course the military industrial complex of the United States with the other countries of the G8 group as junior partners.

Marx and Engels in their *Communist Manifesto* had, while condemning the capitalist system, not failed to note its ability to increase production to an enormous extent. Today, capitalism has entered another phase. The stock markets have provided an opportunity to capitalists to multiply their wealth without entering into the production process at all. The George Soroses of the world can, just with the click of the mouse, turn their millions into billions. I came across a report that Soros had actually criticised globalization and got hold of the book only to find that his criticism of globalization refers to its inability to curb the powers that the national governments still have to regulate and thus hamper the present-day capitalism which has rightly been described as casino capitalism. The recession or what is often being referred to as the meltdown refers to the drop in the indices of all the major stock markets of the world, from the American Dow Jones to the Bombay Stock Exchange Sensex. What was in any case only a bubble has finally burst but it has taken down in its wake millions of Americans and ordinary citizens of the advanced world. These were people who had invested in the great stocks and bonds dream sold by the proponents of globalization as the new weapons of mass attraction.

Asked what he thought of modern civilisation, Gandhi remarked with his typical wry humour: 'It would be a good idea.' A civilisation, the crowning achievement of which are the nuclear arsenals of the world with their capacity to destroy all life on the planet many times over; where progress is measured not by the extent to which it contributes to human welfare and happiness but by the wealth generated; and which is gradually turning the whole world into an inferno; can hardly be called a civilisation. Based as it is on fossil fuels that, at the rate at which they are being consumed, will definitely be exhausted before the end of this century, it is doomed to collapse and yield to a new phase in human evolution in which there will be a transition to a higher level of consciousness, a new race of super men and women spiritually more developed.

II: Failure to Expand

Why has the communist movement in India not been able to expand beyond its three bases in West Bengal, Tripura and Kerala despite its long history? I do not know if I have the right answer but I have my own theory. The communist movement grew in India because of the hard work, sacrifice and courage of hundreds of pioneering cadres, who took part in the freedom struggle, served the poor and exploited peasants and workers, offering them hopes of a bright future in a classless and egalitarian society.

The early entrants in the 1920s and 1930s came from several different streams: from the Indian National Congress-led movement, guiding forces of which were Lokmanya Tilak, Mahatma Gandhi, Jawaharlal Nehru, Sardar Patel, Maulana Azad; the Subhas Bose-led left-nationalist stream; the revolutionary (terrorist) movement of heroic figures such as Bhagat Singh and Surya Sen, to give a few examples. Then there were the trade union and peasant struggles and socialist/communist movements, led by those who were inspired by the ideas of socialist thinkers of various hues in Europe and America, ranging from the Utopian and the Fabian socialists to the Marxists. It was through these struggles and sacrifices that the communists were able to spread their influence and to emerge as an important force in the political arena of the country, not so much in the pre-Independence period as after the adoption of the new Constitution with its introduction of adult franchise and a multi-party democracy.

The ushering in of the new Constitution and the beginning of the universal adult franchise in India, led to a sea change in the socio-political environment. The communist movement and the organizational structure of the Communist Party had been geared to prepare for an armed struggle for the seizure of power. The only controversy was whether it would be on the lines of the Russian revolution or the Maoist Liberation struggle. In the 1948-period, there were attempts to set up bases, such as the one set up in Yenan. The visit of the four-man delegation to Moscow in 1950 resolved the controversy but the party programme and the Tactical Line that came from there continued the old line of combining open and secret work in preparation for an ultimate seizure of power by an armed insurrection.

The series of General Elections from 1952, somewhat unexpectedly, threw up the communists, though small in number, as the main opposition group in the Lok Sabha. Five years and another General Election later, the possibility opened out of the communists coming to power at least in some of the states. In Kerala, they actually did so and, in West Bengal, the number of communists in the assembly kept growing. While the majority in the Party officially denounced the line of the Twentieth Congress of the CPSU regarding the possibility of peaceful transition to socialism, the practice on the ground clearly indicated that the ballot rather than the bullet was becoming the preferred choice of the Party. Winning elections was the first priority and all other activities were put on the backburner.

I have described the changes in the practices and the attitudes of the party leadership. Fighting for party tickets for seats in the municipalities, Assemblies and the Lok Sabha/Rajya Sabha became the norm. Financial and physical resources in terms of funds and volunteers, false voters and musclemen to counter the muscle men of the other Party became part of the strategy of winning elections. Seats began to be sold. I have mentioned earlier how I accidentally witnessed one particular deal. Meanwhile, as is well known, Soviet funds were also coming in and there was the help in the shape of facilities for select party leaders and cadres to go for a change or for treatment in sanatoria in the Soviet Union and in some of the East European countries.

Prior to the 1970s, communists were in power in West Bengal Tripura and Kerala for short spells. Since 1977, Left Front governments, led by the CPI(M), have been in power in West Bengal and Tripura for fairly long spells. In Kerala, the CPI(M)-led Left has been in power on and off during this entire period and is in power at the time of writing. Apart from the corruption and factionalism that are endemic to all governments of different parties in India, a major contribution of this development has been that instead of service to the people even for the Left, the main lever for winning elections appears to be money power, muscle power and patronage in the form of contracts, prize posts, providing employment selectively only to party loyalists and such others.

Apart from this, two other factors seem to be responsible for preventing the communist movement from spreading to other parts of the country. It seems that the main strength of the communist leaders like Lenin and Mao and, later, Gramsci and Togliatti, was that they had their roots in the history, tradition and ethos of their own countries and thus creatively applied Marxist theory to the environmental conditions prevailing there. Mao, in fact, gave a totally different orientation to Marxist theory by making it a peasant revolution.

In India, the country's entire past and all its traditions and thoughts have been rubbished. Rajani Palme Dutt's *India Today* with its categorization of Gandhi ('the Jonah of Indian revolution') as a reactionary and the chief obstacle to the revolution was the Bible of the communists in the early phase. Not that all communists were ignorant of these traditions and ideas. Debiprasad Chattopadhyaya, well versed in Indian philosophy, singled out the Charvak school of philosophy, which is somewhat similar to the hedonistic philosophy that appeared in the West, as the only one relevant to modern India. Others were dismissed as idealistic philosophies incompatible with the theory of Dialectical Materialism, which alone represented the ultimate truth.

I also know vaguely—I have not personally been able to access their articles/books—that Dange and Sardesai have, in some of their writings, tried to go to some of our ancient texts and tried to study to what extent they are relevant to India today. In some of the writings of Professor Hiren Mukherjee too I have found acknowledgement of Rammohan Roy, Sri Aurobindo, Rabindranath Tagore and Gandhi as among the makers of modern India. Notwithstanding all this, in working out the strategy and tactics of the Indian revolution, it was Marxism-Leninism, as interpreted by the Soviet Communist leadership alone, that played a part. Although sometimes there was talk of working out a specifically Indian path, in reality it was the International that decided it. Until 1943, it was the Comintern whose decisions were binding on the Indian party. It was expressly laid down by the Comintern that one of its mandatory conditions for affiliation was that the decisions of the executive committee of the Comintern were binding on affiliated parties. The Indian Party was affiliated. Even after the formal dissolution of the Comintern, it was to Moscow that the Party had to turn in 1950 to resolve the controversy that had arisen after the disastrous Left-Adventurist period. Stalin personally approved the draft programme and Tactical Line given from there to the Indian Party.

Today that programme and Tactical Line stand abandoned, having proved largely irrelevant in present-day conditions. In fact, the practice of the Party, whether the CPI or the CPI(M), especially in states where they are in power, has absolutely nothing that can even remotely be derived from Marxism-Leninism. That does not unfortunately mean that their dependence on foreign sources has ended. It is clearly the Chinese model of unadulterated capitalism that is inspiring the practice of the major communist party, the CPI(M). One also gets to see the peculiar phenomenon of totally different policies being pursued in states where the Party is in power and where it is not. The voice of the Left in Delhi is often totally at variance with the voice of Left in states where it is in power.

Finally, one needs to refer to the active opposition of the Party to the Quit India movement and to its refusal to acknowledge the plain fact that in October-December 1962, China committed aggression against India. Although public memory is short, these events will continue to haunt the communist movement for a long time to come. Unless it comes clean on its past and tries to independently work out its own model of development that puts human development and not the growth of GDP as its objective, it will continue to remain another regional party, indistinguishable from others except for a greater degree of ruthlessness, arrogance, dogmatism and the contempt for democratic norms that it has borrowed from Stalinism.

III My Vision of the Alternative

What should and would be the shape of the better world that we are searching for? The whole of humanity has been engaged in this search ever since the dawn of civilisation: Plato's *Republic;* Ram Raj; *Vasudaiva Kutumbukum* were all attempts to present a vision of a system where there would be harmony and a spirit of universal brotherhood. The French Revolution spelt out the vision of the thinkers of that time in terms that are perhaps more relevant today with their cry of 'Liberty, Equality and Fraternity'. So, it has to be a world where there is freedom, where all have equal opportunities, equal rights and where the whole of mankind is united in fraternal bonds.

Marx's vision of the future society can be seen in his description of the stage of communism in which each one would contribute according to his ability and receive according to his need. It would, of course, be a classless society where there would be no question of exploitation of one class by another. It would also be a society where the state would wither away. There can be quarrel with this vision for a better world.

Perhaps these would be considered to be dreams; utopian ideas that have very little practical validity in today's world. There is no reason to doubt that a process of evolution has been going on ever since the first plants sprouted; the first amoeba appeared. From time to time, there have been great leaps forward and what seemed impossible has been achieved. Higher and higher forms of animals evolved and, finally, we had the *homo sapiens*, the human beings that inhabit the world, all of six billion and more today. The human being is sometimes referred to as a rational animal. Actually, this human being is more than a rational animal; it is one that has the unique capacity to be conscious of itself. This has been a giant leap forward in the process of evolution. There is no reason to think that the process of evolution has now stopped. What will be the next step forward in evolution?

Thinkers like Julian Huxley, Swami Vivekananda and Sri Aurobindo have expressed the view that it will be a development in human consciousness, a leap forward to a higher level. Individuals, perhaps one in a million, have already achieved this level, call it enlightenment, call it *buddhahood*, or the super-conscious state. Vivekananda's clarion call to every human being to realize the divinity that resides within each individual is not a hoax; it is something that is possible. 'Each human being is potentially divine, the effort to realize it is the whole of religion', says Vivekananda. In other words, the possibility of attaining a higher level of spiritual development is there for every individual, provided he or she is willing to make the effort.

Not only is evolution taking place at the individual level, society too is evolving. From the monarchical system, with its concept of the divine right of kings and its Indian version of Ram Rajya, where a benevolent divine figure would rule over the country, we have reached a stage where democracy, the rule of the people, is accepted as the norm. The system of parliamentary democracy, while a step forward, is not yet the rule of the people. It is the rule of a party or a coalition of parties that takes decisions on behalf of the people and rules over them. The only check is that once every five years, or four—as the case may be—people have an opportunity to vote them out of power. As things stand, the party or the coalition of parties that takes its place is usually equally corrupt, self-seeking and geared to helping its own cronies to amass wealth.

This is because in the present system of parliamentary democracy, power does not really vest with the people. In the name of the people, a small caucus of the majority party or the coalition of parties, which is able to muster a majority, carries on the administration and wields absolute power. As history has repeatedly proved, power corrupts and absolute power corrupts absolutely. The slogan of rule of the people, by the people, for the people remains a distant dream.

Clearly this is not the end of the road or the end of history. The process of evolution is going on and will definitely lead to other, more democratic social formations. The emergence of civil society, with its capacity to restrict the absolute power of the state, is an indication of how the common people are acquiring power. The role that civil society is beginning to play provides a glimpse into a future where gradually the state, with its coercive apparatus, would wither away and the people acquire the capacity to carry on the administration. The amendment to the Indian Constitution on Panchayati Raj is another indication of the effort to shift power in favour of the ordinary masses. This effort is largely being thwarted by political parties controlling the panchayats, restricting their freedom to act in the interests of the local people and preventing them from exercising the powers that the Constitution has conferred on them. The highly centralized economic system, where the levers of the economy are in the hands of the centralized state apparatus, on the one hand, and large joint stock corporations, on the other, make the exercise of power at the grass root level virtually impossible.

This may sound as an attempt to look too far into the future; it may be said that it is more important and necessary to discuss the present and to discover what needs to be done today. However, such thinking in terms only of the next election is leading to an endless round where we are running hard but ending up in the same place; sometimes retreating. Howsoever remote the future may appear, there are enough reasons, therefore, to believe that the future is already here. We have reached a point where the possibility of the destruction of the planet is staring us in the face. The threat is emerging from two ends.

The arrival of the nuclear bomb, the power of which has steadily increased, marked a new stage in human history. Here, for the first time, is a weapon the, *brahmastra,* which has the power to destroy all life on earth. The nuclear arsenals of all the countries that form the nuclear club, have increased since the day the first bomb was dropped in Hiroshima and, as is now common knowledge, they can now destroy the world many times over. The horror of Hiroshima and Nagasaki did not lead to any rethinking on our part and we continue to make more and better bombs and better missiles to carry the bombs to the farthest corners of the earth.

More countries, India included, are adding to the world's nuclear arsenal. As the store of oil and other fossil fuels has declined, we are now turning to nuclear energy. Countries that had stopped setting up nuclear reactors because of the obvious risks involved are returning to it. Undoubtedly, others will too and why not? If nuclear energy is our only hope of ensuring energy security, surely the same logic will lead others to the same path. It is no longer a secret that the nuclear bomb is only a little step away from nuclear energy. North Korea has exploded a nuclear device; many other countries have the know-how and have perhaps already developed their nuclear weapons. It is wishful thinking that they are only deterrents and will never be used. In recent years, on more than one occasion there have been flashpoints when nuclear weapons could well have been used. As long as such weapons exist, not only the possibility, but also the probability of their being used is high.

The other looming threat is the speed at which we are destroying the environment. Global warming is one of the many manifestations of the havoc wrought by modern civilisation, industrialization and urbanization, which are its hallmark. The Arctic ice is melting, the Himalayan glaciers are receding and the sea level is rising. The day is not too far off when millions in the coastal regions will be displaced and crowd into the already over populated cities as a new class of refugees. Rivers are drying up; the air and the water that nature has provided in plentiful measure are getting polluted. This is not a distant prospect that we can afford to ignore. All this is already happening and Armageddon is not a flight of fancy but on the agenda of the present generation.

A national of India, Dr. Rajendra K. Pachauri, who heads the Intergovernmental Panel on Climate Change, a committee of scientists set up by the United Nations, has proved that all this is the result of what we are doing in the name of 'development'. Yet we are engaged in the blame game. You, the developed nations of the world started it and are the worst polluters; so you must act while we continue on the same disastrous course of development so that we have as much energy per capita, as much steel, as many cars and other vehicles, as many planes, as many missiles as you have. It would be interesting to examine a letter that Gandhi wrote to Jawaharlal Nehru in 1945 that has been referred to in Kanti Mehta's memoirs. Gandhi suggested that he and Jawaharlal should discuss what the shape of a future India should be like. He appreciated that Nehru's views on the subject were somewhat different from his own. Nevertheless, knowing that Nehru's objective of a bright future for the country was no different from his, he felt that a dialogue between them would be useful. In his letter he stated: 'I am now an old man. I have, therefore, named you as my heir. I must, however, understand my heir and my heir should understand me.' Giving briefly his own vision of the course of development that India should follow he went on to say, 'I am convinced that if India is to attain true freedom and through India the world also . . . sooner or later, the fact must be recognized that people will have to live in villages not in towns, in huts not in palaces. Crores of people will never be able to live in peace with each other in towns and palaces. They will have no recourse but to resort to both violence and untruth.'

Pandit Nehru's ideas were however different. 'I do not understand,' he said, 'why a village should necessarily embody truth and non-violence. A village, normally speaking, is backward intellectually and culturally and no progress can be made from a backward environment.' Gandhiji was not oblivious of the state in which our villages were and, in a subsequent letter, wrote: 'You must not imagine that I am envisaging our village life as it is today. The village of my dreams is still in my mind. After all, every man lives in the world of his dreams. My ideal village will contain intelligent human beings. They will not live in dirt and darkness as animals. Men and women will be free and able to hold their own against anyone in the world. Everyone will have to contribute his quota of manual labour. It is possible to envisage railways, post and telegraph and the like.' The dialogue on this subject never took place as subsequent events, the formation of the interim government with Nehru as the Prime Minister, the riots and the Partition with all the problems that came in its wake, left no scope for the kind of dialogue that had been suggested. Soon after, on the 30 January 1948, Gandhi was assassinated. The light had gone out.

Six decades and eleven Plans later, do we need to hark back to the words of the person whom we call the Father of the Nation and do some rethinking on whether we need to change course? Nehru himself, in his last years, had begun to do precisely this as is evident from a statement he made in 1963 a few months before he died recalling the message of the Mahatma and admitting that a good number of people had not benefited from planning and 'whose poverty was abysmal and most painful'. He further lamented that, howsoever rapidly we advanced towards the machine age, there would be large numbers of our people who would not be touched by it.

My own experience shows that the village of Gandhiji's dreams is not such an absurd idea after all. The percentage of literacy in the group of three villages that comprise Ramgarh is extremely high; definitely not less than 90 per cent. There are a few primary schools and even an English-medium school. Almost 100 years earlier, a swami of the Arya Samaj order, Narayanswamy, set up a school that went up to the matriculation level. Today, it is a government-run intermediate college. The level of female literacy seems to be even higher than that of the males. Apart from the original Arya Samaj Ashram, there are three units of the Sri Aurobindo Ashram. One of the units named Tapogiri holds seminars and camps for students and teachers from Delhi and Pondicherry and organizes discussions on various topics. At its Madhuban centre, I have met people from all parts of the world. Some of them are seekers of Enlightenment; some are on world tours, to spread the message of the conservation of the environment. One European traveller from Prague had travelled in his car-cum-trailer, driving his vehicle on used vegetable oil. He had videos and slide presentations that he displayed in the market place to show that to conserve the environment and arrest the rapidly increasing gases that destroy the environment and lead to global warming, it was necessary that the overwhelming majority of the people of the world took to a vegetarian diet.

Retired professors and writers have settled there enabling intellectual discourse and even the average villager is well aware of developments in the country. The internet has arrived and computer training is imparted to local boys and girls at Madhuban. Two major Hindi newspapers are widely circulated. The filth and the dirt generally associated with villages—and now worse in the towns and cities—are absent. Ethical standards are high and despite the deterioration from the earlier, near Ram Rajya, level, they are much better than those prevailing in cities and towns. It is a fruit-growing area and this is what sustains the local economy. The atmosphere is entirely rural; there is not even a bazar as such; just a few shops. It is where I once hoped to settle down and spend the last years of my life.

I am sure that there are other villages of this nature in India. As part of the public relations exercise of the Bengal Chamber of Commerce and Industry, I helped to organize a development project in a village a few miles north of Calcutta. A team of experts from different disciplines was deputed to work on a whole-time basis for three years. The idea was not to dole out charity but to impart skills and knowledge and help both the agriculture and the small-scale industries of the village. The team was able to make a difference to the whole area, to revive defunct small-scale industries and to improve agricultural incomes. A survey taken three years after the team was withdrawn, showed that much of the effects of the earlier exercise had remained. The whole thing has been documented in a publication in the archives of the Bengal Chamber. I am referring to this to show that even a very limited effort made without any help from the government or aid from foreign sources could achieve so much. How much more would be possible if it were built into the development strategy of the government both at the central and state levels.

Some of the experiments of Dr. Ajit Narain Bose, one-time Secretary in the West Bengal Government's Department of Industry, later member of the State Planning Board and also associated with the National Alliance of Peoples' Movements (NAPM) deserve serious consideration. Not merely at the theoretical level, in experiments conducted at the grassroots in the Midnapur district of West Bengal, he showed how with grass roots planning at the village level, local economies could be lifted out of poverty and the standard of living of the people improved using local resources.

Trapped as we were in the tentacles of globalization and its institutions the World Trade Organization, the World Bank and the IMF; saddled as we are with a foreign debt that is mounting and probably exceeds or is near the $200 billion mark, there are not too many options open to us. Perhaps we can shift our emphasis a bit from urbanization—expected to draw 50 per cent of the population of the country in its sweep in the next few decades—to making our villages a little more liveable, to making agriculture a more exciting and gainful occupation than it is, so that village youth are motivated to stay in the villages rather than to trek to the cities in hoards, with many swelling the ranks of the lumpen proletariat.

There is already a world-wide shortage of foodgrains and in India too the trend is to move away from food to cash crops. Will even the tragic suicides of hundreds of thousands of farmers in the last decade not wake us up to the realization that there is something seriously wrong with our development process? Will even the meltdown of the economies of the most 'developed' countries of the world not make us conscious of the need to strike out a path of our own, more self-reliant, less dependent on the globalized economy, less destructive of the environment?

Such a transformation requires a change in our mind-sets. As long as becoming rich remains the only objective of individuals, improving profitability of public and private sector corporations and growth in GDP the only strategic goal of 'development', we can hardly make any progress in the real sense of the term. Development can only be meaningful if human development and not an abstract market is put at the centre of economic planning. As long as the hedonistic philosophy of 'eat, drink and be merry' remains the only guiding principle of our lives, we will remain stuck in the present iniquitous system.

> A better world is only possible with better human beings and human beings will start getting better when they are able to understand that they are not just animals with animal instincts, not just body and mind but have the unique privilege of possessing a consciousness, a spiritual dimension. It is through the struggle to discover and develop this aspect of their being

that human beings can take themselves, society at large and humanity as a whole to a brighter future and to a new civilisation.

The struggle for a better world, the search for a better social system must go on but it will be successful to the extent that human beings are able to better themselves. This is the essence of what I have learnt from my nearly nine decades of living and the varied experiences that I have had. More importantly, I have realized that to take part in this struggle one has to begin with oneself. In the remaining years of my life—there cannot be many more left—I will keep trying to do precisely this.

Lead kindly Light, amid the encircling gloom,
Lead thou me on!
The night is dark and I am far from home—
Lead thou me on!
Keep Thou my feet; I do not ask to see
The distant scene—one step enough for me.

Afterword

Like the proverbial cat, he has had nine lives and knowing him makes nine lives not quite enough. I first met Jolly Mohan Kaul in the early 1980s, in a world far removed from revolutionary politics, amidst the waters of the Dhakuria Lakes, where he was one of the judges for the Amateur Rowing Association of the East's annual competition being held at the Lake Club. I was then in my early twenties and trying to start a career in the print media. Jolly Kaul had by then completed several kinds of careers; was on the verge of quitting one (public relations) and entering another: economic journalism. That was when our paths met; some thirty years ago.

Even so, I wondered if I was the appropriate person to write the Afterword for this book. Despite our association for nearly three decades, when I met him he was well over his revolutionary past. I knew little about that past save for the fact that it had involved a period of intense activity for more than half a century. Yet, as someone approaching the nineties, Jolly Kaul has been much more than a 'Marxist revolutionary' or a stormy petrel. To me, his thoughts on Gandhism or even on Sri Aurobindo are no less significant than those on Marxism that he adopted heart and soul in his youth. To me, his underlying philosophy of searching for a better world is a demonstrably continuing one, and my exposure to his thinking emboldened me to put pen to paper to recommend his memoirs to a generation that has largely been at the receiving end of the Party's transgressions. This account provides an understanding of the kind of sacrifices that laid the foundations for the Party's mass base in West Bengal that has held the edifice for so many years.

More than anything else, it will provide for people in my generation an explanation of the inducements that led the communist leadership astray.

To be facetious, I had a head start over him in the world of formal economic journalism and, over the 30 years that I have known him, I have seen a matured Jolly Mohan Kaul, who was still intensely active, mentally and physically, and also evolving from a Marxist to a Gandhian to a humanist. In setting down my impressions, I can, perhaps, profile Mr. Kaul as a human being with many more facets than even his book, covering his life-long search for a better world, has revealed. Truth to tell, the Jolly Kaul whom those in-between our ages (I am over 50 and he close to 90) know, is not quite the person whom I know, for I believe that I have had the privilege of getting to know the human being far better than most people who have been close to him in the past, some intimately so.

What never ceased to amaze us—Indrani Kar, Tirtha Roy and myself—is how on earth did he know so much about everything and how on earth did he know everybody. The Chief Minister of the state was his comrade; in the corridors of Writer's Buildings, everyone knew him; at the Bengal Chamber, the Secretary General was his friend; managing directors, here, there, everywhere not only knew him but most called him 'Jolly da'. Editors of newspapers (Sunanda K. Datta-Ray) would drop in to have the simple lunch that he would bring from home that we all shared. Film makers (Chidananda Das Gupta) would drop in to say 'hello'. Economists, artists, bankers, writers, public relations professionals (Adity Shyam, R. P. Gupta . . . you name them), social scientists, scientists, people of exceptional talent—sources that journalists needed years to cultivate—were around us all the time and became our friends too. It was also clear to us that not very many political figures that we knew were considered with such overwhelming affection by people of his generation.

Not for once did we feel that the man who was drawing such illustrious company was an 'exceptional' person. He was actually fun. He and Manish Sarkar (our General Manager), took us rowing, to dinners and made work (at a princely Rs 600 a month) seem great. Office was family business; no boss-subordinate relationship and everybody worked extremely hard. Save the occasional teasing from Manish Sarkar about the 'communist' in our midst, there was hardly a mention of the revolutionary past.

I never did seriously appreciate the significance of my initiation into his multifaceted world at that time. I realize though that the job at the *Statesman* (virtually without an interview) would never have materialized without the silent touch of Jolly Kaul. The editor, Sunanda K. Datta-Ray, was particularly impressed by a piece and Mr. Kaul happened to inform him who the author was. Thereafter, there was an invitation from the *Statesman* to meet C. R. Irani, who 'welcomed me into the family'; he did not really 'interview' me.

Over the years the 'old man' and his wife, Manikuntala Sen, became extremely fond of me—she possibly more than him. I suspect that I was the only person whom she spoke to in the midst of her 'coma' towards the end of her life. I had just been invited to visit America and was giving her the news even as she lay on her bed; eyes tightly shut. I was happy and was trying to convey my joy to her. Suddenly the lady who had been lying with her eyes closed for several days said angrily: 'I don't like that.' America was still an anathema to her.

About Manikuntala and JMK's past, I would only get to know when walking down different parts of Kolkata with him. 'That was our commune'; or 'that was the lane where letters were exchanged between two couriers'—Rainey Park being one of them. Of course, the quality of our dialogue changed over the years to far more important things around societal inequality, things that went wrong in his world of revolutionary politics and why they did, environmental degradation, globalization and its stratifying effect, to Vivekananda, Gandhi . . . There was never a dull moment. Holidays were taken together, movies seen together and meals were frequently shared. He never lost his temper; never allowed any sense of being wronged upset him for long; never went overboard with anything and always remained rational. Did he never err? I have his own confessions about serious errors in managing the politics of his times. Some of them are explained in this book. Others he has not mentioned because it would be impolitic to do so.

By the time Jolly Kaul is 90—have no doubt that he would live well past that age—he would have organized the centenary celebration of Manikuntala—no two people could have deserved each other more—he would have completed the updating of his book on public relations/communications in the twenty-first century; he would have taken innumerable trips to Puri to teach at the Gandhi Labour Foundation; he would have made many trips to Ramgarh, trekking in the hills like a sherpa; he would have written his long-promised book of short stories based on real life experiences. He would, of course, have cooked several meals for me: the keema kabab being my particular favourite; never mind that I may have to go into the kitchen to turn the gas off!

I have shared all his nine lives: the communist, the oarsman/sportsman, the writer, the actor, the public relations professional, the trekker, the economic journalist, the cook, the Gandhian, and he is still all there!

August 2009 Aditi Roy Ghatak

Index

Acharya, Gopal, 158
Acharya, Pankaj, 229
Acharya, Snehangshu, 100, 105, 170, 187, 214
Adhikari, Dr., 91, 119, 121, 122
Ahmad, Muzaffar/Kakababu, 55, 57-58, 150. *See also* Kaul, J.M.
  and Cominform, 142, 302, 303
  in jail, 121, 122, 125, 126, 129, 145, 149, 153, 301
  on Left Adventurism, 131-33
  and M. N. Roy, 147
  and Nazrul Islam, 147, 148, 150
  and 1952 elections, 163, 169
  on Stalin, 148, 149
AITUC, 77, 94, 162. *See also* trade unions
Ali Mazhar, 35-36
All-India Students Federation, 20, 40, 43, 46, 48, 51, 118,
Asaf Ali, Aruna, 266, 268

Banerjee, Abani, 128-29, 141, 302, 314
Banerjee, Subrata, 51, 52
Basavanpunniah, M., 143, 154
Basu, Kamal, 52, 164
Bhaduri, Panchu Gopal, 63-64
Bengal Chamber of Commerce and Industry (BCCI), 21, 279, 281, 291-92, 297, 368
Bengal famine, 1943, 88-90
Bhattacharya, Nepal, 77-78, 83, 104. *See also* trade unions
Bhattacharya, Santosh, 348-49
Birla, B.K., 297-98
Biswas, Debabrata, 51, 53
Bose, Ajit Narain, Dr., 351, 368
Bose, Arun, 20, 21, 26, 27
Bose, Debabrata, 19, 26, 51
Bose, Dilip, 40, 52, 57
Bose, Girindra Sekhar, Dr., 42
Bose, Jyoti, 38, 314, 166, 174, 184, 214
  on Central Committee, 1952, 155
  on China-India war, 237
  inner party struggle, 142, 157
  and J.M. Kaul, 251, 298-99, 312-13
  Provincial Committee, 303
  and success, 39
  on supporting western powers, 66

Bose, Maitrayee, Dr., 79-80, 85, 104. *See also* trade unions
Bose, Subhas Chandra, 37, 39, 81, 86, 116, 299

Calcuta Port union, 79-80. *See also* Kaul, J.M.; trade unions
  communal harmony, 96-98, 108
  Employees Association, 77
  marine section, 82, 109
  strike, 102-05, 116, 132
  worker leaders, 10-111
Cambell, Neville, 41-42, 44
Capital, 19, 260, 268, 282, 291-94, 316, 323, 345, 352
capitalism, 295, 298, 352, 354-58,
Chakravarty, Ambica, 122
Chakravarty, Nirod, 162
Chakravarty, Nripen, 63, 78
Chakravartty, Nikhil, 48, 51, 53, 267, 268, 269, 271
Chakravartty, Renu, 49, 51, 164, 165, 301
Chatterjee, Amiya, 171, 173, 174
Chatterjee, Bela, 300, 301
Chaudhuri, Sachin, 267
Chiang Kai-shek, 190
China-India war, 235, 236, 245, 263. *See also* Communist Party
  Left faction arrests, 247-48, 249
  National Council, 210-12, 243, 246-47, 251
  National Front vs Democratic Front, 191, 193, 224, 225
  Right faction, 250
  split, 237, 251, 254-55
Chinese Communist Party, 225
  asserting leadership, 243-44
  and globalization, 329, 362
  vs India, 233-35, 239
  vs Soviet Union, 232. *See also* Mao Tse-tung
Chittagong Armoury Raid, 14, 122, 142, 169
Chou En-lai, 176, 233-34
Chowdhury, Benoy, 303
Cominform, 142, 156, 192
Comintern, 66, 86, 115, 361
communism, 64, 92, 148, 193, 231, 350, 352-56. *See also* Gorbachev, M.
Communist Manifesto, 43, 357
communist movement, 19, 20, 40, 92, 148, 193, 232, 246, 258-61
Communist Party, 14, 100, 158, 226, 230, 314-15
  Amritsar Party Conference, 224, 226-27, 231, 252. *See also* Kaul, J. M.
  and Bengal famine, 70-71, 88
  Calcutta District Committee, 62, 117, 197, 205, 209,226-28, 246, 252, 255
  Central Committee, 20, 58-59, 64, 65, 119, 153, 155
  Central Party Conference, 1952, 154-55
  Central Secretariat, 209

Centrist Group, 228, 230
Cominform editorial. *See* Cominform
China-India war. *See* China-India war
cultural movement. *See* IPTA; YCI
democratic centralism, 227
and economic policies, 361-62
and elections, 161-64, 188, 200, 201-02
consequences of, 202-03, 358
1946 results, 174
1952 results, 166, 199, 200
factions, 227, 229, 230, 238, 252-53
failure to expand, 357-61
gender bias of, 85, 165, 168, 227, 229-30
as illegal, 41, 51, 54, 119, 121, 124, 154
inner party struggle, 142, 156-57
J.M. Kaul, *xii*, 54, 66, 117. *See also* Kaul, J. M; trade unions
Kerala government, 197-201, 215, 224
Left Adventurism. *See* Left Adventurism
legalization, 66-67
lifestyle, 203-04, 294, 209, 212-15, 313-14
as middle class, 206, 212
MLA expenses, 210
monthly wage, 205, 210-11, 213
Party Centre, 55, 90, 123, 124, 126, 141, 160, 164, 223
party lines, 65, 88, 115, 121, 123, 127, 142, 155, 194. *See also* Left Adventurism
party programme, 154, 162, 169, 175, 360-61. *See also* Congresses
party symbol, 163-64
People's War, 65, 75, 80-81, 85, 86, 87, 118
poor vs rich, 309, 313
post-1977, 254, 360
Provincial Committee Secretariat, 55, 66, 142, 150, 227-28, 303
Soviet funds, 214-15
Second Party Congress, 115, 117, 119-20
Stalin, impact on, 177, 225, 227, 306
Swadhinata, 204-05, 239, 244, 249, 250
Twentieth Congress, CPSU, 189-91, 201, 224
Vijayawada Congress, 239-40, 253, 244
wage structure, 205-08, 210-11
worker cadre neglect, 220-22. *See also* working class
CPI (M), 191, 309-10, 314-15
CPI (ML), 191.
CPSU. *See also* Khrushchev, N.; Stalin
avert Indian party's split, 241
collapse of, 117, 351-52
China policy, 232, 238

CPSU *(contd.)*
and German Non-Aggressive Pact, 86
Masood Ali Khan, 237-38
Mikhail Suslov, 241, 242
Second World War, 40, 54, 62
Stalin's death, 223, 243
Twentieth Party Congress, 33, 61-62, 176, 359
glasnost, 194
Indian Party, 190-94
Stalin, 189. *See also* Khruschev, N.
USSR breakup, 189

Dandekar, N., 275
Dange, S. A., 77, 91, 119, 142, 143, 153, 213, 235-36
Das, Jatin, 15, 125
Dasgupta, Bani, 301, 348
Dasgupta, Promode (PDG), 77, 142, 157, 162, 163, 176, 226, 228, 303
Dasgupta, Rana, 301, 349
Datta, Amlan, 344, 345
Datta-Ray, Sunanda (SKDR), 260, 261, 269, 327, 329, 348
Dialectical Materialsim, 38, 49, 315
Dubcek, Alexander, 62
Dutt, Kalpana, 14, 91, 93
Dutt, Utpal, 167

Elias, Mohammad, 126, 221, 270

fascism, 44-45, 48-49, 54, 55, 66, 86, 177, 86, 177, 299
First World War, 49
food movement, 187-88
Forward Bloc 113-14

Gandhi, M. K., 39, 45, 356. *See also* Mehta, Kanti
against Second World War, 86
assassination, 117
civil disobedience, 4, 14
on modern civilisation, 357
and hunger strikes, 128
on India's future, 366-68
on industrialization, 334, 337, 339-41, 365-66. *See also* Nehru, J.
J.M. Kaul on, 282
Gandhi, Indira, 198
Gandhi Labour Foundation, 333-37, 342, 343
Ganguly, Debkumar, 77, 220
Ganguly, Suhasini, 179
Ghate, S.V., 119, 143
Ghosh, Ajoy, 87, 142, 143, 153, 225, 230-31, 235, 242-43. 246
Ghosh, Ganesh, 114, 142
Ghosh, Krishnapada, 93
Ghosh, Madan, 297
globalization, 328, 340, 343, 355-57. *See also* Mehta, Kanti
Gopalan, A. K., 210-11

Gorbachev, M., 195, 352-53, 354
Great Calcutta Killing, 95-101. *See also* trade unions
Gupta, Bhupesh, 155, 199, 205, 235, 237, 266, 275, 303
Gupta, Indrajit, 47-48, 78, 98, 100, 192
Gupta, Sadhan, 37, 149, 159
Gupta, Somen, 38

Haldar, Gopal. 122
Haldar, Konsari, 164
Halim, Abdul, 144-45
Hitler, Adolf, 52, 54, 86
Hore, Somnath, 163-64
Huda, Shamsul, 122
Huxley, J., 363

Indian National Army (INA), 87, 89, 103, 116
Indian Peoples' Theatre Association (IPTA), 52, 118, 143
Indian National Congress, 358
  China-India war, 234
  and Communist Party, 176, 251, 281
  and elections
    1952, 166-67
    1957, 198
  and Quit India, 37, 85, 86, 95. 116, 262, 300, 326, 362
  on trade unions, 79-81
  and USSR, 190, 191, 224, 232
Indian Oxygen Ltd (BOC), 21, 284, 308, 346
  and affluence, 311
  The Changing Scene, 280
  corporate history, 328
  West Bengal: An Analytical Study, 280-81
Indian Society of Advertisers, 296-97

Jesuit teachers, 21-26, 35, 41
Joshi, P. C., 65, 66-67, 91-93, 118

Kar, Chintamani, 53
Kashmiri Pandits, 29-30
Kaul, B.N., 2
Kaul, J.M., 1, 5, 15
  and AITUC, 77
  brothers
    L.M. Kaul, 5-6, 12, 144, 153, 269, 318, 319
    Major Kaul, 6, 23, 35, 150, 153, 257, 269
    P.M. Kaul, eldest, 6, 9, 32-33, 62, 302
    Victor Kaul, 7, 12, 17-18, 57, 62-63, 153, 178, 257, 265
  on capitalists, 282, 294, 298
  and Communist Party. *See* Communist Party
  and cousin, Suraj Kishen Munshi, 4, 12, 15-16, 38

Kaul, J.M. *(contd.)*
as debater, 35, 36, 40
father, S.M.N., 1-3, 8-11,15, 144, 196, 320
on Eastern Europe, 352, 355
and education
college, 34-38, 42, 45, 54, 273-74
schools, 7-8, 12-14, 15-17, 27-28
finances, 205-07, 259, 263, 265, 270-71, 307-08, 313
on future, 362-68
on Gandhi Labour Foundation, 328, 346. *See also* Mehta, Kanti
on health, 30-31, 345
and ICS, 49, 55, 350
in jail, 1948, 122, 124-25, 135-40. *See also* Ahmad, Muzaffar
Cominform directive, 142
hunger strikes, 128, 134, 141, 144
education, 143
Left Adventurism. *See* Left Adventurism
journalistic debut, 54
Kidderpore commune, 107, 109, 122, 151
on Kuomintang, 190
and Manikuntala Sen, wife, 300-07, 312
election candidate, 165, 168, 303-04
marriage, 176, 178-80, 304, 310-11
and religion, 311-12
mother, Shyamvati, 8, 153
and Marx, Engels, 93, 200, 329
national movement, 14-15
in national Council, 209, 242-43
new careers
advertising, 274, 296-97
BCCI, 280-81
Indian Oxygen Ltd. *See* Indian Oxygen Ltd (BOC)
journalism, 266-69, 288, 328, 329
and PR, 275, 284-85
on panchayats, 363-64
and Party, 46, 49, 195. *See also* Communist Party
Amritsar amendment, 225
candidature, electoral, 165-66
China-India war, 235, 238, 244-46
Democratic Front, 193-94
District Committee Secretary, 1957
leaving Party, 195, 254, 255, 257, 261, 262, 264, 265. *See also* Communist Party
Twentieth Congress, CPSU, 190-91, 194, 195
and political alternative, 362-66, 370-71
and Ramgarh, 153, 318-21, 323, 325-26, 329, 367-68

on religion, 29, 333, 347. *See also* Sen, Manikuntala
sister-in-law, Roopan Kaul, 318, 319, 323
Students Federation, 47-48, 51, 54
student politics, 36-38, 40, 42, 45
on USSR, 262-63, 353, 355-56
and sport, 26, 33, 34
and trade unions, 70-79, 101. *See also* trade unions
going underground, 55-58. *See also* Communist Party
on work, 331-32
World Social Forum, 336
on workers, 282, 298.*See also* trade unions
younger generation, 348
Konar, Harekrishna, 238, 303
Krushchev, N., 148, 177, 194, 227, 233, 238, 251-52
Kumarmangalam, M., 91, 93, 226

Lahiri, Abani, 349-50
Lahiri, Somnath, 61, 77, 123, 192, 228, 248, 257, 300
Lahiri Chaudhuri, D.K., 172
Lama, Dalai, 233
Left Adventurism, 20, 124, 130, 132, 144-45, 160, 192, 209
Central Party conference, 154-55
and middle peasants, 135, 143
no overt opposition, 146
railway strike, 130
and Stalin, 361
'Telengana Path Is Our Path,' 121, 127-28
unions, impact on, 131
workers, 222-23
Lenin, V.I. 162-63
Lucknowi, Saleq, 38

Mainstream, 36, 237, 267-69. *See also* Chakravartty, N.
Mao Tse-tung, 190-91, 241, 243-44
Marxism, 92-93, 200, 215, 329
Mazumdar, Charu, 132, 142, 144
Mitra, Shivshankar, 137
Mitter, Bhaskar, 18-19, 21, 26, 64
Mehta, Balraj, 269
Mehta, Kanti, 339-43
death of, 343-44
Gandhivichar, 334, 339-42, 365
Gandhi Labour Foundation, 332, 335. *See also* GLF
and J.M. Kaul, 333, 335, 343-45
and National Mineworkers Federation, 336
unions, 335, 338, 343
World Social Forum, 335
and workers, 336-38
Menon, Krishna, 233, 269
Momin, Abdul, 122
Mookerjee, S.P., 254
Mukherjee, Bankim, 119, 202-03
Mukherjee Biswanath, 37, 55, 122, 123, 157, 248, 257
Mukherjee, Gita, 122

Mukherjee Hiren, 53, 122, 123-24, 164, 263
Mukherjee, Sadhan, 37
Mukherjee, Saroj, 55
Mukherjee Subhas, 52, 93, 123, 143
Mullik, Geeta, 179
Muslim League, 88-89, 95-97, 98. *See also* Suhrawardy, H. S.

Nag, Leela, 38
Namboodiripad, E.M.S., 87, 197, 213, 299
naval mutiny, 103, 116
Nehru, J., 44, 54, 234, 238, 245
  Bandung, 176, 233
  and China-India war, 251. *See also* Chinese Communist Party
  and Chou En -lai, 233-34
  on development, 175-76, 340-41, 365-66
  on industrialization, 340-41. *See also* Gandhi, M.K.
Nehru, Kamala, 30
Nehru, Motilal, 30

Pachauri, R. K., 366
Palme Dutt, R. 36, 40, 66, 359
Pandit, Jeevanlal, 29
Pandit, Sambhunath, 29
Patriot, 266, 268, 269
Politbureau, 119, 133, 209, 223. *See also* Left Adventurism
Pollitt, Harry, 85-86, 175
Pradhan, Sudhi, 53, 57, 300
Progressive Writers Association, 118
public relations, 282-84, 287-88

Quit India movement. *See* Indian National Congress

Ranadive, B.T. (BTR), 65-66, 77, 118, 154, 162, 211-12, 243
Ramamurti, P., 91
Rao, Rajeswar, 143, 154
Ray, B.C., Dr., 39, 128, 138, 165, 302
refugees, 167
Roy, Ajit, 158, 348
Roy, Dilip, 51
Roy, Dinesh, 205-06
Roy, Shivshankar, 137
Roy, Subhas, 347, 351
Roy, Subodh, 14, 122
Roychowdhury, Sushital, 93, 132, 143
Roy Ghatak, Aditi, 233, 289, 329, 330, 347

Sabherwal, O.P., 269
Sangal, O.P., 268, 269
Sanyal, Prasanta, 40-41, 52, 272-73, 275, 281, 348
Sarkar, Shanti, 301
Second World War, 41, 51, 54, 62, 65, 66, 67, 81, 85
Sehanovis, Chinmohan, 51, 53
Sen, Abani, 72-76

Sen, Abhijit, 21
Sen, Amartya, 88-89
Sen, Amiya Kumar, 273, 275, 279, 280-81
Sen, Bhowani, 38, 49, 119, 123, 131
Sen, Debendra Bijoy, 151-53
Sen, K.C. (Bhaiya), 21
Sen, Manikuntala, 72. *See also* Kaul, J.M.
- absence of women candidates, 165
- arrest, 30, 302
- death, 177, 178, 313, 318
- diksha, 316-17
- election campaign, 171-74
- family, 300
- famine relief, 89-90
- financial straits, 208, 257, 263, 265
- and health, 308-09, 312, 313-15
- in jail, 123, 135, 302
- and Jolly Kaul, 300-01. *See also* Kaul, J. M.
- Mahila Atma Raksha Samiti, 300
- marriage, 304-05, 308. *See also* Kaul.J.M.
- *Nabanna,* 301
- and party factions, 229
- Provincial Committee/ Organizing Committee, 170, 303
- railway strike, 130
- as respected, 300
- school teacher, 271-72
- *Sediner Katha,* 314
- Tebhaga, 315-16
- teachers' movement, 186-87
- tours, 314
- Twentieth Congress, CPSU, 195
- Vijayawada Conference, 239-40

Sen, Mohit, 225, 235,
Sen, Mrinal, 53
Sen, Niranjan, 303
Sen, Sunil, 41
Sengupta, Subroto, 19-20, 27, 52, 56, 274
Shahidi, Pervez, 144
Singh, Ananta, 14, 169-70, 306
South-East Asia Youth Conference, 113-15
Sri Sangha, 38
Stalin, 194, 251-52. *See also* CPSU; USSR
- death, 177, 178
- megalomania, 190
- methods, 119, 134
- Muzaffar Ahmad on, 148
- Second World War, 86
- obedience of communists, 156, 360

Sundarayya, P., 198, 213
Suhrawardy, H.S., 88, 95, 97, 104
Suhrawardy, Shahid, 53

teachers' movement, 186-87
Telengana struggle, [illegible]. See also Left Adventurism
Thapar, Romesh, 267

tram movement, 94, 181-84, 185
trade unions, 70, 106, 142, 158-59, 98
  Beruk and Comens, 72-75
  Bhartia Iron and Steel, 76
  Bombay, 158-59
  capturing of, 83
  Calcutta, 158-59
  Calcutta Port union, 77, 82, 96-98, 100-01, 102-07, 109-11, 116, 132
  capturing of, 83
  Great Calcutta Ki'ling and, 95-98, 100

  vs elections, 201, 202
  Higher income dangers, 338-39. *See also* Mehta, Kanti
  Kshiti Burman, 110, 139
  Makhan Chatterjee, 82, 105, 110, 131, 139
  Molla Bazloo, k110, 218
  Muslim members, 218, 220, 221
  Nepal Bhattacharya, 77, 83, 110
  Parmananda Shyamal, 78, 109
  Ram Sundar Singh, 219-20
  Ram Surath Singh, 139
  strikes, 94, 108-11

Viswanath, 268, 269
Vivekananda, Swami, 23, 311, 315, 349, 362, 336

Wassodevv, Sina, 257, 265-66
Webb, Beatrice, 54, 195, 253
Web, Sidney, 54, 195, 253
working class, 67, 215, 217-222, 335. *See also* Gandhi Labour Foundation; trade unions

Youth Cultural Institute (YCI), 19, 51-53, 267

Zhdhanov, Alexei, 115